UK Manufacturers of Soft Drinks

Profiles of the leading 1150 companies

John D Blackburn

Editor

First Edition

Spring 2019

ISBN-13: 978-1-912736-17-1

ISBN-10: 1-912736-17-9

All rights reserved. No part of this publication may be reproduced, distributed, or transmitted in any form or by any means, including photocopying, recording, or other electronic or mechanical methods, without our prior written permission, except in the case of brief quotations embodied in critical reviews and certain other non-commercial uses permitted by copyright law. For permission requests, please write to us.

Copyright © 2019 Dellam Publishing Limited

Printed in 8pt Nimbus Sans L

Designed by URW++ Design and Development GmbH

Dellam Publishing Limited

2 Heath Drive, Sutton, Surrey, SM2 5RP

Fax: 020 8770 7478   email: enquiries@dellam.com

SAN: 0177881   EAN/GLN: 5030670177882

Table of Contents

1 Acknowledgements iv

2 Introduction v

3 Total Assets League Table 1

- As a measure of size, total assets is preferable to turnover which is influenced by profit margins and whether companies are capital or labour intensive.

4 Age of Companies 7

- Each company is ranked by its date of incorporation. Newcomers are defined as those registered since 2017.

5 Geographic Distribution 15

- Each company is classed by county.

6 Company Profiles 23

- Full company name, date incorporated, net worth, total assets, registered office, activities, shareholders and parent company, directors (with date of birth, nationality and occupation) and number of employees (if available).

7 Index of Directorships 93

- Alphabetical list of directors showing their directorships. If several directors have identical names then their date of birth is shown.

8 Standard Industrial Classification 119

- These codes are used to classify businesses by the type of economic activity in which they are engaged.

9 *finis* 125

Acknowledgements

This is a long and detailed publication containing thousands of facts and figures. It is only to be expected, despite continuous and repeated editing and checking, that errors may occur. In such cases, once we are aware of any, we publish a correction on our website.

Readers are encouraged to check regularly at www.dellam.com/books for any corrections and updates.

Although we take extreme care to ensure accuracy and being up-to-date, we cannot accept responsibility for any errors or omissions.

Contains public sector information licensed under Open Government Licence v3.0. from The Charity Commission (England and Wales) and The Charity Commission for Northern Ireland. © Crown Copyright and database right (2018).

Contains information from the Scottish Charity Register supplied by the Office of the Scottish Charity Regulator and licensed under the Open Government Licence v.2.0. © Crown Copyright and database right (2018).

Contains OS data © Crown copyright and database right (2018)

Contains Royal Mail data © Royal Mail copyright and database right (2018)

Contains National Statistics data © Crown copyright and database right (2018)

Contains Office for National Statistics © Crown copyright and database right (2018)

Maps based on those produced by the Office for National Statistics Geography GIS & Mapping Unit (2012 and 2018).

Contains HM Land Registry data © Crown copyright and database right (2018).

Contains Parliamentary information licensed under the Open Parliament Licence v3.0.

House of Commons Library Briefing Papers licensed under the Open Parliament Licence v3.0.

Contains Food Standards Agency data © Crown copyright and database right (2018).

Contains Eurostat data, 1995-2018, copyright European Commission by the Decision of 12 December 2011.

Maps based on produced by ONS Geography GIS & Mapping Unit.

Contains Companies House data supplied under section 47 and 50 of the Copyright, Designs and Patents Act 1988 and Schedule 1 of the Database Regulations (SI 1997/3032).

We appreciate your interest in our publications, and your comments and suggestions are always welcome. Please contact us at enquiries@dellam.com.

Introduction

This study looks at all companies registered in the United Kingdom where they identify themselves as manufacturers of soft drinks, production of mineral waters and other bottled waters.

This study includes companies that are dormant or non-trading some of which might be latent while others may operate under their owners' names but incorporate to protect the business name. In addition, all newly incorporated companies are included. The study will exclude those companies that do not specifically identify themselves as manufacturers of soft drinks, production of mineral waters and other bottled waters.

The aim of this study is to provide an overview of the key movers and shakers in the UK soft drinks and bottled water sector. Only key data has been isolated, particularly the company's net worth and total assets, but also its full name, date incorporated, registered office, other activities, shareholders, directors (with date of birth, occupation and nationality) and number of employees.

Two indicators of size are used: net worth and total assets. These are preferable to turnover which is influenced by profit margins and whether the companies are capital or labour intensive.

In the years 2016, 2017 and 2018, new company incorporations in the soft drinks and bottled water sector were 111, 278 and 275 respectively.

Breakdown of beverages in the UK is as follows: soft drinks (28%), beer (27%), whisky (25%), cider (7%), gin (3%), mineral water (3%) and others (2%).

Carbonates remain the largest segment worth £6.9 billion.

The breadown for non-alcoholic sector is as follows: cola £1.2 billion; pure juice £851 million; juice drinks £429 million; smoothies £223 million; plain water £616 million; squashes £406 million; traditional mixers £192 million; and fruit carbonates £405 million.

The market for bottled water and fruit juice, neither of which contain added sugar, is unaffected by the sugar levy but nonetheless they do contain naturally-occurring sugars. Despite their natural sugar content, sales of freshly squeezed juices and smoothies were the fastest growing segment.

100% juice is the most important factor in choosing a product.

In terms of Gross Value Added (GVA), beverages (including soft drinks and mineral water) is the largest manufacturing group with a of £6.6 billion in 2015; contributing 23% to the total food and drink manufacturing GVA.

The percentage UK retail price increase from June 2007 to June 2016 for soft drinks was 24% with alcoholic drinks at 17% and coffee, tea, cocoa at 36%

In Great Britain, 57% of those aged 16 years and over in 2017 drank alcohol (29 million people of the population) while 20% did not drink alcohol at all.

Standard cataloguing guidelines for company names in the profile section have been used, but there will be occurrences when the name may not be strictly alphabetical. A certain licence was adopted where it was felt that strictly alphabetical could lead to improper cataloguing. Some company names have been shortened in the league tables for aesthetic reasons.

John D Blackburn
Editor

This page is intentionally left blank

Total Assets League Table

Company	Amount	Company	Amount
ABI SAB Group Holding Limited	£48,913,764,352	Slush Puppie Limited	£13,844,823
Coca-Cola European Partners PLC	£15,913,583,616	JB Drinks Limited	£13,768,087
Diageo Great Britain Limited	£3,436,999,936	Princes Gate Water Limited	£13,554,308
SmithKline Beecham Limited	£2,496,000,000	Konon Limited	£13,540,305
Britvic PLC	£1,664,099,968	Montgomery Waters Limited	£13,048,339
Britvic Soft Drinks Limited	£1,437,943,040	Fentimans Ltd.	£11,622,925
Lucozade Ribena Suntory Limited	£1,394,434,944	Shepley Spring Limited	£11,338,697
Coca-Cola European Partners Great Britain Ltd	£1,293,049,984	Hildon Limited	£10,582,416
Britannia Soft Drinks Limited	£950,691,968	Dayla Holdings Limited	£10,505,968
Refresco Drinks UK Limited	£751,484,992	Dayla Limited	£9,578,971
Coca-Cola Holdings Africa Limited	£585,783,232	Britvic Asset Company No.2 Limited	£9,535,000
Schweppes International Limited	£453,451,424	Thomas Hardy Kendal Limited	£9,162,000
Robinsons Soft Drinks Limited	£371,625,984	Bottlegreen Holdings Limited	£8,236,066
Britvic Overseas Limited	£336,556,992	Clearly Drinks Limited	£7,591,639
Robinsons (Finance) No.2 Limited	£295,481,984	Allson Sparkle Limited	£7,289,341
Coca-Cola HBC Northern Ireland Limited	£295,026,432	James White Drinks Ltd	£6,707,049
A.G. Barr P.L.C.	£288,200,000	Thomas Hardy Burtonwood Limited	£6,525,000
Refresco Beverages UK Limited	£185,803,008	Northumbrian Ice Cream Company Limited	£5,799,730
Britvic International Investments Limited	£170,228,000	Trederwen Springs 2008 Limited	£5,310,754
Nichols PLC	£127,396,000	Heather Ale Limited	£5,044,741
Fevertree Limited	£101,020,128	Caledonian Bottlers PLC	£4,929,933
Total Water Solutions Limited	£87,678,000	Suntory Beverage & Food South Africa Limited	£4,755,399
Beverage Brands (U.K.) Limited	£83,943,024	The Natural Fruit and Beverage Company Limited	£4,363,959
Rubicon Drinks Limited	£82,823,000	Fiji Water (UK) Limited	£4,294,563
Nestle Waters UK Limited	£72,126,000	Kingshill Mineral Water Ltd.	£4,255,915
Hope Sixteen (No.87) Limited	£70,367,000	March Foods Limited	£4,238,437
Highland Spring Limited	£70,362,000	Mariage Freres Royaume Uni Limited	£4,155,805
Cawingredients Limited	£60,866,140	Britvic Asset Company No.1 Limited	£4,028,000
Eden Springs UK Limited	£59,880,000	Big Time Soft Drinks Limited	£3,947,648
Monster Energy Europe Limited	£53,013,208	Vitamin Brands Ltd.	£3,581,257
Merrydown PLC	£51,247,252	Lucozade Ribena Suntory Exports Limited	£3,415,000
Cott Ventures UK Limited	£38,306,000	Ty Nant Spring Water Limited	£3,366,041
Bottle Green Drinks Company Limited	£33,253,072	Luscombe Drinks Limited	£3,015,460
Radnor Hills Mineral Water Company Ltd	£31,864,320	Decantae Mineral Water Limited	£2,866,210
Britvic EMEA Limited	£20,076,000	Simpson's Beverage Supply Company Limited	£2,822,880
JB Drinks Holdings Limited	£19,825,388	Llanllyr Water Company Limited	£2,652,248
Konings Juices & Drinks UK Limited	£19,725,720	Ed's Trading Limited	£2,557,056
Harrogate Spring Water Limited	£19,496,768	Showerings Cider Mill Ltd	£2,506,517
Thomas Hardy Holdings Limited	£19,423,000	Rock's Organic Limited	£2,479,535
Kingsley Beverage Limited	£17,441,068	The Original Drinks and Food Company Ltd	£2,432,643
Coca-Cola International Sales Limited	£17,256,740	Office Watercoolers (S.W.) Limited	£2,329,478
04021465 Limited	£16,639,000	Fonthill Waters Limited	£2,244,408
Woodchester Enterprises Limited	£16,070,285	Maine Soft Drinks Limited	£2,167,888
Belvoir Fruit Farms Drinks Holdings Limited	£15,203,680	Willow Water Limited	£2,159,000
Belvoir Fruit Farms Limited	£15,198,961	Waters & Robson Holdings Limited	£2,110,184
Norbev Limited	£15,103,629	Belu Water Limited	£1,966,644
Princes Gate Spring Water Limited	£14,847,811	Storefast Solutions Limited	£1,923,409
Purity Soft Drinks Limited	£14,429,173	Counterpoint Wholesale (NI) Limited	£1,771,000
Orchid Drinks Limited	£14,113,000	Pressure Coolers Limited	£1,762,930
Buxton Mineral Water Limited	£14,006,000	Scheckter's Organic Beverages Limited	£1,662,964

UK Manufacturers of Soft Drinks

CMB Water Limited	£1,651,816	Ashridge Cider Limited	£458,463
Tarka Springs Limited	£1,649,132	Marlish Waters Limited	£452,257
Plenish Cleanse Ltd	£1,647,191	D & G Drinks Ltd	£432,257
Hartridges Limited	£1,639,382	Cracker Drinks Co. Limited	£428,974
Fillongley Spring Water Limited	£1,607,000	JDM Enterprises Ltd	£403,323
NGN Distribution Limited	£1,597,197	Kolibri Drinks Limited	£400,711
Antrim Hills Spring Water Company Limited	£1,454,623	Ipro Sport Exports Limited	£392,796
Better Fresh Limited	£1,444,693	Pouchlink Ltd	£388,109
Penning Power & Water Limited	£1,438,103	Suncrest Associates Limited	£385,165
Fillongley Ventures Limited	£1,346,000	Artisan Drinks Company Limited	£384,193
Metro Drinks Limited	£1,325,904	Peter Spanton Drinks Ltd	£374,302
P Mulrine and Sons Sales (U.K.) Limited	£1,284,538	Adcocks Drinks Company Limited	£372,270
W.& J.Cruickshank and Company Limited	£1,214,700	Eskimo Joe's Limited	£361,631
Hartpury Heritage Trust	£1,200,023	Seasons Soft Drinks Limited	£351,440
Think Drinks Limited	£1,154,000	Us 4 Slush Limited	£347,388
Blue Keld Springs Limited	£1,127,746	Southdowns Water Co Ltd	£338,135
Portavadie Distillery Limited	£1,110,483	Smoother Spirits Limited	£337,555
Double Dutch Ltd.	£1,097,483	Dash Brands Ltd	£329,261
Glastonbury Spring Water Company Limited	£1,087,706	Soda Folk Ltd	£328,685
Cheddar Water Limited	£1,066,561	Rockbarr Limited	£325,722
The Divine Water Company Limited	£1,057,135	JF Rabbit Ltd	£309,846
Tovali Limited	£1,056,041	Daily Dose Ltd	£294,291
Press London Ltd	£1,009,984	Gunna Drinks Limited	£294,248
Classic Mineral Water Company Limited	£974,074	Lowe Bros. (Cardiff) Limited	£276,561
The Noisy Drinks Co Ltd	£968,769	Precision Hydration Limited	£271,471
Swithland Spring Water Limited	£906,652	Mambo Drinks Limited	£271,370
Berrington Pure Spring Water Limited	£834,028	Mourne Mist Bottled Water Company Ltd	£269,385
Flower of Life Ltd	£812,051	Give Me Tap Limited	£264,806
Fielding Dairies Limited	£797,151	Dalston's Soda Company Ltd	£262,300
Karma Cola UK Ltd	£788,206	Ibis Organics Limited	£261,828
Freedrinks Limited	£781,712	Kul-Kis Limited	£239,760
Wow Food and Drinks Ltd	£719,670	Global Functional Drinks UK Limited	£229,516
Booost Trading Limited	£715,737	Flavour Master Limited	£225,471
The National Forest Spring Water Company Limited	£696,938	New Forest Spring Water Distribution Limited	£220,429
Creative Properties and Investments Ltd	£674,919	Fionnar Springs Ltd.	£212,421
Three Cents Ltd	£639,151	Super Nuva Ltd	£212,330
Citrosoft Drinks Limited	£622,717	LVS Bottling Limited	£211,197
The Deeside Water Company Limited	£622,603	The Start-Up Drinks Lab Limited	£206,699
Soft N Sweet Ltd	£619,012	Alcarelle Limited	£202,600
Swallow Drinks South West Ltd	£602,348	Beechvale Natural Water Ltd	£194,774
Moor Organics Limited	£562,626	Jumpin' Juice Limited	£193,670
Bottling International Ltd	£562,144	Ribble Valley Soft Drinks Limited	£192,997
Speyside Glenlivet (HSL) Company Limited	£543,000	New Forest Spring Water Limited	£192,695
Nix & Kix Ltd	£535,077	Muirhall Water Limited	£190,235
Rosemary Water Limited	£528,207	Refresh Brands Limited	£189,457
Northern Citrus Products Limited	£502,968	Goodness Brands Ltd	£184,965
Mr Fitzpatrick's Limited	£475,900	Sperrin Springs Limited	£181,665
Sutton Spring Limited	£473,368	Ugly Brands Limited	£179,676
Ella Drinks Limited	£470,776	Rainbow Carousel Soft Drinks Limited	£176,082
Red Dragon Water Limited	£463,677	Icely Done Drinks Limited	£174,756

Liquid Fusion Limited	£171,998	Liver Health UK Ltd.	£62,543
Square Root London Limited	£171,353	Anglesey Spring / Dwr Ffynnon Mon / Dwr Mon Ltd	£62,207
C02 Drinks Ltd	£168,620	Ammacus Trading Limited	£59,317
The Meon Spirit Company Ltd	£158,721	Elite Global Nutrition Limited	£59,093
Nourish Foods Limited	£156,903	Made By Brave Limited	£57,843
Omega EFA Limited	£156,107	Linsenlinsen Limited	£57,532
Birmingham Soft Drinks Association Limited (The)	£149,035	Sansu Drinks Ltd	£56,768
Mother Juice Ltd	£145,539	Phoenix Water Coolers Limited	£56,757
Maynard House Limited	£144,402	Club Consultants Ltd	£56,652
Just Bee Drinks Limited	£141,709	Bon Accord Soft Drinks Limited	£56,338
Green Room Brands Limited	£141,258	Outfox Drinks Ltd	£54,554
Spring Water (Devon) Limited	£139,667	Be Gemwater Limited	£53,944
K K Draught Drinks Limited	£130,400	Flow 33 UK Limited	£53,599
Amazing Forest Limited	£129,323	Wardle Spring Water Company Limited	£53,442
Fitch Brew Co Ltd.	£128,424	This Is Holy Water Limited	£53,380
NFSG Ltd.	£128,246	Brain Fud Ltd	£53,068
Juice Man Limited	£124,883	The Temperance Spirit Company Ltd	£52,508
Sekforde Drinks Limited	£124,766	Just Drinking Water Ltd	£51,348
Ice2u Ltd	£114,427	Core Fruit Products Limited	£51,012
The Gourmet Water Company Limited	£112,490	Wunder Workshop Ltd	£50,538
Bax Farm Juice Ltd	£112,089	Ardmore Spring Water Limited	£48,860
Ffynnon Carreg Limited	£108,565	Devonia Water Ltd	£48,831
Sejuiced Limited	£103,593	Alder Spring Limited	£47,953
Brainwave Brands Ltd	£102,509	Healthy Well Being Products Limited	£47,647
Thirsty Soft Drinks Ltd	£99,278	Goldbucks Limited	£47,370
Chia Food (York) Limited	£97,186	Freez Global Ltd.	£47,061
Falcon Soft Drinks Limited	£96,733	The Juice Collective Limited	£46,352
Core Beverage Equipment Ltd	£93,652	Aillo Ltd	£44,182
Mello Drinks Ltd	£92,310	Aqua Esse Limited	£42,916
Third Wave Coffee Ventures Ltd	£91,328	Bladud Spring Limited	£42,341
Grace Under Pressure Ltd	£89,890	Handmade Cider Company Limited	£40,447
Septimus Spyder Soft Drinks Limited	£87,314	PJ Kombucha Limited	£40,238
Cocomojo Group Limited	£87,274	Elsenham Water Limited	£40,235
Double Apple Ltd	£86,519	Classic Holdings Limited	£40,002
Creamright Products, Ltd	£82,008	Dexos Drinks Limited	£39,867
Rejuvenation Water Ltd	£78,248	Limonada Mathe Limited	£39,033
Loch Ness Water Ltd	£77,857	Point Blank Cold Brew Ltd	£38,887
Burst Drink Limited	£76,782	Henny and Joes Ltd	£38,733
Rocktails Drinks Limited	£76,040	Moss Cider Limited	£38,295
Aquadog Mineral Water Ltd	£75,076	Thirsty Planet Limited	£38,260
Phoenix School Drinks Ltd	£74,098	Baroncroft Ltd	£38,235
Herbal Fusions Ltd	£74,001	Beau Drinks Ltd	£37,713
Just Water Limited	£71,662	The Bloomberry Juice Company Limited	£37,150
Norfolk Cordial Ltd	£71,443	Solo Coffee Ltd	£36,710
Gran Steads Ginger Limited	£69,805	Made By Noble Limited	£36,588
Xite Energy Limited	£68,687	Dr Go Ltd	£36,488
Lovely Drinks Limited	£67,554	Samco Retail Ltd	£35,745
Solar Cola Limited	£67,217	Papas Mineral Company Ltd	£35,643
Imprint Marketing Ltd	£63,781	Ryd Food & Drinks Limited	£35,544
&Tailor Ltd	£62,607	Vyking Energy Limited	£35,004

UK Manufacturers of Soft Drinks

dellam

Sleek Still Scottish Water Limited	£33,953	Lurvills Delight Limited	£16,274
Genius Drinks Limited	£33,693	Chosan Drinks Ltd	£16,205
Dorset Ginger Company Limited	£33,586	Lixir Ltd	£16,022
Soho Juice Co Ltd	£33,466	Bumblezest Limited	£15,891
Middle Way Ltd.	£32,153	Sacred Springs Water Company Limited	£15,804
Mad Dog Drinks Limited	£32,129	Impact Sports Science Limited	£15,361
Healthy Hemp Products Ltd	£31,924	Rebel Drinks (London) Limited	£15,199
Faustian Ltd	£31,680	Yarty Cordials Limited	£15,100
East London Juice Co Ltd	£31,558	My Living Water UK Ltd	£14,950
Xtreme Energy Group Limited	£31,451	Coast Drinks Ltd	£14,463
Pembrokeshire Cider Limited	£31,168	Jeffrey's Tonic Ltd	£13,583
Wild Cat Energy Drink Ltd	£31,069	The Urban Cordial Company Limited	£13,279
Blossoms Syrup Limited	£30,472	Alcarelle Holdings Limited	£13,125
Kimpton Apple Press Limited	£30,253	ME Letric Ltd	£12,914
Juice Dub Ltd.	£30,000	Talent Drinks Ltd	£12,100
Enhance Drinks Ltd	£29,743	Kombucha Kat Ltd	£12,047
Etoh Studio Limited	£29,614	Innorbit Ltd	£11,239
Ideas 2 Launch Limited	£29,317	Pearl Soft Drinks Limited	£11,162
Roots Soda Limited	£29,039	Mayag Brands Ltd	£10,326
Willimott House Limited	£29,010	Healthy Juice Co (NI) Ltd	£10,006
Kings Farm Foods Limited	£28,786	Soak Coffee Ltd	£9,977
Hafod Water Limited	£28,529	The Santa Monica Company Ltd	£9,218
The Healthy Protein Co Ltd.	£27,126	Distillers Tonic Limited	£9,027
Evoca Enterprises Limited	£26,673	Healthy Thirst Drinks Limited	£8,966
Hippo & Hedgehog Ltd	£26,144	One Co. of Harrogate Ltd	£8,815
Inginius Limited	£26,116	IDC Irish Drinks Co. Ltd	£8,672
Artemis Brew Ltd	£25,045	Ellive Ltd	£8,645
Yuyo Drinks Ltd	£24,651	Keizen SDK Ltd	£8,520
The Pure Dartmoor Water Company Limited	£23,686	Raw Is More Ltd.	£8,499
Swalevalley Springwater Limited	£23,450	J.H.P Foods Limited	£8,487
BTW Drinks Ltd	£23,039	Two2Three2Four Ltd	£8,459
The Sensible Drinks Company Ltd	£22,975	Syrup Junkie Limited	£8,329
BFT Drinks Limited	£22,091	Wake Drinks Ltd	£8,176
Gaia Brands Ltd	£21,777	Timeless Drinks Ventures Ltd	£7,356
Ultra Beauty Limited	£21,366	Regency Tonic Ltd	£7,300
Darj Limited	£21,125	Innovative Drinks Ltd	£6,940
Sobare Limited	£20,361	We Are Haps Ltd	£6,856
Kuka Coffee Ltd	£19,651	Sleep Soft Drinks Company Ltd	£6,663
The Sussex Mobile Coffee Company Limited	£18,752	Birdhouse Tea Company Limited	£6,636
Koolvibes Limited	£18,448	The Happy Gut Hut Limited	£6,173
Drinks-on-Draught Limited	£18,235	LUHV Limited	£5,817
Bibax Limited	£18,024	Merrily Mulled Ltd	£5,772
Pitstop Coffee Limited	£17,655	Drink Better Limited	£5,646
Areea Limited	£17,466	Zaas Limited	£5,601
Originalsip Ltd	£17,260	Quad Juices Limited	£5,500
The Elaychi Tea Company Ltd	£16,955	The Bily Co Limited	£5,499
Ice Cube Tea Ltd	£16,806	Scotod Ltd	£5,429
Beverage Management Limited	£16,600	Jurassic Spring Water Ltd	£5,351
Karma Water Company Limited	£16,462	115 Design Limited	£5,063
Obeliver Drinks Limited	£16,394	Cen Bottling Company Limited	£4,966

B + K Augustin Limited	£4,873	Magic Potion Energy Drinks International Company Limited	£382
Kendal Cordials Limited	£4,814	Aqua Arbore Ltd.	£349
Wake Energy Drinks Limited	£4,546	Mossdoli Ltd	£336
MacKay & Partners (UK) Limited	£4,219	Blending and Bottling Solutions Limited	£328
Foal Limited	£4,180	Razoo Limited	£292
B4Sport Ltd.	£4,059	Tani-Mola Enterprise Ltd	£282
Miximex Limited	£4,048	Nari Palm Juice Beverages Ltd	£249
Ikoyi Chapmans Limited	£3,848	Grown-Up Foods Ltd	£242
BODI Products Limited	£3,800	Britvic Asset Company No.4 Limited	£230
Jamu Kitchen Ltd	£3,733	Britvic Asset Company No.3 Limited	£229
Bright Barley Company Ltd	£3,489	SMJ Beverages Limited	£222
Acqua Nordica Ltd	£3,452	Vero Drinks Ltd	£198
Enrj Drinks Ltd	£3,060	Two B Limited	£192
Scops Drinks Limited	£2,704	The Water Guru Limited	£175
Clayton's Cold Brewed Coffee Limited	£2,691	Mawsons Traditional Drinks Limited	£174
Benu Distribution Limited	£2,489	Seed Lab Ltd.	£143
UK Premium Brands Limited	£2,250	Cornny Drinks Limited	£125
Woodford & Warner Limited	£2,131	Biofresh Cosmos Ltd	£111
Interactive World Ltd	£2,046	Functional Beverages Ltd	£106
H Two Eau International Limited	£2,009	Hawk Spring Water (S.E.) Limited	£100
Calyx Drinks Ltd	£1,964	The Babywater Company Limited	£100
Boosted Tea (UK) Ltd.	£1,826	Poptails Limited	£100
Mother Root Ltd	£1,768	Belle Beverages Ltd	£100
Barncrofts of London Limited	£1,070	Berkeley Springs Limited	£100
SLO Good Living Ltd	£1,020	South West Juice Co. Ltd	£100
Acqua Eterna Ltd	£1,000	Miss Cola UK Limited	£100
Avid Stacc Ltd	£1,000	The Naivasha Tonic Company Ltd	£100
Nude & Rude Ltd	£1,000	Beyaz Kartal Ltd	£100
Loch Ness Drinks Ltd	£977	MCSS Investments Ltd	£100
Outsider Drinks Ltd.	£970	GB Refreshments Limited	£67
Boo-Chi Limited	£960	Get Nourished Limited	£63
Ayrshire Springs Limited	£951	Kali Engineering Ltd	£50
Floreana Ltd	£931	The East India Company Indian Tonic Water Ltd	£45
Ballmax Beverage Co Limited	£918	Ruudz Limited	£30
Karkade Drinks Limited	£900	Sweet Sally Limited	£26
Aqua Burst Ltd	£833	Fizzy Bugz Limited	£20
Hello Coco Limited	£800	The Juice Doctor Limited	£17
GO4 Beverages Limited	£792	A & S Specialist Supplies Ltd.	£8
Gurkhatise Limited	£791	Polar Krush Limited	£2
Sumo Drinks Ltd	£700	Hill Holme Juice Ltd	£2
Simple Nature Limited	£700	Destructive Lines Ltd	£2
E D Resources Limited	£689	Belfast Bottle Company Limited	£2
Ferment Revolution Limited	£657	St. Davids Spring Water Company Limited	£1
The Soda Factory Limited	£637	Ffynnon Wen Springs Limited	£1
Bouncing Biotics Ltd	£610	Shop-Local-UK Ltd	£1
Norwegian Glacier Water Limited	£542	Sportential Limited	£1
Nelly Tickner Drinks Co. Ltd	£408		

Age of Companies

1800s [5]
Birmingham Soft Drinks Association Ltd
Britannia Soft Drinks Limited
Coca-Cola European Partners GB Ltd
H.D.Rawlings Limited
R.White & Sons Limited

1900-1909
A.G. Barr P.L.C.
Hooper,Struve & Co Ltd

1910-1919
Idris Limited
London Essence Co Ltd
Refresco Beverages UK Limited

1920-1929 [5]
Mandora St. Clements Limited
Nichols PLC
Schweppes International Ltd
Ben Shaws Dispense Drinks Ltd
Sunfresh Soft Drinks Limited

1930-1939 [6]
Britvic Beverages Limited
Britvic Corona Limited
Cambrian Soft Drinks Limited
Hartridges Limited
Purity Soft Drinks Limited
Tizer Limited

1940-1949 [7]
Robert Barr Limited
Coca-Cola HBC Northern Ireland Ltd
Dayla Limited
Merrydown PLC
Simpson's Beverage Supply Co Ltd
Slush Puppie Limited
Southern Table Water Co Ltd

1950-1959 [6]
British Vitamin Products Ltd
Britvic Soft Drinks Limited
Dayla Liquid Packing Limited
Diageo Great Britain Limited
Lowe Bros. (Cardiff) Limited
Tovali Limited

1960-1969
Dayla Holdings Limited
Northern Citrus Products Ltd

1970-1979 [5]
Belfast Bottle Co Ltd
Buxton Mineral Water Limited
Classic Mineral Water Co Ltd
W.& J.Cruickshank and Co Ltd
Highland Spring Limited

1980-1989 [27]
Allson Sparkle Limited
Antrim Hills Spring Water Co Ltd
Beacon Drinks Limited
Big Time Soft Drinks Limited
Britvic EMEA Limited
Britvic International Investments
Calypso Soft Drinks Limited
Citrosoft Drinks Limited
Coca-Cola International Sales Ltd
Decantae Mineral Water Limited
Fielding Dairies Limited
Glastonbury Spring Water Co Ltd
Heather Spring Water Limited
Hildon Limited
Hope Sixteen (No.87) Limited
Kul-Kis Limited
Luscombe Drinks Limited
Maine Soft Drinks Limited
Nestle Waters GB Limited
Nestle Waters UK Limited
Original Drinks Co Ltd.
Refresco (Nelson) Limited
Rubicon Drinks Limited
SmithKline Beecham Limited
Suncrest Associates Limited
Ty Nant Spring Water Limited
James White Drinks Ltd

1990-1994 [21]
Beverage Brands (U.K.) Limited
Caledonian Bottlers PLC
Divine Water Co Ltd
Fentimans Ltd.
Greenbank Drinks Co Ltd
Healthy Thirst Drinks Limited
Heather Ale Limited
Horizon (Contract Drinks) Ltd
J.H.P Foods Limited
Northumbrian Ice Cream Co Ltd
Orchid Drinks Limited
Original Drinks and Food Co Ltd
Original Somerset Certified Water Supply
Pure Choice Watercoolers Ltd
Really Wild Drinks Co Ltd
Refresco Drinks UK Limited
Robinsons Soft Drinks Limited
SMJ Beverages Limited
Scotch Water Co Ltd
Shakespeare Spring Water Co Ltd
Wardle Spring Water Co Ltd

1995 [9]
Blue Keld Springs Limited
Clearly Devon Limited
Hawk Spring Water (S.E.) Ltd
Methuselah 969 Limited
Moorland Mist Limited
Red Devil Energy Drinks Ltd
Rockbarr Limited
Septimus Spyder Soft Drinks Ltd
Whimble Mineral Water & Brewing Co Ltd

1996 [8]
Burnswell Spring (Mauchline) Ltd
Elsenham Water Limited
Galactogen Products Limited
Thomas Hardy Holdings Limited
Life Science Limited
Montgomery Waters Limited
Radnor Hills Mineral Water Co Ltd
Shepley Spring Limited

1997
Drinks-on-Draught Limited
Liquid Ice Water Co Ltd
Seasons Soft Drinks Limited

1998 [12]
ABI SAB Group Holding Limited
Cen Bottling Co Ltd
E D Resources Limited
Ella Drinks Limited
Gleneagles Spring Water Co Ltd.
Thomas Hardy Burtonwood Ltd
Thomas Hardy Kendal Limited
Hartpury Heritage Trust
Llanllyr Water Co Ltd
Nestle Waters (UK) Holdings Ltd
Polar Krush Limited
Swithland Spring Water Limited

1999 [6]
21st Century Coke Co Ltd
Adcocks Drinks Co Ltd
Metro Drinks Limited
Pressure Coolers Limited
Two B Limited
Woodchester Enterprises Ltd

2000 [8]
04021465 Limited
Eden Springs UK Limited
Fonthill Waters Limited
HSW Limited
Harrogate Spring Water Limited
Norbev Limited
Sperrin Springs Limited
Tarka Springs Limited

2001 [12]
Beverage Management Limited
Booost Trading Limited
CMB Water Limited
Core Fruit Products Limited
Falcon Soft Drinks Limited
Kingshill Mineral Water Ltd.
Natural Fruit and Beverage Co Ltd
Office Watercoolers (S.W.) Ltd
Omega EFA Limited
Penning Power & Water Limited
Princes Gate Water Limited
Rainbow Carousel Soft Drinks Ltd

2002 [11]
Babywater Co Ltd
Baroncroft Ltd
Belu Water Limited
Fiji Water (UK) Limited
Fionnar Springs Ltd.
JDM Enterprises Ltd
Just Water Limited
National Forest Spring Water Co Ltd
Ribble Valley Soft Drinks Ltd
Rock's Organic Limited
Taut (UK) Limited

UK Manufacturers of Soft Drinks

2003 [11]
Alder Spring Limited
Blossoms Syrup Limited
Cocaine Limited
Evoca Enterprises Limited
Gaia Brands Ltd
Goldbucks Limited
Hafod Water Limited
Jumpin' Juice Limited
Maynard House Limited
NGN Distribution Limited
Waters & Robson Holdings Ltd

2004 [18]
B + K Augustin Limited
Barzy's Ltd
Berrington Pure Spring Water Ltd
Cheddar Mineral Water Limited
Cheddar Spring Water Limited
Cheddar Water Limited
Fevertree Limited
Gran Steads Ginger Limited
London Fashion Industry Ltd
Mendip Hills Mineral Water Ltd
Mendip Hills Spring Water Ltd
Mourne Mist Bottled Water Co Ltd
Sejuiced Limited
Sutton Spring Limited
Tulchan Spring Water Limited
Us 4 Slush Limited
Vitamin Brands Ltd.
Water Shop Limited

2005 [14]
Ardmore Spring Water Limited
Beechvale Natural Water Ltd
Britvic PLC
Cheddar Natural Mineral Water Ltd
Cheddar Natural Spring Water Ltd
Ed's Trading Limited
Ffynnon Wen Springs Limited
Ibis Organics Limited
MacKay & Partners (UK) Limited
Mawsons Traditional Drinks Ltd
Red Dragon Water Limited
Solar Cola Limited
St. Davids Spring Water Co Ltd
Willow Water Limited

2006 [15]
Bath Natural Mineral Water Ltd
Bath Natural Spring Water Ltd
Bottlegreen Holdings Limited
Enhance Drinks Ltd
Just Drinking Water Ltd
K K Draught Drinks Limited
Mendip Bottle Limited
Noisy Drinks Co Ltd
Pass The Baton Limited
Pearl Soft Drinks Limited
Power Juice Limited
Smoother Spirits Limited
Southdowns Natural Water Ltd
Swalevalley Springwater Ltd
Thirsty Planet Limited

2007 [18]
Ayrshire Springs Limited
Bloomberry Juice Co Ltd
Classic Holdings Limited
Cornish Organic Aloe Vera Ltd
Cracker Drinks Co. Limited
Flavour Master Limited
Highlands Pride Ltd.
Imprint Marketing Ltd
Lovely Drinks Limited
Monster Energy Europe Limited
Moor Organics Limited
Portavadie Distillery Limited
Ruudz Limited
Samco Retail Ltd
Silver Spa Limited
Storefast Solutions Limited
Thirsty Soft Drinks Ltd
Trederwen Springs 2008 Limited

2008 [9]
Braveau Limited
Cawingredients Limited
Mr Freeze (Europe) Limited
Post Hoc Ergo Propter Hoc Ltd
Qibla Cola (Beverages) Ltd
Speyside Glenlivet (HSL) Co Ltd
Spring Cool Soft Drinks Ltd
Sumo Drinks Ltd
Swallow Drinks South West Ltd

2009 [15]
Aqua Burst Ltd
Azerbaijan Juices Limited
Benu Distribution Limited
Big Daddy Beverages Limited
Diesel Brewing Co Ltd.
Elaychi Tea Co Ltd
Endurance Juice Co Ltd
Innorbit Ltd
Kendal Cordials Limited
Ladybird (Drinks) Limited
Lothian Shelf (674) Limited
March Foods Limited
Norwegian Glacier Water Ltd
Phoenix Water Coolers Limited
Woodford & Warner Limited

January-June 2010 [9]
Core Beverage Equipment Ltd
East India Company Indian Tonic Water
Faustian Ltd
Fossick Limited
Handmade Cider Co Ltd
International Soft Drinks Ltd
Scheckter's Organic Beverages Ltd
Scops Drinks Limited
Yo! Cola Ltd

July-December 2010 [10]
Britvic Overseas Limited
C02 Drinks Ltd
Fruitfilm Limited
Fuctivino Ltd
Juice Fabulous Ltd
Mr Fitzpatrick's Limited
Robinsons (Finance) No.2 Ltd
Rok Natural Energy Limited
Spring Water (Devon) Limited
Think Drinks Limited

January-June 2011 [19]
Aillo Ltd
Botanical Alchemy Ltd
Bottle Green Drinks Co Ltd
Brown Box Trading Co Ltd
Clearly Drinks Limited
Creamright Products, Ltd
Deedee's Kitchen Limited
Fillongley Spring Water Ltd
Fillongley Ventures Limited
Give Me Tap Limited
Innovative Drinks Ltd
Karma Water Co Ltd
Kingsley Partners Limited
Liveras Limited
Mad Dog Drinks Limited
Narino Limited
New Forest Spring Water Ltd
Precision Hydration Limited
Tani-Mola Enterprise Ltd

July-December 2011 [16]
5 Hour Energy Limited
J B Bowler Ltd
Britvic Asset Company No.1 Ltd
Britvic Asset Company No.2 Ltd
Britvic Asset Company No.3 Ltd
Britvic Asset Company No.4 Ltd
Everything But The Cow Limited
Impact Sports Science Limited
Inmind Care Services Ltd
Juice Dub Ltd.
Mello Drinks Ltd
Old WCS (Bottlers) Limited
Pure Dartmoor Water Co Ltd
Saapos Ltd
Wild Cat Energy Drink Ltd
Willimott House Limited

January-March 2012 [12]
Berrington Spring Water Ltd
Freedrinks Limited
Gourmet Water Co Ltd
Ideas 2 Launch Limited
JB Drinks Holdings Limited
JB Drinks Limited
Morgan's Exclusive Ltd
Moss Cider Limited
Mr. Whitehead's Drinks Co Ltd.
My Mum's Ltd
Smilk Limited
Sweet Memoirs Limited

April-June 2012 [10]
Belvoir Natural Drinks Co Ltd
Dalston's Soda Co Ltd
Flower of Life Ltd
Ice Cube Tea Ltd
Liquid Fusion Limited
Mariage Freres Royaume Uni Ltd
Obeliver Drinks Limited
Plenish Cleanse Ltd
Poptails Limited
Surrey Food and Drink Innovation Ltd

July-September 2012 [8]
Ayge Limited
Ffynnon Carreg Limited
Floreana Ltd
Green Drink (GB) Ltd
Kimpton Apple Press Limited
My Living Water UK Ltd
Pouchlink Ltd
So-Real Foods Ltd

October-December 2012 [13]
Acqua Eterna Ltd
Better Fresh Limited
Darj Limited
Fyba Ltd.
Interactive World Ltd
Keizen SDK Ltd
Little Miracles (International) Ltd
Little Miracles Drinks Limited
Man Up Energy Limited
Norfolk Cordial Ltd
Oakdale Spring Limited
Roots Soda Limited
Sqwish Squash Limited

January-March 2013 [7]
Global Functional Drinks UK Ltd
LVS Bottling Limited
Phoenix School Drinks Ltd
Press London Ltd
Refresco Developments Limited
Rocktails Drinks Limited
Sacred Springs Water Co Ltd

April-June 2013 [15]
Ashridge Cider Limited
Beau Drinks Ltd
Birdhouse Tea Co Ltd
Boss of Bosses Global Limited
Botanical Drinks Co Ltd
Brainwave Brands Ltd
Buatoc Limited
Counterpoint Wholesale (NI) Ltd
Henny and Joes Ltd
Herbal Fusions Ltd
Juice Man Limited
Jurassic Spring Water Ltd
Meon Spirit Co Ltd
Sansu Drinks Ltd
Southdowns Water Co Ltd

July-September 2013 [16]
Belle Beverages Ltd
Channel Island Water Limited
Cornny Drinks Limited
Deeside Water Company (Holdings) Ltd
Deeside Water Co Ltd
Desert Island Drinks Limited
Healthy Hemp Products Ltd
Lucozade Ribena Suntory Exports Ltd
Lucozade Ribena Suntory Ltd
Powerful Water Co Ltd
Saftiaray & Co Limited
Soda Folk Ltd
Squish Squash Limited
Sweet Sally Limited
Yuyo Drinks Ltd
Zaas Limited

October-December 2013 [17]
Ballmax Beverage Co Limited
Bottling International Ltd
Creative Properties and Investments Ltd
D & G Drinks Ltd
Dr.Shot Ltd.
Genius Drinks Limited
Gingercool Limited
Hedgerow Cordials Limited
Hill Holme Juice Ltd
Juice Shed Co Ltd
Marlish Waters Limited
Monarch Beverages Limited
Princes Gate Spring Water Ltd
Refresh Brands Limited
Square Root London Limited
Suntory Beverage & Food South Africa Ltd
Super Nuva Ltd

January-March 2014 [11]
Chapmans Drinks Limited
Devonia Water Ltd
Ember Drinks Ltd.
Goodness Brands Ltd
Icely Done Drinks Limited
Karma Cola UK Ltd
Mambo Drinks Limited
Muirhall Water Limited
Russia Cola Limited
Sussex Mobile Coffee Co Ltd
Syrup Junkie Limited

April-June 2014 [18]
Blending and Bottling Solutions Ltd
Burst Drink Limited
Cott Ventures UK Limited
Dips Dips Ltd
Eskimo Joe's Limited
Foal Limited
Freez Global Ltd.
Jarrett Health Limited
Just Bee Drinks Limited
KGN London Ltd
Nature's Fountain Limited
Story Drinks Limited
Swing Top Limited
Total Water Solutions Limited
Ultra Beauty Limited
Wow Food and Drinks Ltd
Wunder Workshop Ltd
Yarty Cordials Limited

July-September 2014 [20]
Aquadog Mineral Water Ltd
BTW Drinks Ltd
Club Consultants Ltd
Double Dutch Ltd.
Flow 33 UK Limited
Grace Under Pressure Ltd
Gurkhatise Limited
JF Rabbit Ltd
Limonada Mathe Limited
ME Letric Ltd
Office Beverages Ltd
Point Blank Cold Brew Ltd
Rebel Drinks (London) Limited
Ryd Food & Drinks Limited
Sensible Drinks Co Ltd
Peter Spanton Drinks Ltd
Stonehenge Spring Water Ltd
Thames Vintage Ltd
Wake Energy Drinks Limited
Watermarket Limited

October-December 2014 [8]
Britvic International Support Services
Coca-Cola Holdings Africa Ltd
Malvern Water Co Ltd
Marbella Cartel Ltd
Miximex Limited
NFSG Ltd.
Nix & Kix Ltd
Sharewater Ltd

January 2015 [6]
Berkeley Springs Limited
Bon Accord Soft Drinks Limited
Chia Food (York) Limited
East London Juice Co Ltd
South West Juice Co. Ltd
Ugly Brands Limited

February 2015 [6]
Fizzbang Ltd
Juicy Brands (UK) Ltd.
LUHV Limited
Papas Mineral Co Ltd
Soho Juice Co Ltd
Turn Global Ltd

March 2015 [8]
Acqua Nordica Ltd
Artemis Brew Ltd
Bax Farm Juice Ltd
Chocquers Limited
Choquers Limited
Pitstop Coffee Limited
Rejuvenation Water Ltd
Urban Cordial Co Ltd

April 2015
Aqua Arbore Ltd.
Loch Ness Water Ltd
Ness Scotland Ltd

May 2015 [5]
Areea Limited
Boydall Limited
Chosan Drinks Ltd
Salad Passion Foods Ltd
Third Wave Coffee Ventures Ltd

June 2015
Bibax Limited
Calyx Drinks Ltd
Kingsley Beverage Limited
Prime Sun Limited

July 2015 [6]
Loft 68 Vintage Ltd
Lurvills Delight Limited
Nachure Ltd
Razoo Limited
Rio Coffee Limited
Temperance Spirit Co Ltd

UK Manufacturers of Soft Drinks

August 2015 [6]
Anglesey Spring / Dwr Ffynnon Mon / Dwr Mon
Avid Stacc Ltd
Coca-Cola European Partners PLC
Genii Energy Ltd.
Kings Farm Foods Limited
Nourish Foods Limited

September 2015 [12]
Amazing Forest Limited
Elite Global Nutrition Limited
Evo Drinks Europe Ltd
Healthy Protein Co Ltd.
Juice Doctor Limited
Kolibri Drinks Limited
Montecrysto Limited
Mother Juice Ltd
Prana Drinks Limited
Raw Is More Ltd.
Two Brothers Beverage Co Ltd
Wet Beverages (Global) Ltd

October 2015 [5]
Heritage Health Organics Ltd
Hippo & Hedgehog Ltd
Jurassic Water Limited
Miss Cola UK Limited
Soft N Sweet Ltd

November 2015
Gunna Drinks Limited
Happy Gut Hut Limited
Ikoyi Chapmans Limited

December 2015
Ice Factory Limited
Nari Palm Juice Beverages Ltd
Trove International Limited

January 2016 [6]
Boosted Tea (UK) Ltd.
Brain Fud Ltd
Mission Juice Ltd
Natural Juicing Co Ltd
Steep Soft Drinks Co Ltd
Timeless Drinks Ventures Ltd

February 2016 [15]
A & S Specialist Supplies Ltd.
Clayton's Cold Brewed Coffee Ltd
Daily Dose Ltd
Dash Brands Ltd
Dr Go Ltd
Folkington's (Middle East) Ltd
Juice Collective Limited
Marley and Barley Ltd
One Co. of Harrogate Ltd
SGRIC Limited
SLO Good Living Ltd
Simple Nature Limited
Two2Three2Four Ltd
We Are Haps Ltd
Yemsmoothies Ltd

March 2016 [11]
Bussl Limited
Cocomojo Group Limited
Fruit Diversity Limited
Functional Beverages Ltd
Ipro Sport Exports Limited
Jamu Kitchen Ltd
Koolvibes Limited
Linsenlinsen Limited
New Earth Ventures Ltd
Panacea Drinks Ltd
Pembrokeshire Cider Limited

April 2016 [7]
Admete Ltd
Coast Drinks Ltd
Derbyshire Mineral Waters Ltd
Hello Coco Limited
Liver Health UK Ltd.
Poo Tang Crisps Limited
Solo Coffee Ltd

May 2016 [9]
Alcarelle Holdings Limited
Alcarelle Limited
Fitch Brew Co Ltd.
Merrily Mulled Ltd
Pura Vita Drinks Ltd.
Sekforde Drinks Limited
Sugen Frooth Limited
This Is Holy Water Limited
Youthenergy Drinks Ltd

June 2016 [14]
ARSJ Holding Ltd
Ammacus Trading Limited
Evogue Limited
Fizzy Bugz Limited
Grown-Up Foods Ltd
Inginius Limited
JW Production Limited
Konings Juices & Drinks UK Ltd
Made By Noble Limited
Naivasha Tonic Co Ltd
Red Steel Ltd
Seltza Ltd
Wake Drinks Ltd
Zilch Ltd

July 2016 [10]
Belvoir Fruit Farms Drinks Holdings
Belvoir Fruit Farms Limited
Clear Green Water Limited
Drink Better Limited
Gooddrop Supply Co. Limited
LUHV Drinks Limited
Love Tide Water Limited
Showerings Cider Mill Ltd
Nelly Tickner Drinks Co. Ltd
Vyking Energy Limited

August 2016 [11]
&Tailor Ltd
Aqua Hebrides Limited
Bello's World Limited
Budaquelle Beverages International Ltd
GO4 Beverages Limited
Green Room Brands Limited
H Two Eau International Ltd
P Mulrine and Sons Sales (U.K.) Ltd
Regency Tonic Ltd
Shop-Local-UK Ltd
Sportential Limited

September 2016 [9]
115 Design Limited
Bouncing Biotics Ltd
Bumblezest Limited
Crag Spring Water Limited
Get Nourished Limited
Kixse Limited
Kuka Coffee Ltd
Loch Ness Limited
Pomepure Ltd

October 2016 [10]
Ammo Your Ammunition to Greatness
Biofresh Cosmos Ltd
Botanical Soda Works Limited
Bright Barley Co Ltd
Ice2u Ltd
Mayag Brands Ltd
Outfox Drinks Ltd
Quad Juices Limited
Tea GB International Limited
Xtreme Energy Group Limited

November 2016 [6]
BODI Products Limited
Essence PH10 Limited
Goat Drinks Ltd
Magic Potion Energy Drinks International
Milkshake and Co London Ltd
Rosemary Water Limited

December 2016
Enrj Drinks Ltd
Kombucha Kat Ltd
Salcombe Cider Co Ltd

January 2017 [18]
Aqua Esse Limited
Avobravo Limited
Be Gemwater Limited
Distillers Tonic Limited
Edinburgh Artesian Water Co Ltd
Goodnatured Co Ltd.
H2go Drinks Ltd
Icetails Ltd
Isle of Skye Spring Water Co Ltd
Kemetic Cooks Ltd
Kingston upon Hull Liqour Co Ltd
Loch Ness Tonic Ltd
Loch Ness Tonic Water Ltd
Nozbo Drinks Limited
Rocx Energy Ltd
Soak Coffee Ltd
Temperance Drinks Limited
Village Orchard Ltd

February 2017 [17]
Craft Soft Drinks Community Ltd
Dorset Ginger Co Ltd
ECIG Retail Europe Limited
Healthy Well Being Products Ltd
IDC Irish Drinks Co. Ltd
Jeffrey's Tonic Ltd
Kali Engineering Ltd
Konon Limited
Lixir Ltd
Naturally Buzzin Energy Products Ltd
Sleek Still Scottish Water Ltd
Talent Drinks Ltd
Tapwater Corporation Limited
Thirsty Beasts Drinks Ltd
Water Guru Limited
Xite Energy Limited
Xorb Energy Limited

March 2017 [13]
Artisan Drinks Co Ltd
Bladud Spring Limited
Boo-Chi Limited
Elan League UK Ltd
Ellive Ltd
GB Refreshments Limited
HD Water Limited
Loch Ness Drinks Ltd
Lupe Kombucha Ltd.
Middle Way Ltd.
Roo Drinks Limited
Thirstea Drinks Limited
Vero Drinks Ltd

April 2017 [9]
Destructive Lines Ltd
Double Apple Ltd
Etoh Studio Limited
Karkade Drinks Limited
Momo Kombucha Ltd
Originalsip Ltd
Outsider Drinks Ltd.
Pura Panela Ltd
Seed Lab Ltd.

May 2017 [20]
Armagh Juice Co Ltd
B20 Water Ltd
Barncrofts of London Limited
Bily Co Limited
Carbon Drinks Limited
Cold Bru Tea Limited
Ferment Revolution Limited
Gallybird Tonic Co Ltd
Made By Brave Limited
Mother Root Ltd
New Forest Spring Water Distribution Ltd
Nude & Rude Ltd
Nude Drinks Limited
Nutrapharm Ltd
Saicho Ltd.
Shindig Promotions Ltd
Bertrand Tailor Limited
UK Dorset Ltd
Vitapure Drinks Co Ltd
Zombie Energy Limited

June 2017 [22]
B4Sport Ltd.
BFT Drinks Limited
Beyaz Kartal Ltd
DRII Limited
Delicious Retail Ltd
Dry Beverages Limited
Exoteeque Limited
Exotic Beverages Limited
Halo Drinks Co Ltd
Healthy Juice Co (NI) Ltd
Hell Energy Ltd
Hydrade Drinks Limited
Lionade Ltd
Mighty Flames Ltd
Peel and Spice Ltd
Polconut Ltd
SK Global Brands Ltd
Santa Monica Co Ltd
Session Brewing Co. Limited
Soda Factory Limited
Start-Up Drinks Lab Limited
Tea Rocks Ltd

July 2017 [8]
Craft Mixers Co Ltd
Drinkology Limited
Freak Cocktails Ltd
Microbiome Technologies Ltd
Mother Nature's Drinks Limited
New Life Water Limited
Wisdom Superfoods CIC
Yummy Juice Co Ltd

August 2017 [15]
Bespokery Ltd
Bitter Salvation Ltd
Caledonian Cola Co Ltd
Clearwater Drink Limited
Country Garden Drinks Co Ltd
Dry Drinks and Teas Co Ltd
Fuse Drinks Ltd
Genie Drinks Ltd
House of Symbols Ltd
Nele Drinks Limited
Portable Marketing Solutions Ltd
Skwishee Ltd
Sobare Limited
Sober Drinks Limited
Yeast Meets West Limited

September 2017 [13]
Ballantyne McLean Limited
DRGN Global Ltd.
Dexos Drinks Limited
Good Beverage Co Ltd
Hydration Station Ltd
Kendal Brewery Ltd
Malvern Bottling Works Limited
Positive Potions Limited
Pump House Water Ltd
SRP Equipe Limited
Smith & Harrison Ltd
Three Cents Ltd
UK Premium Brands Limited

October 2017 [14]
Agua Fresca Ltd.
H20miles Ltd
Koala Karma UK Limited
Korko Limited
Luxbev Limited
Luxuryshakes Ltd
Moores of Warwick Limited
Mossdoli Ltd
Mr Holmes Flavored Syrups Ltd
Mylkman Ltd
Neu Water Limited
PJ Kombucha Limited
Rhythm Nutrition Ltd
Strawhill Estate Spirits Co Ltd

November 2017 [12]
Alitasa Ltd
Bad Girls Brew Limited
Explorer Coffees Ltd
Frozen Brothers Limited
Hangin Drinks Limited
Happy Curations Limited
Infinite Session Ltd
Intelligent Brews Co Ltd
Mother Kombucha Ltd
Unique Drinks Limited
White Smoke Distillery Ltd
Zuddha Water Limited

December 2017 [17]
Amino Drinks Limited
Bigla Brewing Co Ltd
Bloody Drinks Limited
Bowser Limited
Bowser Properties Limited
Bowser Tonic Limited
Cornish Kombucha Limited
Edinburgh Tonic Ltd
Elementhree Ltd
Food and Drink Development Co Ltd
Hullabaloos Lemonade Limited
Livitus Limited
Natural Food and Drink Co Ltd
Roiss Mineral Water Limited
Wise Herb Co Ltd
Wolfe's Drinks Limited
Xite Beverages Limited

January 2018 [23]
40 Kola Ltd
Alpha Energy Drink Limited
Ankerwycke Water Limited
Birch Boost Ltd
Bounce Back Drinks Limited
Charlie T's Ltd
Copper Stag Ltd
ECF Global Ltd
Enchanted Forest Milks Limited
Equilibrium Food & Drink Ltd
Good Water Trading Ltd
Hawkins Drinks Limited
Lord Eden Beverages Ltd
Lord Eden Ltd
MCSS Investments Ltd
Neue Water Limited
Oxidize Limited
Pickle Shot Limited
Raviom Limited
Rebel Drinks Accra Limited

UK Manufacturers of Soft Drinks

Scotod Ltd
Sopro Drinks Ltd
Vivo Water Ltd

February 2018 [19]
Alive Beverages Limited
Amor Food and Beverages Holdings Ltd
Beyond Alcohol Ltd
Burble Foods and Beverages Ltd
Chastity Limited
Cornfield Foods and Beverages Ltd
Crosby Beverages Ltd
Distinate Ltd
Eauvolution Limited
Havok Energy Drink. Ltd
Holos London Ltd
House of Balmoral Ltd
Lytewater Limited
Morninglory Ltd
N'ife Limited
Saint Patricks Ltd
Shlurpies Ltd.
Theodore Global Limited
WTRplus Ltd

March 2018 [23]
411 Beverages Limited
AB Vaults Group Limited
Amaize Drinks Limited
Artio Foods Ltd
Boil and Broth Ltd
Cardinal Drinks Ltd
Chakra Chai Limited
Ginsense Ltd
Hawkshead Gin and Spirit Co Ltd
Istok Foods Limited
Juice Supply Limited
Kompassion Ltd
London Botanical Drinks Ltd
Macro Munch Ltd
Naneau Limited
Neptune SA Ltd
Pure Spring Aqua Ltd
Red Bandit Limited
Slimmers World Sports Drinks Ltd
Viva Riva Beverage Co Ltd
Vivo Viva Beverages Limited
Watkins Drinks Limited
Wild Husk Limited

April 2018 [20]
Afrimalt International Limited
Alcro Commercials Limited
Alive Water Ltd
Alkali Water Limited
Alko Vintages UK Ltd
Anglo African Food & Beverages Holding
Brewski Coffee Ltd
Cheese Burger Limited
Dakena-One International Ltd
Elfie Drinks Co Ltd
Fab World Limited
Funk Beverages Ltd
Jolly's Drinks Limited
Juice Junkies Limited
Moringa Superfoods UK Limited
Nairamalt UK Limited
Pharmaco Group Limited
Qishui Limited
Tiny Mighty People Ltd
Wildeve Ltd

May 2018 [27]
APE2O Limited
Akme Coffee Limited
Alive & Kicking Fermented Foods Ltd
Andina Coffee Co. Ltd
Arosuk Ltd
Corduroy Ideas Limited
Devon Soda Co Limited
Faultless Drinks Limited
Glucofit Limited
Hedgerow Soft Drinks Ltd
ICB Advisory Limited
Ice People Limited
Jellani Ltd
Kombuchaye Ltd
Lemon Factory Ltd
Lintaru DGL Ltd
My Little Potion Ltd
Oxford Juice Co Ltd
Pentire Drinks Limited
Piff Juice Limited
Punchline Ltd
Saft Drinks Ltd
Schnapps Limited
Sea Buck Limited
Yorkshire Soft Drinks Ltd
Your Water Ltd
Zireson Enterprises Limited

June 2018 [16]
70s Booch Ltd
Artathlon Beverages Limited
Artathlon Water Limited
Brewberry Limited
Crystalstore Ltd
Edinburgh Kombucha Ltd
Fruito Soft Drinks Limited
Giantcandyco Limited
Johnson Supplies UK Ltd
Nerissimo Luxury Espresso Ltd
Paisley Drinks Co. Ltd
Saffron Water Limited
Sendivogius Limited
Shrubb Ltd
Upper Harglodd Farm Ltd
Waterful Ltd

July 2018 [22]
Awlgold Ltd
Boostvitaminwater Ltd
Cantaker Ltd
Conscious Drinks Limited
Cybora Ltd
Danjan Ventures Ltd
Drinks for Beauty Ltd
Finn Capital Ltd
Fruito Beverages (Africa) Ltd
Highdrate Ltd
Hike Coffee Ltd
Hoods Cordial Ltd
Humble Bumble Ltd
Lady Eden Ltd
Molly Rose Drinks Ltd
Mount Valley Beverages Ltd
Phutures Limited
Proper Good Brands Limited
Refreshing Intercepted Limited
J Water Disabled Children Ltd
Whollywater Ltd
Zowell Ltd

August 2018 [20]
Cure T.H.A.S.D. Limited
El Natural Ltd
Frey Drinks Limited
Green Monkey Drinks Ltd
O.T.C Beverages Limited
Permeske Ltd
Reluminate Ltd
Rigdeplot Ltd
Roar Loud Limited
Salicaria Ltd
Saltcoats Mineral Water Co Ltd
Shandy Shack Ltd
Sipsup Limited
Skep Drinks Limited
Sodahouseco Limited
TMF Trading Limited
Titonic Ltd
UK Brighton Food & Nutrition Research Centre
Wotar Ltd
Zion Manufacturing Ltd

September 2018 [29]
AA Group Holdings Ltd
Aberrucia Ltd
Ad Hoque Ltd
Agilebody Ltd
Bax Botanics Limited
Driver's Drinks Co Ltd
Eastcott Drinks Ltd
Emery Brand Ltd
Enso Goods Limited
GB Heritage Ltd
Gibraltar Gin Co Ltd
Glaisher & Ames Ltd
Good Remedy Limited
Honu Sodas UK Limited
Innovate Energy Drinks Ltd
Kore Kombucha Ltd
NR Enterprise Limited
No Longer Bax Botanics Limited
Pointeer Ltd
Signpost Brewery Ltd
Spirit of Shanti Ltd
Strada Soft Drinks Ltd
Superfoods Nutrition Ltd
Tasty Kameleon Ltd
Vitte Nutrition Ltd
Water Group Ltd
Yee Energy Ltd
Youthenergy East Africa Ltd
Zero Proof International Ltd

October 2018 [30]
413 Limited
Adapt Kombucha Limited
Alexionut Ltd
Benefit Water Ltd
CBD Revolution Ltd
Captains Original Ltd
Chaiwala Limited
Connect Beverages Ltd
Drinks Group Holdings Ltd
Earth Plant Co Ltd
Enterprises Beyond Reason Ltd
Ginsecco Ltd
Green Foods International Ltd
Henrysuper Roots Drinks Ltd
Immunoguardian Ltd
Lifeline Holdings Limited

Love Tonic Ltd
Mildenhall Bottling Co Ltd
Mobay Drinks Ltd
Nutricana Ltd
Ocentek Ltd
Our Northern Stars Limited
Pivotal Drinks Ltd
Pop in Tea Limited
Qiblah Beverages Limited
Real Natural UK Ltd
TBD Brew Co Ltd
Tasteuk Limited
Vine Springs Ltd
Your Mind Body Soul Limited

November 2018 [32]
Artemis Import & Export Ltd
Bliiss Ltd
Blue Raspberry Investments Ltd
CBD Tonic & Mixers Limited
Can of Wagon Ltd
Celtic Soul Drinks Limited
Chilled Water Ltd
Common Goods Group Limited
Dove Foods Ltd
Drinks Cubed Ltd
Edible Hedgerow Ltd
Exotica Beverages Ltd
Fake Brews Ltd
Faraday Drinks Ltd
Fizzbang Beverage Co Ltd
A & C Green Food and Beverage Ltd
Guffaw Ltd
Hendre Distillery Ltd
Hon Limited
Jeffries Group Ltd
Kapyani Limited
Lough Neagh Distillers - 1837 Ltd
Lucid Beverage Research Ltd
Qiblah Products Limited
Rainbow Beverages Ltd

Sweet Leaves Ltd
Syncrobia Ltd
Teabase Ltd
Three Spirit Drinks Ltd
Two Keys Ltd
UK Blue Ribbon Group Beer Co., Ltd
Westmoor Botanicals Limited

December 2018 [14]
Alcohol Free Drinks Limited
Alyke Health Limited
Aquacan Limited
FYA Peppa Kitchen Ltd
Faractive Limited
Goodlives Panacea Blend Ltd
Steven Hatch Operations Consultancy Ltd
Leanteen Limited
Liverpool Canning Co Ltd
Mighty Drinks Ltd.
Ryan-Knight Enterprises Ltd
Tassology Limited
V-Storm Energy Ltd
Zero Proof UK Limited

January 2019 [20]
Bennu Rising Ltd.
Bread Drink Lab Limited
CBDMEhealthy Limited
Caraway and Peel Limited
Carrington's Coffee Co Ltd
Dangercode Ltd
Efcon UK Ltd
HYP Water Ltd
Hidden Orchard Ltd
JSJuices Ltd
Kubera Group International Ltd
MB Drinks Ltd
Mangogo Ltd
Package Water Solutions Ltd
Paradise Rum Limited
Rootfire Ltd

SIP Kombucha Ltd
Space Chef Ltd
Tanfield Springs Ltd
Vitosha Wine Ltd

February 2019 [35]
Adaquo H20 Ltd
Ardross Castle Water Co Ltd
Birken Tree (Scotland) Limited
Bless Up Beverages Ltd
Bolbol Imports Ltd
Bright Smoothies Ltd
Canncrest Drinks Limited
Cotton & Cane Ltd
Cure Project Limited
Dee's Greens Limited
Do Drink Co Ltd
Duo Drinks Ltd
Eliya Europe Ltd
Endo Sport Ltd
Green Leaf Liquids Limited
Gut Drinks Ltd
H2can Ltd
HIH Frankly Irresistible Ltd
Kingdon Callea Ltd
Live Kindly Drinks Co Ltd
Ma3 Drinks Ltd
Mag Marketing Limited
Marah Drinks Limited
Ocean Tears Ltd
Original Free Drinks Co Ltd
Paradise Drinks Co. Limited
Persian Roze Ltd
Refreshing Drinks Co Ltd
Sai Water UK Limited
Seafire Brewing Co. Ltd
Sips MCR Ltd
Spruce Water Limited
Trip Drink Ltd
Vida Water Ltd
Wild Life Botanicals Ltd

Geographic Distribution by County

Co Antrim [15]
Antrim Hills Spring Water Co Ltd
Belfast Bottle Co Ltd
Bottle Green Drinks Co Ltd
Coca-Cola HBC Northern Ireland Ltd
Cocomojo Group Limited
Counterpoint Wholesale (NI) Ltd
Intelligent Brews Co Ltd
Kul-Kis Limited
Maine Soft Drinks Limited
Nele Drinks Limited
Norbev Limited
Panacea Drinks Ltd
Scotod Ltd
Spring Cool Soft Drinks Ltd
TBD Brew Co Ltd

Co Armagh [10]
Ardmore Spring Water Limited
Armagh Juice Co Ltd
Boosted Tea (UK) Ltd.
Classic Holdings Limited
Classic Mineral Water Co Ltd
Functional Beverages Ltd
Healthy Juice Co (NI) Ltd
Lough Neagh Distillers - 1837 Ltd
Nourish Foods Limited
Strawhill Estate Spirits Co Ltd

Co Down [5]
Mourne Mist Bottled Water Co Ltd
Papas Mineral Co Ltd
Shindig Promotions Ltd
Soak Coffee Ltd
Titonic Ltd

Co Fermanagh
Beechvale Natural Water Ltd

Co Londonderry
IDC Irish Drinks Co. Ltd

Co Tyrone
P Mulrine and Sons Sales (U.K.) Ltd
Sperrin Springs Limited

Aberdeenshire [5]
ARSJ Holding Ltd
Aqua Hebrides Limited
Deeside Water Company (Holdings) Ltd
Deeside Water Co Ltd
Nozbo Drinks Limited

Angus
Ella Drinks Limited
Red Steel Ltd
Scotch Water Co Ltd

Argyll & Bute
Portavadie Distillery Limited

Ayrshire [5]
Ayrshire Springs Limited
Burnswell Spring (Mauchline) Ltd
K K Draught Drinks Limited
Natural Fruit and Beverage Co Ltd
Saltcoats Mineral Water Co Ltd

Banffshire
W.& J.Cruickshank and Co Ltd

Clackmannanshire
Heather Ale Limited

Dumfries & Galloway
Molly Rose Drinks Ltd

Dunbartonshire
Middle Way Ltd.
Smoother Spirits Limited

Fife [8]
Allson Sparkle Limited
Alyke Health Limited
Gooddrop Supply Co. Limited
A & C Green Food and Beverage Ltd
House of Balmoral Ltd
Nerissimo Luxury Espresso Ltd
Seafire Brewing Co. Ltd
Skwishee Ltd

Inverness-shire
Fionnar Springs Ltd.
Love Tonic Ltd

Isle of Skye
Isle of Skye Spring Water Co Ltd

Lanarkshire [19]
Alive Water Ltd
Andina Coffee Co. Ltd
Robert Barr Limited
A.G. Barr P.L.C.
Bounce Back Drinks Limited
Caledonian Cola Co Ltd
Chastity Limited
Clear Green Water Limited
Foal Limited
Get Nourished Limited
Ginsecco Ltd
Grown-Up Foods Ltd
Heather Spring Water Limited
Hippo & Hedgehog Ltd
JW Production Limited
Kingshill Mineral Water Ltd.
Muirhall Water Limited
Old WCS (Bottlers) Limited
Sportential Limited

Perthshire [6]
Birken Tree (Scotland) Limited
Highland Spring Limited
Highlands Pride Ltd.
Hope Sixteen (No.87) Limited
Lothian Shelf (674) Limited
Speyside Glenlivet (HSL) Co Ltd

Perth & Kinross
Gleneagles Spring Water Co Ltd.

Renfrewshire
Braveau Limited
Craft Soft Drinks Community Ltd
Paisley Drinks Co. Ltd
Start-Up Drinks Lab Limited

Ross & Cromarty
Loch Ness Drinks Ltd
Loch Ness Limited
Ness Scotland Ltd

Ross-shire
Ardross Castle Water Co Ltd
Loch Ness Tonic Ltd
Loch Ness Tonic Water Ltd
Loch Ness Water Ltd

Selkirkshire
Goodnatured Co Ltd.

Stirlingshire
B4Sport Ltd.
Seltza Ltd

Anglesey
Positive Potions Limited

Bedfordshire [7]
Double Apple Ltd
Falcon Soft Drinks Limited
Loft 68 Vintage Ltd
Milkshake and Co London Ltd
Theodore Global Limited
Waterful Ltd
Zilch Ltd

Berkshire [23]
Ammo Your Ammunition to Greatness
Amor Food and Beverages Holdings Ltd
Ayge Limited
Beyond Alcohol Ltd
Boydall Limited
Cornny Drinks Limited
Cracker Drinks Co. Limited
Ember Drinks Ltd.
Faractive Limited
Food and Drink Development Co Ltd
Green Room Brands Limited
Imprint Marketing Ltd
Innorbit Ltd
JF Rabbit Ltd
MCSS Investments Ltd
Monarch Beverages Limited
Natural Food and Drink Co Ltd
Paradise Drinks Co. Limited
Ryd Food & Drinks Limited
Thirsty Beasts Drinks Ltd
Three Spirit Drinks Ltd
Wild Husk Limited
Wise Herb Co Ltd

Buckinghamshire [18]
Alexionut Ltd
Blossoms Syrup Limited
Bright Barley Co Ltd
Dayla Holdings Limited
Dayla Limited
Drinks-on-Draught Limited
Frozen Brothers Limited
Gurkhatise Limited
Ice People Limited
Kingsley Partners Limited
Mandora St. Clements Limited
Ocean Tears Ltd
Rubicon Drinks Limited

UK Manufacturers of Soft Drinks

Saft Drinks Ltd
Slush Puppie Limited
Taut (UK) Limited
Tizer Limited
Yo! Cola Ltd

Cambridgeshire [12]
Adcocks Drinks Co Ltd
B + K Augustin Limited
E D Resources Limited
Fielding Dairies Limited
Finn Capital Ltd
House of Symbols Ltd
Inmind Care Services Ltd
Kingsley Beverage Limited
March Foods Limited
Moringa Superfoods UK Limited
Rhythm Nutrition Ltd
V-Storm Energy Ltd

Cardiganshire
Do Drink Co Ltd
Ice Cube Tea Ltd
Llanllyr Water Co Ltd
Ty Nant Spring Water Limited

Carmarthenshire
Hafod Water Limited
Tovali Limited

Cheshire [19]
Adapt Kombucha Limited
Ammacus Trading Limited
Beverage Management Limited
Blending and Bottling Solutions Ltd
Carrington's Coffee Co Ltd
Ellive Ltd
Faultless Drinks Limited
Fruitfilm Limited
GB Heritage Ltd
Thomas Hardy Burtonwood Ltd
Thomas Hardy Holdings Limited
Thomas Hardy Kendal Limited
Hon Limited
Jeffrey's Tonic Ltd
Juice Shed Co Ltd
Lytewater Limited
Mag Marketing Limited
Samco Retail Ltd
Thirsty Soft Drinks Ltd

Cleveland
Cure T.H.A.S.D. Limited
Salicaria Ltd

Clwyd
Wake Drinks Ltd
Wake Energy Drinks Limited

Co Durham
JDM Enterprises Ltd
Zombie Energy Limited

Cornwall [6]
Cornish Kombucha Limited
Devon Soda Co Limited
Hidden Orchard Ltd
Rocktails Drinks Limited
Sea Buck Limited
Sugen Frooth Limited

Cumbria [6]
Hawkshead Gin and Spirit Co Ltd
Ibis Organics Limited
Kendal Brewery Ltd
Kendal Cordials Limited
LVS Bottling Limited
Morninglory Ltd

Derbyshire [9]
BFT Drinks Limited
Calypso Soft Drinks Limited
Derbyshire Mineral Waters Ltd
Mr Freeze (Europe) Limited
Peel and Spice Ltd
Refresco (Nelson) Limited
Refresco Developments Limited
Refresco Drinks UK Limited
Roiss Mineral Water Limited

Devon [16]
21st Century Coke Co Ltd
Ashridge Cider Limited
Bloomberry Juice Co Ltd
Clearly Devon Limited
Devonia Water Ltd
Jolly's Drinks Limited
Just Water Limited
Luscombe Drinks Limited
Methuselah 969 Limited
Moorland Mist Limited
Naturally Buzzin Energy Products Ltd
Pure Dartmoor Water Co Ltd
Salcombe Cider Co Ltd
Scops Drinks Limited
Sweet Leaves Ltd
Tarka Springs Limited

Dorset [8]
115 Design Limited
Boil and Broth Ltd
Dorset Ginger Co Ltd
Jurassic Spring Water Ltd
Kubera Group International Ltd
Precision Hydration Limited
We Are Haps Ltd
Yuyo Drinks Ltd

Dyfed
Ffynnon Carreg Limited
Liquid Ice Water Co Ltd

Essex [23]
A & S Specialist Supplies Ltd.
Afrimalt International Limited
Aquacan Limited
Artio Foods Ltd
Big Daddy Beverages Limited
Burst Drink Limited
C02 Drinks Ltd
CBD Revolution Ltd
Chosan Drinks Ltd
Dips Dips Ltd
Elsenham Water Limited
Frey Drinks Limited
Gibraltar Gin Co Ltd
Hill Holme Juice Ltd
Lionade Ltd
Miss Cola UK Limited
Nairamalt UK Limited

Neptune SA Ltd
New Earth Ventures Ltd
Rio Coffee Limited
Shop-Local-UK Ltd
Skep Drinks Limited
Sweet Sally Limited

Glamorgan [10]
El Natural Ltd
Heritage Health Organics Ltd
International Soft Drinks Ltd
Lowe Bros. (Cardiff) Limited
Lurvills Delight Limited
Mambo Drinks Limited
Neu Water Limited
Prana Drinks Limited
Rigdeplot Ltd
Tapwater Corporation Limited

Gloucestershire [23]
Bottlegreen Holdings Limited
Brewberry Limited
Distillers Tonic Limited
Hartpury Heritage Trust
Innovate Energy Drinks Ltd
Kuka Coffee Ltd
Life Science Limited
MacKay & Partners (UK) Limited
Merrydown PLC
NFSG Ltd.
Office Watercoolers (S.W.) Ltd
Qishui Limited
Rocx Energy Ltd
Sacred Springs Water Co Ltd
Seed Lab Ltd.
Sodahouseco Limited
Solo Coffee Ltd
Super Nuva Ltd
Woodchester Enterprises Ltd
Xite Beverages Limited
Xite Energy Limited
Xorb Energy Limited
Xtreme Energy Group Limited

Gwynedd
Ffynnon Wen Springs Limited
St. Davids Spring Water Co Ltd

Hampshire [28]
Bowser Limited
Bowser Properties Limited
Bowser Tonic Limited
CBD Tonic & Mixers Limited
Etoh Studio Limited
Explorer Coffees Ltd
Fossick Limited
Hartridges Limited
Hildon Limited
Jurassic Water Limited
LUHV Drinks Limited
LUHV Limited
Meon Spirit Co Ltd
Mildenhall Bottling Co Ltd
Mr. Whitehead's Drinks Co Ltd.
Naneau Limited
New Forest Spring Water Distribution Ltd
New Forest Spring Water Ltd
Nude Drinks Limited
Rock's Organic Limited
Shandy Shack Ltd

Smilk Limited
Southdowns Natural Water Ltd
Southdowns Water Co Ltd
Two2Three2Four Ltd
Us 4 Slush Limited
Vitosha Wine Ltd
Yarty Cordials Limited

Herefordshire [8]
Berrington Pure Spring Water Ltd
Berrington Spring Water Ltd
GB Refreshments Limited
HYP Water Ltd
Malvern Water Co Ltd
Real Natural UK Ltd
Whimble Mineral Water & Brewing Co Ltd
Youthenergy Drinks Ltd

Hertfordshire [52]
Alcarelle Holdings Limited
Alcarelle Limited
Beau Drinks Ltd
Britannia Soft Drinks Limited
British Vitamin Products Ltd
Britvic Asset Company No.1 Ltd
Britvic Asset Company No.2 Ltd
Britvic Asset Company No.3 Ltd
Britvic Asset Company No.4 Ltd
Britvic Beverages Limited
Britvic Corona Limited
Britvic EMEA Limited
Britvic International Investments
Britvic International Support Services
Britvic Overseas Limited
Britvic PLC
Britvic Soft Drinks Limited
Cantaker Ltd
Conscious Drinks Limited
Craft Mixers Co Ltd
Creamright Products, Ltd
Eauvolution Limited
Greenbank Drinks Co Ltd
HIH Frankly Irresistible Ltd
Hangin Drinks Limited
Hooper,Struve & Co Ltd
Icely Done Drinks Limited
Idris Limited
J.H.P Foods Limited
Juice Dub Ltd.
Liveras Limited
Luxuryshakes Ltd
Orchid Drinks Limited
Post Hoc Ergo Propter Hoc Ltd
Proper Good Brands Limited
H.D.Rawlings Limited
Really Wild Drinks Co Ltd
Red Devil Energy Drinks Ltd
Robinsons (Finance) No.2 Ltd
Robinsons Soft Drinks Limited
Rootfire Ltd
SIP Kombucha Ltd
Scheckter's Organic Beverages Ltd
Soda Folk Ltd
Southern Table Water Co Ltd
Sunfresh Soft Drinks Limited
Talent Drinks Ltd
R.White & Sons Limited
Woodford & Warner Limited
Youthenergy East Africa Ltd
Zero Proof International Ltd
Zero Proof UK Limited

Isle of Anglesey
Anglesey Spring / Dwr Ffynnon Mon / Dwr Mon

Isle of Wight
Kixse Limited

Kent [24]
Bax Farm Juice Ltd
Bouncing Biotics Ltd
CMB Water Limited
Core Fruit Products Limited
Desert Island Drinks Limited
Efcon UK Ltd
Fizzbang Ltd
Goldbucks Limited
Hawk Spring Water (S.E.) Ltd
Hydration Station Ltd
Innovative Drinks Ltd
Ipro Sport Exports Limited
Jarrett Health Limited
Juice Fabulous Ltd
Karkade Drinks Limited
Korko Limited
Man Up Energy Limited
Moor Organics Limited
Original Drinks Co Ltd.
Original Drinks and Food Co Ltd
Phoenix School Drinks Ltd
Ryan-Knight Enterprises Ltd
Storefast Solutions Limited
Tea Rocks Ltd

Lancashire [45]
411 Beverages Limited
Awlgold Ltd
B20 Water Ltd
Bily Co Limited
Bless Up Beverages Ltd
Botanical Soda Works Limited
Calyx Drinks Ltd
Cen Bottling Co Ltd
Chaiwala Limited
Chilled Water Ltd
Citrosoft Drinks Limited
Clearwater Drink Limited
Connect Beverages Ltd
Crag Spring Water Limited
Crystalstore Ltd
Dakena-One International Ltd
Dove Foods Ltd
Elaychi Tea Co Ltd
Flavour Master Limited
Freez Global Ltd.
Fuctivino Ltd
Fyba Ltd.
H2go Drinks Ltd
Ice2u Ltd
Just Bee Drinks Limited
Ladybird (Drinks) Limited
Mawsons Traditional Drinks Ltd
Mello Drinks Ltd
Mr Fitzpatrick's Limited
Mr Holmes Flavored Syrups Ltd
Northern Citrus Products Ltd
Omega EFA Limited
Refreshing Intercepted Limited
Ribble Valley Soft Drinks Ltd
Rockbarr Limited
Roo Drinks Limited

Sensible Drinks Co Ltd
Simpson's Beverage Supply Co Ltd
Sips MCR Ltd
Steep Soft Drinks Co Ltd
Strada Soft Drinks Ltd
Third Wave Coffee Ventures Ltd
Unique Drinks Limited
Wardle Spring Water Co Ltd
Yee Energy Ltd

Leicestershire [12]
Amazing Forest Limited
Bottling International Ltd
Hell Energy Ltd
Jeffries Group Ltd
Lady Eden Ltd
Lord Eden Beverages Ltd
Lord Eden Ltd
MB Drinks Ltd
Spirit of Shanti Ltd
Swithland Spring Water Limited
Wild Cat Energy Drink Ltd
Zuddha Water Limited

Lincolnshire [5]
Boss of Bosses Global Limited
Cocaine Limited
Country Garden Drinks Co Ltd
London Fashion Industry Ltd
Rainbow Carousel Soft Drinks Ltd

London [294]
413 Limited
AA Group Holdings Ltd
AB Vaults Group Limited
ABI SAB Group Holding Limited
Acqua Eterna Ltd
Acqua Nordica Ltd
Admete Ltd
Akme Coffee Limited
Alcohol Free Drinks Limited
Alcro Commercials Limited
Alitasa Ltd
Alive & Kicking Fermented Foods Ltd
Alive Beverages Limited
Alko Vintages UK Ltd
Alpha Energy Drink Limited
Amino Drinks Limited
Anglo African Food & Beverages Holding
Aqua Arbore Ltd.
Aqua Esse Limited
Aquadog Mineral Water Ltd
Arosuk Ltd
Artathlon Beverages Limited
Artathlon Water Limited
Artemis Import & Export Ltd
Avobravo Limited
Azerbaijan Juices Limited
BODI Products Limited
BTW Drinks Ltd
Babywater Co Ltd
Bad Girls Brew Limited
Barncrofts of London Limited
Barzy's Ltd
Belle Beverages Ltd
Bello's World Limited
Belu Water Limited
Benu Distribution Limited
Berkeley Springs Limited
Bespokery Ltd
Better Fresh Limited

UK Manufacturers of Soft Drinks

Bibax Limited
Biofresh Cosmos Ltd
Bitter Salvation Ltd
Bloody Drinks Limited
Bolbol Imports Ltd
Boo-Chi Limited
Booost Trading Limited
Boostvitaminwater Ltd
Botanical Alchemy Ltd
Botanical Drinks Co Ltd
J B Bowler Ltd
Brewski Coffee Ltd
Buatoc Limited
Bumblezest Limited
Burble Foods and Beverages Ltd
Bussl Limited
CBDMEhealthy Limited
Cambrian Soft Drinks Limited
Can of Wagon Ltd
Canncrest Drinks Limited
Captains Original Ltd
Caraway and Peel Limited
Cardinal Drinks Ltd
Chakra Chai Limited
Channel Island Water Limited
Coast Drinks Ltd
Coca-Cola Holdings Africa Ltd
Coca-Cola International Sales Ltd
Cold Bru Tea Limited
Common Goods Group Limited
Copper Stag Ltd
Cornfield Foods and Beverages Ltd
Cotton & Cane Ltd
Creative Properties and Investments Ltd
Crosby Beverages Ltd
Cure Project Limited
D & G Drinks Ltd
DRGN Global Ltd.
Daily Dose Ltd
Dalston's Soda Co Ltd
Darj Limited
Dash Brands Ltd
Dee's Greens Limited
Deedee's Kitchen Limited
Delicious Retail Ltd
Dexos Drinks Limited
Diageo Great Britain Limited
Double Dutch Ltd.
Drinks Cubed Ltd
Dry Drinks and Teas Co Ltd
Duo Drinks Ltd
ECF Global Ltd
Earth Plant Co Ltd
East India Company Indian Tonic Water
Eastcott Drinks Ltd
Elan League UK Ltd
Elementhree Ltd
Enchanted Forest Milks Limited
Endurance Juice Co Ltd
Enrj Drinks Ltd
Everything But The Cow Limited
Evoca Enterprises Limited
Evogue Limited
Exotica Beverages Ltd
FYA Peppa Kitchen Ltd
Fake Brews Ltd
Faustian Ltd
Ferment Revolution Limited
Fevertree Limited
Fiji Water (UK) Limited
Fizzbang Beverage Co Ltd
Fizzy Bugz Limited

Flow 33 UK Limited
Freedrinks Limited
Fruito Beverages (Africa) Ltd
Fruito Soft Drinks Limited
Funk Beverages Ltd
Fuse Drinks Ltd
Genie Drinks Ltd
Genius Drinks Limited
Giantcandyco Limited
Give Me Tap Limited
Glaisher & Ames Ltd
Global Functional Drinks UK Ltd
Good Beverage Co Ltd
Good Remedy Limited
Good Water Trading Ltd
Green Drink (GB) Ltd
H Two Eau International Ltd
H20miles Ltd
H2can Ltd
HD Water Limited
Halo Drinks Co Ltd
Happy Curations Limited
Havok Energy Drink. Ltd
Healthy Protein Co Ltd.
Henrysuper Roots Drinks Ltd
Highdrate Ltd
Holos London Ltd
Honu Sodas UK Limited
Hydrade Drinks Limited
Ideas 2 Launch Limited
Immunoguardian Ltd
Infinite Session Ltd
Interactive World Ltd
Istok Foods Limited
JB Drinks Holdings Limited
JB Drinks Limited
JSJuices Ltd
Jamu Kitchen Ltd
Jellani Ltd
Juice Supply Limited
Juicy Brands (UK) Ltd.
Kali Engineering Ltd
Kapyani Limited
Karma Cola UK Ltd
Kemetic Cooks Ltd
Kimpton Apple Press Limited
Kolibri Drinks Limited
Kompassion Ltd
Konon Limited
Koolvibes Limited
Leanteen Limited
Lifeline Holdings Limited
Limonada Mathe Limited
Linsenlinsen Limited
Lintaru DGL Ltd
Little Miracles (International) Ltd
Little Miracles Drinks Limited
Liverpool Canning Co Ltd
Lixir Ltd
London Botanical Drinks Ltd
London Essence Co Ltd
Lucid Beverage Research Ltd
Lupe Kombucha Ltd.
Luxbev Limited
Ma3 Drinks Ltd
Marah Drinks Limited
Mariage Freres Royaume Uni Ltd
Mayag Brands Ltd
Merrily Mulled Ltd
Mighty Drinks Ltd.
Momo Kombucha Ltd
Morgan's Exclusive Ltd

Mossdoli Ltd
Mother Juice Ltd
Mother Kombucha Ltd
Mother Nature's Drinks Limited
Mother Root Ltd
Mount Valley Beverages Ltd
My Little Potion Ltd
Mylkman Ltd
N'ife Limited
NR Enterprise Limited
Nature's Fountain Limited
Neue Water Limited
Nix & Kix Ltd
Nutricana Ltd
Obeliver Drinks Limited
Original Free Drinks Co Ltd
Originalsip Ltd
Outsider Drinks Ltd.
Oxidize Limited
Pentire Drinks Limited
Persian Roze Ltd
Pharmaco Group Limited
Phutures Limited
Pitstop Coffee Limited
Pivotal Drinks Ltd
Plenish Cleanse Ltd
Poptails Limited
Power Juice Limited
Press London Ltd
Pressure Coolers Limited
Punchline Ltd
Pura Vita Drinks Ltd.
Quad Juices Limited
Rainbow Beverages Ltd
Raviom Limited
Raw Is More Ltd.
Razoo Limited
Rebel Drinks (London) Limited
Rebel Drinks Accra Limited
Refreshing Drinks Co Ltd
Rejuvenation Water Ltd
Reluminate Ltd
Roar Loud Limited
Rosemary Water Limited
Russia Cola Limited
SGRIC Limited
SK Global Brands Ltd
SLO Good Living Ltd
SMJ Beverages Limited
Saffron Water Limited
Saftiaray & Co Limited
Saint Patricks Ltd
Salad Passion Foods Ltd
Sansu Drinks Ltd
Schweppes International Ltd
Sejuiced Limited
Sendivogius Limited
Sharewater Ltd
Signpost Brewery Ltd
So-Real Foods Ltd
Sobare Limited
Soho Juice Co Ltd
South West Juice Co. Ltd
Peter Spanton Drinks Ltd
Spruce Water Limited
Square Root London Limited
Superfoods Nutrition Ltd
Sweet Memoirs Limited
Syncrobia Ltd
TMF Trading Limited
Bertrand Tailor Limited
Tassology Limited

Tasteuk Limited
Tasty Kameleon Ltd
Teabase Ltd
Thames Vintage Ltd
Thirstea Drinks Limited
This Is Holy Water Limited
Three Cents Ltd
Nelly Tickner Drinks Co. Ltd
Timeless Drinks Ventures Ltd
Tiny Mighty People Ltd
Trip Drink Ltd
Trove International Limited
Turn Global Ltd
Two B Limited
Two Keys Ltd
UK Blue Ribbon Group Beer Co., Ltd
UK Brighton Food & Nutrition Research Centre
UK Dorset Ltd
UK Premium Brands Limited
Ugly Brands Limited
Ultra Beauty Limited
Urban Cordial Co Ltd
Vero Drinks Ltd
Vine Springs Ltd
Vitamin Brands Ltd.
Vitte Nutrition Ltd
Vivo Water Ltd
Waters & Robson Holdings Ltd
Whollywater Ltd
Wild Life Botanicals Ltd
Wolfe's Drinks Limited
Wotar Ltd
Wow Food and Drinks Ltd
Wunder Workshop Ltd
Yeast Meets West Limited
Yemsmoothies Ltd
Your Mind Body Soul Limited
Yummy Juice Co Ltd
Zowell Ltd

Lothian

Edinburgh Kombucha Ltd
Kombuchaye Ltd
ME Letric Ltd

Merseyside [20]

Alder Spring Limited
Baroncroft Ltd
Beacon Drinks Limited
Budaquelle Beverages International Ltd
Cott Ventures UK Limited
Dayla Liquid Packing Limited
Decantae Mineral Water Limited
ECIG Retail Europe Limited
Gingercool Limited
Goodlives Panacea Blend Ltd
Moss Cider Limited
Nichols PLC
Noisy Drinks Co Ltd
Package Water Solutions Ltd
Pearl Soft Drinks Limited
Permeske Ltd
Ben Shaws Dispense Drinks Ltd
Soda Factory Limited
Total Water Solutions Limited
Willow Water Limited

Middlesex [43]

Ankerwycke Water Limited
Aqua Burst Ltd
Areea Limited
Beyaz Kartal Ltd
Brain Fud Ltd
Club Consultants Ltd
Coca-Cola European Partners GB Ltd
Coca-Cola European Partners PLC
Dangercode Ltd
Distinate Ltd
Emery Brand Ltd
Evo Drinks Europe Ltd
Exotic Beverages Limited
Fab World Limited
GO4 Beverages Limited
Gaia Brands Ltd
Galactogen Products Limited
Hello Coco Limited
Humble Bumble Ltd
ICB Advisory Limited
Ice Factory Limited
KGN London Ltd
Keizen SDK Ltd
Lucozade Ribena Suntory Exports Ltd
Lucozade Ribena Suntory Ltd
Monster Energy Europe Limited
My Mum's Ltd
Nari Palm Juice Beverages Ltd
Nude & Rude Ltd
Paradise Rum Limited
Polconut Ltd
Pop in Tea Limited
Portable Marketing Solutions Ltd
Pouchlink Ltd
Pure Spring Aqua Ltd
Saapos Ltd
Sai Water UK Limited
Shlurpies Ltd.
SmithKline Beecham Limited
Spring Water (Devon) Limited
Suntory Beverage & Food South Africa Ltd
Tani-Mola Enterprise Ltd
Zaas Limited

Midlothian [13]

70s Booch Ltd
Beverage Brands (U.K.) Limited
Bon Accord Soft Drinks Limited
Caledonian Bottlers PLC
Drink Better Limited
Edinburgh Artesian Water Co Ltd
Edinburgh Tonic Ltd
Floreana Ltd
Healthy Hemp Products Ltd
Liver Health UK Ltd.
Roots Soda Limited
Sleek Still Scottish Water Ltd
Tulchan Spring Water Limited

Monmouthshire

Hendre Distillery Ltd
Juice Junkies Limited
Sober Drinks Limited

Norfolk [6]

Artisan Drinks Co Ltd
Fonthill Waters Limited
Steven Hatch Operations Consultancy Ltd
Live Kindly Drinks Co Ltd
Norfolk Cordial Ltd
Zion Manufacturing Ltd

Northamptonshire [8]

5 Hour Energy Limited
Core Beverage Equipment Ltd
Herbal Fusions Ltd
Outfox Drinks Ltd
Refresh Brands Limited
Village Orchard Ltd
Watkins Drinks Limited
Zireson Enterprises Limited

Northumberland [5]

Blue Raspberry Investments Ltd
Fentimans Ltd.
Marlish Waters Limited
Northumbrian Ice Cream Co Ltd
Polar Krush Limited

Nottinghamshire [14]

Ballmax Beverage Co Limited
Belvoir Fruit Farms Drinks Holdings
Belvoir Fruit Farms Limited
Belvoir Natural Drinks Co Ltd
Benefit Water Ltd
Bliiss Ltd
Drinks Group Holdings Ltd
Edible Hedgerow Ltd
Hoods Cordial Ltd
National Forest Spring Water Co Ltd
Nutrapharm Ltd
Piff Juice Limited
Saicho Ltd.
Two Brothers Beverage Co Ltd

Oxfordshire [9]

Charlie T's Ltd
Drinkology Limited
Ed's Trading Limited
Inginius Limited
Koala Karma UK Limited
Kombucha Kat Ltd
Oxford Juice Co Ltd
Pump House Water Ltd
Wisdom Superfoods CIC

Pembrokeshire [6]

NGN Distribution Limited
Pembrokeshire Cider Limited
Princes Gate Spring Water Ltd
Princes Gate Water Limited
Shrubb Ltd
Upper Harglodd Farm Ltd

Powys

Hedgerow Soft Drinks Ltd
Montgomery Waters Limited
Radnor Hills Mineral Water Co Ltd
Trederwen Springs 2008 Limited

Somerset [40]
04021465 Limited
Bath Natural Mineral Water Ltd
Bath Natural Spring Water Ltd
Bigla Brewing Co Ltd
Bladud Spring Limited
Bread Drink Lab Limited
Brown Box Trading Co Ltd
Cheddar Mineral Water Limited
Cheddar Natural Mineral Water Ltd
Cheddar Natural Spring Water Ltd
Cheddar Spring Water Limited
Cheddar Water Limited
Corduroy Ideas Limited
Cornish Organic Aloe Vera Ltd
Glastonbury Spring Water Co Ltd
Glucofit Limited
Henny and Joes Ltd
Hullabaloos Lemonade Limited
Impact Sports Science Limited
Juice Collective Limited
Kingdon Callea Ltd
Kore Kombucha Ltd
Lovely Drinks Limited
Mendip Bottle Limited
Mendip Hills Mineral Water Ltd
Mendip Hills Spring Water Ltd
Mission Juice Ltd
Naivasha Tonic Co Ltd
Office Beverages Ltd
Original Somerset Certified Water Supply
Refresco Beverages UK Limited
Ruudz Limited
Sekforde Drinks Limited
Showerings Cider Mill Ltd
Soft N Sweet Ltd
Swallow Drinks South West Ltd
Think Drinks Limited
Water Shop Limited
Watermarket Limited
Your Water Ltd

Staffordshire [5]
Enso Goods Limited
Hawkins Drinks Limited
Rok Natural Energy Limited
Septimus Spyder Soft Drinks Ltd
Space Chef Ltd

Suffolk [7]
Ballantyne McLean Limited
Hedgerow Cordials Limited
Kings Farm Foods Limited
Konings Juices & Drinks UK Ltd
Maynard House Limited
James White Drinks Ltd
White Smoke Distillery Ltd

Surrey [38]
Aillo Ltd
Amaize Drinks Limited
Celtic Soul Drinks Limited
Chocquers Limited
Choquers Limited
Divine Water Co Ltd
Dr Go Ltd
Dr.Shot Ltd.
East London Juice Co Ltd
Elfie Drinks Co Ltd
Eliya Europe Ltd
Enhance Drinks Ltd
Essence PH10 Limited
Exoteeque Limited
Genii Energy Ltd.
Grace Under Pressure Ltd
Gunna Drinks Limited
Gut Drinks Ltd
Healthy Thirst Drinks Limited
Juice Doctor Limited
Juice Man Limited
Jumpin' Juice Limited
Liquid Fusion Limited
Mad Dog Drinks Limited
Miximex Limited
Mobay Drinks Ltd
Nachure Ltd
Narino Limited
O.T.C Beverages Limited
Ocentek Ltd
Pomepure Ltd
Prime Sun Limited
Sipsup Limited
Surrey Food and Drink Innovation Ltd
Syrup Junkie Limited
Tea GB International Limited
Vitapure Drinks Co Ltd
Willimott House Limited

Sussex [33]
APE2O Limited
Agua Fresca Ltd.
Buxton Mineral Water Limited
Clayton's Cold Brewed Coffee Ltd
Drinks for Beauty Ltd
Driver's Drinks Co Ltd
Eden Springs UK Limited
Enterprises Beyond Reason Ltd
Folkington's (Middle East) Ltd
Gallybird Tonic Co Ltd
Gran Steads Ginger Limited
Guffaw Ltd
Icetails Ltd
Just Drinking Water Ltd
Made By Brave Limited
Made By Noble Limited
Marley and Barley Ltd
Metro Drinks Limited
Microbiome Technologies Ltd
Natural Juicing Co Ltd
Nestle Waters (UK) Holdings Ltd
Nestle Waters GD Limited
Nestle Waters UK Limited
Pure Choice Watercoolers Ltd
Red Dragon Water Limited
Regency Tonic Ltd
Session Brewing Co. Limited
Silver Spa Limited
Solar Cola Limited
Sussex Mobile Coffee Co Ltd
Vida Water Ltd
WTRplus Ltd
Wildeve Ltd

Tyne & Wear [15]
40 Kola Ltd
Adaquo H20 Ltd
Brainwave Brands Ltd
Clearly Drinks Limited
Diesel Brewing Co Ltd.
Hike Coffee Ltd
Karma Water Co Ltd
Love Tide Water Limited
Our Northern Stars Limited
Pickle Shot Limited
Point Blank Cold Brew Ltd
Powerful Water Co Ltd
Sopro Drinks Ltd
Sumo Drinks Ltd
J Water Disabled Children Ltd

Warwickshire [15]
&Tailor Ltd
Avid Stacc Ltd
Birch Boost Ltd
Chapmans Drinks Limited
Fillongley Spring Water Ltd
Fillongley Ventures Limited
Fruit Diversity Limited
Goodness Brands Ltd
Ikoyi Chapmans Limited
Moores of Warwick Limited
Qibla Cola (Beverages) Ltd
Shakespeare Spring Water Co Ltd
Simple Nature Limited
Temperance Drinks Limited
Wet Beverages (Global) Ltd

West Midlands [27]
Aberrucia Ltd
Ad Hoque Ltd
Agilebody Ltd
Bennu Rising Ltd.
Big Time Soft Drinks Limited
Birmingham Soft Drinks Association Ltd
Elite Global Nutrition Limited
Endo Sport Ltd
Ginsense Ltd
Green Foods International Ltd
Green Monkey Drinks Ltd
Happy Gut Hut Limited
Healthy Well Being Products Ltd
Horizon (Contract Drinks) Ltd
Johnson Supplies UK Ltd
Lemon Factory Ltd
Livitus Limited
Macro Munch Ltd
Magic Potion Energy Drinks International
Mighty Flames Ltd
PJ Kombucha Limited
Phoenix Water Coolers Limited
Purity Soft Drinks Limited
SRP Equipe Limited
Story Drinks Limited
Suncrest Associates Limited
Swing Top Limited

Wiltshire [6]
Handmade Cider Co Ltd
My Living Water UK Ltd
Penning Power & Water Limited
Squish Squash Limited
Sqwish Squash Limited
Stonehenge Spring Water Ltd

Worcestershire
Be Gemwater Limited
Malvern Bottling Works Limited
Pass The Baton Limited
Water Guru Limited

Yorkshire [58]

Alkali Water Limited
Artemis Brew Ltd
Bax Botanics Limited
Birdhouse Tea Co Ltd
Blue Keld Springs Limited
Bright Smoothies Ltd
Carbon Drinks Limited
Cawingredients Limited
Cheese Burger Limited
Chia Food (York) Limited
Cybora Ltd
DRII Limited
Danjan Ventures Ltd
Destructive Lines Ltd
Dry Beverages Limited
Equilibrium Food & Drink Ltd
Eskimo Joe's Limited
Faraday Drinks Ltd
Fitch Brew Co Ltd.
Flower of Life Ltd
Freak Cocktails Ltd
Goat Drinks Ltd
Gourmet Water Co Ltd
Green Leaf Liquids Limited
HSW Limited
Harrogate Spring Water Limited
Kingston upon Hull Liqour Co Ltd
Mangogo Ltd
Marbella Cartel Ltd
Montecrysto Limited
New Life Water Limited
No Longer Bax Botanics Limited
Norwegian Glacier Water Ltd
Oakdale Spring Limited
One Co. of Harrogate Ltd
Pointeer Ltd
Poo Tang Crisps Limited
Pura Panela Ltd
Qiblah Beverages Limited
Qiblah Products Limited
Red Bandit Limited
Santa Monica Co Ltd
Schnapps Limited
Seasons Soft Drinks Limited
Shepley Spring Limited
Slimmers World Sports Drinks Ltd
Smith & Harrison Ltd
Sutton Spring Limited
Swalevalley Springwater Ltd
Tanfield Springs Ltd
Temperance Spirit Co Ltd
Thirsty Planet Limited
Viva Riva Beverage Co Ltd
Vivo Viva Beverages Limited
Vyking Energy Limited
Water Group Ltd
Westmoor Botanicals Limited
Yorkshire Soft Drinks Ltd

Company Profiles

&Tailor Ltd
Incorporated: 5 August 2016
Net Worth: £45,801 *Total Assets:* £62,607
Registered Office: 30 Binley Road, Coventry, Warwicks, CV3 1JA
Major Shareholder: Cristina Vila Vives
Officers: Cristina Vila Vives [1982] Director [Spanish]

04021465 Limited
Incorporated: 26 June 2000 *Employees:* 96
Net Worth Deficit: £26,068,000 *Total Assets:* £16,639,000
Registered Office: Mallard Court, Express Park, Bridgwater, Somerset, TA6 4RN
Officers: Aart Cornelis Duijzer, Secretary; Aart Cornelis Duijzer [1963] Director [Dutch]

115 Design Limited
Incorporated: 19 September 2016 *Employees:* 2
Net Worth: £2,887 *Total Assets:* £5,063
Registered Office: The Studio, c/o Street Farm, Burton Street, Marnhull, Sturminster Newton, Dorset, DT10 1PP
Shareholder: Matthew Pepper
Officers: Amber Pepper [1979] Director; Matthew Pepper [1975] Director

21st Century Coke Co. Ltd.
Incorporated: 20 January 1999
Registered Office: Point House, Exeter Road, Bishops Tawton, Barnstaple, Devon, EX32 0EN
Officers: Steven Taylor, Secretary; John William Taylor [1948] Director/Retired; Steven James Taylor [1983] Director/Builder

40 Kola Ltd
Incorporated: 11 January 2018
Registered Office: 19 Osborne Road, Newcastle upon Tyne, NE2 2AH
Shareholders: Daniel John Young; Kieran Dougan
Officers: Kieran Dougan, Secretary; Kieran Dougan [1992] Director; Daniel John Young [1992] Director

411 Beverages Limited
Incorporated: 5 March 2018
Registered Office: 111 Blackburn Street, Radcliffe, Manchester, M26 3WQ
Major Shareholder: Tassaduq Ashraf
Officers: Tasadduq Ali Ashraf [1978] Director

413 Limited
Incorporated: 30 October 2018
Registered Office: 20 Ledbury House, East Dulwich, London, SE22 8AN
Major Shareholder: Adebowale Johnson
Officers: Adebowale Johnson [1984] Director/Business Executive

5 Hour Energy Limited
Incorporated: 6 September 2011
Registered Office: Winwick Hall, Winwick, Northampton, NN6 7PD
Major Shareholder: Bruce Philip Green
Officers: Bruce Philip Green [1944] Director/Consultant

70s Booch Ltd
Incorporated: 27 June 2018
Registered Office: 16 Hillview, Edinburgh, EH4 2AF
Major Shareholder: Rory Paterson
Officers: Rory Paterson [1991] Director

A & S Specialist Supplies Ltd.
Incorporated: 8 February 2016
Net Worth Deficit: £5,227 *Total Assets:* £8
Registered Office: 69 Campbell Avenue, Ilford, Essex, IG6 1EB
Shareholders: Aine Mary Eireannach; Sanjeev Kumar Choraria
Officers: Sanjeev Kumar Choraria [1970] Director; Aine Mary Plimmer [1971] Director

AA Group Holdings Ltd
Incorporated: 3 September 2018
Registered Office: 85 Great Portland Street, London, W1W 7LT
Major Shareholder: Adwoa Kuffour Akoto
Officers: Adwoa Kuffour Akoto [1990] Director/Entrepreneur

AB Vaults Group Limited
Incorporated: 8 March 2018
Registered Office: 5 Academy House, 1 Thunderer Street, London, E13 9DP
Major Shareholder: Samuel Ndungu
Officers: Samuel N K Banks [1988] Director/Entrepreneur [Kenyan]

Aberrucia Ltd
Incorporated: 12 September 2018
Registered Office: Suite 4, 43 Hagley Road, Stourbridge, W Midlands, DY8 1QR
Major Shareholder: Ryan Gandy
Officers: Rannie Ayson [1987] Director [Filipino]

ABI SAB Group Holding Limited
Incorporated: 17 March 1998 *Employees:* 177
Previous: Sabmiller Limited
Net Worth: £48,800,354,304 *Total Assets:* £48,913,764,352
Registered Office: Bureau, 90 Fetter Lane, London, EC4A 1EN
Parent: ABI UK Holding 2 Limited
Officers: Kevin Jean-Frederic Douws [1982] Director [Belgian]; Sibil Jiang [1990] Director [Australian]; Stephen John Turner [1966] Director/Accountant

Acqua Eterna Ltd
Incorporated: 6 November 2012
Net Worth: £1,000 *Total Assets:* £1,000
Registered Office: 17 Ensign House, Admirals Way, Canary Wharf, London, E14 9XQ
Officers: Andrew Fomychov [1966] Director

Acqua Nordica Ltd
Incorporated: 26 March 2015
Net Worth: £1,902 *Total Assets:* £3,452
Registered Office: 17 Ensign House, Admirals Way, Canary Wharf, London, E14 9XQ
Shareholder: Birgir Loftsson
Officers: Andrew Fomychov [1966] Director/Manager; Birgir Loftsson [1967] Director/Manager [Icelander]

Ad Hoque Ltd
Incorporated: 5 September 2018
Registered Office: 316 Farm Street, Birmingham, B19 2UF
Major Shareholder: Radhwan Hoque
Officers: Radhwan Hoque [1993] Sales Director

Adapt Kombucha Limited
Incorporated: 10 October 2018
Registered Office: Suite 7, 2-4 Trafford Road, Alderley Edge, Cheshire, SK9 7NN
Shareholders: Damian Gregory; Joel Ndunda
Officers: Damian Gregory [1977] Director [Irish]; Joel Ndunda [1985] Director [American]

UK Manufacturers of Soft Drinks

Adaquo H20 Ltd
Incorporated: 22 February 2019
Registered Office: 40-46 Side, Newcastle upon Tyne, NE1 3JA
Major Shareholder: Polat Cosar Akcicek
Officers: Polat Cosar Akcicek [1995] Director

Adcocks Drinks Company Limited
Incorporated: 8 April 1999
Net Worth: £6,350 Total Assets: £372,270
Registered Office: Crease Drove, Crowland, Peterborough, PE6 0BN
Shareholders: John Keith Adcock; Darren Mitchell Adcock
Officers: John Keith Adcock, Secretary; John Keith Adcock [1969] Director

Admete Ltd
Incorporated: 4 April 2016
Registered Office: Office Q, 35a Astbury Road, London, SE15 2NL
Major Shareholder: Boris Lendak
Officers: Boris Lendak [1962] Director [Slovak]

Afrimalt International Limited
Incorporated: 26 April 2018
Registered Office: Flat 801, Jute Court, Abbey Road, Barking, Essex, IG11 7FT
Major Shareholder: Olumolawa Oludotun Olusi
Officers: Olumolawa Oludotun Olusi [1977] Director [Nigerian]

Agilebody Ltd
Incorporated: 18 September 2018
Registered Office: Office 1, PMJ House, Highlands Road, Shirley, Solihull, W Midlands, B90 4ND
Major Shareholder: Libby Kelly
Officers: Ralph Christian Gonzales [1984] Director [Filipino]

Agua Fresca Ltd.
Incorporated: 16 October 2017
Registered Office: 28 Priory Street, Lewes, E Sussex, BN7 1HH
Major Shareholder: Noah Preston
Officers: Noah Preston [1994] Director

Aillo Ltd
Incorporated: 19 January 2011
Net Worth: £17,394 Total Assets: £44,182
Registered Office: 35 Chaldon Way, Coulsdon, Surrey, CR5 1DJ
Major Shareholder: Naveed Aslam
Officers: Toseef Aslam, Secretary; Naveed Aslam [1970] Director

Akme Coffee Limited
Incorporated: 15 May 2018
Registered Office: Arena B2, 71 Ashfield Road, London, N4 1FF
Major Shareholder: Johann Dumelie
Officers: Johann Dumelie [1981] Director [French]

Alcarelle Holdings Limited
Incorporated: 18 May 2016
Net Worth: £11,968 Total Assets: £13,125
Registered Office: c/o Numerii Ltd, Park House, 15-23 Greenhill Crescent, Watford, Herts, WD18 8PH
Shareholders: David Orren; David John Nutt
Officers: Philip Edwards, Secretary; Philip Aubrey Edwards [1951] Director/Accountant; David Nutt [1951] Director/University Professor; David Orren [1956] Director/Consultant

Alcarelle Limited
Incorporated: 18 May 2016
Net Worth: £2,000 Total Assets: £202,600
Registered Office: c/o Numerii Ltd, Park House, 15-23 Greenhill Crescent, Watford, Herts, WD18 8PH
Shareholders: David John Nutt; David Orren
Officers: Philip Edwards, Secretary; Philip Aubrey Edwards [1951] Director/Accountant; David Nutt [1951] Director/University Professor; David Orren [1956] Director/Consultant

Alcohol Free Drinks Limited
Incorporated: 31 December 2018
Registered Office: 13a Basement Flat, 13 Richmond Way, Shepherds Bush, London, W12 8LQ
Major Shareholder: Jolyon Paul Jago
Officers: Jolyon Paul Jago [1974] Director/Chief Executive

Alcro Commercials Limited
Incorporated: 18 April 2018
Registered Office: 71-75 Shelton Street, London, WC2H 9JQ
Major Shareholder: Hugo Valdes-Vera
Officers: Hugo Valdes-Vera [1973] Director

Alder Spring Limited
Incorporated: 3 November 2003 Employees: 1
Net Worth Deficit: £65,156 Total Assets: £47,953
Registered Office: Granite Building, 6 Stanley Street, Liverpool, L1 6AF
Shareholders: Marian Tracey Langford; Stanley Morphet
Officers: Marian Tracey Langford [1966] Director/Sales Manager; Charles David Morphet [1964] Director/Motor Engineer; Stanley Morphet [1969] Director/Production Engineer

Alexionut Ltd
Incorporated: 16 October 2018
Registered Office: 57 North Eleventh Street, Milton Keynes, Bucks, MK9 3BU
Major Shareholder: Ionut Alexandru Mustacioara
Officers: Ionut Alexandru Mustacioara [1991] Director [Romanian]

Alitasa Ltd
Incorporated: 23 November 2017
Registered Office: 13 Benwick Close, London, SE16 2HE
Major Shareholder: Juste Juozapaityte
Officers: Juste Juozapaityte, Secretary; Juste Juozapaityte [1990] Director [Lithuanian]

Alive & Kicking Fermented Foods Ltd
Incorporated: 25 May 2018
Registered Office: 71-75 Shelton Street, Covent Garden, London, WC2H 9JQ
Major Shareholder: Joseph Michael Mead Hunter
Officers: Joseph Michael Mead Hunter, Secretary; Joseph Michael Mead Hunter [1960] Director

Alive Beverages Limited
Incorporated: 6 February 2018
Registered Office: 45 Tasman Road, London, SW9 9LZ
Officers: Emma Garvey [1982] Director/Drinks Manufacturer; Victoria Hamilton [1983] Director/Drinks Manufacturer

Alive Water Ltd
Incorporated: 4 April 2018
Registered Office: 48 Cartvale Road, Glasgow, G42 9SW
Major Shareholder: Rohail Gilani
Officers: Rohail Gilani [1991] Director/Manager [Pakistani]

Alkali Water Limited
Incorporated: 30 April 2018
Registered Office: First Point Business Park, Doncaster, S Yorks, DN4 5JP
Major Shareholder: Niall Aadya Mason
Officers: Niall Aadya Mason [1997] Director/Professional Footballer

Alko Vintages UK Ltd
Incorporated: 19 April 2018
Registered Office: 71-75 Shelton Street, Covent Garden, London, WC2H 9JQ
Shareholders: Archard Lwihula Kati; Elkanah Ondieki Oenga
Officers: Archard Lwihula Kato [1960] Director [New Zealander]; Elkanah Ondieki Oenga [1984] Director [Kenyan]

Allson Sparkle Limited
Incorporated: 19 September 1984 *Employees:* 54
Net Worth: £5,053,407 *Total Assets:* £7,289,341
Registered Office: Unit S and Warehouse 5, Telford Road, Eastfield Industrial Estate, Glenrothes, Fife, KY7 4NX
Shareholders: Nicola Drysdale; Colin Jonathon Drysdale
Officers: Colin Jonathon Drysdale [1966] Executive Director; Nicola Drysdale [1969] Director

Alpha Energy Drink Limited
Incorporated: 31 January 2018
Registered Office: Kemp House, 160 City Road, London, EC1V 2NX
Officers: Arnon Satayaprakorb [1971] Director/Businessman [American]

Alyke Health Limited
Incorporated: 19 December 2018
Registered Office: 1 The Paddock, The Square, Letham, Cupar, Fife, KY15 7RP
Major Shareholder: Jon-Paul Kitching
Officers: Jon-Paul Kitching [1979] Director/Chief Executive

Amaize Drinks Limited
Incorporated: 8 March 2018
Registered Office: Flat 7, 26 Normanton Road, South Croydon, Surrey, CR2 7AR
Officers: Jon Del Mar, Secretary; Jonathan Quintanilla Del Mar [1975] Director/Soft Drink Producer

Amazing Forest Limited
Incorporated: 11 September 2015
Net Worth Deficit: £526 *Total Assets:* £129,323
Registered Office: 18 Granville Avenue, Oadby, Leicester, LE2 5FL
Major Shareholder: Pavel Shparkovich
Officers: Pavel Shparkovich [1986] Director

Amino Drinks Limited
Incorporated: 21 December 2017
Registered Office: 3rd Floor, 86-90 Paul Street, London, EC2A 4NE
Officers: Simon Carty [1988] Director/Founder

Ammacus Trading Limited
Incorporated: 2 June 2016
Net Worth: £8,012 *Total Assets:* £59,317
Registered Office: 78 Park Lane, Poynton, Stockport, Cheshire, SK12 1RE
Major Shareholder: Amanda Louise Duran Gleave
Officers: Amanda Louise Duran Gleave [1972] Director; Simon Andrew Gleave [1965] Director/Property Manager

Ammo Your Ammunition to Greatness Limited
Incorporated: 7 October 2016
Registered Office: 4 Rochfords Gardens, Slough, Berks, SL2 5XJ
Officers: Sharmarke Haydar Ali [1993] Director

Amor Food and Beverages Holdings Limited
Incorporated: 19 February 2018
Registered Office: 70-72 Alma Road, Windsor, Berks, SL4 3EZ
Major Shareholder: Craig Hodge
Officers: Craig Hodge [1971] Director

Andina Coffee Co. Ltd
Incorporated: 31 May 2018
Registered Office: 38 Gardenside Avenue, Glasgow, G32 8DY
Major Shareholder: Maria Paz Varela Hernandez
Officers: Maria Paz Varela Hernandez [1990] Director/Finance Assistant [Colombian]

Anglesey Spring / Dwr Ffynnon Mon / Dwr Mon Ltd
Incorporated: 25 August 2015 *Employees:* 1
Net Worth Deficit: £2,080 *Total Assets:* £62,207
Registered Office: Tyn Pwll, Tyn Pwll, Pentraeth, Isle of Anglesey, LL75 8UL
Major Shareholder: David Wyn Thomas
Officers: David Wyn Thomas [1988] Director/Bottled Water

Anglo African Food & Beverages Holding Ltd
Incorporated: 11 April 2018
Registered Office: 71-75 Shelton Street, London, WC2H 9JQ
Shareholders: Adebayo Adeosun; Carl Buddhasingh
Officers: Adebayo Adeosun [1966] Director; Carl Buddhasingh [1963] Director

Ankerwycke Water Limited
Incorporated: 25 January 2018
Registered Office: 3 Brook Business Centre, Cowley Mill Road, Uxbridge, Middlesex, UB8 2FX
Shareholders: Jeremy Hugh Crame; Janet Pamela Winifred Crame
Officers: Janet Pamela Winifred Crame [1955] Director; Jeremy Hugh Crame [1951] Director

Antrim Hills Spring Water Company Limited
Incorporated: 6 October 1989 *Employees:* 7
Net Worth: £1,228,660 *Total Assets:* £1,454,623
Registered Office: 100 Irish Hill Road, Ballyclare, Co Antrim, BT39 9NL
Major Shareholder: Brian Samuel Geary
Officers: Brian Samuel Geary, Secretary; Brian Samuel Geary [1965] Director; Peter Jonathon Geary [1968] Director; Rosemary Wilson Geary [1940] Director

APE2O Limited
Incorporated: 17 May 2018
Registered Office: Aberdeen House, South Road, Haywards Heath, W Sussex, RH16 4NG
Major Shareholder: Anthony Newman
Officers: Anthony Newman [1972] Director

Aqua Arbore Ltd.
Incorporated: 30 April 2015
Net Worth Deficit: £18,409 *Total Assets:* £349
Registered Office: F25 Waterfront Studios, 1 Dock Road, London, E16 1AH
Officers: Mehdi Meghzifene [1989] Director/Sales & Distribution [Algerian]; Nicholas Edward Puckrin [1988] Director/Production & Supply [South African]

Aqua Burst Ltd
Incorporated: 7 June 2009
Net Worth Deficit: £48,762 *Total Assets:* £833
Registered Office: 21 Kingshill Drive, Harrow, Middlesex, HA3 8TD
Major Shareholder: Davin Pattni
Officers: Kantilal Pattni, Secretary; Davin Pattni [1977] Director

Aqua Esse Limited
Incorporated: 4 January 2017 *Employees:* 2
Net Worth Deficit: £10,225 *Total Assets:* £42,916
Registered Office: Summit House, 170 Finchley Road, London, NW3 6BP
Shareholders: Dianne Skurray; Vladimir Svalov
Officers: Dianne Skurray [1964] Director/Consultant [Australian]

Aqua Hebrides Limited
Incorporated: 30 August 2016
Registered Office: Johnstone House, 52-54 Rose Street, Aberdeen, AB10 1HA
Shareholders: Michael Kinnaird; Sara Jennifer Aboud
Officers: Sara Jennifer Aboud [1978] Director/Development Officer; Michael Kinnaird [1958] Director

Aquacan Limited
Incorporated: 6 December 2018
Registered Office: Grangewood House, Bakers Lane, Ingatestone, Essex, CM4 0BZ
Major Shareholder: Melissa Binder
Officers: Melissa Binder [1976] Director

Aquadog Mineral Water Ltd
Incorporated: 22 September 2014
Net Worth Deficit: £86,677 *Total Assets:* £75,076
Registered Office: Suite 1, 3rd Floor, 11-12 St James's Square, London, SW1Y 4LB
Shareholders: Vladimir Raiman; Dipl. Ing. Marek Jankovic
Officers: Peter Alexander Sokol [1996] Director [Slovak]

Ardmore Spring Water Limited
Incorporated: 25 November 2005
Net Worth: £10,284 *Total Assets:* £48,860
Registered Office: 81 Upper Damolly Road, Newry, Co Armagh, BT34 1QW
Major Shareholder: Ronan McElherron
Officers: Mary McElherron, Secretary; Ronan McElherron [1967] Director/Manager of Water Cooler Business [Irish]

Ardross Castle Water Company Ltd
Incorporated: 6 February 2019
Registered Office: Ardross Castle, Ardross, Alness, Ross-shire, IV17 0YE
Major Shareholder: Donald Emmanuel McTaggart
Officers: Donald Emmanuel McTaggart [1961] Director

Areea Limited
Incorporated: 11 May 2015
Net Worth Deficit: £14,559 *Total Assets:* £17,466
Registered Office: Suite 7-4, Alperton House, Bridgewater Road, Wembley, Middlesex, HA0 1EH
Major Shareholder: Antimo Farid Mire
Officers: Antimo Farid Mire [1990] Director/Chief Executive Officer [Italian]

Armagh Juice Company Limited
Incorporated: 8 May 2017
Registered Office: 73 Drumnasoo Road, Portadown, Co Armagh, BT62 4EX
Officers: Kelly Crawford [1981] Director; Helen Troughton [1954] Director; Mark Troughton [1983] Director; Philip Troughton [1953] Director

Arosuk Ltd
Incorporated: 12 May 2018
Registered Office: 20-22 Wenlock Road, London, N1 7GU
Officers: Fatih Yildirim [1981] Director

ARSJ Holding Ltd
Incorporated: 16 June 2016
Registered Office: 23b Diamond Lane, Aberdeen, AB10 1WB
Major Shareholder: Andrius Ratkevicius
Officers: Simas Jarasunas [1991] Director/Co-Founder [Lithuanian]; Andrius Ratkevicius [1991] Director [Lithuanian]

Artathlon Beverages Limited
Incorporated: 29 June 2018
Registered Office: 22 Naylor House, 10 John Fearon Walk, London, W10 4NX
Major Shareholder: Panayiotis Neufelt
Officers: Panayiotis Neufelt [1967] Director [Greek]

Artathlon Water Limited
Incorporated: 29 June 2018
Registered Office: 22 Naylor House, 10 John Fearon Walk, London, W10 4NX
Major Shareholder: Panayiotis Neufelt
Officers: Panayiotis Neufelt [1967] Director [Greek]

Artemis Brew Ltd
Incorporated: 25 March 2015 *Employees:* 4
Net Worth Deficit: £11,036 *Total Assets:* £25,045
Registered Office: Innisfree, Northfield Lane, Womersley, N Yorks, DN6 9BB
Major Shareholder: Ben Lewis Barker
Officers: Ben Lewis Barker [1993] Director

Artemis Import & Export Ltd
Incorporated: 14 November 2018
Registered Office: 305 Hertford Road, Edmonton, London, N9 7ET
Major Shareholder: Pervin Cuvalcioglu
Officers: Pervin Cuvalcioglu [1979] Director/Businesswoman [Cypriot]

Artio Foods Ltd
Incorporated: 12 March 2018
Registered Office: 52 Beams Way, Billericay, Essex, CM11 2NN
Major Shareholder: Mike Grainger
Officers: Michael Grainger [1992] Director

Artisan Drinks Company Limited
Incorporated: 9 March 2017 *Employees:* 2
Net Worth: £345,506 *Total Assets:* £384,193
Registered Office: 22-26 King Street, King's Lynn, Norfolk, PE30 1HJ
Major Shareholder: Steven William Cooper
Officers: Michael John Andrews [1969] Director; Steven William Cooper [1970] Director; Mark Davidson [1960] Director [South African]; Alan Walsh [1982] Director

Ashridge Cider Limited
Incorporated: 2 April 2013
Net Worth Deficit: £5,175 *Total Assets:* £458,463
Registered Office: Barkingdon Farm, Staverton, Totnes, Devon, TQ9 6AN
Major Shareholder: Jason Mitchell
Officers: Jason Mitchell [1952] Director

B + K Augustin Limited
Incorporated: 4 August 2004
Net Worth: £2,425 *Total Assets:* £4,873
Registered Office: 4 St Francis Drive, The Scholar, Chatteris, Cambs, PE16 6BS
Major Shareholder: Kim Kent Augustin
Officers: Kim Augustin, Secretary; Bethael Augustin [1964] Director; Kim Augustin [1970] Director

Avid Stacc Ltd
Incorporated: 13 August 2015
Net Worth: £1,000 *Total Assets:* £1,000
Registered Office: 34 Gardeners End, Rugby, Warwicks, CV22 7RQ
Parent: David Arweny
Officers: David Arweny, Secretary; David Arweny [1966] Director/Consultant

Avobravo Limited
Incorporated: 17 January 2017
Registered Office: 318 Norbury Avenue, London, SW16 3RL
Major Shareholder: Hamza Zaveri
Officers: Hamza Zaveri [1990] Director

Awlgold Ltd
Incorporated: 18 July 2018
Registered Office: Suite 6, First Floor, Wordsworth Mill, Wordsworth Street, Bolton, Lancs, BL1 3ND
Major Shareholder: Abbey Huelin
Officers: Laila Puno [1979] Director [Filipino]

Ayge Limited
Incorporated: 29 August 2012
Registered Office: 8 Planner Walk, Wokingham, Berks, RG40 1GU
Officers: Ibrahim Abubakar Garba, Secretary; Ibrahim Abubakar Garba [1972] Director/Finance Manager

Ayrshire Springs Limited
Incorporated: 5 July 2007 *Employees:* 1
Net Worth Deficit: £205,737 *Total Assets:* £951
Registered Office: Meikle Garclaugh, New Cumnock, E Ayrshire, KA18 4NS
Officers: Louise McClounie, Secretary; Ruth McClounie [1941] Director; William McClounie [1938] Director; William Lindsay McClounie [1972] Director

Azerbaijan Juices Limited
Incorporated: 26 March 2009
Registered Office: 7th Floor, 9 Berkeley Street, London, W1J 8DW
Major Shareholder: Nijat Heydarov
Officers: Gillian Ralston Jordan [1963] Director

B20 Water Ltd
Incorporated: 2 May 2017
Registered Office: 112 Gardner Road, Prestwich, Manchester, M25 3JE
Major Shareholder: Daniel Jessid Losada
Officers: Daniel Jessid Losada [1986] Director/Drinks Dispenser

B4Sport Ltd.
Incorporated: 5 June 2017
Net Worth Deficit: £206 *Total Assets:* £4,059
Registered Office: Suite 3, Scion House, Stirling University, Innovation Park, Stirling, FK9 4NF
Major Shareholder: Mohsin Laginaf
Officers: Mohsin Laginaf [1988] Director

The Babywater Company Limited
Incorporated: 16 January 2002
Net Worth Deficit: £29,241 *Total Assets:* £100
Registered Office: 62 Wilson Street, London, EC2A 2BU
Officers: Oonagh Chloe Lander [1970] Director

Bad Girls Brew Limited
Incorporated: 7 November 2017
Registered Office: 22a Thorney Crescent, London, SW11 3TT
Major Shareholder: Barbara Elizabeth Gorna
Officers: Barbara Elizabeth Gorna, Secretary; Barbara Elizabeth Gorna [1955] Director

Ballantyne McLean Limited
Incorporated: 25 September 2017
Registered Office: 23 Fox Meadow, Barking, Ipswich, Suffolk, IP6 8HS
Shareholders: Caryl Jackson; Sharon Anna Ballantyne
Officers: Sharon Anna Ballantyne [1978] Director; Cary McLean [1965] Director

Ballmax Beverage Co Limited
Incorporated: 8 October 2013 *Employees:* 1
Net Worth Deficit: £77,285 *Total Assets:* £918
Registered Office: Pendennis House, 169 Eastgate, Worksop, Notts, S80 1QS
Major Shareholder: Lydia Mee
Officers: Lydia Mee [1993] Director

Barncrofts of London Limited
Incorporated: 5 May 2017
Net Worth Deficit: £2,532 *Total Assets:* £1,070
Registered Office: 8 Pomona House, Evelyn Street, London, SE8 5RS
Major Shareholder: Matthew Dollive
Officers: Matthew Dollive [1982] Director/Entrepreneur

Baroncroft Ltd
Incorporated: 11 December 2002
Net Worth Deficit: £39,651 *Total Assets:* £38,235
Registered Office: Unit 6, 1 Merton Street, St Helens, Merseyside, WA9 1HX
Major Shareholder: Gregory Fildes
Officers: Jacqueline Fildes, Secretary; Gregory Fildes [1948] Director

Robert Barr Limited
Incorporated: 28 October 1946
Registered Office: Westfield House, 4 Mollins Road, Cumbernauld, N Lanarks, G68 9HD
Parent: A.G. Barr P.L.C.
Officers: Julie Anne Barr, Secretary; Julie Anne Barr [1973] Director/Company Secretary; Stuart Lorimer [1966] Finance Director

UK Manufacturers of Soft Drinks dellam

A.G. Barr P.L.C.
Incorporated: 30 June 1904 Employees: 976
Net Worth: £201,900,000 Total Assets: £288,200,000
Registered Office: Westfield House, 4 Mollins Road, Cumbernauld, N Lanarks, G68 9HD
Officers: Julie Anne Barr, Company Secretary; William Robin Graham Barr [1938] Director/Chartered Accountant; Susan Verity Barratt [1965] Director; Martin Andrew Griffiths [1966] Director; Jonathan David Kemp [1971] Commercial Director; Stuart Lorimer [1966] Finance Director; Andrew Lewis Memmott [1964] Director; John Ross Nicolson [1953] Director; Pamela Powell [1963] Director [American]; David James Ritchie [1969] Director [Irish]; Nicholas Barry Edward Wharton [1966] Director/Chartered Accountant; Roger Alexander White [1965] Director/Chief Executive

Barzy's Ltd
Incorporated: 2 February 2004
Registered Office: 15 Arodene Road, Bixton Hill, London, SW2 2BQ
Major Shareholder: Neville Williams
Officers: Augustina Marian Williams, Secretary; Neville George Williams [1966] Director

Bath Natural Mineral Water Limited
Incorporated: 11 October 2006
Registered Office: David Urch, Carscliff, Upper Draycott Road, Cheddar, Somerset, BS27 3YL
Shareholder: Tabitha Sarah-Jane Urch
Officers: Virginia Urch, Secretary; David Lawrence Urch [1951] Director; Duncan Winston Urch [1980] Director/Helicopter Pilot; Tabitha Sarah-Jane Urch [1978] Director/Property Agent; Virginia Urch [1952] Director/Farmer

Bath Natural Spring Water Limited
Incorporated: 10 October 2006
Registered Office: David Urch, Carscliff, Upper Draycott Road, Cheddar, Somerset, BS27 3YL
Shareholder: Tabitha Sarah-Jane Urch
Officers: Virginia Urch, Secretary; David Lawrence Urch [1951] Director; Duncan Winston Urch [1980] Director/Helicopter Pilot; Tabitha Sarah-Jane Urch [1978] Director/Property Agent; Virginia Urch [1952] Director/Farmer

Bax Botanics Limited
Incorporated: 24 September 2018
Registered Office: 1 Thornton Bridge Cottages, Thornton Bridge, Helperby, York, YO61 2RH
Shareholders: Rosemary Jane Badger Bax; Christopher Martin Bax
Officers: Christopher Martin Bax [1966] Director; Rosemary Jane Badger Bax [1964] Director

Bax Farm Juice Ltd
Incorporated: 10 March 2015 Employees: 4
Net Worth Deficit: £76,898 Total Assets: £112,089
Registered Office: Hempstead Farm, Tonge, Sittingbourne, Kent, ME9 9BJ
Officers: Julie Hadlow, Secretary; Edward Doubleday [1985] Director/Farm Worker; Dr Oliver Peter Doubleday [1952] Director/Farmer; Oliver Christopher Doubleday [1991] Director/Researcher; Philip Doubleday [1988] Director/Farm Worker

Be Gemwater Limited
Incorporated: 9 January 2017 Employees: 4
Net Worth Deficit: £229,627 Total Assets: £53,944
Registered Office: The Courtyard, 10 Belle Vue Terrace, Malvern, Worcs, WR14 4PZ
Shareholders: Richard Kirk Polack; Richard Kirk Polack
Officers: Judith Dorothy Polack, Secretary; Robert Barry McCarthy [1973] Director/Production Manager [South African]; Richard Kirk Polack [1963] Director/Self Employed

Beacon Drinks Limited
Incorporated: 20 June 1983
Registered Office: Laurel House, Woodlands Park, Ashton Road, Newton-le-Willow, St Helens, Merseyside, WA12 0HH
Parent: Nichols PLC
Officers: Timothy John Croston, Secretary; Timothy John Croston [1963] Director

Beau Drinks Ltd
Incorporated: 25 June 2013
Net Worth Deficit: £602,541 Total Assets: £37,713
Registered Office: 6-7 Castle Gate, Hertford, SG14 1HD
Major Shareholder: Dawn Pritchard
Officers: Dawn Pritchard [1973] Director

Beechvale Natural Water Ltd
Incorporated: 12 January 2005
Net Worth Deficit: £23,684 Total Assets: £194,774
Registered Office: 21 Topped Mountain Road, Cavanacross, Tempo, Enniskillen, Co Fermanagh, BT94 3DD
Officers: Maureen Elizabeth Kelly, Secretary; Eamon Charles Kelly [1956] Director [Irish]; Maureen Elizabeth Kelly [1955] Director/Cook [Irish]

Belfast Bottle Company Limited
Incorporated: 20 April 1978
Net Worth: £2 Total Assets: £2
Registered Office: Galgorm Industrial Estate, 7 Corbally Road, Ballymena, Co Antrim, BT42 1JQ
Major Shareholder: Nicholas McKenna
Officers: Nicholas McKenna, Secretary; Margherita McKenna [1946] Director/Housewife; Nicholas McKenna [1947] Director

Belle Beverages Ltd
Incorporated: 26 July 2013
Net Worth Deficit: £46,646 Total Assets: £100
Registered Office: The Howarth Armsby Suite, New Broad Street House, 35 New Broad Street, London, EC2M 1NH
Major Shareholder: Nanaesi Idun
Officers: Nanaesi Idun [1975] Director

Bello's World Limited
Incorporated: 25 August 2016
Registered Office: 83 Warrior Square, Manor Park, London, E12 5RR
Major Shareholder: Nurudeen Bello
Officers: Nurudeen Bello [1989] Director

Belu Water Limited
Incorporated: 23 September 2002 Employees: 11
Net Worth: £530,913 Total Assets: £1,966,644
Registered Office: 62 Hatton Garden, London, EC1N 8LR
Officers: Charlotte Sera Harrington [1977] Director/Chief Operating Officer; Matthew John King [1976] Director/Chartered Accountant; Karen Jane Lynch [1969] Managing Director; Peter Tyson [1950] Director

Belvoir Fruit Farms Drinks Holdings Limited
Incorporated: 27 July 2016 Employees: 84
Net Worth: £8,451,392 Total Assets: £15,203,680
Registered Office: Belvoir Fruit Farms, Barkestone Lane, Bottesford, Nottingham, NG13 0DH
Major Shareholder: Richard John Peverel Manners
Officers: Stephen Christopher Bridgens [1953] Director/Chartered Accountant; Richard John Peverel Manners [1963] Director; Anthony Henry Westropp [1944] Director

Belvoir Fruit Farms Limited
Incorporated: 26 July 2016 *Employees:* 84
Net Worth: £8,383,773 *Total Assets:* £15,198,961
Registered Office: Belvoir Fruit Farms, Barkestone Lane, Bottesford, Nottingham, NG13 0DH
Parent: Belvoir Fruit Farms Drinks Holdings Limited
Officers: Stephen Christopher Bridgens [1953] Director/Chartered Accountant; Francis William Fitzgibbons [1960] Production Director; Lee Bruce Hemmings [1977] Director; Richard John Peverel Manners [1963] Director; Paul Andrew Parkins [1974] Director/Chief Operating Officer; Anthony Henry Westropp [1944] Director

Belvoir Natural Drinks Company Limited
Incorporated: 21 June 2012
Registered Office: Belvoir Fruit Farms, Barkestone Lane, Bottesford, Nottingham, NG13 0DH
Major Shareholder: Richard John Peverel Manners
Officers: Richard John Peverel Manners [1963] Director/MD

Benefit Water Ltd
Incorporated: 10 October 2018
Registered Office: 52a Westgate, Southwell, Notts, NG25 0JX
Major Shareholder: Gavin Lloyd Cox
Officers: Gavin Lloyd Cox [1973] Director

Bennu Rising Ltd.
Incorporated: 31 January 2019
Registered Office: Fort Dunlop, Fort Parkway, Birmingham, B24 9FE
Shareholders: Joseph Burris; Mizani Bennu
Officers: Joseph Burris [1988] Director/Entrepreneur

Benu Distribution Limited
Incorporated: 28 August 2009
Net Worth Deficit: £3,337 *Total Assets:* £2,489
Registered Office: 1 Kings Avenue, London, N21 3NA
Parent: Berrywhite Group Ltd
Officers: Andrew Willfred Mark Jennings [1971] Director

Berkeley Springs Limited
Incorporated: 6 January 2015
Net Worth: £94 *Total Assets:* £100
Registered Office: F20A Waterfront Studios, 1 Dock Road, London, E16 1AH
Major Shareholder: Ali Hassan
Officers: Ali Hassan [1978] Director [Pakistani]

Berrington Pure Spring Water Limited
Incorporated: 19 August 2004
Net Worth: £207,515 *Total Assets:* £834,028
Registered Office: Berrington Spring Water Limited, Little Berrington Farm, Marden, Hereford, HR1 3EY
Shareholders: Ben Phiip Rendell; Henry Alexander Tomlin
Officers: Henry Alexander Tomlin, Secretary; Rhodri Alun Lewis [1982] Director; Benjamin Phillip Rendell [1974] Director/Self Employed; Henry Alexander Tomlin [1974] Director/Bank Manager

Berrington Spring Water Limited
Incorporated: 13 February 2012
Registered Office: Little Berrington Farm, Marden, Hereford, HR1 3EY
Officers: Matt Crocker [1983] Director; Rhodri Alun Lewis [1982] Director; Benjamin Phillip Rendell [1974] Director; Benjamin Richardson [1981] Director; Henry Alexander Tomlin [1974] Director

Bespokery Ltd
Incorporated: 31 August 2017
Registered Office: 701 Maypole Court, Geoff Cade Way, London, E3 4RP
Major Shareholder: Jason Fachler
Officers: Jason Fachler [1987] Director/Financial Analyst [American]

Better Fresh Limited
Incorporated: 11 October 2012
Net Worth Deficit: £910,911 *Total Assets:* £1,444,693
Registered Office: 61 Grosvenor Street, London, W1K 3JE
Shareholder: Benjamin Guy Arbib
Officers: Kate Elizabeth Inshaw, Secretary; Benjamin Guy Arbib [1980] Director; Vincent Soe on Heilbron [1971] Director/Consultant [Dutch]; Hamish Spencer Murray McCall [1972] Director/Consultant; Carlos Gustavo Valdetaro Lins de Albuquerque [1978] Director/Consultant [Brazilian]

Beverage Brands (U.K.) Limited
Incorporated: 8 March 1993 *Employees:* 110
Net Worth: £56,286,920 *Total Assets:* £83,943,024
Registered Office: 4th Floor, 115 George Street, Edinburgh, EH2 4JN
Parent: SHS Group Ltd
Officers: Arthur William Richmond, Secretary; Elaine Birchall [1966] Director [Irish]; Arthur William Richmond [1966] Director; Joseph Sloan [1946] Director

Beverage Management Limited
Incorporated: 5 June 2001 *Employees:* 1
Previous: The Feel Good Drinks Company Limited
Net Worth Deficit: £1,287,318 *Total Assets:* £16,600
Registered Office: Grosvenor House, 20 Barrington Road, Altrincham, Cheshire, WA14 1HB
Officers: Malte Vogel [1978] Finance Director [German]

Beyaz Kartal Ltd
Incorporated: 16 June 2017
Net Worth: £100 *Total Assets:* £100
Registered Office: First Floor, Dean House, 193 High Street, Enfield, Middlesex, EN3 4EA
Officers: Ramazan Karakas [1979] Director [Swedish]

Beyond Alcohol Ltd
Incorporated: 1 February 2018
Registered Office: 150 Wharfedale Road, Winnersh Triangle, Berks, RG41 5RB
Shareholders: Meeta Sethna Gournay; Charlotte Tatiana Mary Mercer; Dashiel Reuben Lilley
Officers: Meeta Sethna Gournay [1980] Director [American]; Dashiel Reuben Lilley [1983] Director; Charlotte Tatiana Mary Mercer [1984] Director

BFT Drinks Limited
Incorporated: 9 June 2017
Net Worth Deficit: £29,093 *Total Assets:* £22,091
Registered Office: Summerfield, Back Lane, Shirley, Ashbourne, Derbys, DE6 3AS
Shareholders: Liam Matthew Tyler; Andrew Mark Bell; Jonathan Mark Fuller
Officers: Andrew Mark Bell [1992] Director/Founder; Jonathan Mark Fuller [1990] Director/Founder; Liam Matthew Tyler [1993] Director/Founder

Bibax Limited
Incorporated: 20 June 2015
Net Worth Deficit: £113,425 *Total Assets:* £18,024
Registered Office: 71-75 Shelton Street, Covent Garden, London, WC2H 9JQ
Shareholders: Jan-Oliver Sell; Koby Gordon Roger Woodman
Officers: Jan-Oliver Sell, Secretary; Jan-Oliver Sell [1976] Director; Koby Gordon Roger Woodman [1978] Director

Big Daddy Beverages Limited
Incorporated: 20 April 2009
Registered Office: 49 Cruick Avenue, South Ockendon, Essex, RM15 6EL
Major Shareholder: Kelechi Imo
Officers: Kelechi Kenneth Imo [1980] Director

Big Time Soft Drinks Limited
Incorporated: 3 November 1987 *Employees:* 48
Net Worth: £2,366,363 *Total Assets:* £3,947,648
Registered Office: 29 Waterloo Road, Wolverhampton, W Midlands, WV1 4DJ
Shareholders: Mohinder Singh Athwal; Kashmir Kaur
Officers: Kashmir Kaur, Secretary; Kamaljit Athwal [1979] Director; Mohinder Singh Athwal [1952] Director; Ravinder Kaur Kang [1974] Director; Kashmir Kaur [1951] Director

Bigla Brewing Company Ltd
Incorporated: 18 December 2017
Registered Office: 1 St Marys Park Road, Portishead, Bristol, BS20 6SN
Major Shareholder: Yavor Kostadinchev
Officers: Yavor Kostadinchev [1981] Director [Bulgarian]

The Bily Co Limited
Incorporated: 10 May 2017
Net Worth: £1,714 *Total Assets:* £5,499
Registered Office: 143 Ayres Road, Old Trafford, Manchester, M16 9WR
Major Shareholder: Duane Bryan
Officers: Duane Bryan, Secretary; Duane Bryan [1982] Director

Biofresh Cosmos Ltd
Incorporated: 21 October 2016
Net Worth Deficit: £9,859 *Total Assets:* £111
Registered Office: 258 Merton Road, London, SW18 5JL
Major Shareholder: Muhammad Saad Khan
Officers: Muhammad Saad Khan [1984] Director/Certified Chartered Accountant; Christos Papadimitrakopoulos [1970] Director [Greek]

Birch Boost Ltd
Incorporated: 8 January 2018
Registered Office: 1st Floor, Packwood House, Guild Street, Stratford upon Avon, Warwicks, CV37 6RP
Major Shareholder: Patrick Birch
Officers: Dr Patrick Birch [1990] Director/Founder

Birdhouse Tea Company Limited
Incorporated: 15 May 2013 *Employees:* 2
Net Worth Deficit: £48,868 *Total Assets:* £6,636
Registered Office: 63 Bawtry Road, Bramley, Rotherham, S Yorks, S66 2TN
Shareholders: Julie English; Rebecca Lauren English
Officers: Julie English [1957] Director; Rebecca Lauren English [1988] Director

Birken Tree (Scotland) Limited
Incorporated: 12 February 2019
Registered Office: 2 Pitheavlis Cottages, Perth, PH2 0PZ
Shareholders: Robert William Clamp; Gabrielle Parrot
Officers: Robert William Clamp [1966] Director; Gabrielle Parrot [1989] Director [French]

Birmingham Soft Drinks Association Limited (The)
Incorporated: 29 October 1887
Net Worth: £145,488 *Total Assets:* £149,035
Registered Office: 88 Aldridge Road, Perry Barr, Birmingham, B42 2TP
Officers: Anthony Graham Curtis, Secretary; Graham Stanley Millichip [1938] Director/Soft Drinks Manufacturer; Barry John Stevens [1946] Director/Soft Drinks Manufacturer

Bitter Salvation Ltd
Incorporated: 16 August 2017
Registered Office: 190 New Kings Road, London, SW6 4NF
Shareholders: Alexandra Lynette Dover; Alexander Thomas Dover
Officers: Alexander Thomas Dover [1975] Director; Alexandra Lynette Dover [1988] Director

Bladud Spring Limited
Incorporated: 22 March 2017
Net Worth Deficit: £84,069 *Total Assets:* £42,341
Registered Office: Business Control, Red Lion Yard, 102 Frome Road, Bath, BA2 2PP
Officers: Mark Jason Keith Allen [1969] Director; Rachel Ingeborg Mary Allen [1971] Director; Jonathan Willis [1962] Director

Blending and Bottling Solutions Limited
Incorporated: 8 May 2014
Net Worth: £78 *Total Assets:* £328
Registered Office: Oak Tree House, Lyons Lane, Appleton, Warrington, Cheshire, WA4 5NA
Shareholder: Oliver Daniel Lewis
Officers: Oliver Daniel Lewis, Secretary; Mark Peter Lewis [1956] Director/Self Employed; Oliver Daniel Lewis [1991] Director/Self Employed; Tracy Jane Lewis [1964] Director/Self Employed

Bless Up Beverages Ltd
Incorporated: 15 February 2019
Registered Office: 27 Pendle Court, Leigh, Lancs, WN7 3AB
Shareholders: Jordan Lewis Ayrton Morris; Jake Christopher Laithwaite; Troy Peter Sanford
Officers: Jake Christopher Laithwaite [1995] Director/Barman; Jordan Lewis Ayrton Morris [1993] Director/Chef; Troy Peter Sanford [1985] Director/Chef

Bliiss Ltd
Incorporated: 15 November 2018
Registered Office: Unit 1955, 109 Vernon House, Friar Lane, Nottingham, NG1 6DQ
Major Shareholder: Berenge Nathalie Grove-Stephensen
Officers: Berenge Nathalie Grove-Stephensen [1980] Director

Bloody Drinks Limited
Incorporated: 5 December 2017
Registered Office: 13A Chadwick Road, London, E11 1NE
Shareholders: Henry Robert Spencer Farnham; William Trevorian Stuart Best
Officers: William Trevorian Stuart Best [1985] Director/Entrepreneur; Henry Robert Spencer Farnham [1985] Director/Entrepreneur

The Bloomberry Juice Company Limited
Incorporated: 18 June 2007 *Employees:* 1
Net Worth: £1,817 *Total Assets:* £37,150
Registered Office: 165 High Street, Honiton, Devon, EX14 1LQ
Shareholders: Christopher Blair Jones; Sarah Jones
Officers: Christopher Blair Jones [1953] Director; Sarah Jane Jones [1956] Director

Blossoms Syrup Limited
Incorporated: 21 July 2003 *Employees:* 1
Net Worth Deficit: £53,007 *Total Assets:* £30,472
Registered Office: April Cottage, Beacons Bottom, High Wycombe, Bucks, HP14 3XG
Major Shareholder: Aude Marie Claude Dupont Dudley
Officers: Mark Jonathon Cheyney Dudley, Secretary/Director; Aude Marie Claude Jacques Dupont Dudley [1970] Director [French]

Blue Keld Springs Limited
Incorporated: 22 December 1995 *Employees:* 22
Net Worth: £693,397 *Total Assets:* £1,127,746
Registered Office: Joseph Marr House, Units 18-20 Langthwaite Business Park, South Kirkby, W Yorks, WF9 3AP
Officers: Bridget Stickney Marr [1961] Director; Charles Roger Marr [1960] Director; Philip Edward Marr [1984] Director; Polly Anna Metcalfe [1986] Director; Annabelle Amy Tyson [1983] Director; Nicholas Giles Wharton [1966] Director

Blue Raspberry Investments Ltd
Incorporated: 16 November 2018
Registered Office: 87 Station Road, Ashington, Northumberland, NE63 8RS
Shareholders: Allison Goldfinch; Paul John Goldfinch
Officers: Allison Goldfinch [1975] Director; Paul John Goldfinch [1973] Director

BODI Products Limited
Incorporated: 17 November 2016
Net Worth Deficit: £3,760 *Total Assets:* £3,800
Registered Office: 34 South Molton Street, London, W1K 5RG
Officers: Olusoji Adamo, Secretary; Olusoji Adamo [1967] Sales Director; Giles Augustus Craig [1967] Managing Director

Boil and Broth Ltd
Incorporated: 5 March 2018
Registered Office: P O Box 7169, Poole, Dorset, BH15 9EL
Shareholder: Rachel Susan Down
Officers: Rachel Susan Down [1979] Managing Director; Simon Edward Down [1968] Director

Bolbol Imports Ltd
Incorporated: 15 February 2019
Registered Office: 20-22 Wenlock Road, London, N1 7GU
Major Shareholder: Ali Mansour
Officers: Ali Mansour [1992] Director

Bon Accord Soft Drinks Limited
Incorporated: 14 January 2015 *Employees:* 1
Net Worth Deficit: £45,838 *Total Assets:* £56,338
Registered Office: 6 St Colme Street, Edinburgh, EH3 6AD
Parent: Bon Accord Soft Drinks Holdings Limited
Officers: Nathan Paul Burrough [1979] Director; Karen Margaret Knowles [1985] Director/Account Manager

Boo-Chi Limited
Incorporated: 24 March 2017
Net Worth Deficit: £5,020 *Total Assets:* £960
Registered Office: 85 Walm Lane, London, NW2 4QL
Major Shareholder: Eaoifa Forward
Officers: Eaoifa Forward [1984] Director/Owner

Booost Trading Limited
Incorporated: 19 June 2001
Net Worth Deficit: £210,344 *Total Assets:* £715,737
Registered Office: 255 Putney Bridge Road, London, SW15 2PU
Officers: Patrick John O'Flaherty, Secretary/Consultant; Patrick John O'Flaherty [1968] Director/Consultant; Karen Margaret O'Neill [1971] Director/Branding Consultant

Boosted Tea (UK) Ltd.
Incorporated: 26 January 2016 *Employees:* 2
Net Worth Deficit: £62,001 *Total Assets:* £1,826
Registered Office: Boosted Tea, 3rd Floor, 29 Market Street, Portadown, Craigavon, Co Armagh, BT62 3LD
Shareholder: Arin Necmi Cubuk
Officers: Arin Cubuk [1992] Director; Jamie Curran [1996] Director

Boostvitaminwater Ltd
Incorporated: 9 July 2018
Registered Office: International House, 12 Constance Street, London, E16 2DQ
Officers: Mazeer Hussain [1987] Director

Boss of Bosses Global Limited
Incorporated: 7 May 2013
Registered Office: 18 Sandtoft Close, Lincoln, LN6 3PE
Major Shareholder: Jeb Screw You
Officers: Jeb Screw You [1962] Director/Entrepreneur

Botanical Alchemy Ltd
Incorporated: 17 March 2011
Registered Office: 47 Deodar Road, London, SW15 2NU
Major Shareholder: Susan Claire Lettice
Officers: Claire Lettice [1961] Director/Consultant

The Botanical Drinks Company Limited
Incorporated: 12 April 2013
Registered Office: 47 Deodar Road, Putney, London, SW15 2NU
Major Shareholder: Susan Claire Lettice
Officers: Susan Claire Lettice [1961] Director

Botanical Soda Works Limited
Incorporated: 10 October 2016
Registered Office: Holly Bank Barn, Crag Road, Warton, Carnforth, Lancs, LA5 9PL
Shareholders: Catherine Walsh; Callum Byerley
Officers: Callum James Byerley [1990] Director/Soft Drinks Producer; Catherine Anne Walsh [1979] Director/Soft Drinks Producer

Bottle Green Drinks Company Limited
Incorporated: 14 February 2011
Net Worth: £100,100 *Total Assets:* £33,253,072
Registered Office: SHS House, 199 Airport Road West, Belfast, BT3 9ED
Parent: SHS Group Ltd
Officers: Arthur Richmond, Secretary; Elaine Birchall [1966] Director [Irish]; Arthur Richmond [1968] Director; Karen Salters [1970] Director

Bottlegreen Holdings Limited
Incorporated: 9 August 2006
Net Worth: £1,434,486 *Total Assets:* £8,236,066
Registered Office: Manderson House, 5230 Valiant Court, Delta Way, Brockworth, Gloucester, GL3 4FE
Parent: Bottle Green Drinks Company Limited
Officers: Arthur Richmond, Secretary; Elaine Birchall [1966] Director [Irish]; Arthur William Richmond [1966] Director/Accountant; Karen Salters [1970] Director

UK Manufacturers of Soft Drinks   dellam

Bottling International Ltd
Incorporated: 11 October 2013 Employees: 10
Previous: Jeffries Vintage Drinks Ltd
Net Worth Deficit: £283,263 Total Assets: £562,144
Registered Office: Park House, 37 Clarence Street, Leicester, LE1 3RW
Major Shareholder: Lee Thomas John Jeffries
Officers: Lee Thomas John Jeffries [1981] Sales Director; Maurice Newton [1965] Director

Bounce Back Drinks Limited
Incorporated: 19 January 2018
Registered Office: Clockwise Offices, 77 Renfrew Street, Glasgow, G2 3BZ
Major Shareholder: Vandana Pillai
Officers: Vandana Pillai [1989] Director [Indian]

Bouncing Biotics Ltd
Incorporated: 19 September 2016
Net Worth: £610 Total Assets: £610
Registered Office: 22 Birdham Close, Bromley, Kent, BR1 2HF
Officers: Bernadette Harrison [1977] Director; Jenny Tomei [1990] Director

J B Bowler Ltd
Incorporated: 19 September 2011
Registered Office: 47 Deodar Road, London, SW15 2NU
Officers: Claire Lettice [1961] Director/Consultant

Bowser Limited
Incorporated: 14 December 2017
Registered Office: 5 Poole Road, Bournemouth, BH2 5QL
Major Shareholder: Rupert Holloway
Officers: Emily Etherton, Secretary; Frederick Gamper, Secretary; Rupert Holloway [1984] Managing Director

Bowser Properties Limited
Incorporated: 15 December 2017
Registered Office: 5 Poole Road, Bournemouth, BH2 5QL
Shareholders: Rupert Holloway; Bowser Limited
Officers: Emily Etherton, Secretary; Frederick Gamper, Secretary; Rupert Holloway [1984] Managing Director

Bowser Tonic Limited
Incorporated: 15 December 2017
Registered Office: 5 Poole Road, Bournemouth, BH2 5QL
Shareholders: Rupert Holloway; Bowser Limited
Officers: Emily Etherton, Secretary; Frederick Gamper, Secretary; Rupert Holloway [1984] Managing Director

Boydall Limited
Incorporated: 23 May 2015
Registered Office: 2 Sheep Fair Way, Lambourn, Hungerford, Berks, RG17 7LQ
Officers: Hannah Mary Boydall [1993] Director/Manager; Patrick Vincent Boydall [1995] Director/Manager

Brain Fud Ltd
Incorporated: 14 January 2016 Employees: 3
Net Worth: £8,118 Total Assets: £53,068
Registered Office: Suite 2, Fountain House, 1a Elm Park, Stanmore, Middlesex, HA7 4AU
Major Shareholder: Esther Ihuoma Udeh
Officers: Jessica Katharine Gould [1995] Director/Entrepreneur; Mark Udeh [1993] Director; Philip Enyinnaya Udeh [1981] Director

Brainwave Brands Ltd
Incorporated: 21 May 2013
Previous: Brainwave Drinks Ltd
Net Worth: £99,093 Total Assets: £102,509
Registered Office: Gateshead International Business Centre, Mulgrave Terrace, Gateshead, Tyne & Wear, NE8 1AN
Shareholder: Richard Frederick Veltrop-Baister
Officers: Nikola Hrstic [1959] Director; Richard Frederick Veltrop-Baister [1981] Director

Braveau Limited
Incorporated: 27 May 2008
Registered Office: Sandyford Abattoir, Sandyford Road, Paisley, Renfrewshire, PA3 4HP
Officers: Allan Jess [1961] Director; David Campbell Jess [1958] Director

The Bread Drink Lab Limited
Incorporated: 22 January 2019
Registered Office: Suite 15, Yeovil Innovation Centre, Barracks Close, Copse Road, Yeovil, Somerset, BA22 8RN
Major Shareholder: Jonathann Cocogne
Officers: Jonathann Cocogne [1981] Director/Bar Manager [French]

Brewberry Limited
Incorporated: 22 June 2018
Registered Office: Keepers, Minchinhampton, Stroud, Glos, GL6 9AN
Major Shareholder: Henry Edward Stephen Davidson Binns
Officers: Henry Edward Stephen Davidson Binns [1997] Director

Brewski Coffee Ltd
Incorporated: 3 April 2018
Registered Office: 20-22 Wenlock Road, London, N1 7GU
Major Shareholder: Callum Ruffman
Officers: Callum Ruffman [1990] Director/Project Manager

Bright Barley Company Ltd
Incorporated: 14 October 2016
Net Worth Deficit: £110,438 Total Assets: £3,489
Registered Office: FMC, Unit 16 Manor Courtyard, Hughenden Avenue, High Wycombe, Bucks, HP13 5RE
Major Shareholder: Jiali Jiang
Officers: Jiali Jiang [1989] Director and Vice General Manager [Chinese]

Bright Smoothies Ltd
Incorporated: 21 February 2019
Registered Office: 49 Westfield Road, Leeds, LS3 1DF
Major Shareholder: Lewis Dan Challinor
Officers: Lewis Dan Challinor [1994] Director/Student

Britannia Soft Drinks Limited
Incorporated: 5 March 1896
Net Worth: £163,152,000 Total Assets: £950,691,968
Registered Office: Breakspear Park, Breakspear Way, Hemel Hempstead, Herts, HP2 4TZ
Parent: Britvic PLC
Officers: Judith Moore, Secretary; Mathew James Dunn [1974] Director/Chief Financial Officer; Peter Simon Litherland [1964] Director/Chief Executive; Alexandra Clare Thomas [1974] Director/General Counsel and Company Secretary

British Vitamin Products Limited
Incorporated: 19 July 1950
Registered Office: Breakspear Park, Breakspear Way, Hemel Hempstead, Herts, HP2 4TZ
Parent: Britvic Soft Drinks Limited
Officers: Judith Moore, Secretary; Mathew James Dunn [1974] Director/Chief Financial Officer; Peter Simon Litherland [1964] Director/Chief Executive; Alexandra Clare Thomas [1974] Director/General Counsel and Company Secretary

Britvic Asset Company No.1 Limited
Incorporated: 23 August 2011
Net Worth: £4,027,000 *Total Assets:* £4,028,000
Registered Office: Breakspear Park, Breakspear Way, Hemel Hempstead, Herts, HP2 4TZ
Parent: Britannia Soft Drinks Limited
Officers: Judith Moore, Secretary; Mathew James Dunn [1974] Director/Chief Financial Officer; Peter Simon Litherland [1964] Director/Chief Executive; Alexandra Clare Thomas [1974] Director/General Counsel and Company Secretary

Britvic Asset Company No.2 Limited
Incorporated: 23 August 2011
Net Worth: £467,000 *Total Assets:* £9,535,000
Registered Office: Breakspear Park, Breakspear Way, Hemel Hempstead, Herts, HP2 4TZ
Parent: Britannia Soft Drinks Limited
Officers: Judith Moore, Secretary; Mathew James Dunn [1974] Director/Chief Financial Officer; Peter Simon Litherland [1964] Director/Chief Executive; Alexandra Clare Thomas [1974] Director/General Counsel and Company Secretary

Britvic Asset Company No.3 Limited
Incorporated: 23 August 2011
Net Worth: £129 *Total Assets:* £229
Registered Office: Breakspear Park, Breakspear Way, Hemel Hempstead, Herts, HP2 4TZ
Parent: Britannia Soft Drinks Limited
Officers: Judith Moore, Secretary; Mathew James Dunn [1974] Director/Chief Financial Officer; Peter Simon Litherland [1964] Director/Chief Executive; Alexandra Clare Thomas [1974] Director/General Counsel and Company Secretary

Britvic Asset Company No.4 Limited
Incorporated: 18 October 2011
Net Worth: £130 *Total Assets:* £230
Registered Office: Breakspear Park, Breakspear Way, Hemel Hempstead, Herts, HP2 4TZ
Parent: Britannia Soft Drinks Limited
Officers: Judith Moore, Secretary; Mathew James Dunn [1974] Director/Chief Financial Officer; Peter Simon Litherland [1964] Director/Chief Executive; Alexandra Clare Thomas [1974] Director/General Counsel and Company Secretary

Britvic Beverages Limited
Incorporated: 26 November 1938
Registered Office: Breakspear Park, Breakspear Way, Hemel Hempstead, Herts, HP2 4TZ
Parent: Britvic Soft Drinks Limited
Officers: Judith Moore, Secretary; Mathew James Dunn [1974] Director/Chief Financial Officer; Peter Simon Litherland [1964] Director/Chief Executive; Alexandra Clare Thomas [1974] Director/General Counsel and Company Secretary

Britvic Corona Limited
Incorporated: 20 December 1938
Registered Office: Breakspear Park, Breakspear Way, Hemel Hempstead, Herts, HP2 4TZ
Parent: Britvic Soft Drinks Limited
Officers: Judith Moore, Secretary; Mathew James Dunn [1974] Director/Chief Financial Officer; Peter Simon Litherland [1964] Director/Chief Executive; Alexandra Clare Thomas [1974] Director/General Counsel and Company Secretary

Britvic EMEA Limited
Incorporated: 13 October 1986 *Employees:* 42
Net Worth Deficit: £52,337,000 *Total Assets:* £20,076,000
Registered Office: Breakspear Park, Breakspear Way, Hemel Hempstead, Herts, HP2 4TZ
Parent: Britannia Soft Drinks Limited
Officers: Judith Moore, Secretary; Christophe Garcia [1975] Director [French]; Hessel Douwe de Jong [1969] International Managing Director [Dutch]; Stephen Andrew Smith [1972] Director

Britvic International Investments Limited
Incorporated: 13 October 1986
Net Worth: £169,670,000 *Total Assets:* £170,228,000
Registered Office: Breakspear Park, Breakspear Way, Hemel Hempstead, Herts, HP2 4TZ
Parent: Britannia Soft Drinks Limited
Officers: Judith Moore, Secretary; Mathew James Dunn [1974] Director/Chief Financial Officer; Peter Simon Litherland [1964] Director/Chief Executive; Alexandra Clare Thomas [1974] Director/General Counsel and Company Secretary

Britvic International Support Services Limited
Incorporated: 15 October 2014
Registered Office: Breakspear Park, Breakspear Way, Hemel Hempstead, Herts, HP2 4TZ
Parent: Britvic International Investments Limited
Officers: Judith Moore, Secretary; Mathew James Dunn [1974] Director/Chief Financial Officer; Alexandra Clare Thomas [1974] Director/General Counsel and Company Secretary

Britvic Overseas Limited
Incorporated: 17 August 2010
Net Worth: £74,459,000 *Total Assets:* £336,556,992
Registered Office: Breakspear Park, Breakspear Way, Hemel Hempstead, Herts, HP2 4TZ
Parent: Britannia Soft Drinks Limited
Officers: Judith Moore, Secretary; Mathew James Dunn [1974] Director/Chief Financial Officer; Peter Simon Litherland [1964] Director/Chief Executive; Alexandra Clare Thomas [1974] Director/General Counsel and Company Secretary

Britvic PLC
Incorporated: 27 October 2005 *Employees:* 4,781
Net Worth: £377,300,000 *Total Assets:* £1,664,099,968
Registered Office: Breakspear Park, Breakspear Way, Hemel Hempstead, Herts, HP2 4TZ
Officers: Jonathan Mark Adelman, Secretary; Suniti Kiransinh Chauhan [1974] Director/Finance [American]; Susan Michelle Clark [1964] Director; John Patrick Daly [1956] Director [Irish]; Mathew James Dunn [1974] Director/Chief Financial Officer; Christopher William Eccleshare [1955] Director; Peter Simon Litherland [1964] Director/Chief Executive; Ian Philip McHoul [1960] Director/Chief Financial Officer; Euan Angus Sutherland [1969] Director

UK Manufacturers of Soft Drinks   dellam

Britvic Soft Drinks Limited
Incorporated: 16 March 1953 *Employees:* 1,903
Net Worth: £768,606,016 *Total Assets:* £1,437,943,040
Registered Office: Breakspear Park, Breakspear Way, Hemel Hempstead, Herts, HP2 4TZ
Parent: Britannia Soft Drinks Limited
Officers: Alexandra Clare Thomas, Secretary; Matthew Robert Barwell [1966] Strategic Marketing & Innovation Director; Mathew James Dunn [1974] Director/Chief Financial Officer; Richard Paul Graham [1968] Director/General Manager; Clive Alastair Hooper [1964] Director; Peter Simon Litherland [1964] Director/Chief Executive

Brown Box Trading Co Ltd
Incorporated: 3 June 2011
Registered Office: 7 Kiln Park, Searle Crescent, Weston-Super-Mare, Somerset, BS23 3XP
Major Shareholder: Elliott Howell Johnson
Officers: Elliott Johnson [1977] Director

BTW Drinks Ltd
Incorporated: 28 August 2014 *Employees:* 1
Net Worth Deficit: £127,615 *Total Assets:* £23,039
Registered Office: 214 Bermondsey Street, London, SE1 3TQ
Officers: Nick Alessandro Crispini [1980] Director

Buatoc Limited
Incorporated: 15 April 2013
Registered Office: 6a Watford Way, London, NW4 3AD
Officers: Odili Anthony Cliffe [1986] Director/Accountant

Budaquelle Beverages International Ltd
Incorporated: 18 August 2016
Registered Office: Unit 42 Price Street Business Centre, Price Street, Birkenhead, Merseyside, CH41 4JQ
Major Shareholder: Laszlo Ficsor
Officers: Laszlo Ficsor [1956] Director/Businessman [German]

Bumblezest Limited
Incorporated: 1 September 2016
Net Worth Deficit: £34,485 *Total Assets:* £15,891
Registered Office: 24 Forthbridge Road, London, SW11 5NY
Major Shareholder: Daniel Watson
Officers: Daniel Watson [1979] Director/Drinks Manufacturer

Burble Foods and Beverages Limited
Incorporated: 8 February 2018
Registered Office: 71-75 Shelton Street, Covent Garden, London, WC2H 9JQ
Major Shareholder: Tolulope Ayomide Agbeyo
Officers: Tolulope Ayomide Agbeyo [1994] Director [Nigerian]

Burnswell Spring (Mauchline) Limited
Incorporated: 30 September 1996
Net Worth Deficit: £79,502
Registered Office: The Pumphouse, 1 Burngrange Lane, Mauchline, E Ayrshire, KA5 6EL
Shareholders: Andrew Cooper; David McMichael Cooper
Officers: Catherine Nimmo Cooper, Secretary; Andrew Cooper [1944] Director/Kitchen Fitter & Joiner

Burst Drink Limited
Incorporated: 17 June 2014
Net Worth: £5,163 *Total Assets:* £76,782
Registered Office: Unit G, Lea Road Trading Estate, Lea Road, Waltham Abbey, Essex, EN9 1AE
Major Shareholder: Mindel Deborah Rubin
Officers: Mindel Rubin, Secretary; Mindel Deborah Rubin [1980] Director

Bussl Limited
Incorporated: 14 March 2016
Previous: Hydrogenated Water Ltd
Registered Office: 71-75 Shelton Street, Covent Garden, London, WC2H 9JQ
Major Shareholder: Fiona Jayne Swailes
Officers: Conrad Swailes, Secretary; Fiona Jayne Swailes [1966] Managing Director

Buxton Mineral Water Limited
Incorporated: 5 July 1977
Net Worth: £11,525,000 *Total Assets:* £14,006,000
Registered Office: 1 City Place, Gatwick, W Sussex, RH6 0PA
Parent: Nestle Holdings (U.K.) PLC
Officers: Michel Beneventi [1971] Managing Director of Nestle Waters UK [Swiss]; Charles David Hardy Roberts [1974] Director/Factory Manager; Richard James Shaw [1974] Director/Management Accountant

C02 Drinks Ltd
Incorporated: 7 October 2010
Net Worth: £42,570 *Total Assets:* £168,620
Registered Office: 19-20 Bourne Court, Southend Road, Woodford Green, Essex, IG8 8HD
Parent: Langhedge Holdings Limited
Officers: Serge Smadja, Secretary; Serge Noel Smadja [1954] Director [French]

Caledonian Bottlers PLC
Incorporated: 23 August 1993 *Employees:* 46
Net Worth: £3,784,607 *Total Assets:* £4,929,933
Registered Office: 4th Floor, 115 George Street, Edinburgh, EH2 4JN
Parent: Beverage Brands (UK) Ltd
Officers: Arthur Richmond, Secretary; Elaine Birchall [1966] Director [Irish]; Arthur William Richmond [1966] Director

The Caledonian Cola Company Ltd
Incorporated: 22 August 2017
Registered Office: 272 Blue Square Business Centre, Bath Street, Glasgow, G2 4JR

Calypso Soft Drinks Limited
Incorporated: 30 April 1981
Registered Office: Citrus Grove, Sideley, Kegworth, Derby, DE74 2FJ
Shareholder: Cooke Bros (Tattenhall) Limited
Officers: David John Saint [1964] Managing Director

Calyx Drinks Ltd
Incorporated: 11 June 2015
Net Worth Deficit: £4,544 *Total Assets:* £1,964
Registered Office: 6 Hart Street, Burnley, Lancs, BB11 2SG
Shareholders: Michael Peter Andrew Bass; Raphael Adesina Ogunrinde
Officers: Michael Peter Andrew Bass [1967] Director; Raphael Adesina Ogunrinde [1981] Director; Rev Andrew Wickens [1963] Director

Cambrian Soft Drinks Limited
Incorporated: 4 April 1930
Registered Office: 33 Cavendish Square, London, W1G 0PW
Officers: Andrew Maxwell Coppel [1950] Director; Colin David Elliot [1964] Director

Can of Wagon Ltd
Incorporated: 1 November 2018
Registered Office: 65 Wellington Road, London, E7 9BY
Shareholder: Suresh Kumar Basra
Officers: Suresh Kumar Basra [1970] Director/House Husband

Canncrest Drinks Limited
Incorporated: 5 February 2019
Registered Office: 119 The Hub, 300 Kensal Road, London, W10 5BE
Parent: Canncrest Limited
Officers: David Channing Gibson [1974] Director

Cantaker Ltd
Incorporated: 18 July 2018
Registered Office: Ground Floor Office, 108 Fore Street, Hertford, SG14 1AB
Major Shareholder: Anthony Derbyshire
Officers: Charise Pampanga [1993] Director [Filipino]

Captains Original Ltd
Incorporated: 29 October 2018
Registered Office: 20-22 Wenlock Road, London, N1 7GU
Shareholders: Howard James Corrigan; Michael Thomas Sweeney
Officers: Edward Corrigan, Secretary; Howard James Corrigan [1980] Director/Wine Merchant; Michael Thomas Sweeney [1968] Director/Civil Engineer

Caraway and Peel Limited
Incorporated: 30 January 2019
Registered Office: 168 Peckham Rye, London, SE22 9QA
Major Shareholder: Lauren Winsor
Officers: Lauren Winsor [1982] Director/Photographer

Carbon Drinks Limited
Incorporated: 11 May 2017
Registered Office: 32 Gillygate, Pontefract, W Yorks, WF8 1PQ
Officers: Adrian Howell [1967] Director

Cardinal Drinks Ltd
Incorporated: 14 March 2018
Registered Office: 3 Liskeard Gardens, London, SE3 0PE
Major Shareholder: Emma Bailey
Officers: Emma Bailey [1977] Director

Carrington's Coffee Company Ltd
Incorporated: 23 January 2019
Registered Office: 49 Church Lane, Lowton, Warrington, Cheshire, WA3 2AS
Shareholders: Alexander Nicholas Carrington; Suzanne Ellen Ruth Wimbourne
Officers: Alexander Nicholas Carrington [1988] Director; Suzanne Ellen Ruth Wimbourne [1989] Director

Cawingredients Limited
Incorporated: 20 June 2008 Employees: 173
Net Worth: £22,491,476 Total Assets: £60,866,140
Registered Office: Caw House, Conygarth Way, Leeming Bar Business Park, Leeming Bar, Northallerton, N Yorks, DL7 9FD
Major Shareholder: Andrew James Cawthray
Officers: Mark Kevin Adamson [1984] Director/Chartered Accountant; Elizabeth Burkhardt [1986] Director; Andrew James Cawthray [1957] Director; Susan Cawthray [1958] Director; Hannah Harrison [1983] Director; Peter Richard Harrison [1979] Director; Andrew David Holt [1959] Director/Solicitor

The CBD Revolution Ltd
Incorporated: 31 October 2018
Registered Office: 12 Woodberry Close, Leigh on Sea, Essex, SS9 4QT
Major Shareholder: Daren Robert Palmer
Officers: Daren Robert Palmer [1976] Director

CBD Tonic & Mixers Limited
Incorporated: 9 November 2018
Registered Office: 5 Cricket Close, Crawley, Winchester, Hants, SO21 2PX
Major Shareholder: Simon Paul Hobson
Officers: Simon Paul Hobson [1980] Director/Businessman

CBDMEhealthy Limited
Incorporated: 21 January 2019
Registered Office: 25 Balham High Road, London, SW12 9AL
Shareholders: Kyriacos Stylianou; Ali Al Khyami; Nick Giorgio
Officers: Ali Al Khyami [1979] Director; Nick Giorgio [1969] Director; Kyriacos Stylianou [1971] Director

Celtic Soul Drinks Limited
Incorporated: 30 November 2018
Registered Office: 12 York Road, Richmond, Surrey, TW10 6DR
Major Shareholder: Craig Hutchison
Officers: Craig Hutchison [1975] Director/Founder

Cen Bottling Company Limited
Incorporated: 24 September 1998
Net Worth Deficit: £80,898 Total Assets: £4,966
Registered Office: Unit 46 Cariocca Business Park, Hellidon Close, Manchester, M12 4AH
Parent: Odeiga House Limited
Officers: Olalekan Kamorudeen Kaffo [1979] Director/IT [Nigerian]; Marie Terez Laraba Osammor [1993] Director

Chaiwala Limited
Incorporated: 7 October 2018
Registered Office: 4 Borrowdale Drive, Rochdale, Lancs, OL11 3JZ
Officers: Muhammad Ejaz [1978] Director/Sales Manager

Chakra Chai Limited
Incorporated: 6 March 2018
Registered Office: 39 Kingsmill Terrace, London, NW8 6AA
Major Shareholder: Hoda Mohajerani
Officers: Hoda Mohajerani [1971] Founder & Director

Channel Island Water Limited
Incorporated: 1 August 2013
Registered Office: 300 City Road, London, EC1Y 2AB
Major Shareholder: Andrew Rupert Grimwood
Officers: Andrew Rupert Grimwood [1964] Director/Accountant

Chapmans Drinks Limited
Incorporated: 14 January 2014
Registered Office: 3 Theatre Court, Theatre Street, Warwick, CV34 4DY
Major Shareholder: Garry Mark Robinson
Officers: Garry Mark Robinson [1966] Director

Charlie T's Ltd
Incorporated: 16 January 2018
Registered Office: Spring House, Pound Lane, Stanton St John, Oxford, OX33 1HF
Major Shareholder: Charles Michael Harnden
Officers: Charles Michael Harnden [1993] Director; Karin Harnden [1960] Director

Chastity Limited
Incorporated: 7 February 2018
Registered Office: 2324 Great Western Road, Glasgow, G15 6SE
Major Shareholder: Roddy Nicoll
Officers: Rodryke Nicoll, Secretary; Janice Grace Condron [1966] Director; Rodryke Nicoll [1966] Director

Cheddar Mineral Water Limited
Incorporated: 23 August 2004
Registered Office: Carscliffe, Upper Draycott Road, Cheddar, Somerset, BS27 3YL
Shareholder: Tabitha Sarah-Jane Urch
Officers: Virginia Urch, Secretary; David Lawrence Urch [1951] Director; Duncan Winston Urch [1980] Director; Tabitha Sarah-Jane Urch [1978] Director; Virginia Urch [1952] Director

Cheddar Natural Mineral Water Limited
Incorporated: 31 January 2005
Registered Office: Carscliffe, Upper Draycott Road, Cheddar, Somerset, BS27 3YL
Shareholder: Tabitha Sarah-Jane Urch
Officers: Virginia Urch, Secretary/Farmer; David Lawrence Urch [1951] Director; Duncan Winston Urch [1980] Director; Tabitha Sarah-Jane Urch [1978] Director

Cheddar Natural Spring Water Limited
Incorporated: 27 January 2005
Registered Office: Carscliffe Farm, Upper Draycott Road, Cheddar, Somerset, BS27 3YL
Shareholder: Tabitha Sarah-Jane Urch
Officers: Virginia Urch, Secretary; David Lawrence Urch [1951] Director; Duncan Winston Urch [1980] Director; Tabitha Sarah-Jane Urch [1978] Director; Virginia Urch [1952] Director

Cheddar Spring Water Limited
Incorporated: 23 August 2004
Registered Office: Carscliffe, Upper Draycott Road, Cheddar, Somerset, BS27 3YL
Shareholder: Tabitha Sarah-Jane Urch
Officers: Virginia Urch, Secretary; David Lawrence Urch [1951] Director; Duncan Winston Urch [1980] Director; Tabitha Sarah-Jane Urch [1978] Director; Virginia Urch [1952] Director

Cheddar Water Limited
Incorporated: 23 August 2004 *Employees:* 3
Net Worth: £250,024 *Total Assets:* £1,066,561
Registered Office: Carscliffe, Upper Draycott Road, Cheddar, Somerset, BS27 3YL
Shareholders: David Lawrence Urch; Tabitha Sarah-Jane Urch
Officers: Virginia Urch, Secretary; David Lawrence Urch [1951] Director; Duncan Winston Urch [1980] Director; Tabitha Sarah-Jane Urch [1978] Director; Virginia Urch [1952] Director

Cheese Burger Limited
Incorporated: 24 April 2018
Registered Office: c/o Burger Chef Limited, Bridge House, 64-72 Mabgate, Leeds, LS9 7DZ
Major Shareholder: Robert (Elias) Wilson
Officers: Robert Wilson [1941] Director (CEO)

Chia Food (York) Limited
Incorporated: 9 January 2015 *Employees:* 3
Net Worth: £41,544 *Total Assets:* £97,186
Registered Office: 2 Clifton Moor Business Village, James Nicolson Link, York, YO30 4XG
Shareholders: Timothy Alfred Taylor; Lisa Christine Clarke
Officers: Lisa Christine Clarke [1971] Director/Project Manager

Chilled Water Ltd
Incorporated: 20 November 2018
Registered Office: Unit D2, Ennis Close, Roundthorn Industrial Estate, Manchester, M23 9LE
Major Shareholder: Asif Ayub
Officers: Asif Ayub [1970] Managing Director

Chocquers Limited
Incorporated: 5 March 2015
Registered Office: 49 Upper Selsdon Road, South Croydon, Surrey, CR2 8DG
Officers: Paul Abdul-Abbass Audu [1966] Director/Consultant; Sharon Johnson [1962] Director/Consultant

Choquers Limited
Incorporated: 4 March 2015
Registered Office: 49 Upper Selsdon Road, South Croydon, Surrey, CR2 8DG
Officers: Paul Abdul-Abbass Audu [1966] Director/Consultant; Sharon Johnson [1962] Director/Consultant

Chosan Drinks Ltd
Incorporated: 12 May 2015
Net Worth Deficit: £95,592 *Total Assets:* £16,205
Registered Office: 6 Albrighton Croft, Highwoods, Colchester, Essex, CO4 9RB
Major Shareholder: Eliza Miranda Maurice Jones
Officers: Eliza Miranda Maurice Jones [1958] Director/Manufacturer

Citrosoft Drinks Limited
Incorporated: 30 November 1987 *Employees:* 9
Net Worth: £500,184 *Total Assets:* £622,717
Registered Office: 11 Nicholas Street, Burnley, Lancs, BB11 2AL
Shareholders: Michelle Jayne Spence; Patricia Abraham
Officers: Lesley May Keegan, Secretary; Malcolm Joseph Abraham [1942] Director; Patricia Anne Abraham [1943] Director; Michelle Jayne Spence [1965] Director

Classic Holdings Limited
Incorporated: 12 June 2007
Net Worth: £40,000 *Total Assets:* £40,002
Registered Office: 12 Church Place, Lurgan, Craigavon, Co Armagh, BT66 6EY
Officers: Liam Duffy [1972] Director [Irish]; Gerard Watters [1972] Director/Chartered Accountant [Irish]

Classic Mineral Water Company Limited
Incorporated: 9 July 1976 *Employees:* 17
Net Worth: £310,075 *Total Assets:* £974,074
Registered Office: 12 Church Place, Lurgan, Craigavon, Co Armagh, BT66 6EY
Parent: Classic Holdings Limited
Officers: Liam Duffy [1972] Director [Irish]; Gerard Watters [1972] Director/Chartered Accountant [Irish]

Clayton's Cold Brewed Coffee Limited
Incorporated: 2 February 2016
Net Worth Deficit: £1,126 *Total Assets:* £2,691
Registered Office: Lodsworth House, Lodsworth, Petworth, W Sussex, GU28 9BY
Major Shareholder: Christian John Cameron Summers
Officers: Christian John Cameron Summers [1995] Director/Manager

Clear Green Water Limited
Incorporated: 21 July 2016
Registered Office: 4 Hazel Wood, Wishaw, N Lanarks, ML2 8XZ
Major Shareholder: Stephen Hughes
Officers: Stephen Hughes [1987] Director

Clearly Devon Limited
Incorporated: 17 August 1995
Registered Office: 95 Grassendale Avenue, Plymouth, PL2 2JP
Officers: Roger James Mitchell, Secretary; Julia Christine Cider [1970] Director/Teacher; Rachael Jane Mitchell [1968] Director/Manager

Clearly Drinks Limited
Incorporated: 26 January 2011 *Employees:* 73
Previous: CBL Drinks Limited
Net Worth: £1,926,171 *Total Assets:* £7,591,639
Registered Office: Riverside Industrial Estate, Riverside Road, Sunderland, Tyne & Wear, SR5 3JG
Parent: Clearly Drinks Group Limited
Officers: Geoffrey Mark Hodgson [1961] Director; Michael Alan Howard [1969] Director; Damian Jon Stevenson [1967] Director

Clearwater Drink Limited
Incorporated: 14 August 2017
Registered Office: 170 Withington Road, Manchester, M16 8JN
Major Shareholder: Shekha Ahmed Omar
Officers: Shekha Ahmed Omar [1968] Director/Manager

Club Consultants Ltd
Incorporated: 17 July 2014
Net Worth Deficit: £27,854 *Total Assets:* £56,652
Registered Office: c/o 447 Kenton Road, Harrow, Middlesex, HA3 0XY
Officers: Timothy Lawrence Luscombe [1957] Director/Consultant; Russell Paul West [1968] Director/IT Consultant

CMB Water Limited
Incorporated: 30 April 2001 *Employees:* 22
Net Worth: £866,390 *Total Assets:* £1,651,816
Registered Office: Walmer Court Farm, 466 Dover Road, Upper Walmer, Deal, Kent, CT14 7NA
Shareholders: William Bomer; Selma Isabella Henrietta Bomer
Officers: William Bomer, Secretary; Sarah Bomer [1942] Director; William Bomer [1967] Managing Director; Eion Campbell [1979] Director; Barry Bernard Iverson [1953] Director/Manager

Coast Drinks Ltd
Incorporated: 25 April 2016
Net Worth Deficit: £2,463 *Total Assets:* £14,463
Registered Office: 80 Highbury Park, London, N5 2XE
Shareholders: Joseph Michael McCanta; Richard Samuel Watson
Officers: Joseph Michael McCanta [1980] Director/Brand Ambassador [American]; Richard Samuel Watson [1983] Director

Coca-Cola European Partners Great Britain Limited
Incorporated: 24 July 1888 *Employees:* 3,440
Previous: Coca-Cola Enterprises Limited
Net Worth: £739,393,024 *Total Assets:* £1,293,049,984
Registered Office: Pemberton House, Bakers Road, Uxbridge, Middlesex, UB8 1EZ
Parent: Coca-Cola European Partners Holdings Great Britain Limited
Officers: Huma Allana, Secretary; Huma Allana [1975] Company Secretary/Director; Michael Clark [1970] Director; Leendert Pieter Den Hollander [1969] Director/Vice President & General Manager CCE Ltd [Dutch]; Frank Govaerts [1961] Director/European General Counsel [Belgian]; Ed Owen Walker [1967] Director

Coca-Cola European Partners PLC
Incorporated: 4 August 2015 *Employees:* 24
Net Worth: £5,847,109,120 *Total Assets:* £15,913,583,616
Registered Office: Pemberton House, Bakers Road, Uxbridge, Middlesex, UB8 1EZ
Officers: Clare Wardle, Secretary; Jan Bennink [1956] Director [Dutch]; Francisco Javier Crespo Benitez [1965] Director [American]; Christine Cross [1951] Director; Sol Daurella [1966] Director/Chairperson; Javier Ferran [1956] Director; Irial Finan [1957] Director/Executive Vice President [Irish]; Damian Paul Gammell [1970] Director [Irish]; Nathalie Laurence Gaveau [1975] Director [French]; Alvaro Gomez-Trenor Aguilar [1952] Director [Spanish]; Philip Humann [1945] Director [American]; Orrin Henry Ingram II [1960] Director [American]; Thomas Johnson [1949] Director [American]; Alfonso Libano Daurella [1954] Director [Spanish]; Mario Rotllant Sola [1951] Director [Spanish]; Jose Ignacio Comenge Sanchez Real [1951] Director [Spanish]; Garry Watts [1956] Director/Chairman of BTG PLC; Curtis Welling [1949] Director [American]

Coca-Cola HBC Northern Ireland Limited
Incorporated: 25 June 1945 *Employees:* 434
Net Worth: £63,295,496 *Total Assets:* £295,026,432
Registered Office: 12 Lissue Road, Lisburn, Co Antrim, BT28 2SZ
Parent: CC Beverage Holdings II BV
Officers: Rebecca Louise Jones, Secretary; Mel Drohan [1967] Director/Chief Financial Officer [Irish]; Matthieu Antoine Jean Seguin [1968] Director/General Manager [French]

Coca-Cola Holdings Africa Limited
Incorporated: 11 December 2014
Net Worth: £585,754,944 *Total Assets:* £585,783,232
Registered Office: Ingrid Cope, c/o Beverage Services Limited, 1a Wimpole Street, London, W1G 0EA
Parent: The Coca-Cola Company
Officers: Mellenefi Van Wyk Louw [1969] Director/Legal Entity Controller [South African]; Mpumelelo Mazibuko [1976] Director/Attorney (Legal Counsel) [South African]

Coca-Cola International Sales Limited
Incorporated: 5 November 1984 *Employees:* 5
Net Worth: £14,480,374 *Total Assets:* £17,256,740
Registered Office: 1a Wimpole Street, London, W1G 0EA
Parent: Coca-Cola Holdings (United Kingdom) Limited
Officers: Ingrid Natalie Cope [1972] Director/Solicitor; Scott Edward Roche [1964] Finance Director [Canadian]; Ruben Christiaan Stephaan Rutten [1977] Finance Director [Belgian]; Margaret Ann Stewart [1972] HR Director [Irish]; Jonathan Mark Woods [1968] Director/Franchise Operations Manager

Cocaine Limited
Incorporated: 19 May 2003
Registered Office: 18 Sandtoft Close, Lincoln, LN6 3PE
Major Shareholder: Jeb Screw You
Officers: Jebaraj Screw You [1962] Director/Businessman

Cocomojo Group Limited
Incorporated: 11 March 2016
Net Worth Deficit: £1,002 *Total Assets:* £87,274
Registered Office: 12 Enterprise Crescent, Lisburn, Co Antrim, BT28 2BP
Major Shareholder: Ronald Andrew Hill
Officers: Ronald Andrew Hill [1976] Director

Cold Bru Tea Limited
Incorporated: 10 May 2017
Registered Office: 72 Great Titchfield Street, London, W1W 7QW
Officers: Faraz Ahmad [1982] Director; Osman Ahmed [1982] Director

Common Goods Group Limited
Incorporated: 8 November 2018
Registered Office: 76 Bathgate Road, London, SW19 5PH
Shareholders: Julian Liban; Justin Lyndan Linnebank; Guy Steven Laurie
Officers: Guy Steven Laurie [1990] Director; Julian Liban [1990] Director; Justin Lyndan Linnebank [1989] Director [Dutch]

Connect Beverages Ltd
Incorporated: 30 October 2018
Registered Office: 36 Higher Shady Lane, Bromley Cross, Bolton, Lancs, BL7 9AQ
Major Shareholder: Rachel Louise Jones
Officers: Rachel Louise Jones [1989] Managing Director

Conscious Drinks Limited
Incorporated: 18 July 2018
Registered Office: 44 Rectory Lane, Kings Langley, Herts, WD4 8EY
Shareholders: James Daniel Jacoby; Vanessa Tanis Jacoby
Officers: James Daniel Jacoby [1976] Director; Vanessa Tanis Jacoby [1981] Director

Copper Stag Ltd
Incorporated: 22 January 2018
Registered Office: 4 Abbey Mansion Mews, London, SE24 0DD
Major Shareholder: William Thomas Bushell
Officers: William Thomas Bushell [1986] Managing Director

Corduroy Ideas Limited
Incorporated: 17 May 2018
Registered Office: 39 Seymour Road, Bishopston, Bristol, BS7 9HS
Major Shareholder: Rupert William Conroy Gwillim
Officers: Rupert William Conroy Gwillim [1995] Director and Company Secretary

Core Beverage Equipment Ltd
Incorporated: 7 May 2010
Previous: Nene Valley Orchards Limited
Net Worth: £54,320 *Total Assets:* £93,652
Registered Office: 3 Everdon Park, Heartlands Business Park, Daventry, Northants, NN11 8YJ
Officers: Jonathan George Llewellyn Chaplin [1961] Director/Marketing Consultant

Core Fruit Products Limited
Incorporated: 13 December 2001
Net Worth Deficit: £104,208 *Total Assets:* £51,012
Registered Office: Upper Mystole Park Farm, Pennypot Lane, Mystole, Canterbury, Kent, CT4 7BT
Shareholder: John Walter James Brown
Officers: Wendy Dorothea Simpson Brown, Secretary/Financial Advisor; John Walter James Brown [1956] Director/Farmer; Wendy Dorothea Simpson Brown [1954] Director/Financial Advisor

Cornfield Foods and Beverages Limited
Incorporated: 8 February 2018
Registered Office: 71-75 Shelton Street, Covent Garden, London, WC2H 9JQ
Major Shareholder: Tolulope Ayomide Agbeyo
Officers: Tolulope Ayomide Agbeyo [1994] Director [Nigerian]

Cornish Kombucha Limited
Incorporated: 22 December 2017
Registered Office: Cleswyth, Creegbrawse, Redruth, Cornwall, TR16 5QF
Major Shareholder: Ben John Laskey
Officers: Ben John Laskey [1975] Director

Cornish Organic Aloe Vera Ltd
Incorporated: 2 May 2007
Registered Office: Carscliff, Upper Draycott Road, Cheddar, Somerset, BS27 3YL
Shareholder: David Lawrence Urch
Officers: Virginia Urch, Secretary; David Lawrence Urch [1951] Director; Virginia Urch [1952] Director/Farmer

Cornny Drinks Limited
Incorporated: 16 September 2013
Net Worth Deficit: £458 *Total Assets:* £125
Registered Office: 69 Bantry Road, Slough, SL1 5FD
Major Shareholder: Yaw Amponsah
Officers: Vivian Amponsah [1985] Director/Businesswoman; Yaw Amponsah [1983] Director [Ghanaian]

Cott Ventures UK Limited
Incorporated: 12 May 2014 *Employees:* 3
Net Worth: £12,176,000 *Total Assets:* £38,306,000
Registered Office: c/o Aimia Foods Limited, Penny Lane, Haydock, St Helens, Merseyside, WA11 0QZ
Parent: Cott Retail Brands Limited
Officers: Jason Robert Ausher [1973] Director [American]; Claire Duffy [1976] Director/Solicitor; Steven Kitching [1964] Director; Matthew James Vernon [1975] Director

Cotton & Cane Ltd
Incorporated: 25 February 2019
Registered Office: 20-22 Wenlock Road, London, N1 7GU
Major Shareholder: Carol Cooper
Officers: Carol Cooper [1967] Director

Counterpoint Wholesale (NI) Limited
Incorporated: 24 June 2013 *Employees:* 8
Net Worth Deficit: £626,000 *Total Assets:* £1,771,000
Registered Office: 42-46 Fountain Street, Belfast, BT1 5EF
Parent: Robinsons Soft Drinks Ltd
Officers: Kevin Ronald Donnelly [1967] Country Director [Irish]; Mathew James Dunn [1974] Director/Chief Financial Officer; Declan Daniel Morgan [1979] Director [Irish]

The Country Garden Drinks Company Limited
Incorporated: 30 August 2017
Registered Office: Chestnut House, Stewton Lane, Louth, Lincs, LN11 8SB
Shareholders: Matthew James Hamilton; Emma Hamilton
Officers: Emma Hamilton [1986] Director; Matthew James Hamilton [1991] Director

Cracker Drinks Co. Limited
Incorporated: 12 April 2007 *Employees:* 4
Net Worth Deficit: £10,966 *Total Assets:* £428,974
Registered Office: Victoria House, 26 Queen Victoria Street, Reading, Berks, RG1 1TG
Shareholders: Fruit Drinks Limited; Monksmead Partnership LLP
Officers: Christopher Nigel Banks [1959] Director; John James Clifford Lovell [1955] Director; Sohail Anwar Rasul [1960] Director/Chartered Accountant; Nicholas Robert Theakston [1955] Director

The Craft Mixers Company Limited
Incorporated: 31 July 2017
Registered Office: Holtsmere Manor, Holtsmere End Lane, Redbourn, St Albans, Herts, AL3 7AW
Major Shareholder: Thomas James Wiggett
Officers: Alexander Edward Jollivet [1989] Managing Director; Thomas James Wiggett [1990] Managing Director

The Craft Soft Drinks Community Ltd
Incorporated: 21 February 2017
Registered Office: Unit D5, Kelburn Business Park, Port Glasgow, Inverclyde, PA14 6BL
Officers: Hannah Magdaline Fisher [1983] Director; Craig Robert Strachan [1988] Director

The Crag Spring Water Limited
Incorporated: 28 September 2016
Registered Office: Bruilimar House, Jubilee Road, Middleton, Manchester, M24 2LX
Officers: Doran Barry Binder [1972] Director; Melissa Jane Binder [1976] Director

Creamright Products, Ltd
Incorporated: 7 February 2011
Net Worth: £61,276 *Total Assets:* £82,008
Registered Office: 34a Watling Street, Radlett, Herts, WD7 7NN
Major Shareholder: Jay Douglas Meester
Officers: Jay Douglas Meester, Secretary [American]; Jay Douglas Meester [1956] Director/Import/Distributor [American]

Creative Properties and Investments Ltd
Incorporated: 27 November 2013
Net Worth: £674,618 *Total Assets:* £674,919
Registered Office: 15 Stratton Street, London, W1J 8LQ
Major Shareholder: Andreas Yanakopoulos
Officers: Georgios Chondrorizos [1967] Director [Greek]; Andreas Yanakopoulos [1963] Director [Greek]

Crosby Beverages Ltd
Incorporated: 19 February 2018
Registered Office: 193 Drayton Bridge Road, London, W13 0JH
Major Shareholder: Odi Olali
Officers: Rhys Johnson [1991] Director; Odi Olali [1990] Director

W.& J.Cruickshank and Company Limited
Incorporated: 5 May 1978 *Employees:* 4
Net Worth: £1,178,406 *Total Assets:* £1,214,700
Registered Office: Cunningholes Industrial Estate, March Road, Buckie, Banffshire, AB56 4DA
Major Shareholder: William Cruickshank
Officers: William Cruickshank [1942] Director

Crystalstore Ltd
Incorporated: 25 June 2018
Registered Office: Suite 6, First Floor, Wordsworth Mill, Wordsworth Street, Bolton, Lancs, BL1 3ND
Major Shareholder: Arron Lee Chaloner
Officers: Darwin Tenorio [1980] Director [Filipino]

The Cure Project Limited
Incorporated: 12 February 2019
Registered Office: 5 Fleet Place, London, EC4M 7RD
Major Shareholder: Kendra Aga Khan
Officers: Kendra Aga Khan [1988] Director [American]

Cure T.H.A.S.D. Limited
Incorporated: 15 August 2018
Registered Office: Flat 10, 84 High Street, Norton, Stockton on Tees, Cleveland, TS20 1DR
Major Shareholder: Christoper Iles
Officers: Christoper Iles [1984] Director

Cybora Ltd
Incorporated: 11 July 2018
Registered Office: Suite 1, Fielden House, 41 Rochdale Road, Todmorden, W Yorks, OL14 6LD
Major Shareholder: Ben Murray
Officers: Kate Maloloy On [1997] Director [Filipino]

D & G Drinks Ltd
Incorporated: 17 December 2013
Net Worth: £371,249 *Total Assets:* £432,257
Registered Office: Studio 2.05, Food Exchange, New Covent Garden Market, London, SW8 5EL
Shareholder: Damien Kennedy
Officers: Damien Kennedy [1983] Director/Entrepreneur [Irish]; Rory Gordon MacGregor Lawson [1981] Director/Sports Personality; Ronan Phillips [1975] Finance Director [Irish]

Daily Dose Ltd
Incorporated: 16 February 2016
Net Worth Deficit: £247,656 *Total Assets:* £294,291
Registered Office: 2 Sunray Avenue, London, SE24 9PY
Major Shareholder: George Thomas Huges-Davies
Officers: Sara Frances Mary Cohen, Secretary; George Hughes-Davies [1993] Director/Self Employed

Dakena-One International Limited
Incorporated: 23 April 2018
Registered Office: 3 Eyre Street, Hulme, Manchester, M15 6HD
Officers: Helen Olukemi King [1965] Managing Director

Dalston's Soda Company Ltd
Incorporated: 4 April 2012 *Employees:* 8
Previous: Dalston Cola Company Ltd
Net Worth Deficit: £6,960 *Total Assets:* £262,300
Registered Office: 2nd Floor, 33 Queen Street, London, EC4R 1AP
Shareholder: Duncan O' Brien
Officers: Daniel James Broughton [1980] Director; Duncan Anthony Daniel Benedict O'Brien [1985] Director/Sustainability Professional

Dangercode Ltd
Incorporated: 22 January 2019
Registered Office: Unit 5, 2nd Floor, Red Lion Court, Alexandra Road, Hounslow, Middlesex, TW3 1JS
Major Shareholder: Mohamed Aweys
Officers: Mohamed Aweys [1988] Director [Italian]

Danjan Ventures Ltd
Incorporated: 25 July 2018
Registered Office: 42 Woodheys Park, Kingswood, Hull, HU7 3AJ
Major Shareholder: Janet Morton
Officers: Janet Morton [1968] Director

Darj Limited
Incorporated: 24 December 2012
Net Worth Deficit: £241,635 *Total Assets:* £21,125
Registered Office: c/o Francis Oyewole, 49 Green Lanes, Green Lanes, London, N16 9BU
Shareholder: Francis Oyewole
Officers: Francis Oyewole [1991] Director

Dash Brands Ltd
Incorporated: 19 February 2016 *Employees:* 2
Net Worth: £124,794 *Total Assets:* £329,261
Registered Office: The Waterworks, 52 Grosvenor Gardens, London, SW1W 0AU
Officers: Bradley Berman [1983] Director/Vice President - Bodybio, Inc [American]; Jack Harry Scott [1990] Director/Co-Founder; Alexander William Lowndes Wright [1991] Director/Co-Founder

Dayla Holdings Limited
Incorporated: 26 January 1961 *Employees:* 93
Net Worth: £6,414,306 *Total Assets:* £10,505,968
Registered Office: Unit 2, 50 Aylesbury Road, Aston Clinton, Aylesbury, Bucks, HP22 5AH
Shareholders: Timothy John Cooper; Susan Frances Lapham
Officers: Timothy John Cooper, Secretary; Timothy John Cooper [1957] Director/Soft Drinks Factor - Manufacturer

Dayla Limited
Incorporated: 31 December 1943 *Employees:* 93
Net Worth: £4,593,204 *Total Assets:* £9,578,971
Registered Office: Unit 2, 50 Aylesbury Road, Aston Clinton, Aylesbury, Bucks, HP22 5AH
Shareholders: Dayla Holdings Limited; Timothy John Cooper; Susan Frances Lapham
Officers: Peter Brine Lapham, Secretary; Daniel Cooper [1988] Commercial Director; Timothy John Cooper [1957] Director/Soft Drinks Factor Manufacturer; James Lapham [1980] Director; Peter Brine Lapham [1949] Director

Dayla Liquid Packing Limited
Incorporated: 21 April 1958
Registered Office: Laurel House, Woodlands Park, Ashton Road, Newton-le-Willows, St Helens, Merseyside, WA12 0HH
Parent: Nichols PLC
Officers: Tim Croston, Secretary; Timothy John Croston [1963] Director

Decantae Mineral Water Limited
Incorporated: 25 September 1985 *Employees:* 35
Net Worth: £831,005 *Total Assets:* £2,866,210
Registered Office: c/o Aimia Foods Limited, Penny Lane, Haydock, St Helens, Merseyside, WA11 0QZ
Parent: Total Water Solutions Limited
Officers: Jason Robert Ausher [1973] Director [American]; Claire Duffy [1976] Director/Solicitor; Steven Kitching [1964] Director; Ian Spooner [1962] Director; Matthew James Vernon [1975] Director

Dee's Greens Limited
Incorporated: 22 February 2019
Registered Office: 119 High Street, London, NW10 4TR
Major Shareholder: Hashi Ali Yusuf
Officers: Hashi Ali Yusuf [1993] Director/Management Consultant

Deedee's Kitchen Limited
Incorporated: 29 March 2011
Net Worth Deficit: £57,072
Registered Office: Flat D, 172 Holland Road, London, W14 8AH
Major Shareholder: Zeh Rose Danielle Drogba
Officers: Danielle Drogba, Secretary; Danielle Drogba [1980] Director [French]

The Deeside Water Company (Holdings) Limited
Incorporated: 19 August 2013
Registered Office: The Capitol, 431 Union Street, Aberdeen, AB11 6DA
Shareholder: Lemuria Enterprises Limited
Officers: George Alexander Simpson [1943] Director; Martin John Simpson [1968] Director

The Deeside Water Company Limited
Incorporated: 20 August 2013 *Employees:* 11
Net Worth: £221,942 *Total Assets:* £622,683
Registered Office: The Capitol, 431 Union Street, Aberdeen, AB11 6DA
Parent: The Deeside Water Company (Holdings) Limited
Officers: George Alexander Simpson [1943] Director; Martin John Simpson [1968] Director

Delicious Retail Ltd
Incorporated: 21 June 2017
Registered Office: 106 Crowborough Road, London, SW17 9QG
Major Shareholder: Luke Raskino
Officers: Luke Dominic Raskino [1973] Director

Derbyshire Mineral Waters Limited
Incorporated: 18 April 2016
Registered Office: St Helen's House, King Street, Derby, DE1 3EE
Officers: Helen Claire Salloway [1961] Director; Stephen Michael Salloway [1956] Director/Surveyor; Amanda Jane Wells [1957] Director; Gary John Wells [1960] Director

Desert Island Drinks Limited
Incorporated: 20 September 2013
Registered Office: Barnfield Farm, Gravesend Road, Wrotham, Sevenoaks, Kent, TN15 7JR
Major Shareholder: James Edwards
Officers: James Edwards, Secretary; James Edwards [1954] Director/Businessman

Destructive Lines Ltd
Incorporated: 11 April 2017
Net Worth: £2 *Total Assets:* £2
Registered Office: 51 Clarkegrove Road, Sheffield, S10 2NH
Shareholders: Adam Alexander Martin; Thomas Edward Soden
Officers: Adam Alexander Martin [1978] Director/Designer; Thomas Edward Soden [1983] Director

Devon Soda Co Limited
Incorporated: 23 May 2018
Registered Office: Netley House, Callington, Cornwall, PL17 8BG
Parent: Rocktails Drinks Ltd
Officers: Katie May Bain [1983] Marketing Director; Christopher George Yandell [1981] Director

Devonia Water Ltd
Incorporated: 26 March 2014 *Employees:* 2
Net Worth Deficit: £9,685 *Total Assets:* £48,831
Registered Office: Orchard House, Clyst St Mary, Exeter, Devon, EX5 1BR
Officers: Neil Osbern Nigel Graham [1960] Director/Manager

Dexos Drinks Limited
Incorporated: 14 September 2017
Net Worth Deficit: £3,991 *Total Assets:* £39,867
Registered Office: 2nd Floor, 130 Shaftesbury Avenue, London, W1D 5EU
Parent: Dexos Holdings Limited
Officers: Peter Charles Clark [1961] Director/Accountant; Kamila Laura Sitwell [1974] Director/Soft Drinks [Polish]; Vincent Lucien Sitwell [1971] Director/Marketing & Soft Drinks

Diageo Great Britain Limited
Incorporated: 5 May 1952 *Employees:* 1,238
Net Worth: £2,988,000,000 *Total Assets:* £3,436,999,936
Registered Office: Lakeside Drive, Park Royal, London, NW10 7HQ
Parent: Grand Metropolitan Limited
Officers: Gavin Paul Crickmore [1958] Director/Chartered Accountant; James Matthew Crayden Edmunds [1974] Director/Solicitor; Sharon Lynnette Fennessy [1967] Director/Group Treasurer [Irish]; Kerryn Louise Haynes [1970] Director/Accountant; David Heginbottom [1970] Director/Group Treasurer; Hina Patel [1979] Director/Company Secretary Senior Assistant; Gabor Zeisler [1973] Director/General Manager [Hungarian]

The Diesel Brewing Co Ltd.
Incorporated: 29 June 2009
Previous: The Diesel Energy Drink Co Ltd
Registered Office: 1 Well Lane, Low Fell, Gateshead, Tyne & Wear, NE9 6JZ
Shareholders: Raymond Callan; Bob Senior
Officers: Raymond Callan [1961] Director/Licensed Wholesaler; Bob Senior [1954] Director

Dips Dips Ltd
Incorporated: 7 April 2014
Registered Office: 41 High Street, Barkingside, Ilford, Essex, IG6 2AD
Major Shareholder: Hershil Patel
Officers: Hershil Patel [1980] Director/Sales Executive

Distillers Tonic Limited
Incorporated: 13 January 2017
Net Worth: £181 *Total Assets:* £9,027
Registered Office: Suite 2, 18 High Street, Thornbury, Glos, BS35 2AH
Shareholders: Michael Colin Kain; Felicity Eleanor Hall
Officers: Felicity Eleanor Hall, Secretary; Felicity Eleanor Hall [1968] Director/Distiller; Michael Colin Kain [1971] Director/Distiller

Distinate Ltd
Incorporated: 12 February 2018
Registered Office: 2 Goodwood Avenue, Enfield, Middlesex, EN3 5RP
Officers: Danyal Adam Hussain [1995] Director; Rahul Patel [1997] Director

The Divine Water Company Limited
Incorporated: 18 October 1994 *Employees:* 23
Net Worth: £510,494 *Total Assets:* £1,057,135
Registered Office: The Cottage, 2 Castlefield Road, Reigate, Surrey, RH2 0SH
Parent: Wolvers Holdings Limited
Officers: Horst Werner Rauter, Secretary; Horst Werner Rauter [1944] Director; James Werner Rauter [1974] Managing Director; Sylvia Christine Rauter [1945] Director

The Do Drink Company Ltd
Incorporated: 12 February 2019
Registered Office: Cnwc Y Cneuen, Llangeitho, Tregaron, Ceredigion, SY25 6SU
Shareholders: Lisa Margaret Bowen; James Richard Dominic Taplin
Officers: Lisa Margaret Bowen [1973] Director/Marketing Executive; James Richard Dominic Taplin [1973] Director/Entrepreneur

Dorset Ginger Company Limited
Incorporated: 22 February 2017 *Employees:* 1
Net Worth Deficit: £35,361 *Total Assets:* £33,586
Registered Office: 87 North Road, Poole, Dorset, BH14 0LT
Major Shareholder: Nicholas Paul Good
Officers: Nicholas Paul Good [1965] Director; Timea Good [1979] Director

Double Apple Ltd
Incorporated: 3 April 2017
Net Worth: £73,574 *Total Assets:* £86,519
Registered Office: 247 Runley Road, Luton, Beds, LU1 1TY
Major Shareholder: Bilal Ahmed
Officers: Bilal Ahmed [1990] Director/Business Person [Pakistani]

Double Dutch Ltd.
Incorporated: 18 September 2014
Net Worth: £802,859 *Total Assets:* £1,097,483
Registered Office: 23-25 Portman Close, London, W1H 6BS
Shareholders: Raissa Catherina de Haas; Joyce de Haas
Officers: Joyce Michelle de Haas [1990] Director/Chief Operating Officer [Dutch]; Raissa Catherina de Haas [1990] Chief Executive Director [Dutch]; Paul Jonathan Kerr [1954] Director/Chartered Accountant

Dove Foods Ltd
Incorporated: 28 November 2018
Registered Office: Unit 9-10 Dove Cottage Mill, Duckworth Street, Darwen, Lancs, BB3 1AR
Major Shareholder: Zubair Ugradar
Officers: Zubair Ugradar [1976] Director

Dr Go Ltd
Incorporated: 29 February 2016
Net Worth: £1,755 *Total Assets:* £36,488
Registered Office: Oaklyn House, Walliswood, Dorking, Surrey, RH5 5RD
Shareholders: Gunter Graubach; Sarah Chan
Officers: Neil Graham Oughton, Secretary; Neil Graham Oughton [1957] Director/Consultant

Dr.Shot Ltd.
Incorporated: 18 November 2013
Registered Office: 6 Parry Close, Epsom, Surrey, KT17 2PB
Officers: Clayton Ritchard Grover [1992] Director; Elizabeth Ann Russell [1989] Director

DRGN Global Ltd.
Incorporated: 26 September 2017
Registered Office: 47 Marylebone Lane, London, W1U 2NT
Major Shareholder: Vishal Sodha
Officers: Vishal Sodha [1978] Director

DRII Limited
Incorporated: 9 June 2017
Registered Office: Caw House, Conygarth Way, Leeming Bar Business Park, Leeming Bar, N Yorks, DL7 9FD
Shareholders: Andrew James Cawthray; Peter Richard Harrison
Officers: Andrew James Cawthray [1957] Director; Peter Richard Harrison [1979] Director

Drink Better Limited
Incorporated: 28 July 2016
Net Worth Deficit: £15,039 *Total Assets:* £5,646
Registered Office: Glenlinden, 1 Spylaw Avenue, Edinburgh, EH13 0LW
Officers: Andrew Ligertwood [1979] Director/Beverages; Gillian Ligertwood [1979] Director/Beverages

Drinkology Limited
Incorporated: 3 July 2017
Registered Office: 65 Cherwell Drive, Marston, Oxford, OX3 0ND
Shareholders: Sukhveer Singh Mattu; Amandeep Kaur Vig
Officers: Sukhveer Singh Mattu [1990] Director/Accountant; Amandeep Kaur Vig [1985] Director/Accountant

Drinks Cubed Ltd
Incorporated: 6 November 2018
Registered Office: 27 Old Gloucester Street, London, WC1N 3AX
Major Shareholder: Ravinder Singh Sandhu
Officers: Ravinder Singh Sandhu [1979] Director/Chairman

UK Manufacturers of Soft Drinks

Drinks for Beauty Ltd
Incorporated: 27 July 2018
Registered Office: 7 Baywood Gardens, Brighton, BN2 6BN
Officers: Mark Galvin [1974] Director [Irish]; Vian Nga Nguyen [1983] Director [Swedish]

The Drinks Group Holdings Ltd
Incorporated: 3 October 2018
Registered Office: Mercury House, Shipstones Business Centre, Northgate, Nottingham, NG7 7FN
Major Shareholder: Peter Robson
Officers: Peter Robson, Secretary; Peter Robson [1959] Director

Drinks-on-Draught Limited
Incorporated: 13 January 1997
Net Worth: £8,062 *Total Assets:* £18,235
Registered Office: 327 Chartridge Lane, Chartridge, Chesham, Bucks, HP5 2SQ
Major Shareholder: Andros Kontos
Officers: Donya Edwards, Secretary; Donya Edwards [1962] Director/PA Secretary; Andros Kontos [1962] Director/Businessman

The Driver's Drinks Company Limited
Incorporated: 13 September 2018
Registered Office: Yew Tree House, Lewes Road, Forest Row, E Sussex, RH18 5AA
Major Shareholder: Hamish Christian Gordon
Officers: Hamish Christian Gordon [1971] Director

Dry Beverages Limited
Incorporated: 9 June 2017
Registered Office: Caw House, Conygarth Way, Leeming Bar Business Park, Leeming Bar, N Yorks, DL7 9FD
Shareholders: Andrew James Cawthray; Peter Richard Harrison
Officers: Andrew James Cawthray [1957] Director; Peter Richard Harrison [1979] Director

Dry Drinks and Teas Company Ltd
Incorporated: 8 August 2017
Registered Office: 41 Cathcart Road, London, SW10 9JG
Officers: Martina Angelova Hajjar [1973] Director

Duo Drinks Ltd
Incorporated: 25 February 2019
Registered Office: 71 Silverthorne Road, London, SW8 3HH
Shareholders: Jack Francis de Montmorency Carbutt; Augustus David Hill
Officers: Jack Francis de Montmorency Carbutt [1994] Director; Augustus David Hill [1994] Director

E D Resources Limited
Incorporated: 26 June 1998
Net Worth: £689 *Total Assets:* £689
Registered Office: Botanic House, 100 Hills Road, Cambridge, CB2 1PH
Major Shareholder: Paul Jonathan Bendit
Officers: Frances Bendit, Secretary; Paul Jonathan Bendit [1959] Director

The Earth Plant Co Ltd
Incorporated: 23 October 2018
Registered Office: 3 St Georges Avenue, London, NW9 0JT
Major Shareholder: Keval Joshi
Officers: Keval Joshi [1976] Director

The East India Company Indian Tonic Water Ltd
Incorporated: 18 March 2010
Net Worth: £45 *Total Assets:* £45
Registered Office: 39 St James's Street, London, SW1A 1JD
Major Shareholder: Robin Chapman
Officers: Robin Chapman [1947] Director/Solicitor

East London Juice Co Ltd
Incorporated: 7 January 2015
Net Worth: £10,698 *Total Assets:* £31,558
Registered Office: Beech Cottage, Farnham Lane, Haslemere, Surrey, GU27 1HG
Major Shareholder: Charisse Lindsey Baker
Officers: Charisse Baker [1982] Sales Director [Canadian]

Eastcott Drinks Ltd
Incorporated: 4 September 2018
Registered Office: 20-22 Wenlock Road, London, N1 7GU
Shareholders: Andrew George Colley; James Paul Sullivan
Officers: Andrew George Colley [1969] Director; James Paul Sullivan [1970] Director

Eauvolution Limited
Incorporated: 5 February 2018
Registered Office: 64 Beech Hill, Barnet, Herts, EN4 0JJ
Shareholder: Fiona McSharry
Officers: Fiona McSharry [1978] Director [Irish]

ECF Global Ltd
Incorporated: 23 January 2018
Registered Office: 20-22 Wenlock Road, London, N1 7GU
Officers: Rev Freedom Ikechukwu Egbune [1960] Project Director

ECIG Retail Europe Limited
Incorporated: 20 February 2017
Registered Office: 121 Waterside, 10 William Jessop Way, Liverpool, L3 1ED
Major Shareholder: James Leary
Officers: James Leary [1985] Director/Accountant

Ed's Trading Limited
Incorporated: 29 June 2005 *Employees:* 1
Net Worth: £1,058,189 *Total Assets:* £2,557,056
Registered Office: The Ascott Suite, Greystones House, Burford Road, Chipping Norton, Oxon, OX7 5XA
Shareholder: Edward Rigg
Officers: Rachel Firth Rigg, Secretary; Edward Rigg [1979] Director

Eden Springs UK Limited
Incorporated: 1 September 2000 *Employees:* 380
Net Worth: £15,251,000 *Total Assets:* £59,880,000
Registered Office: Unit D, Fleming Centre, Fleming Way, Crawley, W Sussex, RH10 9NN
Parent: Cott Corporation
Officers: Ron Zev Frieman [1955] Director [American]; Brian Richard Macpherson [1971] Deputy Managing Director; Shane Perkey [1976] Director [American]

Edible Hedgerow Ltd
Incorporated: 29 November 2018
Registered Office: Ingenuity Lab, Ingenuity Centre, Haydn Green Institute, Wollaton Road, Nottingham, NG8 1BB
Shareholders: Jennifer Louise Loxton; Victoria Louise Sedman
Officers: Dr Jennifer Louise Loxton [1978] Director; Dr Victoria Louise Sedman [1979] Director

Edinburgh Artesian Water Company Ltd
Incorporated: 4 January 2017
Registered Office: 1 Margaret Rose Loan, Edinburgh, EH10 7EQ
Major Shareholder: Charles Thomson McKinlay
Officers: Charles Thomson McKinlay [1948] Director/Retired

Edinburgh Kombucha Ltd
Incorporated: 22 June 2018
Registered Office: 53 Clayknowes Place, Musselburgh, E Lothian, EH21 6UQ
Major Shareholder: Norma Jane Findlay
Officers: Norma Jane Findlay [1978] Director/Occupational Therapist

Edinburgh Tonic Ltd
Incorporated: 11 December 2017
Registered Office: 17-21 East Mayfield, Edinburgh, EH9 1SE
Major Shareholder: Charles Alexander Herd
Officers: Charles Alexander Herd [1968] Director

Efcon UK Ltd
Incorporated: 10 January 2019
Registered Office: 21 The Fairway, Bromley, Kent, BR1 2JZ
Officers: Anahita Unger [1961] Director; Elena Unger [1997] Director; Philip Unger [1981] Director; Samira Unger [1990] Director

El Natural Ltd
Incorporated: 22 August 2018
Registered Office: 6 Maes Y Sarn, Pentyrch, Cardiff, CF15 9QQ
Major Shareholder: James Frederick Cashin
Officers: James Frederick Cashin [1989] Director

Elan League UK Ltd
Incorporated: 14 March 2017
Registered Office: Kemp House, 160 City Road, London, EC1V 2NX
Officers: Aklane Adu [1979] Director/Secretary; Babatunde Adu [1978] Director/Secretary

The Elaychi Tea Company Ltd
Incorporated: 30 June 2009 *Employees:* 1
Net Worth: £628 *Total Assets:* £16,955
Registered Office: 184 Chorley Road, Walton-le-Dale, Preston, Lancs, PR5 4PD
Major Shareholder: Stephen Jervis
Officers: Stephen Jervis [1959] Director/Catering Supplies

Elementhree Ltd
Incorporated: 27 December 2017
Registered Office: Unit 5 Millennium Business Centre, 3 Humber Road, London, NW2 6DW
Major Shareholder: Will Afolabi Daniels-Dada
Officers: Will Afolabi Daniels-Dada [1972] Director/Builder; Olufunmilayo Olufemi-Dada [1966] Director/Businesswoman

Elfie Drinks Co Ltd
Incorporated: 16 April 2018
Registered Office: Limeway Cottage, Hogspudding Lane, Newdigate, Dorking, Surrey, RH5 5DS
Shareholders: Christopher James Collis; Jacqueline Joan Collis
Officers: Christopher James Collis [1962] Director

Elite Global Nutrition Limited
Incorporated: 4 September 2015
Net Worth Deficit: £101,759 *Total Assets:* £59,093
Registered Office: Elite House, 691-693 Warwick Road, Solihull, W Midlands, B91 3DA
Major Shareholder: David Paul Hoey
Officers: David Paul Hoey [1966] Director; Luke Dominic Hoey [1997] Director

Eliya Europe Ltd
Incorporated: 28 February 2019
Registered Office: 15 The Borough, Brockham, Betchworth, Surrey, RH3 7NB
Major Shareholder: Bjorn Filip Botvid Johansson
Officers: Bjorn Filip Botvid Johansson [1978] Director [Swedish]

Ella Drinks Limited
Incorporated: 20 October 1998
Net Worth: £103,308 *Total Assets:* £470,776
Registered Office: Wandershiell, Aldbar, Brechin, Angus, DD9 6SY
Shareholders: Anne Thomson; John Stephen Gallagher
Officers: Anne Thomson, Secretary; John Stephen Gallagher [1952] Director; Anne Thomson [1954] Director

Ellive Ltd
Incorporated: 6 March 2017
Net Worth: £2,354 *Total Assets:* £8,645
Registered Office: 2 Southwood Close, Marple, Stockport, Cheshire, SK6 7PN
Shareholders: Elena Gaal; Gyorgy Eduard Gaal
Officers: Elena Gaal [1974] Director; Gyorgy Eduard Gaal [1970] Director/Nurse

Elsenham Water Limited
Incorporated: 16 January 1996
Net Worth Deficit: £195,224 *Total Assets:* £40,235
Registered Office: Water Circle, City Meadows, Stansted, Essex, CM22 6DR
Parent: Cheergrey Limited
Officers: Iain Edward Anderson, Secretary; Michael Robert Johnstone [1945] Director/Investor

Ember Drinks Ltd.
Incorporated: 11 March 2014
Registered Office: 1 St Nicholas Cottages, Poplar Lane, Hurst, Reading, Berks, RG10 0DL
Major Shareholder: James Oliver Girdler
Officers: James Oliver Girdler [1991] Director/Owner

Emery Brand Ltd
Incorporated: 1 September 2018
Registered Office: 43 Bridgewater Road, Wembley, Middlesex, HA0 1AQ
Major Shareholder: Thurairajasingam Nanthakumar
Officers: Thurairajasingam Nanthakumar [1972] Director [Sri Lankan]

Enchanted Forest Milks Limited
Incorporated: 25 January 2018
Registered Office: Flat 3, Churchfield Mansions, 321-345 New Kings Road, London, SW6 4RA
Officers: Kelsey Wright [1985] Director/Food Services

Endo Sport Ltd
Incorporated: 4 February 2019
Registered Office: 791 Stratford Road, Birmingham, B11 4DG
Major Shareholder: Pardeep Singh Sooch
Officers: Pardeep Singh Sooch [1985] Director

Endurance Juice Company Limited
Incorporated: 14 April 2009
Registered Office: 6 Pulford Road, London, N15 6SP
Major Shareholder: Michael Osizimhete Okpapi
Officers: John Ikhaobomhe Okpapi, Secretary; John Ikhaobomhe Okpapi [1989] Director/Company Secretary & Deputy Chief Executive Officer; Michael Osizimhete Okpapi [1959] Director/Chairman & Chief Executive Officer

Enhance Drinks Ltd
Incorporated: 30 August 2006
Net Worth Deficit: £7,454 Total Assets: £29,743
Registered Office: Unit 106, 30 Red Lion Street, Richmond, Surrey, TW9 1RB
Shareholders: Gillian Caseberry; James Malcolmson
Officers: James Malcolmson [1970] Director

Enrj Drinks Ltd
Incorporated: 9 December 2016
Net Worth Deficit: £14,717 Total Assets: £3,060
Registered Office: 58 Radnor Walk, London, SW3 4BN
Major Shareholder: Nicholas Benjamin Bush
Officers: Dr. Nicholas Benjamin Bush [1992] Medical Doctor, Director

Enso Goods Limited
Incorporated: 26 September 2018
Registered Office: 380 Werrington Road, Stoke on Trent, Staffs, ST2 9AB
Major Shareholder: Josh Dion Bradley Heath
Officers: Josh Dion Bradley Heath [1994] Director/Entrepreneur

Enterprises Beyond Reason Ltd
Incorporated: 15 October 2018
Registered Office: 41 Mill Road, Lancing, W Sussex, BN15 0PZ
Shareholders: Edmund Mortimer; Anna Aleksandrova
Officers: Anna Aleksandrova [1989] Creative Director [Latvian]; Edmund Mortimer [1991] Director

Equilibrium Food & Drink Ltd
Incorporated: 8 January 2018
Registered Office: 231 London Road, Sheffield, S2 4NF
Shareholders: Anthony James Lowe; Wendy Ann Lowe
Officers: Anthony James Lowe [1963] Director

Eskimo Joe's Limited
Incorporated: 15 April 2014
Net Worth Deficit: £466,328 Total Assets: £361,631
Registered Office: Sanderson House, Station Road, Horsforth, Leeds, LS18 5NT
Officers: Laura Rebecca Peters [1988] Director

Essence PH10 Limited
Incorporated: 1 November 2016
Registered Office: 11 Church Road, Great Bookham, Leatherhead, Surrey, KT23 3PB
Parent: Essence Water Inc
Officers: Joel Gabriel [1974] Director [American]

Etoh Studio Limited
Incorporated: 25 April 2017
Net Worth Deficit: £22,077 Total Assets: £29,614
Registered Office: 89 Leigh Road, Eastleigh, Hants, SO50 9DQ
Major Shareholder: Omar Sharif Mohamed Bakhaty
Officers: Omar Sharif Mohamed Bakhaty [1988] Director

Everything But The Cow Limited
Incorporated: 15 July 2011
Registered Office: 67 Westow Street, Upper Norwood, London, SE19 3RW
Shareholders: Lisa Jane Clement; Karen Marie Burleton; Keith Heller
Officers: Karen Marie Burleton [1966] Director; Lisa Jane Clement [1967] Director; Keith Louis Heller [1948] Director [Canadian]

Evo Drinks Europe Ltd
Incorporated: 11 September 2015
Registered Office: 2 Ryefied Court, Joel Street, Northwood, Middlesex, HA6 1LP
Parent: Evo Drinks PLC
Officers: Helge Hoefer [1968] Director [German]; Max Maerker [1998] Director [German]

Evoca Enterprises Limited
Incorporated: 28 May 2003
Net Worth Deficit: £326,213 Total Assets: £26,673
Registered Office: 12-15 Hatherley Mews, London, E17 4QP
Major Shareholder: Intisar Qasim
Officers: Mian Muhammad Asif Salahuddin, Secretary/Director Operations; Intisar Qasim [1976] Managing Director

Evogue Limited
Incorporated: 14 June 2016
Registered Office: 38 Park Street, Mayfair, London, W1K 2JF
Major Shareholder: Andreas Yanakopoulos
Officers: Georgios Chondrorizos [1967] Director [Greek]

Exoteeque Limited
Incorporated: 12 June 2017
Net Worth Deficit: £7,808
Registered Office: 118-120 London Road, Mitcham, Surrey, CR4 3LB
Major Shareholder: Connie Petronella Parillon
Officers: Connie Petronella Parillon [1967] Director/Administrator

Exotic Beverages Limited
Incorporated: 19 June 2017
Registered Office: 54 Hillbury Avenue, Harrow, Middlesex, HA3 8EW
Officers: George Myrants, Secretary; Radha Nagrecha Gagneja [1982] Director/Accountant; Davendra Parbat Khimani [1972] Director

Exotica Beverages Ltd
Incorporated: 29 November 2018
Registered Office: Third Floor, 207 Regent Street, London, W1B 3HH
Major Shareholder: Anjam Saddiq
Officers: Anjam Saddiq [1977] Director

Explorer Coffees Ltd
Incorporated: 8 November 2017
Registered Office: 1 Pepys Close, Gosport, Hants, PO12 2BJ
Major Shareholder: Simon Neil Hallsworth
Officers: Kay Hallsworth [1973] Director; Neil Hallsworth [1973] Director

Fab World Limited
Incorporated: 24 April 2018
Registered Office: 43 Postmasters Lodge Exchange Walk, Pinner, Middlesex, HA5 5AD
Shareholder: Pradeep Khanduja
Officers: Pradeep Khanduja [1976] Director/IT Consultant

Fake Brews Ltd
Incorporated: 26 November 2018
Registered Office: 45 Canford Road, London, SW11 6PB
Major Shareholder: Timothy Norman Hirst
Officers: Timothy Norman Hirst [1983] Director/Management Consultant

Falcon Soft Drinks Limited
Incorporated: 6 February 2001 *Employees:* 3
Net Worth Deficit: £28,502 *Total Assets:* £96,733
Registered Office: 71 High Street, Great Barford, Bedford, MK44 3LF
Shareholders: Alan William Nicholson; Victoria Rosina Kathleen Nicholson
Officers: Victoria Rosina Kathleen Nicholson, Secretary; Alan William Nicholson [1947] Director/Engineer; Victoria Rosina Kathleen Nicholson [1944] Director/Administrator; Paul John Phillips [1963] Director

Faractive Limited
Incorporated: 7 December 2018
Registered Office: Trinity Cottage, Church Road, Sunningdale, Ascot, Berks, SL5 0NJ
Major Shareholder: David John Farrell
Officers: David John Farrell [1975] Director/Operations Manager

Faraday Drinks Ltd
Incorporated: 21 November 2018
Registered Office: Trust House, 5 New Augustus Street, Bradford, W Yorks, BD1 5LL
Major Shareholder: Omar Bahadur
Officers: Omar Bahadur [1995] Director/Salesman

Faultless Drinks Limited
Incorporated: 31 May 2018
Registered Office: 1 Mount Pleasant, Prestbury Road, Macclesfield, Cheshire, SK10 3BZ
Major Shareholder: Thomas James Groves
Officers: Thomas James Groves [1981] Director

Faustian Ltd
Incorporated: 8 April 2010
Net Worth Deficit: £105,872 *Total Assets:* £31,680
Registered Office: Third Floor, 207 Regent Street, London, W1B 3HH
Major Shareholder: Nina Faust
Officers: Nina Faust [1976] Director/Entrepreneur [Luxembourger]

Fentimans Ltd.
Incorporated: 13 September 1994 *Employees:* 55
Net Worth: £3,498,928 *Total Assets:* £11,622,925
Registered Office: Fearless House, Beaufront Park, Alnwick Road, Hexham, Northumberland, NE46 4TU
Major Shareholder: Eldon Arthur Robson
Officers: Eldon Arthur Robson, Secretary; Ian David Bray [1963] Director; David Charlton [1952] Director/Chartered Accountant; Eldon Arthur Robson [1950] Director/Manager

Ferment Revolution Limited
Incorporated: 12 May 2017 *Employees:* 3
Net Worth Deficit: £3,181 *Total Assets:* £657
Registered Office: 86a Yerbury Road, London, N19 4RS
Shareholders: Nicole Schubert-Nicolas; Clare Susannah Gerrard; Teresa Elizabeth Franke
Officers: Teresa Elizabeth Franke [1974] Director/Entrepreneur; Clare Susannah Gerrard [1963] Director/Entrepreneur; Nicole Schubert-Nicolas [1977] Director/Entrepreneur [German]

Fevertree Limited
Incorporated: 19 November 2004 *Employees:* 51
Net Worth: £58,507,144 *Total Assets:* £101,020,128
Registered Office: Kildare House, 3 Dorset Rise, London, EC4Y 8EN
Parent: Fevertree Drinks PLC
Officers: Charles Timothy Rolls [1957] Director of Drinks Company; Timothy Daniel Gray Warrillow [1975] Director/Marketing

Ffynnon Carreg Limited
Incorporated: 27 July 2012
Net Worth Deficit: £8,759 *Total Assets:* £108,565
Registered Office: Room 1, 7 Meadows Bridge, Parc Menter, Cross Hands, Llanelli, Dyfed, SA14 6RA
Shareholders: Kulveerpal Singh Sura; Gurkirpal Singh Sura
Officers: Gurkirpal Singh Sura [1986] Director/Manager; Kulveerpal Singh Sura [1988] Director/Manager

Ffynnon Wen Springs Limited
Incorporated: 14 July 2005
Net Worth: £1 *Total Assets:* £1
Registered Office: Bryn Gwynfa Farm, Carmel, Caernarfon, Gwynedd, LL54 7AP
Major Shareholder: Michael Rees Thomas
Officers: Sarah Elisabeth Roberts [1973] Director/Graphic Design; Michael Rees Thomas [1950] Director/Consultant

Fielding Dairies Limited
Incorporated: 10 September 1985
Net Worth: £435,521 *Total Assets:* £797,151
Registered Office: Unit 8 Imperial Way, Eagle Buiness Park, Yaxley, Peterborough, PE7 3GP
Major Shareholder: Heather Mary Skews
Officers: Timothy Collins [1964] Director

Fiji Water (UK) Limited
Incorporated: 21 February 2002 *Employees:* 7
Net Worth: £2,871,175 *Total Assets:* £4,294,563
Registered Office: 21 Bedford Square, London, WC1B 3HH
Shareholders: Stewart Allen Resnick; Lynda Rae Resnick
Officers: Craig Bryan Cooper, Secretary; Craig Bryan Cooper [1967] Director/Attorney [American]

Fillongley Spring Water Limited
Incorporated: 8 March 2011 *Employees:* 15
Net Worth: £1,329,000 *Total Assets:* £1,607,000
Registered Office: Fillongley Spring Water, Tamworth Road, Fillongley, Coventry, Warwicks, CV7 8DZ
Parent: Fillongley Ventures Limited
Officers: Jill Lee-Young, Secretary; Roy Ian Lawson Dexter [1968] Finance Director; Kevin John Matthews [1957] Director; John Martin Murphy [1967] Director; Gregory Pritchett [1972] Director

Fillongley Ventures Limited
Incorporated: 23 June 2011
Net Worth: £400,000 *Total Assets:* £1,346,000
Registered Office: Tamworth Road, Fillongley, Coventry, Warwicks, CV7 8DZ
Parent: Angel Springs Holdings Ltd.
Officers: Jill Lee-Young, Secretary; Roy Ian Lawson Dexter [1968] Finance Director; Kevin John Matthews [1957] Operations Director; Gregory Pritchett [1972] Director

Finn Capital Ltd
Incorporated: 19 July 2018
Registered Office: Farm Cottage, Cardinals Green, Horseheath, Cambridge, CB21 4QX
Major Shareholder: Edward Finnbar Brown
Officers: Edward Finnbar Brown [1993] Director/Chartered Accountant

Fionnar Springs Ltd.
Incorporated: 25 April 2002 *Employees:* 4
Net Worth: £33,891 *Total Assets:* £212,421
Registered Office: 4th Floor, Metropolitan House, 31-33 High Street, Inverness, IV1 1HT
Major Shareholder: Alexander Ross Farquhar
Officers: Alexander Ross Farquhar [1934] Director

Fitch Brew Co Ltd.
Incorporated: 18 May 2016
Net Worth: £119,311 *Total Assets:* £128,424
Registered Office: Milton House, West End, Sutton-on-the-Forest, N Yorks, YO61 1DS
Major Shareholder: Emily Fitchett
Officers: Andrew Stephen Deeley [1984] Finance Director; Emily Fitchett [1988] Director

The Fizzbang Beverage Company Ltd
Incorporated: 23 November 2018
Registered Office: 20-22 Wenlock Road, London, N1 7GU
Major Shareholder: David Charles Pearce
Officers: Mark Trigg, Secretary; Mark David Albert Trigg, Secretary; Graham Hodges [1966] Technical and Operations Director; David Charles Pearce [1967] Director; Mark Trigg [1966] Sales and Marketing Director

Fizzbang Ltd
Incorporated: 20 February 2015
Net Worth Deficit: £9,655
Registered Office: Arnold Court, Back Street, Leeds, Maidstone, Kent, ME17 1TG
Officers: David Charles Pearce [1967] Director; Sarah Jane Pearce [1970] Director

Fizzy Bugz Limited
Incorporated: 22 June 2016
Net Worth Deficit: £2,719 *Total Assets:* £20
Registered Office: 10 Oxford Gate, Brook Green, London, W6 7DA
Major Shareholder: Sophia Salem
Officers: Sophia Salem [1979] Director/Business Owner

Flavour Master Limited
Incorporated: 10 January 2007 *Employees:* 4
Net Worth: £132,842 *Total Assets:* £225,471
Registered Office: Unit 17d, Cinnamon Brow Business Park, Makerfield Way, Ince in Makerfield, Wigan, Lancs, WN2 2PR
Officers: Andrew Grahame Hulme [1960] Director

Floreana Ltd
Incorporated: 18 September 2012
Net Worth Deficit: £9,520 *Total Assets:* £931
Registered Office: 104 Springfield, Edinburgh, EH6 5SD
Major Shareholder: Simon James Mitchell
Officers: Simon James Mitchell [1971] Director

Flow 33 UK Limited
Incorporated: 16 September 2014 *Employees:* 1
Net Worth Deficit: £111,448 *Total Assets:* £53,599
Registered Office: 63 Hampstead House, 176 Finchley Road, London, NW3 6BT
Major Shareholder: Ilan Azouri
Officers: Ilan Azouri [1969] Director [Israeli]

Flower of Life Ltd
Incorporated: 30 April 2012 *Employees:* 16
Net Worth: £319,250 *Total Assets:* £812,051
Registered Office: Unit 2a Orchard Business Park, Scout Road, Hebden Bridge, W Yorks, HX7 5HZ
Shareholder: Daniel Shevek Spayne
Officers: Jacob Alexander Rogers, Secretary; Patrick William Elio Leoni Sceti [1983] Director; Jacob Alexander Rogers [1986] Director/Secretary; Daniel Shevek Spayne [1979] Director

Foal Limited
Incorporated: 16 April 2014
Net Worth Deficit: £17,623 *Total Assets:* £4,180
Registered Office: Flat 1/1, 2 Hanson Park, Glasgow, G31 2HA
Major Shareholder: Craig Robert Strachan
Officers: Craig Robert Strachan [1988] Managing Director

Folkington's (Middle East) Ltd
Incorporated: 29 February 2016
Registered Office: The Workshop, Endlewick House, Arlington, E Sussex, BN26 6RU
Major Shareholder: Paul Jonathan Bendit
Officers: Frances Katherine Bendit, Secretary; Paul Jonathan Bendit [1959] Director

Fonthill Waters Limited
Incorporated: 15 November 2000 *Employees:* 22
Net Worth: £981,390 *Total Assets:* £2,244,408
Registered Office: 29 Turbine Way, Swaffham, Norfolk, PE37 7XD
Shareholder: Jonathan Michael Brown
Officers: Sally Louise Warburton, Secretary; Bailey Abramovitz [1962] Director [Canadian]; Jonathan Michael Brown [1955] Director; Simon Richard Francis Hardy [1959] Director; Brian Knight [1936] Director; Sally Louise Warburton [1963] Finance Director

The Food and Drink Development Company Limited
Incorporated: 19 December 2017
Registered Office: 12 Dewe Lane, Burghfield, Reading, Berks, RG30 3SU
Major Shareholder: Ketan Harshad Joshi
Officers: Carolynne Joshi, Secretary; Dev Ketan Kong Joshi [1994] Director; Jay Ketan Kong Joshi [1992] Director; Dr Ketan Harshad Joshi [1961] Director

Fossick Limited
Incorporated: 9 February 2010
Registered Office: 6 Charlecote Mews, Staple Gardens, Winchester, Hants, SO23 8SR
Major Shareholder: Simon Hill
Officers: Simon Hill [1979] Director

Freak Cocktails Ltd
Incorporated: 19 July 2017
Registered Office: Queen Street Chambers, 68 Queen Street, Sheffield, S1 1WR
Major Shareholder: Lance Barry Worthington
Officers: Lance Barry Worthington [1968] Director/Photographer

Freedrinks Limited
Incorporated: 10 January 2012 Employees: 6
Net Worth Deficit: £1,339,592 Total Assets: £781,712
Registered Office: Acre House, 11-15 William Road, London, NW1 3ER
Parent: Freedrinks Holdings Limited
Officers: Igor Sosin [1967] Director/Entrepreneur [Russian]; Dragan Zarkovic [1954] Director [Serbian]

Freez Global Ltd.
Incorporated: 28 April 2014 Employees: 1
Net Worth Deficit: £21,463 Total Assets: £47,061
Registered Office: 109-111 Blackburn Street, Radcliffe, Manchester, M26 3WQ
Major Shareholder: Tasadduq Ali Ashraf
Officers: Tasadduq Ali Ashraf [1978] Director/Salesman

Frey Drinks Limited
Incorporated: 14 August 2018
Registered Office: 90 Archer Avenue, Southend on Sea, Essex, SS2 4QT
Shareholders: Hadley-James Henry Brown; Max Foster
Officers: Hadley-James Henry Brown [1993] Director; Max Foster [1994] Director/Graphic Designer

Frozen Brothers Limited
Incorporated: 1 November 2017
Registered Office: c/o Slush Puppie Ltd, Coronation Road, Cressex Business Park, High Wycombe, Bucks, HP12 3TA
Major Shareholder: Mark Jeffrey Peters
Officers: Mark Jeffrey Peters [1958] Managing Director

Fruit Diversity Limited
Incorporated: 22 March 2016
Registered Office: Dudley House, Abbey Hill, Kenilworth, Warwicks, CV8 1LU
Shareholders: Annette Denise Magraw; James Edmund Grenville Magraw
Officers: Annette Denise Magraw [1965] Director/Trade Mark Consultant; James Edmund Grenville Magraw [1960] Director/Chartered Accountant

Fruitfilm Limited
Incorporated: 31 August 2010
Registered Office: 349 Bramhall Lane, Stockport, Cheshire, SK3 8TP
Shareholder: Zaheer Ahmad
Officers: Zaheer Ahmad [1971] Director

Fruito Beverages (Africa) Limited
Incorporated: 23 July 2018
Registered Office: 65 Samuel Street, London, SE18 5LF
Parent: Fruito (UK) Limited
Officers: Adekunle Akanji Ademola [1955] Director/Consultant

Fruito Soft Drinks Limited
Incorporated: 25 June 2018
Registered Office: 65 Samuel Street, London, SE18 5LF
Parent: Topmost Foods Limited
Officers: Adekunle Akanji Ademola [1955] Director

Fuctivino Ltd
Incorporated: 5 July 2010
Registered Office: 1 Astley House, Whitehall Road, Darwen, Lancs, BB3 2LH
Parent: Michael Burke
Officers: Michael Burke [1949] Director

Functional Beverages Ltd
Incorporated: 31 March 2016
Net Worth Deficit: £9,250 Total Assets: £106
Registered Office: 7 Ballymacnab Road, Tassagh, Co Armagh, BT60 2QS
Major Shareholder: Caoimhin Michael Rafferty
Officers: Caoimhin Michael Rafferty [1998] Director/Student [Irish]

Funk Beverages Ltd
Incorporated: 23 April 2018
Registered Office: 21 Rockmount Road, London, SE19 3SZ
Major Shareholder: Lucy Madeleine Smith
Officers: Lucy Madeleine Smith [1982] Director/Marketing [New Zealander]

Fuse Drinks Ltd
Incorporated: 7 August 2017
Registered Office: 3 Elliot Hill, Blackheath, London, SE13 7EB
Major Shareholder: Paul Thomas Hudson
Officers: Paul Thomas Hudson [1985] Director; Natalia Stukan [1985] Director [Russian]

FYA Peppa Kitchen Ltd
Incorporated: 20 December 2018
Registered Office: 25 Nash Road, London, SE4 2QH
Major Shareholder: Novelette Ann-Marie Williams
Officers: Novelette Ann-Marie Williams [1975] Director/Chief Executive

Fyba Ltd.
Incorporated: 11 October 2012
Registered Office: Pelton Fold Barn, Bury Road, Turton, Bolton, Lancs, BL7 0BS
Major Shareholder: Karl Bradley Seddon
Officers: Karl Bradley Seddon [1989] Director

Gaia Brands Ltd
Incorporated: 11 March 2003
Net Worth Deficit: £13,821 Total Assets: £21,777
Registered Office: 5 Whitegate Gardens, Harrow Weald, Middlesex, HA3 6BW
Major Shareholder: Gary Simon Leigh
Officers: Roma Bendel, Secretary; Gary Simon Leigh [1965] Director/Marketing

Galactogen Products Limited
Incorporated: 29 October 1996
Registered Office: Cadbury House, Sanderson Road, Uxbridge, Middlesex, UB8 1DH
Parent: Reading Scientific Services Limited
Officers: Tracey Jayne Gale [1965] Finance Director; Rachel Ann Henton [1969] Director/General Manager

Gallybird Tonic Co Ltd
Incorporated: 31 May 2017
Registered Office: Yew Tree House, Lewes Road, Forest Row, E Sussex, RH18 5AA
Major Shareholder: Fiona Victoria Louise Kemp
Officers: Fiona Kemp [1974] Director

GB Heritage Ltd
Incorporated: 21 September 2018
Registered Office: Beck House, King Street, Knutsford, Cheshire, WA16 6DX
Major Shareholder: Siobhan Cathrina Maria Brady
Officers: Siobhan Cathrina Maria Brady [1972] Sales Director

GB Refreshments Limited
Incorporated: 7 March 2017
Net Worth Deficit: £2,076 *Total Assets:* £67
Registered Office: Sunnybank Cottage, Much Marcle, Ledbury, Herefords, HR8 2NH
Major Shareholder: Benjamin James Davis
Officers: Benjamin James Davis [1993] Director

Genie Drinks Ltd
Incorporated: 30 August 2017
Registered Office: 34 Hadyn Park Road, London, W12 9AG
Shareholders: William Edward Read; Alexander St. John Webster
Officers: William Edward Read [1978] Director; Alexander St. John Webster [1978] Director

Genii Energy Ltd.
Incorporated: 27 August 2015
Registered Office: 34 Tynemouth Road, Mitcham, Surrey, CR4 2BN
Major Shareholder: Freddie Gabriel Scobey
Officers: Samuel James Welbank, Secretary; Freddie Scobey [1990] Director/Management Consultant; Sam James Welbank [1991] Director/Management Consultant

Genius Drinks Limited
Incorporated: 10 October 2013
Net Worth Deficit: £138,022 *Total Assets:* £33,693
Registered Office: 57 Warwick Road, London, SW5 9HB
Major Shareholder: Hilary Jane Marsh
Officers: Hilary Jane Marsh [1959] Director/Entrepreneur

Get Nourished Limited
Incorporated: 15 September 2016 *Employees:* 1
Net Worth Deficit: £4,119 *Total Assets:* £63
Registered Office: c/o Christie Griffith, 19 Woodside Place, Glasgow, G3 7QL
Major Shareholder: David Andrew Charles Towse
Officers: David Andrew Charles Towse [1979] Director/Business Owner

Giantcandyco Limited
Incorporated: 22 June 2018
Registered Office: 130 Old Street, London, EC1V 9BD
Officers: Damian Wingham, Secretary; Damian Paul Wingham [1975] Director

The Gibraltar Gin Company Limited
Incorporated: 21 September 2018
Registered Office: Morants Hall, Colchester Road, Great Bromley, Colchester, Essex, CO7 7TN
Major Shareholder: Michael Joseph Volf
Officers: Michael Joseph Volf [1959] Director/Owner Care Group

Gingercool Limited
Incorporated: 24 October 2013
Registered Office: 17a Anfield Road, Anfield, Liverpool, L4 0TE
Shareholder: Martin James Cooke
Officers: Martin James Cooke [1967] Director/Business Consultant; Ewan Brian Vickers [1974] Director [Jamaican]

Ginsecco Ltd
Incorporated: 12 October 2018
Registered Office: 17 Whitelaw Street, Glasgow, G20 0DG
Shareholders: Jonathan McCall; Craig Gibson
Officers: Craig Gibson [1983] Director/Engineer; Jonathan McCall [1982] Director/Engineer

Ginsense Ltd
Incorporated: 21 March 2018
Registered Office: Ward End Park House, Washwood Heath Road, Birmingham, B8 2HB
Major Shareholder: Pete Freerunner Simpson
Officers: Pete Freerunner Simpson [1974] Director

Give Me Tap Limited
Incorporated: 26 May 2011
Net Worth Deficit: £43,224 *Total Assets:* £264,806
Registered Office: 12 Clarendon Road, Edmonton, London, N18 2AJ
Parent: Give Me Tap, Inc.
Officers: Frank Mensah, Secretary; Dr Edwin Kwaku Broni Mensah [1985] Director

Glaisher & Ames Ltd
Incorporated: 17 September 2018
Registered Office: 5 Warfield Road, London, NW10 5LA
Shareholders: George Woulfe Glaisher; Alexander Edmund Ames
Officers: George Woulfe Glaisher [1992] Director

Glastonbury Spring Water Company Limited
Incorporated: 4 October 1988 *Employees:* 24
Net Worth: £840,855 *Total Assets:* £1,087,706
Registered Office: 14 Queen Square, Bath, BA1 2HN
Officers: Caroline Mary Tucker, Secretary; Caroline Mary Tucker [1950] Director/Secretary; David Peter Tucker [1976] Director/Manager; Ian Christopher Tucker [1950] Director

Gleneagles Spring Water Company Ltd.
Incorporated: 27 April 1998
Registered Office: c/o Highland Spring Ltd, Stirling Street, Blackford, Auchterarder, Perth & Kinross, PH4 1QA
Officers: Leslie Montgomery, Secretary/Director; Maher Al-Tajir [1957] Director [Emirati/British]; Leslie Montgomery [1963] Director

Global Functional Drinks UK Limited
Incorporated: 8 March 2013
Net Worth Deficit: £15,342,891 *Total Assets:* £229,516
Registered Office: 2nd Floor, 13 John Princes Street, London, W1G 0JR
Officers: Igor Popov [1965] Director/Legal Officer [Russian]

Glucofit Limited
Incorporated: 14 May 2018
Registered Office: 203 Dovercourt Road, Bristol, BS7 9SF
Major Shareholder: John Dunkerley
Officers: John Dunkerley [1986] Director

GO4 Beverages Limited
Incorporated: 15 August 2016
Net Worth: £344 *Total Assets:* £792
Registered Office: 8 Eastmead Avenue, Greenford, Middlesex, UB6 9RA
Officers: Nathanael Lasme [1959] Director [Ivorian]

Goat Drinks Ltd
Incorporated: 1 November 2016
Net Worth Deficit: £4,209
Registered Office: 7 Finkle Street, Thirsk, N Yorks, YO7 1DA
Major Shareholder: Colette Safhill
Officers: Colette Safhill [1973] Director/Therapist

Goldbucks Limited
Incorporated: 18 June 2003
Net Worth: £14,928 *Total Assets:* £47,370
Registered Office: 195 Bourne Vale, Bromley, Kent, BR2 7LX
Major Shareholder: Djahit Ismail
Officers: Djahit Ismail, Secretary; Djahit Ismail [1948] Director/Businessman [Cypriot]

Good Beverage Company Limited
Incorporated: 11 September 2017
Registered Office: 29 Elbe Street, London, SW6 2QP
Shareholder: Jasbinder Singh Ball
Officers: Parisha Kanani, Secretary; Jasbinder Singh Ball [1972] Director/Chartered Accountant

Good Remedy Limited
Incorporated: 4 September 2018
Registered Office: 71 Airedale Avenue, London, W4 2NN
Major Shareholder: Damian Guy Routley
Officers: Damian Guy Routley [1978] Director

Good Water Trading Ltd
Incorporated: 26 January 2018
Registered Office: 61 Chelsea Manor Street, London, SW3 5RZ
Shareholders: Leona Bodina Mani; Leona Bodina Mani
Officers: Leona Bodina Mani [1969] Director

Gooddrop Supply Co. Limited
Incorporated: 21 July 2016
Registered Office: 1 The Paddock, Letham, Cupar, Fife, KY15 7RP
Major Shareholder: Jon-Paul Kitching
Officers: Jon-Paul Kitching [1979] Director/Founder

Goodlives Panacea Blend Ltd
Incorporated: 31 December 2018
Registered Office: 2a Eastbank Street, Southport, Merseyside, PR8 1DW
Major Shareholder: Peter Armstrong
Officers: Peter Armstrong [1980] Managing Director

The Goodnatured Company Ltd.
Incorporated: 31 January 2017
Registered Office: Upper Flat, Craigpark House, Craigpark Gardens, Galashiels, Selkirkshire, TD1 3HZ
Major Shareholder: Heloise Brown
Officers: David Charles Alexander Brown [1965] Accounts Director; Heloise Brown [1974] Director/Entrepreneur [South African]

Goodness Brands Ltd
Incorporated: 13 March 2014
Net Worth: £19,867 *Total Assets:* £184,965
Registered Office: 30 Binley Road, Coventry, Warwicks, CV3 1JA
Major Shareholder: Gary Mark Barnshaw
Officers: Gary Mark Barnshaw [1966] Managing Director; Stephen Cram [1960] Director; David Jervis Smith [1964] Director/Sales & Marketing

The Gourmet Water Company Limited
Incorporated: 28 March 2012 *Employees:* 2
Net Worth: £32,068 *Total Assets:* £112,490
Registered Office: Rosemary, Copgrove, Harrogate, N Yorks, HG3 3SZ
Parent: Averre Group Limited
Officers: Jayne Tracy Averre, Secretary; Jayne Tracy Averre [1965] Director/Entrepreneur; Raymond James Averre [1963] Director/Entrepreneur

Grace Under Pressure Ltd
Incorporated: 17 July 2014
Net Worth Deficit: £535,029 *Total Assets:* £89,890
Registered Office: Unit 12 Trade City, Avro Way, Brooklands Business Park, Weybridge, Surrey, KT13 0YF
Shareholders: Jamie Moulding; Jessica Mary Moulding
Officers: Jamie Moulding [1974] Director; Jessica Mary Moulding [1986] Director

Gran Steads Ginger Limited
Incorporated: 4 August 2004
Net Worth: £25,444 *Total Assets:* £69,805
Registered Office: 6 Thornhill Close, Hove, E Sussex, BN3 8JL
Shareholders: Christopher Royston Knox; Rosemary Ann Knox
Officers: Rosemary Ann Knox, Secretary; Christopher Royston Knox [1952] Director/Production Manager; Rosemary Ann Knox [1954] Director/Company Secretary

Green Drink (GB) Ltd
Incorporated: 14 September 2012
Registered Office: 19 Varley Parade, London, NW9 6RR
Shareholder: Anuj Joshi
Officers: Anuj Joshi [1990] Director/Analyst

A & C Green Food and Beverage Limited
Incorporated: 21 November 2018
Registered Office: 59 Bonnygate, Cupar, Fife, KY15 4BY
Officers: Giorgio Cozzolino Cozzolino [1964] Director [Italian]

Green Foods International Ltd
Incorporated: 30 October 2018
Registered Office: 40 Parliament Street, Small Heath, Birmingham, B10 0QJ
Major Shareholder: Sheikh Mohammed Goyas Uddin
Officers: Sheikh Mohammed Goyas Uddin [1970] Director/Businessman

Green Leaf Liquids Limited
Incorporated: 25 February 2019
Registered Office: 45a Balby Road, Doncaster, S Yorks, DN4 0RD
Shareholders: Kuldip Chopra; Ravinder Paul Pabial
Officers: Kuldip Chopra [1977] Director/Civil Servant; Ravinder Paul Pabial [1978] Director/Accounts Manager

Green Monkey Drinks Ltd
Incorporated: 1 August 2018
Registered Office: County Ground, Edgbaston Road, Birmingham, B5 7QU
Shareholders: Sandip Jhooty; Serge Davies; Shaban Hussain
Officers: Serge Davies [1990] Director; Shaban Hussain [1974] Director; Manjit Jhooty [1974] Director; Nicholas Mark Smith [1969] Director

Green Room Brands Limited
Incorporated: 17 August 2016 *Employees:* 3
Net Worth Deficit: £1,220,289 *Total Assets:* £141,258
Registered Office: Fourth Floor, Abbots House, Abbey Street, Reading, Berks, RG1 3BD
Shareholder: Hurstmere Investments Limited
Officers: William Joseph Coker [1965] Director; Gerard Anthony Reidy [1942] Director/Retired [Irish]; Nicolai Henrik Skaanild [1974] Director [Danish]; Andrew Charles Williams [1964] Director; Paul James Woodward [1969] Director/Self Employed/CEO

UK Manufacturers of Soft Drinks

Greenbank Drinks Company Limited
Incorporated: 24 October 1991
Registered Office: Breakspear Park, Breakspear Way, Hemel Hempstead, Herts, HP2 4TZ
Parent: Orchid Drinks Limited
Officers: Judith Moore, Secretary; Mathew James Dunn [1974] Director/Chief Financial Officer; Peter Simon Litherland [1964] Director/Chief Executive; Alexandra Clare Thomas [1974] Director/General Counsel and Company Secretary

Grown-Up Foods Ltd
Incorporated: 2 June 2016
Net Worth Deficit: £1,896 *Total Assets:* £242
Registered Office: 2nd Floor, Clyde Offices, 48 West George Street, Glasgow, G2 1BP
Shareholders: Charles Rowden Beard; Sarah Dougan
Officers: Charles Rowden Beard [1959] Director; Sarah Dougan [1963] Director

Guffaw Ltd
Incorporated: 12 November 2018
Registered Office: 9 Park View Rise, Telscombe Cliffs, Peacehaven, E Sussex, BN10 7NQ
Major Shareholder: Ghomdim Jose Fabrice Cheta
Officers: Ghomdim Jose Fabrice Cheta [1995] Director/Administrator

Gunna Drinks Limited
Incorporated: 30 November 2015 *Employees:* 3
Net Worth Deficit: £23,985 *Total Assets:* £294,248
Registered Office: Ward House, 6 Ward Street, Guildford, Surrey, GU1 4LH
Shareholders: Melvin George William Jay; Melvin George William Jay
Officers: Melvin George William Jay [1964] Director

Gurkhatise Limited
Incorporated: 30 September 2014
Net Worth Deficit: £48,792 *Total Assets:* £791
Registered Office: Brandon House, 90 The Broadway, Chesham, Bucks, HP5 1EG
Major Shareholder: Ranjeet Singh Sagoo
Officers: Ranjeet Singh Sagoo [1979] Director

Gut Drinks Ltd
Incorporated: 13 February 2019
Registered Office: 9 Abbots Close, Guildford, Surrey, GU2 7RW
Shareholders: Andrew John Routley; Jeremy Charles Hiscocks
Officers: James Andrew Taylor [1964] Director

H Two Eau International Limited
Incorporated: 19 August 2016
Net Worth: £3 *Total Assets:* £2,009
Registered Office: Flat 1, 75 Egerton Gardens, London, SW3 2BY
Shareholders: Brigidino Fiordilino; Andreas Breijs; Levico Acque SRL.
Officers: Andreas Breijs, Secretary; Brigidino Fiordilino [1964] Director/Trade Agent [Italian]

H20miles Ltd
Incorporated: 3 October 2017
Registered Office: 20-22 Wenlock Road, London, N1 7GU
Officers: Roy Uziel Moed [1953] Director

H2can Ltd
Incorporated: 6 February 2019
Registered Office: 72 Aylward, London, E1 0ER
Major Shareholder: Nicholas Robinson
Officers: Nicholas Robinson [1981] Director/Personal Trainer [Australian]

H2go Drinks Ltd
Incorporated: 9 January 2017
Registered Office: Lindum House, Lees New Road, Oldham, Lancs, OL4 5PP
Major Shareholder: Reece Best
Officers: Reece Best [1993] Director/Owner

Hafod Water Limited
Incorporated: 24 April 2003 *Employees:* 3
Net Worth: £16,489 *Total Assets:* £28,529
Registered Office: The Hafodneddyn Estate, Broad Oak, Llandeilo, Carmarthenshire, SA19 7AE
Shareholders: David Howard Royal; Christopher Howard Royal
Officers: David Howard Royal, Secretary/Partner; Anne-Marie Royal [1980] Finance Director; Christopher Howard Royal [1943] Director/Partner; David Howard Royal [1977] Director/Partner

Halo Drinks Company Limited
Incorporated: 30 June 2017
Registered Office: First Floor, The London Office, 85 Great Portland Street, London, W1W 7LT
Shareholder: Angel Business Club Nominees Ltd
Officers: Natalia Franchini Gliorsi, Secretary; Dominic Peter Clive Berger [1969] Director; Ian Michael Minton [1982] Director; Steven Christopher Wilkinson [1980] Director

Handmade Cider Company Limited
Incorporated: 4 May 2010 *Employees:* 1
Net Worth Deficit: £4,601 *Total Assets:* £40,447
Registered Office: The Old Cider Shed, Slaughterford Mill, Slaughterford, Chippenham, Wilts, SN14 8RJ
Major Shareholder: Denis France
Officers: Denis France [1967] Director

Hangin Drinks Limited
Incorporated: 21 November 2017
Registered Office: 35 Deerswood Avenue, Hatfield, Herts, AL10 8RX
Shareholders: Samuel Marchant; Oliver Vagg; Thomas Sexton
Officers: Samuel Marchant [1996] Director; Thomas Sexton [1991] Director; Oliver Vagg [1996] Director

Happy Curations Limited
Incorporated: 29 November 2017
Registered Office: Floor 4, 15-19 Great Titchfield Street, London, W1W 8AZ
Major Shareholder: Nathan McKenzie Clemes
Officers: Nathan McKenzie Clemes [1989] Director [Canadian]; Antonia Alexandra Jamison [1972] Director; Dr Ketan Harshad Joshi [1961] Director; Neville John Portelli [1959] Director

The Happy Gut Hut Limited
Incorporated: 4 November 2015
Net Worth: £1,298 *Total Assets:* £6,173
Registered Office: 70 Summer Lane, Birmingham, B19 3NG
Officers: Alyn Norris [1972] Director/Sales

Thomas Hardy Burtonwood Limited
Incorporated: 10 July 1998 *Employees:* 43
Net Worth: £468,000 *Total Assets:* £6,525,000
Registered Office: Bold Lane, Burtonwood, Warrington, Cheshire, WA5 4TH
Officers: Gary Alexander Todd [1966] Site Director; Neil Mark Voss [1969] Director; Jonathan Christopher Ward [1978] Director; Margaret Rae Ward [1944] Director

Thomas Hardy Holdings Limited
Incorporated: 27 December 1996 *Employees:* 114
Net Worth: £12,852,000 *Total Assets:* £19,423,000
Registered Office: Bold Lane, Burtonwood, Warrington, Cheshire, WA5 4TH
Officers: Neil Mark Voss [1969] Director; Jonathan Christopher Ward [1978] Director; Margaret Rae Ward [1944] Director

Thomas Hardy Kendal Limited
Incorporated: 29 December 1998 *Employees:* 64
Net Worth: £6,922,000 *Total Assets:* £9,162,000
Registered Office: Bold Lane, Burtonwood, Warrington, Cheshire, WA5 4TH
Officers: Peter Michael Armstrong [1965] Site Director; Neil Mark Voss [1969] Director; Jonathan Christopher Ward [1978] Director; Margaret Rae Ward [1944] Director

Harrogate Spring Water Limited
Incorporated: 16 August 2000 *Employees:* 74
Net Worth: £4,716,504 *Total Assets:* £19,496,768
Registered Office: Harlow Moor Road, Harrogate, N Yorks, HG2 0QB
Parent: Harrogate Water Brands Limited
Officers: Anthony Joseph Cain [1948] Director; James Anthony Cain [1973] Director; Simon David Knaggs [1966] Operations Director; Robert James Pickering [1964] Director; Damien Michael Wilkinson [1969] Finance Director

Hartpury Heritage Trust
Incorporated: 6 March 1998
Net Worth: £1,184,356 *Total Assets:* £1,200,023
Registered Office: Orchard Centre, Blackwells End, Hartpury, Gloucester, GL19 3DB
Officers: Holly Bridget Chapman, Secretary; Margaret Bailey [1961] Director; Holly Bridget Chapman [1956] Museum Director; James Roger Chapman [1950] Director/Retired Solicitor; Pauline Drury [1950] Director/Teacher; John Griffiths Evans [1937] Director; Mary Rose McGhee [1935] Director/Ward Clerk

Hartridges Limited
Incorporated: 7 April 1934 *Employees:* 10
Net Worth: £1,363,028 *Total Assets:* £1,639,382
Registered Office: Hartridges, The Maltings, Hambledon, Waterlooville, Hants, PO7 4AE
Parent: Hartridges Group Limited
Officers: Christopher Simon Hartridge, Secretary; Charlotte Amelia Hartridge [1982] Director/Investor Relations at a Hedge Fund; Christopher Simon Hartridge [1949] Director/Mineral Water Manufacturer; Edward Thomas Hartridge [1981] Director

Steven Hatch Operations Consultancy Ltd
Incorporated: 27 December 2018
Registered Office: Market House, Church Street, Harleston, Norfolk, IP20 9BB
Shareholders: Steven Hatch; Allison Hatch
Officers: Allison Hatch [1965] Director; Steven Hatch [1963] Director

Havok Energy Drink. Ltd
Incorporated: 28 February 2018
Registered Office: 20-22 Wenlock Road, London, N1 7GU
Major Shareholder: Shashidhar Kalenahalli Gubbanna
Officers: Shashidhar Kalenahalli Gubbanna [1944] Director/Businessman [Indian]

Hawk Spring Water (S.E.) Limited
Incorporated: 20 October 1995
Net Worth: £100 *Total Assets:* £100
Registered Office: Conway House, Pattenden Lane, Marden, Kent, TN12 9QD
Parent: Water Wellbeing Limited
Officers: Benjamin Raymond Stanley McGannan [1967] Director

Hawkins Drinks Limited
Incorporated: 15 January 2018
Registered Office: 3 All Saints Croft, Burton on Trent, Staffs, DE14 3EA
Major Shareholder: Martin John Hawkins
Officers: Martin John Hawkins [1957] Director

Hawkshead Gin and Spirit Co Ltd
Incorporated: 16 March 2018
Registered Office: Gilmarver Flat, Wordsworth Street, Hawkshead, Cumbria, LA22 0PA
Major Shareholder: Mark Warburton
Officers: Mark Warburton [1964] Director

HD Water Limited
Incorporated: 16 March 2017
Registered Office: 19 Seymour Place, London, W1H 5BG
Shareholders: Shaikh Khalifa Mohamed Ateyatalla Alkhalifa; Omer Ahmed Rana
Officers: Khalifah Mohamed Ateyatalla Alkhalifa [1983] Director/Business Consultant [Bahraini]; Omer Ahmed Rana [1980] Director/Strategist

Healthy Hemp Products Ltd
Incorporated: 27 August 2013
Previous: Loveburgh Raw Limited
Net Worth: £239 *Total Assets:* £31,924
Registered Office: Unit 5, 1 Dryden Road, Bilston Glen Industrial Estate, Loanhead, Midlothian, EH20 9LZ
Major Shareholder: Jaskarn Singh Nottay
Officers: Jaskarn Nottay [1985] Director/Graphic Design, Printing & Advertising

Healthy Juice Co (NI) Ltd
Incorporated: 12 June 2017
Net Worth: £1,040 *Total Assets:* £10,006
Registered Office: 67 Rathfriland Road, Newry, Co Armagh, BT34 1LD
Major Shareholder: Amanda Kearns
Officers: Amanda McGeown [1990] Director/Nutritionist [Irish]

The Healthy Protein Co Ltd.
Incorporated: 8 September 2015
Net Worth Deficit: £19,265 *Total Assets:* £27,126
Registered Office: 6a Burgoyne Road, London, N4 1AD
Major Shareholder: Rafael Rozenson
Officers: Rafael Rozenson [1979] Director

Healthy Thirst Drinks Limited
Incorporated: 1 October 1991
Net Worth Deficit: £83,280 *Total Assets:* £8,966
Registered Office: Thornycroft Farm, Thorncroft Drive, Leatherhead, Surrey, KT22 8JD
Shareholders: Frank Christoffel Van Ooijen; Jules Van Harn; Guy Woodall; Sheila Catherine Woodall
Officers: Frank Christoffel Van Ooijen, Secretary; Jules Van Harn [1975] Director [Dutch]; Frank Christoffel Van Ooijen [1965] Director/MD [Dutch]; Dr Guy Woodall [1954] Director; Sheila Catherine Woodall [1955] Director

Healthy Well Being Products Limited
Incorporated: 13 February 2017
Net Worth Deficit: £519,694 *Total Assets:* £47,647
Registered Office: 146 Wisley Way, Birmingham, B32 2JX
Officers: Boota Sanghera [1969] Director

Heather Ale Limited
Incorporated: 19 April 1994 *Employees:* 62
Net Worth: £2,378,768 *Total Assets:* £5,044,741
Registered Office: Eglinton Store, Kelliebank, Alloa, Clackmannanshire, FK10 1NT
Major Shareholder: Scott John Williams
Officers: Scott John Williams, Secretary; Bruce Andrew Williams [1960] Director/Brewing Supplies; Scott John Williams [1964] Director/Brewer

Heather Spring Water Limited
Incorporated: 30 October 1987
Registered Office: 229 St Vincent Street, Glasgow, G2 5QY
Major Shareholder: Stanley Ian Bernard
Officers: Stanley Ian Bernard, Secretary; Deirdre Bernard [1950] Director; Stanley Ian Bernard [1947] Director

Hedgerow Cordials Limited
Incorporated: 9 October 2013
Registered Office: Green Farm Cottage, Oak Road, Thurston, Bury St Edmunds, Suffolk, IP31 3SN
Major Shareholder: Charlotte Grant
Officers: Charlotte Mary Maconarchy Grant [1986] Director

Hedgerow Soft Drinks Ltd
Incorporated: 21 May 2018
Registered Office: Heartsease Farm, Knighton, Powys, LD7 1LU
Shareholders: John Christopher Evans; William Walter Watkins
Officers: John Evans [1962] Director; William Walter Watkins [1965] Director

Hell Energy Ltd
Incorporated: 19 June 2017
Registered Office: 10 Evington Valley Road, Leicester, LE5 5LJ
Major Shareholder: Hao Sun
Officers: Hao Sun [1976] Director [Chinese]

Hello Coco Limited
Incorporated: 28 April 2016
Net Worth: £100 *Total Assets:* £800
Registered Office: 110 Viglen House, Alperton Lane, Wembley, Middlesex, HA0 1HD
Major Shareholder: Hemanth Patak
Officers: Heman Pathak [1959] Director/Businessman

Hendre Distillery Ltd
Incorporated: 13 November 2018
Registered Office: Hendre Glyn Farm, Upper Llanover, Abergavenny, Monmouthshire, NP7 9ER
Major Shareholder: Sioned Haf Leyshon
Officers: Sioned Haf Leyshon [1989] Director; Alan John Williams [1953] Director; Victoria Nancy Williams [1961] Director

Henny and Joes Ltd
Incorporated: 22 May 2013 *Employees:* 1
Net Worth: £4,542 *Total Assets:* £38,733
Registered Office: The Locks House, Brassmill Lane, Bath, BA1 3JW
Major Shareholder: Ashley Bailey
Officers: Ashley Bailey, Secretary; Ashley Bailey [1988] Director/Bar Manager

Henrysuper Roots Drinks Ltd
Incorporated: 23 October 2018
Registered Office: 20-22 Wenlock Road, London, N1 7GU
Major Shareholder: Keith Henry
Officers: Keith Henry [1966] Director

Herbal Fusions Ltd
Incorporated: 24 June 2013
Net Worth Deficit: £29,818 *Total Assets:* £74,001
Registered Office: 2 New Terrace, Byfield, Daventry, Northants, NN11 6UY
Major Shareholder: Graham Trevitt
Officers: Tom Alexander Scott Dye [1984] Director; Graham Trevitt [1955] Director

Heritage Health Organics Ltd
Incorporated: 8 October 2015
Registered Office: 5 Woodland Way, Heolgerrig, Merthyr Tydfil, CF48 1SQ
Shareholders: Lynn Heritage; Yvonne Heritage
Officers: Yvonne Heritage, Secretary; Lynn Heritage [1948] Managing Director; Yvonne Heritage [1955] Director/Company Secretary

Hidden Orchard Ltd
Incorporated: 30 January 2019
Registered Office: Unit 1a Herniss Business Park, Longdowns, Cornwall, TR10 9BZ
Major Shareholder: Jeffrey Charles Richard Bradley
Officers: Jeffrey Charles Richard Bradley, Secretary; Jeffrey Charles Richard Bradley [1976] Director/Drinks Producer

Highdrate Ltd
Incorporated: 23 July 2018
Registered Office: 19b Station Parade, Uxbridge Road, London, W5 3LD
Major Shareholder: Elvis Anthony Collis
Officers: Elvis Anthony Collis [1984] Director

Highland Spring Limited
Incorporated: 13 March 1979 *Employees:* 519
Net Worth: £12,191,000 *Total Assets:* £70,362,000
Registered Office: Stirling Street, Blackford, Perthshire, PH4 1QA
Officers: Leslie Montgomery, Secretary/Chief Executive; Mohammed Mahdi Al Tajir [1931] Director [Emirati]; Khalid Mohamed Mahdi Altajir [1958] Director/Businessman [Emirati]; Maher Altajir [1957] Director [Emirati]; Leslie Montgomery [1963] Director/Chief Executive

Highlands Pride Ltd.
Incorporated: 27 June 2007
Registered Office: 1 Aspen Court, High Street, Crieff, Perthshire, PH7 3HZ
Shareholder: Charles Duncan Brown
Officers: Charles Duncan Brown, Secretary; Charles Duncan Brown [1947] Horticulturist/Director; Robert John Grafham [1952] Director

HIH Frankly Irresistible Limited
Incorporated: 15 February 2019
Registered Office: c/o Hillier Hopkins LLP, First Floor, Radius House, 51 Clarendon Road, Watford, Herts, WD17 1HP
Major Shareholder: Philomena Catherine Shiels
Officers: Philomena Catherine Shiels, Secretary; Philomena Catherine Shiels [1967] Director/Therapist

Hike Coffee Ltd
Incorporated: 11 July 2018
Registered Office: 104 Sandringham Road, Newcastle upon Tyne, NE3 1PY
Major Shareholder: William John Edward Anderson
Officers: William John Edward Anderson [1984] Director

Hildon Limited
Incorporated: 27 November 1984 *Employees:* 65
Net Worth: £2,935,419 *Total Assets:* £10,582,416
Registered Office: Hildon Ltd, Broughton, Hants, SO20 8DQ
Shareholders: Balaji Ramamoorthy; Hildon House Ltd
Officers: Munjurpet Narayanan Kannan [1968] Director/Chartered Accountant [Indian]; Avi David Sklut [1977] Director/General Manager [American]

Hill Holme Juice Ltd
Incorporated: 9 October 2013
Net Worth: £2 *Total Assets:* £2
Registered Office: Ground Floor, Southway House, 29 Southway, Colchester, Essex, CO2 7BA
Shareholders: Nigel Peter Lane; Claire Louise Lane
Officers: Clare Louise Lane [1965] Director; Nigel Peter Lane [1964] Director

Hippo & Hedgehog Ltd
Incorporated: 27 October 2015 *Employees:* 2
Net Worth: £26,054 *Total Assets:* £26,144
Registered Office: 172 Warriston Street, Glasgow, G33 2LD
Shareholders: Paul Andrew Blackler; Isatou Njai
Officers: Paul Blackler [1983] Director/Finance; Isatou Njai [1994] Director/Co-Founder [Gambian]

Holos London Ltd
Incorporated: 12 February 2018
Registered Office: 58 Crowthorne Close, Southfields, London, SW18 5RX
Major Shareholder: Thomas Michael Partridge
Officers: Christine Gilland Robinson [1984] Director; Naomi Joy Partridge [1984] Director; Thomas Michael Partridge [1981] Director/Chief Executive

Hon Limited
Incorporated: 13 November 2018
Registered Office: Ricoh, Church Lane, Farndon, Chester, CH3 6QD
Major Shareholder: Bernadette Frances Maddocks
Officers: Bernadette Frances Maddocks [1964] Director

Honu Sodas UK Limited
Incorporated: 7 September 2018
Registered Office: 73 Hillway, London, N6 6AB
Shareholders: Caitlin Mary Egen; Gregg Michael Egen
Officers: Gregg Michael Egen, Secretary; Caitlin Mary Egen [1991] Director/Chief Executive; Gregg Michael Egen [1955] Director

Hoods Cordial Ltd
Incorporated: 9 July 2018
Registered Office: Apt 6, St Peters Church Walk, Nottingham, NG1 2JR
Shareholders: Nicholas Graham; Russell Wheatley
Officers: Nicholas Graham [1982] Director/Manager

Hooper,Struve & Company Limited
Incorporated: 29 December 1900
Registered Office: Breakspear Park, Breakspear Way, Hemel Hempstead, Herts, HP2 4TZ
Parent: Britvic Soft Drinks Limited
Officers: Judith Moore, Secretary; Mathew James Dunn [1974] Director/Chief Financial Officer; Peter Simon Litherland [1964] Director/Chief Executive; Alexandra Clare Thomas [1974] Director/General Counsel and Company Secretary

Hope Sixteen (No.87) Limited
Incorporated: 26 March 1986 *Employees:* 519
Net Worth: £8,272,000 *Total Assets:* £70,367,000
Registered Office: Stirling Street, Blackford, Perthshire, PH4 1QA
Officers: Leslie Montgomery, Finance Director; Mohammed Mahdi Al Tajir [1931] Director [Emirati]; Maher Altajir [1957] Director [Emirati]; Leslie Montgomery [1963] Director

Horizon (Contract Drinks) Limited
Incorporated: 28 May 1991
Registered Office: Anchor Brook Business Park, Wharf Approach, Aldridge, W Midlands, WS9 8BX
Major Shareholder: Barry John Stevens
Officers: Andrew Cooper [1979] Finance Director; Barry John Stevens [1946] Director/Soft Drinks Wholesaler; David Barry Stevens [1979] Director

House of Balmoral Ltd
Incorporated: 23 February 2018
Registered Office: 56 Canon Byrne Glebe, Kirkcaldy, Fife, KY1 2RE
Major Shareholder: Scott MacDougall
Officers: Scott MacDougall [1969] Director/Actor

House of Symbols Ltd
Incorporated: 17 August 2017
Registered Office: 2 The Old School House, St Catherines Court, Church Street, Litlington, Royston, Cambs, SG8 0QL
Major Shareholder: Abigail Leek
Officers: Abigail Leek [1983] Director

HSW Limited
Incorporated: 7 March 2000
Registered Office: Harlow Moor Road, Harrogate, N Yorks, HG2 0QB
Shareholder: Anthony Joseph Cain
Officers: Anthony Lancelot Parker, Secretary; Anthony Joseph Cain [1948] Director

Hullabaloos Lemonade Limited
Incorporated: 21 December 2017
Registered Office: 12 Parkfield, Axbridge, Somerset, BS26 2DD
Shareholder: Randa Abdullah-Hucker
Officers: Randa Abdullah-Hucker [1977] Director/Business Owner; Leigh Hucker [1973] Director/Business Owner

Humble Bumble Ltd
Incorporated: 13 July 2018
Registered Office: 2nd Floor, College House, 17 King Edwards Road, Ruislip, Middlesex, HA4 7AE
Major Shareholder: Ian Scarborough
Officers: Ian Scarborough [1988] Director/Graphic Design

Hydrade Drinks Limited
Incorporated: 23 June 2017
Registered Office: International House, 12 Constance Street, London, E16 2DQ
Officers: Neil Alexander Shand McDonald [1984] Director

Hydration Station Ltd
Incorporated: 4 September 2017
Registered Office: c/o Evans & Evans, 24a St Radigunds Road, Dover, Kent, CT17 0JY
Major Shareholder: Adrian Eliot Evans
Officers: Adrian Eliot Evans [1971] Director

HYP Water Ltd
Incorporated: 30 January 2019
Registered Office: 25 St Marys Lane, Burghill, Hereford, HR4 7QL
Major Shareholder: Nicholas Mark Warwick Entwisle
Officers: Nicholas Mark Warwick Entwisle [1997] Director

Ibis Organics Limited
Incorporated: 25 May 2005
Net Worth: £60,711 *Total Assets:* £261,828
Registered Office: Bank House, Kirkbride, Wigton, Cumbria, CA7 5HR
Shareholders: William Graham Irving; Charles Graham Irving
Officers: William Graham Irving, Director and Secretary; Charles Graham Irving [1946] Director; William Graham Irving [1972] Director and Secretary

ICB Advisory Limited
Incorporated: 11 May 2018
Registered Office: 5 Jardine House, Harrovian Business Village, Bessborough Road, Harrow, Middlesex, HA1 3EX
Shareholder: Ian Christopher Beaumont
Officers: Ian Christopher Beaumont [1973] Director

Ice Cube Tea Ltd
Incorporated: 18 June 2012
Net Worth Deficit: £10,933 *Total Assets:* £16,806
Registered Office: 81 Bridge Street, Lampeter, Ceredigion, SA48 7AB
Major Shareholder: Huw Pritchard Edwards
Officers: Huw Pritchard Edwards [1978] Director/Food Inspector

Ice Factory Limited
Incorporated: 23 December 2015
Registered Office: 94 Mornington Road, Greenford, Middlesex, UB6 9HW
Major Shareholder: Govind Thethy
Officers: Govind Thethy [1989] Director/Electrical Consultant

The Ice People Limited
Incorporated: 10 May 2018
Registered Office: The Entertainer, Boughton Business Park, Bell Lane, Amersham, Bucks, HP6 6GL
Officers: Stuart James Grant [1984] Director

Ice2u Ltd
Incorporated: 24 October 2016
Net Worth Deficit: £10,239 *Total Assets:* £114,427
Registered Office: Hare and Hounds, Ormskirk Road, Skelmersdale, Lancs, WN8 9AA
Major Shareholder: Robert Lesbirel
Officers: Robert Carl LesbIreland [1980] Director

Icely Done Drinks Limited
Incorporated: 31 March 2014
Net Worth: £85,331 *Total Assets:* £174,756
Registered Office: 4 Rawmec Business Park, Plumpton Road, Hoddesdon, Herts, EN11 0EE
Major Shareholder: Eleftherios Christodoulou
Officers: Eleftherios Christodoulou [1982] Founder/Managing Director

Icetails Ltd
Incorporated: 30 January 2017
Registered Office: 48 Addison Way, Bognor Regis, W Sussex, PO22 9HY
Major Shareholder: Thomas David Parsons
Officers: Thomas David Parsons [1993] Director/Draftsman

IDC Irish Drinks Co. Ltd
Incorporated: 15 February 2017
Net Worth Deficit: £29,879 *Total Assets:* £8,672
Registered Office: 70 Woodside Road, Newbuildings, Co Londonderry, BT47 2QF
Major Shareholder: Giles Aaron Hay
Officers: Giles Aaron Hay [1997] Director/Security Manager

Ideas 2 Launch Limited
Incorporated: 21 February 2012
Net Worth Deficit: £77,460 *Total Assets:* £29,317
Registered Office: 30 Percy Street, London, W1T 2DB
Shareholders: Hua He; Sophia Nadur
Officers: Dr Hua HE [1962] Director/Doctor [French]; Sophia Nadur [1967] Director/Lawyer [British/Trinidadian]

Idris Limited
Incorporated: 9 April 1919
Registered Office: Breakspear Park, Breakspear Way, Hemel Hempstead, Herts, HP2 4TZ
Parent: Britvic Soft Drinks Limited
Officers: Judith Moore, Secretary; Mathew James Dunn [1974] Director/Chief Financial Officer; Peter Simon Litherland [1964] Director/Chief Executive; Alexandra Clare Thomas [1974] Director/General Counsel and Company Secretary

Ikoyi Chapmans Limited
Incorporated: 25 November 2015
Net Worth Deficit: £21,955 *Total Assets:* £3,848
Registered Office: 3 Theatre Court, Warwick, CV34 4DY
Shareholders: Garry Robinson; Michael John Robinson
Officers: Garry Robinson [1966] Director; Michael John Robinson [1963] Director

Immunoguardian Ltd
Incorporated: 29 October 2018
Registered Office: 20-22 Wenlock Road, London, N1 7GU
Major Shareholder: Zubaida Khan
Officers: Zubaida Khan [1969] Director/Carer

Impact Sports Science Limited
Incorporated: 7 October 2011
Net Worth Deficit: £41,880 *Total Assets:* £15,361
Registered Office: Unit 18 North Street Workshops, North Street, Stoke-Sub-Hamdon, Somerset, TA14 6QR
Major Shareholder: Clare Louise Gardner
Officers: Benjamin Peter Cobbett [1982] Director/Sports Scientist; Clare Louise Gardner [1974] Director

Imprint Marketing Ltd
Incorporated: 8 October 2007
Net Worth: £60,527 *Total Assets:* £63,781
Registered Office: 3 Burnham Grove, Bracknell, Berks, RG42 2LJ
Shareholders: Joanne Claire Pritchard; Gregory Noel Pritchard
Officers: Gregory Noel Pritchard, Secretary; Joanne Claire Pritchard [1980] Director

Infinite Session Ltd
Incorporated: 1 November 2017
Registered Office: 32 Chroma Mansions, 14 Penny Brookes Street, London, E20 1BP
Shareholders: Christopher John Hannaway; Thomas Eamon Hannaway
Officers: Christopher John Hannaway [1989] Director; Thomas Eamon Hannaway [1987] Director

Inginius Limited
Incorporated: 20 June 2016
Net Worth Deficit: £45,055 *Total Assets:* £26,116
Registered Office: 18 Wentworth Road, Thame, Oxon, OX9 3XQ
Shareholders: Andrew Graham Peerless; Michele Carole Bodart
Officers: Michele Bodart, Secretary; Michele Carole Bodart [1960] Director; Andrew Graham Peerless [1956] Director

Inmind Care Services Ltd
Incorporated: 15 August 2011
Registered Office: 1 Hornbeam Road, Hampton Hargate, Peterborough, Cambs, PE7 8FY
Officers: Candy Mary Bainn [1974] Director/Health & Social Care, Education and Training [Ghanaian]

Innorbit Ltd
Incorporated: 20 July 2009
Net Worth Deficit: £119,688 *Total Assets:* £11,239
Registered Office: 12 Dewe Lane, Burghfield, Reading, Berks, RG30 3SU
Shareholders: Ketan Harshad Joshi; Carol Joshi
Officers: Dr Ketan Joshi, Secretary; Carolynne Joshi [1959] Director; Dev Ketan Kong Joshi [1994] Director; Jay Ketan Kong Joshi [1992] Director; Dr Ketan Joshi [1961] Director

Innovate Energy Drinks Ltd
Incorporated: 4 September 2018
Registered Office: 1 St Margaret's Terrace, 1 St Margarets Road, Cheltenham, Glos, GL50 4DT
Shareholders: Conner Victor Crotchett; Angela Nunes
Officers: Conner Victor Crotchett [1974] Director [Irish]; Angela Nunes [1969] Director

Innovative Drinks Ltd
Incorporated: 15 April 2011
Net Worth: £6,940 *Total Assets:* £6,940
Registered Office: Chelsworth, Church Road, Hartley, Longfield, Kent, DA3 8DL
Shareholders: Sarbjeet Singh Bhangle; Harminder Singh Ahluwalia
Officers: Harminder Singh Ahluwalia [1982] Managing Director; Sarbjeet Singh Bhangle [1983] Managing Director; Fabrizio Parente [1960] Director [Italian]

The Intelligent Brews Company Ltd
Incorporated: 6 November 2017
Registered Office: 19-21 Balmoral Road, Belfast, BT12 6QA
Major Shareholder: Scott James Marks
Officers: Scott James Marks [1991] Director/Entrepreneur

Interactive World Ltd
Incorporated: 9 October 2012 *Employees:* 4
Net Worth Deficit: £37,685 *Total Assets:* £2,046
Registered Office: 19 The Mall, Ealing, London, W5 2PJ
Shareholders: Bogdan Jaminski; Marissa Jaminska
Officers: Marissa Jaminska [1959] Director [Polish]; Bogdan Jaminski [1960] Director [Polish]

International Soft Drinks Ltd
Incorporated: 13 April 2010
Registered Office: Morgan House, Brian Crescent, Porthcawl, Bridgend, CF36 5LE
Major Shareholder: Frederick Lindsay Morgan
Officers: Frederick Lindsay Morgan [1945] Director

Ipro Sport Exports Limited
Incorporated: 15 March 2016
Net Worth: £41,490 *Total Assets:* £392,796
Registered Office: 84 High Street, Broadstairs, Kent, CT10 1JJ
Shareholder: Michael Patrick Smyth
Officers: Andrew James Felton [1955] Director; Michael Patrick Smyth [1972] Director

Isle of Skye Spring Water Company Limited
Incorporated: 11 January 2017
Registered Office: Rhu An Dunain, Peinmore, Portree, Isle of Skye, IV51 9LG
Officers: William MacCaskill [1969] Director

Istok Foods Limited
Incorporated: 23 March 2018
Registered Office: 92 Mapleton Road, London, SW18 4GB
Major Shareholder: Gem Orr
Officers: Gem Orr [1994] Director

J.H.P Foods Limited
Incorporated: 15 July 1994
Net Worth: £121 *Total Assets:* £8,487
Registered Office: 2 The Comyns, Bushey Heath, Bushey, Herts, WD23 1HP
Officers: John Henry Pike, Secretary; Angela Cecilia Pike [1937] Director/Housewife; John Henry Pike [1936] Director/Farmer

Jamu Kitchen Ltd
Incorporated: 29 March 2016
Net Worth: £2,486 *Total Assets:* £3,733
Registered Office: Flat 13, 4 Triangle Road, London, E8 3SP
Major Shareholder: Tanita de Ruijt
Officers: Tanita de Ruijt [1990] Director/www.jamukitchen.co.uk [Dutch]

Jarrett Health Limited
Incorporated: 10 June 2014
Registered Office: Barnes Roffe Accountants, Charles Lake House, Claire Causeway, Crossways Business Park, Dartford, Kent, DA2 6QA
Officers: Pearl Ann Jarrett [1962] Director

JB Drinks Holdings Limited
Incorporated: 15 March 2012 Employees: 75
Net Worth Deficit: £11,792,126 Total Assets: £19,825,388
Registered Office: 17 Waterloo Place, London, SW1Y 4AR
Parent: Langholm Capital 2008 LLP
Officers: Rooney Anand [1964] Director/Chief Executive; Sarah Jane Baldwin [1970] Director/Chief Executive Officer; Albert Edward Bernard Wiegman [1952] Director

JB Drinks Limited
Incorporated: 15 March 2012
Net Worth Deficit: £12,076,634 Total Assets: £13,768,087
Registered Office: 17 Waterloo Place, London, SW1Y 4AR
Parent: JB Drinks Holdings Limited
Officers: Sarah Jane Baldwin [1970] Director/Chief Executive Officer; Albert Edward Bernard Wiegman [1952] Director

JDM Enterprises Ltd
Incorporated: 14 November 2002
Net Worth Deficit: £11,508 Total Assets: £403,323
Registered Office: Office 97 Viewpoint, Derwentside Business Centre, Consett, Co Durham, DH8 6BN
Major Shareholder: James Darrin Mead
Officers: James Darrin Mead [1971] Director

Jeffrey's Tonic Ltd
Incorporated: 28 February 2017 Employees: 2
Net Worth Deficit: £18,119 Total Assets: £13,583
Registered Office: 15 Lockwood View, Chester, CH2 1EZ
Shareholders: Michael Edward Robinson; Maureen Stella Robinson
Officers: Steven Frehley [1965] Sales Director; Louise Jayne Palmer [1965] Technical Director; Benjamin Edward Robinson [1983] Director; Maureen Stella Robinson [1956] Product Development Director; Michael Edward Robinson [1957] Managing Director

Jeffries Group Ltd
Incorporated: 26 November 2018
Registered Office: 15 Bath Lane, Leicester, LE3 5BF
Major Shareholder: Joseph Julian Levy
Officers: Lee Jeffries [1981] Director; Joseph Julian Levy [1981] Director/Property Developer; Richard Anthony Parker [1952] Financial Director; Leon Williamson [1980] Director

Jellani Ltd
Incorporated: 10 May 2018
Registered Office: 71-75 Shelton Street, London, WC2H 9JQ
Shareholders: Kayode Alynsola Obatbru; Bamidele Omotosho
Officers: Kayode Akinsola Obateru [1983] Director/IT Manager; Dr Bamidele Omotosho [1982] Director/Medical Doctor

JF Rabbit Ltd
Incorporated: 12 September 2014 Employees: 3
Net Worth: £283,886 Total Assets: £309,846
Registered Office: 20 King Street, Maidenhead, Berks, SL6 1DT
Shareholder: Felix Tanzer
Officers: Felix Tanzer [1985] Director

Johnson Supplies UK Ltd
Incorporated: 21 June 2018
Registered Office: Unit 41 Birch Road East, Witton, Birmingham, B6 7DA
Shareholder: Neville Johnson
Officers: Elajabeth Francis, Secretary; Neville Johnson [1967] Director/Production Manager

Jolly's Drinks Limited
Incorporated: 20 April 2018
Registered Office: Harscombe House, 1 Darklake View, Estover, Plymouth, PL6 7TL
Parent: Digmala Limited
Officers: Tara Michelle Bond [1967] Owner Director; Richard Alan Burrows [1971] Director/Business Owner

JSJuices Ltd
Incorporated: 2 January 2019
Registered Office: 71-75 Shelton Street, London, WC2H 9JQ
Major Shareholder: Javan Simpson
Officers: Javan Simpson [1994] Director

The Juice Collective Limited
Incorporated: 10 February 2016 Employees: 2
Net Worth Deficit: £119,630 Total Assets: £46,352
Registered Office: 6 Charlotte Street, Bath, BA1 2NE
Major Shareholder: Emma Frampton
Officers: Emma Frampton [1989] Director

The Juice Doctor Limited
Incorporated: 23 September 2015
Net Worth Deficit: £902 Total Assets: £17
Registered Office: 73 Bennetts Way, Shirley, Croydon, Surrey, CR0 8AF
Major Shareholder: Hewitt Grant
Officers: Hewitt Grant [1972] Director

Juice Dub Ltd.
Incorporated: 5 December 2011
Net Worth: £30,000 Total Assets: £30,000
Registered Office: 2 Cowslip Meadow, Northchurch, Berkhamsted, Herts, HP4 1FN
Officers: Matthew William Thompson [1980] Director/Catering Professional

Juice Fabulous Ltd
Incorporated: 31 August 2010
Previous: Impactalay Ltd
Registered Office: 5 Westbrook Cottages, Margate, Kent, CT9 5BE
Major Shareholder: Kelly O'Reilly
Officers: Kelly O'Reilly [1973] Director/Care Worker; Terence William Simpson [1941] Director

Juice Junkies Limited
Incorporated: 19 April 2018
Registered Office: Newbridge Cottage, Newport, TF10 8EG
Officers: Gareth Liam Hodgkins [1967] Director

Juice Man Limited
Incorporated: 24 June 2013
Net Worth: £86,877 Total Assets: £124,883
Registered Office: The Old Rectory, Church Street, Weybridge, Surrey, KT13 8DE
Major Shareholder: Andrew James Cooper
Officers: Andrew James Cooper [1981] Director/Mode & Actor

The Juice Shed Company Limited
Incorporated: 21 November 2013
Registered Office: Unit A, Third Avenue, Poynton Industrial Estate, Poynton, Stockport, Cheshire, SK12 1YL
Major Shareholder: Andrew Webb
Officers: Andrew John Webb [1959] Director/Manager

Juice Supply Limited
Incorporated: 20 March 2018
Registered Office: 2 Sunray Avenue, Herne Hill, London, SE24 9PY
Officers: George Hughes-Davies [1993] Director

Juicy Brands (UK) Ltd.
Incorporated: 27 February 2015
Registered Office: 20-22 Wenlock Road, London, N1 7GU
Officers: Lajos Janos Bese [1954] Director [Hungarian]

Jumpin' Juice Limited
Incorporated: 20 February 2003
Net Worth: £101,600 *Total Assets:* £193,670
Registered Office: 9 Forest Way, Ashtead, Surrey, KT21 1JN
Major Shareholder: Ivor Samuel Lyons
Officers: Shelley Atkins, Secretary; Ivor Samuel Lyons [1971] Director/Caterer

Jurassic Spring Water Ltd
Incorporated: 5 April 2013
Net Worth: £378 *Total Assets:* £5,351
Registered Office: Herston Yards Farm, Washpond Lane, Swanage, Dorset, BH19 3DJ
Major Shareholder: Robert Farmer
Officers: Robert Farmer [1952] Holiday Park Director

Jurassic Water Limited
Incorporated: 19 October 2015
Registered Office: Oakley Court, 6 Outram Road, Southsea, Hants, PO5 1QR
Major Shareholder: John Gerrard Cole
Officers: John Cole [1958] Director/Publican

Just Bee Drinks Limited
Incorporated: 8 May 2014
Net Worth: £83,076 *Total Assets:* £141,709
Registered Office: The Just Bee Hive, 1st Floor, Joshua Brooks Building, 106 Princess Street, Manchester, M1 6NG
Shareholders: Andrew James Sugden; Joe Harper
Officers: Ian Jonathan Bye [1963] Director; Timothy John Croston [1963] Director; Joseph Harper [1984] Director/Accountant; Simon Maxwell Saul Leonard [1978] Director; Andrew Sugden [1985] Director/Accountant

Just Drinking Water Ltd
Incorporated: 6 February 2006
Net Worth Deficit: £10,009 *Total Assets:* £51,348
Registered Office: 8 Pondside, Haywards Heath, W Sussex, RH16 4TH
Major Shareholder: Neil David Tomlinson
Officers: Neil David Tomlinson, Secretary; Alison Tomlinson [1964] Director; Neil David Tomlinson [1962] Director/Marketing Professional

Just Water Limited
Incorporated: 29 May 2002 *Employees:* 1
Net Worth: £17,310 *Total Assets:* £71,662
Registered Office: Leeward House, Fitzroy Road, Exeter Business Park, Exeter, Devon, EX1 3LJ
Shareholders: Colin John Dyer; Pauline Dianne Dyer
Officers: Pauline Dianne Dyer, Secretary; Colin John Dyer [1957] Director/Farmer; Pauline Dianne Dyer [1961] Director/Farmer

JW Production Limited
Incorporated: 26 June 2016
Net Worth Deficit: £238
Registered Office: 16 Manse Road, Mount Vernon, Glasgow, G32 0RA
Shareholders: Megan Ftizgerald; Daniel Quigley
Officers: Megan FitzGenerald [1989] Director

K K Draught Drinks Limited
Incorporated: 13 March 2006
Net Worth: £48,425 *Total Assets:* £130,400
Registered Office: Unit 16 James Little Street, Kilmarnock, E Ayrshire, KA1 4AT
Major Shareholder: James McDougall
Officers: James McDougall, Secretary; James McDougall [1968] Director; Andrew Murray [1979] Director

Kali Engineering Ltd
Incorporated: 13 February 2017
Net Worth Deficit: £11,777 *Total Assets:* £50
Registered Office: 71-75 Shelton Street, Covent Garden, London, WC2H 9JQ
Major Shareholder: Michael Dennis Kay
Officers: Michael Dennis Kay [1953] Director/Retired

Kapyani Limited
Incorporated: 9 November 2018
Registered Office: 152 City Road, London, EC1V 2NX
Shareholders: Amina Buba; Georgina Sowemimo
Officers: Amina Buba [1987] Director; Georgina Sowemimo [1989] Director [Nigerian]

Karkade Drinks Limited
Incorporated: 19 April 2017 *Employees:* 1
Net Worth Deficit: £4,136 *Total Assets:* £900
Registered Office: The White House, Clifton Marine Parade, Gravesend, Kent, DA11 0DY
Major Shareholder: Christopher Peter Bowen
Officers: Christopher Peter Bowen [1960] Director

Karma Cola UK Ltd
Incorporated: 25 February 2014 *Employees:* 8
Net Worth Deficit: £1,422,751 *Total Assets:* £788,206
Registered Office: Unit 1, 22 Pakenham Street, London, WC1X 0LB
Parent: Wayfairer Limited
Officers: Simon Cosmo Coley [1964] Director [New Zealander]; Christopher John Morrison [1960] Director [New Zealander]; Matthew John Morrison [1972] Director [New Zealander]; Prince Albert Tucker [1958] Director

Karma Water Company Limited
Incorporated: 12 April 2011 *Employees:* 1
Net Worth Deficit: £43,167 *Total Assets:* £16,462
Registered Office: Somerford Buildings, Norfolk Street, Sunderland, Tyne & Wear, SR1 1EE
Major Shareholder: Valerie Colling
Officers: Valerie Colling [1972] Director; Jonathan Paul Gold [1961] Director/Venture Capitalist

Keizen SDK Ltd
Incorporated: 27 December 2012
Previous: Justcocktail Ltd
Net Worth Deficit: £85,409 *Total Assets:* £8,520
Registered Office: 136 Rabournmead Drive, Northolt, Middlesex, UB5 6YL
Major Shareholder: Ade Teslim Lawal
Officers: Ade Teslim Lawal [1975] Director/Consultant; Toju Maduemezia [1978] Director/HR Consultant [Nigerian]

Kemetic Cooks Ltd
Incorporated: 11 January 2017
Registered Office: 52 Hardinge Crescent, London, SE18 6TB
Major Shareholder: Dwayne Thompson
Officers: Dwayne Thompson [1979] Director

Kendal Brewery Ltd
Incorporated: 19 September 2017
Registered Office: Masons Yard 24, 22 Stramongate, Kendal, Cumbria, LA9 4BN
Shareholders: Jonathan Gillis Ritson; Darren Lincoln
Officers: Darren Lincoln [1968] Director/Joiner

Kendal Cordials Limited
Incorporated: 6 July 2009
Net Worth Deficit: £5,188 Total Assets: £4,814
Registered Office: 25 Main Street, Staveley, Kendal, Cumbria, LA8 9LU
Major Shareholder: Helen Victoria Hindle
Officers: Helen Victoria Hindle [1970] Director

KGN London Ltd
Incorporated: 28 April 2014
Registered Office: Unit 23 Phoenix Distribution Park, Phoenix Way, Hounslow, Middlesex, TW5 9NB
Officers: Salinder Kaur Gill [1979] Director

Kimpton Apple Press Limited
Incorporated: 23 July 2012 Employees: 2
Net Worth Deficit: £41,888 Total Assets: £30,253
Registered Office: 90 Jermyn Street, London, SW1Y 6JD
Major Shareholder: John Henry Clarke
Officers: John Henry Clarke [1959] Director/Consultant

Kingdon Callea Ltd
Incorporated: 15 February 2019
Registered Office: Mentone, Timsbury Road, High Littleton, Bristol, BS39 6HL
Shareholder: Richard Geoffrey Howard
Officers: Savannah Alalia [1980] Director/Market Consultant; Richard Geoffrey Howard [1963] Director

Kings Farm Foods Limited
Incorporated: 11 August 2015
Net Worth Deficit: £24,700 Total Assets: £28,786
Registered Office: Kings Farm, Cranley Green, Eye, Suffolk, IP23 7NX
Major Shareholder: Matthew Graham Havers
Officers: Roxanne Radcliffe, Secretary; Matthew Graham Havers [1988] Director; Roxanne Radcliffe [1988] Director

Kingshill Mineral Water Ltd.
Incorporated: 11 July 2001 Employees: 12
Net Worth: £2,623,789 Total Assets: £4,255,915
Registered Office: 145 St Vincent Street, Glasgow, G2 5JF
Shareholder: Ronald Mark Hounsell
Officers: Paul Martin, Secretary; Ronald Mark Hounsell [1961] Director; Richard James Madden [1953] Director/Project Management Consultant; Paul Martin [1965] Director/Accountant

Kingsley Beverage Limited
Incorporated: 19 June 2015 Employees: 3
Net Worth Deficit: £563,458 Total Assets: £17,441,068
Registered Office: 2 Waterworth Road, Alwalton, Peterborough, Cambs, PE7 3AG
Officers: Christopher John Bradshaw [1969] Managing Director; Jose Manuel Da Camara [1964] Director/Chartered Accountant [Portuguese]; Rogerio Correia Diniz [1967] Director/Logistics Specialist [Portuguese]; Carla Hinge [1973] Director

Kingsley Partners Limited
Incorporated: 11 April 2011
Registered Office: 2 Crossways Business Centre, Bicester Road, Kingswood, Aylesbury, Bucks, HP18 0RA
Major Shareholder: Rebecca Louise Kingsley-Bates
Officers: Rebecca Kingsley-Bates, Secretary; Paul Kingsley-Bates [1965] Director; Rebecca Louise Kingsley-Bates [1968] Director

The Kingston upon Hull Liqour Company Limited
Incorporated: 9 January 2017
Registered Office: 51 Chantry Way East, Swanland, North Ferriby, E Yorks, HU14 3QF
Officers: Iain Todd [1969] Director

Kixse Limited
Incorporated: 26 September 2016
Registered Office: 35 Adelaide Grove, East Cowes, Isle of Wight, PO32 6DD
Officers: Claire Western, Secretary; Philip Edward Palmer [1949] Director; LEA Western [1967] Director

Koala Karma UK Limited
Incorporated: 17 October 2017
Registered Office: 6 Kings Orchard, Brightwell-Cum-Sotwell, Wallingford, Oxon, OX10 0QY
Shareholder: Rachel Mary Rowntree
Officers: Gary Booker [1970] Director; Rachel Mary Rowntree [1978] Director

Kolibri Drinks Limited
Incorporated: 7 September 2015
Previous: Dexos Drinks Ltd.
Net Worth Deficit: £55,047 Total Assets: £400,711
Registered Office: 2nd Floor, 130 Shaftesbury Avenue, London, W1D 5EU
Parent: Dexos Holdings Limited
Officers: Peter Charles Clark [1961] Director/Accountant; Kamila Laura Sitwell [1974] Director/Soft Drinks Expert [Polish]; Vincent Lucien Sitwell [1971] Director/Marketing Agency

Kombucha Kat Ltd
Incorporated: 6 December 2016 Employees: 1
Net Worth: £5,647 Total Assets: £12,047
Registered Office: 8 King Edward Street, Oxford, OX1 4HL
Major Shareholder: Sam Edmund Martingell
Officers: Paul Edmund Martingell, Secretary; Sam Edmund Martingell [1985] Director/Owner

Kombuchaye Ltd
Incorporated: 21 May 2018
Registered Office: 4e Stoneybank Terrace, Musselburgh, E Lothian, EH21 6NL
Officers: Lewis Jones [1993] Director/Chef

Kompassion Ltd
Incorporated: 29 March 2018
Registered Office: Unit 30, 86b Wallis Road, London, E9 5LN
Major Shareholder: Jonathan Alexander Katona
Officers: Jonathan Alexander Katona [1987] Director [Hungarian]

Konings Juices & Drinks UK Limited
Incorporated: 1 June 2016 *Employees:* 89
Net Worth: £1,385,239 *Total Assets:* £19,725,720
Registered Office: Konings Juices & Drinks UK Ltd, Stoke Road, Boxford, Sudbury, Suffolk, CO10 5AF
Parent: New-Kon NV
Officers: Dirk Stany Urbain Jozef Ghislain Maris [1964] Director/Chief Executive Officer [Belgian]; Anne Marina Moors [1988] Director [Belgian]; Luc Leon Alfons Nulens [1964] Director/Chief Operating Officer [Belgian]

Konon Limited
Incorporated: 2 February 2017
Net Worth: £11,877,676 *Total Assets:* £13,540,305
Registered Office: Unit 5 Lewis House, School Road, London, NW10 6TD
Parent: Aphea Fund Ltd-Mayfair Group Fund
Officers: Andreas Yanakopoulos [1963] Director [Greek]

Koolvibes Limited
Incorporated: 30 March 2016 *Employees:* 2
Net Worth Deficit: £1,475 *Total Assets:* £18,448
Registered Office: 776-778 International House, Barking Road, London, E13 9PJ
Shareholder: Gillian Gibbs
Officers: Gillian Gibbs, Secretary; Gillian Gibbs-Sawyers [1974] Director/Registered Nurse; Michael Sawyers [1978] Director/Chef

Kore Kombucha Ltd
Incorporated: 5 September 2018
Registered Office: 3 Read Mead, Glastonbury, Somerset, BA6 8DN
Shareholders: Geoffrey Nigel John King; Aniko King
Officers: Aniko King [1976] Production Director; Geoffrey Nigel John King [1953] Sales Director

Korko Limited
Incorporated: 6 October 2017
Registered Office: 9FD Maidstone Road, Blue Bell Hill, Chatham, Kent, ME5 9QP
Major Shareholder: Hermina Korko Lartey
Officers: Hermina Korko Lartey [1977] Director/Cook

Kubera Group International Ltd
Incorporated: 7 January 2019
Registered Office: 13 Wareham Road, Lytchett Matravers, Poole, Dorset, BH16 6FH
Major Shareholder: Joshua Delano Taylor
Officers: Joshua Delano Taylor [1993] Director

Kuka Coffee Ltd
Incorporated: 9 September 2016
Net Worth Deficit: £2,423 *Total Assets:* £19,651
Registered Office: Glebe Farm, Great Rissington, Cheltenham, Glos, GL54 2LH
Shareholders: John Arthur Bowden; George Hugh Rynn Arthur Spooner
Officers: Nicholas Beer [1994] Director/Barista; John Arthur Bowden [1994] Director/Events Manager; George Hugh Rynn Arthur Spooner [1994] Director/Entrepreneur

Kul-Kis Limited
Incorporated: 13 March 1985 *Employees:* 3
Net Worth: £174,405 *Total Assets:* £239,760
Registered Office: 1a Alexandra Park Avenue, Belfast, BT15 3AU
Major Shareholder: John Elliott
Officers: John Elliott, Secretary; John Elliott [1960] Director/Chemist; Rosemary Francis Elliott [1960] Director/Communications

Lady Eden Ltd
Incorporated: 5 July 2018
Registered Office: The Stables, Station Drive, Kirby Muxloe, Leicester, LE9 2ET
Major Shareholder: Simon Phillip Michaels
Officers: Simon Phillip Michaels [1972] Director/Businessman

Ladybird (Drinks) Limited
Incorporated: 7 July 2009
Registered Office: 1a First Avenue, Ashton on Ribble, Preston, Lancs, PR2 1JQ
Major Shareholder: Matthew John Watkinson
Officers: Matthew John Watkinson [1986] Director

Leanteen Limited
Incorporated: 24 December 2018
Registered Office: 318 Norbury Avenue, London, SW16 3RL
Major Shareholder: Hamza Zaveri
Officers: Hamza Zaveri [1990] Director/Lawyer

The Lemon Factory Ltd
Incorporated: 11 May 2018
Registered Office: 193 Friary Road, Birmingham, B20 1AA
Shareholders: Aneil Lal; Perjeet Nijran
Officers: Aneil Lal [1987] Director; Perjeet Nijran [1986] Director

Life Science Limited
Incorporated: 30 December 1996
Registered Office: 10 Forest Vale Road, Forest Vale Industrial Estate, Cinderford, Glos, GL14 2PH
Major Shareholder: Executors of Mr Alvin Clive Matthews
Officers: David John Twiss [1975] Director

Lifeline Holdings Limited
Incorporated: 8 October 2018
Registered Office: 201 Sphere Apartments, 25 St Paul's Way, London, E3 4YE
Shareholders: Christen Dali; Khaleelah Estella-Jean Jones
Officers: Christen Dali [1992] Director [Belgian]; Dr Khaleelah Estella-Jean Jones [1988] Director [American]

Limonada Mathe Limited
Incorporated: 23 July 2014
Net Worth: £30,138 *Total Assets:* £39,033
Registered Office: 3rd Floor, 86-90 Paul Street, London, EC2A 4NE
Shareholders: Jacopo Pintaldi; Adrien Meyer
Officers: Thomas Alexander Anderson [1990] Director; Hortense Decaux [1990] Director/Consultant [French]; Adrien Meyer [1992] Director [French]; Jacopo Pintaldi [1991] Director [Italian]

Linsenlinsen Limited
Incorporated: 8 March 2016
Net Worth: £10,271 *Total Assets:* £57,532
Registered Office: 50b Westbourne Gardens, London, W2 5NS
Major Shareholder: Caroline Abdon
Officers: Anna Caroline Abdon [1981] Director [Swedish]

Lintaru DGL Ltd
Incorporated: 7 May 2018
Registered Office: 15 Tonbridge Crescent, Queensbury, London, HA3 9LA
Major Shareholder: Alexandru Lintaru
Officers: Alexandru Lintaru [1988] Director/Driver [Romanian]

Lionade Ltd
Incorporated: 27 June 2017
Registered Office: 95 Kent Road, Grays, Essex, RM17 6DE
Officers: Eugen Guglia [1950] Director/Consultant [Austrian]

Liquid Fusion Limited
Incorporated: 23 April 2012
Net Worth: £3,527 *Total Assets:* £171,998
Registered Office: Wey Court West, Union Road, Farnham, Surrey, GU9 7PT
Major Shareholder: Edward Swete
Officers: Edward Swete [1981] Managing Director

Liquid Ice Water Company Limited
Incorporated: 3 March 1997
Registered Office: 108a Lammas Street, Carmarthen, Dyfed, SA31 3AP
Officers: David Richard Griffiths, Secretary; Terry Baugh Griffiths [1946] Director

Little Miracles (International) Limited
Incorporated: 29 November 2012
Net Worth Deficit: £901,443
Registered Office: Aston House, Cornwall Avenue, London, N3 1LF
Major Shareholder: Per Algot Enevoldsen
Officers: Mark Jonathan Catton [1987] Director; Frederik Senger [1985] Director [Danish]

Little Miracles Drinks Limited
Incorporated: 15 October 2012
Net Worth Deficit: £10,206,962
Registered Office: Aston House, Cornwall Avenue, London, N3 1LF
Major Shareholder: Mark Jonathan Catton
Officers: Mark Jonathan Catton [1967] Director

The Live Kindly Drinks Company Limited
Incorporated: 4 February 2019
Registered Office: 74 The Close, Norwich, NR1 4DR
Parent: Arrhenius Holdings Limited
Officers: Robert Bell [1979] Director/Chartered Accountant; Jonathon Mark Lansley [1962] Director/Business Manager

Liver Health UK Ltd.
Incorporated: 4 April 2016 *Employees:* 1
Net Worth: £45,631 *Total Assets:* £62,543
Registered Office: Floor 3, 1-4 Atholl Crescent, Edinburgh, EH3 8HA
Shareholders: De Silva Asanka; Pharos Limited
Officers: Igor Pierre Boyadjian [1974] Managing Director [French]; Harald Peter Burchardt [1986] Director [German]; Asanka de Silva [1977] Director/Marketer

Liveras Limited
Incorporated: 6 January 2011
Registered Office: The Grove, Hadley Green Road, Barnet, Herts, EN5 5PY
Major Shareholder: Luke John Liveras
Officers: Luke John Liveras [1991] Director

Liverpool Canning Company Limited
Incorporated: 19 December 2018
Registered Office: The London Office, First Floor, 85 Great Portland Street, London, W1W 7LT
Major Shareholder: Dominic Peter Clive Berger
Officers: Natalia Franchini Gliorsi, Secretary; Dominic Peter Clive Berger [1969] Director; Ian Michael Minton [1982] Director

Livitus Limited
Incorporated: 27 December 2017
Registered Office: 2 St Philips Place, Birmingham, B3 2RB
Shareholders: Oyedele Abidemi Olaoye; Thomas Aymen Jabrane
Officers: Dr Thomas Aymen Jabrane [1982] Director/Entrepreneur [French]; Oyedele Abidemi Olaoye [1985] Director/Entrepreneur

Lixir Ltd
Incorporated: 22 February 2017 *Employees:* 2
Net Worth Deficit: £25,149 *Total Assets:* £16,022
Registered Office: 20-22 Wenlock Road, London, N1 7GU
Shareholders: Jordan John Palmer; Matthew Devendra Mahatme
Officers: Matthew Devendra Mahatme [1993] Director; Jordan John Palmer [1994] Director; Samuel Paul Romaine [1995] Director

Llanllyr Water Company Limited
Incorporated: 13 October 1998
Net Worth: £733,033 *Total Assets:* £2,652,248
Registered Office: Talsarn, Lampeter, Ceredigion, SA48 8QB
Parent: Llanllyr Source Limited
Officers: Ian Michael Stuart Downie, Secretary; Patrick Robert Cooper Gee [1963] Director; Seth Romans [1974] Director [American]; John Frank Wallington [1972] Director

Loch Ness Drinks Ltd
Incorporated: 8 March 2017
Net Worth Deficit: £2,913 *Total Assets:* £977
Registered Office: Beinn Bhurie, 3 Hillpark Brae, Munlochy, Ross & Cromarty, IV8 8PL
Officers: John Philip Oag [1970] Managing Director

Loch Ness Limited
Incorporated: 15 September 2016
Registered Office: 3 Hillpark Brae, Munlochy, Ross & Cromarty, IV8 8PL
Officers: John Philip Oag [1970] Director/Sales

Loch Ness Tonic Ltd
Incorporated: 17 January 2017
Registered Office: Beinn Bhurie, Hillpark Brae, Munlochy, Ross-shire, IV8 8PL
Major Shareholder: John Philip Oag
Officers: John Philip Oag [1970] Director

Loch Ness Tonic Water Ltd
Incorporated: 17 January 2017
Registered Office: Beinn Bhurie, Hillpark Brae, Munlochy, Ross-shire, IV8 8PL
Major Shareholder: John Philip Oag
Officers: John Philip Oag [1970] Director

Loch Ness Water Ltd
Incorporated: 22 April 2015
Net Worth Deficit: £65,823 *Total Assets:* £77,857
Registered Office: Beinn Bhurie, Hillpark Brae, Munlochy, Ross-shire, IV8 8PL
Shareholders: John Philip Oag; Donna Park
Officers: John Philip Oag [1970] Director/Sales

Loft 68 Vintage Ltd
Incorporated: 14 July 2015
Previous: Experience Alchemy Ltd.
Registered Office: 15 Bell Close, Cublington, Leighton Buzzard, Beds, LU7 0LH
Officers: Jordan Grace [1993] Director/Beverages

London Botanical Drinks Limited
Incorporated: 16 March 2018
Registered Office: 39-45 Bermondsey Street, London, SE1 3XF
Shareholders: Paul Mathew; Bloodandsand Limited
Officers: Daniel Paul Hatton [1982] Ventures Director; Paul Mathew [1976] Director/Drinks Consultant

London Essence Company Limited (The)
Incorporated: 4 October 1918
Registered Office: 9 Roding Road, Beckton, London, E6 6LF
Parent: Britvic Soft Drinks Limited
Officers: Judith Moore, Secretary; Mathew James Dunn [1974] Director/Chief Financial Officer; Peter Simon Litherland [1964] Director/Chief Executive; Alexandra Clare Thomas [1974] Director/General Counsel and Company Secretary

London Fashion Industry Limited
Incorporated: 26 July 2004
Registered Office: 18 Sandtoft Close, Lincoln, LN6 3PE
Major Shareholder: Jeb Screw You
Officers: Jebaraj Screw You [1962] Director/Businessman

Lord Eden Beverages Ltd
Incorporated: 5 January 2018
Registered Office: The Stables, Station Drive, Kirby Muxloe, Leicester, LE9 2ET
Major Shareholder: Simon Phillip Michaels
Officers: Simon Phillip Michaels [1972] Director/Businessman

Lord Eden Ltd
Incorporated: 5 January 2018
Registered Office: The Stables, Station Drive, Kirby Muxloe, Leicester, LE9 2ET
Major Shareholder: Simon Phillip Michaels
Officers: Simon Phillip Michaels [1972] Director/Businessman

Lothian Shelf (674) Limited
Incorporated: 23 October 2009
Registered Office: Stirling Street, Blackford, Perthshire, PH4 1QA
Officers: Mark Alexander Steven, Secretary; Maher Al Tajir [1957] Director; Leslie Montgomery [1963] Director/Chief Executive

Lough Neagh Distillers - 1837 Ltd
Incorporated: 26 November 2018
Registered Office: Inverlodge, 51 Bannfoot Road, Derrytrasna, Co Armagh, BT66 6PH
Major Shareholder: Vernon Fox
Officers: Vernon Fox [1973] Director [Irish]

Love Tide Water Limited
Incorporated: 11 July 2016
Registered Office: Somerford Buildings, Norfolk Street, Sunderland, Tyne & Wear, SR1 1EE
Major Shareholder: Valerie Colling
Officers: Valerie Colling [1972] Director

Love Tonic Ltd
Incorporated: 3 October 2018
Registered Office: 135 Culduthel Road, Inverness, IV2 4EF
Shareholders: Donald Sinclair Lawson; Gary Ronald Morren
Officers: Donald Sinclair Lawson [1959] Director; Gary Ronald Morren [1967] Director

Lovely Drinks Limited
Incorporated: 1 June 2007 *Employees:* 3
Net Worth: £115 *Total Assets:* £67,554
Registered Office: The Old Sawmill, Home Farm, Barrow Court Lane, Barrow Gurney, Bristol, BS48 3RW
Major Shareholder: Richard Antony Freeman
Officers: Richard Antony Freeman [1955] Director/Consultant

Lowe Bros. (Cardiff) Limited
Incorporated: 19 June 1959 *Employees:* 3
Net Worth: £167,224 *Total Assets:* £276,561
Registered Office: 27 Azalea Close, Cardiff, CF23 7HR
Officers: David John Sansom, Secretary; David Paul Cheetham [1961] Director; David John Sansom [1958] Director/Secretary

Lucid Beverage Research Ltd
Incorporated: 26 November 2018
Registered Office: Kemp House, 160 City Road, London, EC1V 2NX
Major Shareholder: Saul Johnson
Officers: Saul Johnson, Secretary; Saul Johnson [1993] Director/Teacher

Lucozade Ribena Suntory Exports Limited
Incorporated: 8 August 2013 *Employees:* 3
Net Worth: £40,000 *Total Assets:* £3,415,000
Registered Office: 2 Longwalk Road, Stockley Park, Uxbridge, Middlesex, UB11 1BA
Parent: Lucozade Ribena Suntory Limited
Officers: Louis-Francois Amand Gombert [1967] Director [French]; Mary Elizabeth Guest [1980] Director; Carol Robert [1979] Director; Peter James Thomlinson [1967] Director/Chief Financial Officer

Lucozade Ribena Suntory Limited
Incorporated: 10 July 2013 *Employees:* 720
Net Worth: £864,452,992 *Total Assets:* £1,394,434,944
Registered Office: 2 Longwalk Road, Stockley Park, Uxbridge, Middlesex, UB11 1BA
Parent: Suntory Beverage & Food Limited
Officers: Mary Guest, Secretary; Mary Elizabeth Guest [1980] Director and Company Secretary; Peter John Harding [1964] Director/Chief Operating Officer; Toby Peter McKeever [1969] Director; Jaime Antonio Mussons Freixas [1961] Director/Chief Marketing Officer [Spanish]; Carol Robert [1979] Director; Takayuki Sanno [1968] Director [Japanese]; Craig William Shelden [1964] Director/Chief Financial Officer [Australian]; Tetsu Tanaka [1967] Director [Japanese]; Peter James Thomlinson [1967] Director/Chief Financial Officer; Yuji Yamazaki [1957] Director [Japanese]

LUHV Drinks Limited
Incorporated: 5 July 2016
Previous: LUHV Limited
Registered Office: 7 Bournemouth Road, Chandler's Ford, Eastleigh, Hants, SO53 3DA
Parent: LUHV Drinks Limited
Officers: Christopher Beech [1982] Managing Director

LUHV Limited
Incorporated: 5 February 2015
Previous: LUHV Drinks Limited
Net Worth Deficit: £38,369 *Total Assets:* £5,817
Registered Office: 7 Bournemouth Road, Chandler's Ford, Eastleigh, Hants, SO53 3DA
Major Shareholder: Christopher Beech
Officers: Christopher Beech [1982] Managing Director and Salesman

Lupe Kombucha Ltd.
Incorporated: 17 March 2017
Registered Office: Flat 15a, 91 Gloucester Terrace, London, W2 3HB
Officers: Elaine Emily Ho [1988] Director/Founder

Lurvills Delight Limited
Incorporated: 24 July 2015
Net Worth Deficit: £15,396 Total Assets: £16,274
Registered Office: The Maltings, East Tyndall Street, Cardiff, CF24 5EA
Major Shareholder: David John Steward
Officers: David John Steward [1962] Director/Sales and Marketing

Luscombe Drinks Limited
Incorporated: 30 November 1987
Net Worth: £1,705,460 Total Assets: £3,015,460
Registered Office: Luscombe Drinks Limited, Dean Court, Lower Dean, Buckfastleigh, Devon, TQ11 0LT
Shareholder: Gabriel Luscombe David
Officers: James Mark Spreadbury, Secretary; Gabriel Luscombe David [1965] Director; Venetia David [1973] Director; James Spreadbury [1984] Director/Chartered Accountant

Luxbev Limited
Incorporated: 4 October 2017
Registered Office: 71-75 Shelton Street, Covent Garden, London, WC2H 9JQ
Major Shareholder: Hernando Ramirez
Officers: Hernando Ramirez, Secretary; Hernando Ramirez [1969] Director [French]

Luxuryshakes Ltd
Incorporated: 18 October 2017
Registered Office: Luxuryshakes Ltd, Suite 146, Churchill House, Stirling Way, Borehamwood, Herts, WD6 2HP
Major Shareholder: Andrew Jonathan Sherick
Officers: Andrew Jonathan Sherick [1971] Director

LVS Bottling Limited
Incorporated: 10 January 2013
Net Worth Deficit: £455,770 Total Assets: £211,197
Registered Office: Unit 1A Townfoot Industrial Estate, Brampton, Cumbria, CA8 1SW
Major Shareholder: Navinder Kaur Gill
Officers: Navinder Kaur Gill [1977] Director/Computer Analyst

Lytewater Limited
Incorporated: 26 February 2018
Registered Office: 78 Park Lane, Poynton, Stockport, Cheshire, SK12 1RE
Major Shareholder: Simon Gleave
Officers: Simon Gleave [1965] Director/Business Manager

Ma3 Drinks Ltd
Incorporated: 11 February 2019
Registered Office: 152 Forest Road, London, E17 6JQ
Major Shareholder: Uzma Khan
Officers: Uzma Khan [1983] Director

MacKay & Partners (UK) Limited
Incorporated: 8 February 2005
Net Worth: £3,560 Total Assets: £4,219
Registered Office: 24 St Birinus Court, Gassons Road, Lechlade, Glos, GL7 3BU
Officers: Sarah Louise MacKay, Company Secretary; Hugh Kenneth St Clair MacKay [1955] Director/Accountant

Macro Munch Ltd
Incorporated: 29 March 2018
Registered Office: Suite 52, 51 Pinfold Street, Birmingham, B2 4AY
Major Shareholder: Idrees Rabani
Officers: Idrees Rabani [1995] Director

Mad Dog Drinks Limited
Incorporated: 17 March 2011
Net Worth Deficit: £72,766 Total Assets: £32,129
Registered Office: 99 Westmead Road, Sutton, Surrey, SM1 4HX
Major Shareholder: Ross Leonard Van Geest
Officers: Gillian Denise Van Geest, Secretary; Richard Donald John Bennett [1970] Director; Ross Leonard Van Geest [1979] Director

Made By Brave Limited
Incorporated: 18 May 2017
Net Worth Deficit: £1,770 Total Assets: £57,843
Registered Office: Lampool Corner, Maresfield, Uckfield, E Sussex, TN22 3DS
Shareholders: Kate Rebecca Prince; Annelie Whitfield
Officers: Kate Rebecca Prince [1973] Director; Annelie Whitfield [1974] Director/Naturopath

Made By Noble Limited
Incorporated: 28 June 2016
Net Worth Deficit: £13,575 Total Assets: £36,588
Registered Office: Lampool Corner, Maresfield, Uckfield, E Sussex, TN22 3DS
Shareholder: Kate Rebecca Prince
Officers: Kate Rebecca Prince [1973] Director; Simon Charles Prince [1972] Director

Mag Marketing Limited
Incorporated: 27 February 2019
Registered Office: 1 Huxley Terrace, Bowdon, Altrincham, Cheshire, WA14 3ET
Officers: Rebecca Martin [1980] Director/Sales and Marketing Consultant

Magic Potion Energy Drinks International Company Limited
Incorporated: 10 November 2016
Net Worth Deficit: £1,318 Total Assets: £382
Registered Office: 17 Bufferys Close, Solihull, W Midlands, B91 3UX
Major Shareholder: Jatinder Singh Sehmi
Officers: Mandeep Singh Sehmi, Secretary; Jatinder Singh Sehmi [1978] Director

Maine Soft Drinks Limited
Incorporated: 13 April 1987 Employees: 107
Net Worth: £715,733 Total Assets: £2,167,888
Registered Office: 35 Ballymena Road, Ballymoney, Co Antrim, BT53 7EX
Shareholders: Samuel Harkness; Bruce Harkness
Officers: Samuel Harkness, Secretary; Bruce Harkness [1947] Director; Derrick Harkness [1971] Director; Jonathan Harkness [1974] Director; Priscilla Ann Harkness [1948] Director; Samuel Harkness [1937] Director

Malvern Bottling Works Limited
Incorporated: 22 September 2017
Registered Office: Old Bottling Works, 10 Belle Vue Terrace, Malvern, Worcs, WR14 4PZ
Parent: Be Gemwater Ltd
Officers: Richard Kirk Polack [1963] Director

The Malvern Water Company Limited
Incorporated: 13 October 2014
Registered Office: The Old Coach House, Parkway, Ledbury, Herefords, HR8 2JG
Major Shareholder: Guy Deacon Trezona
Officers: Guy Deacon Trezona [1961] Director

Mambo Drinks Limited
Incorporated: 18 February 2014
Previous: Sales Inspiration Limited
Net Worth: £187,243 *Total Assets:* £271,370
Registered Office: 4 Swansea Road, Penllergaer, Swansea, SA4 9AQ
Officers: Samantha Atkinson [1985] Director/Commercial Manager; David Hugh Jones [1964] Managing Director

Man Up Energy Limited
Incorporated: 17 December 2012
Registered Office: 70 Latham Road, Bexleyheath, Kent, DA6 7NQ
Major Shareholder: Daniel Alexander Albert McGovern
Officers: Daniel Alexander Albert McGovern [1991] Director

Mandora St. Clements Limited
Incorporated: 11 May 1921
Registered Office: Crossley Drive, Magna Park, Milton Keynes, Bucks, MK17 8FL
Parent: A.G. Barr P.L.C.
Officers: Julie Anne Barr, Company Secretary; Stuart Lorimer [1966] Finance Director; Roger Alexander White [1965] Director/Chief Executive

Mangogo Ltd
Incorporated: 2 January 2019
Registered Office: John Banner Centre, 620 Attercliffe Road, Sheffield, S9 3QS
Major Shareholder: Jerome Tagore Jacob
Officers: Jerome Tagore Jacob [1991] Director/Consultant

Marah Drinks Limited
Incorporated: 1 February 2019
Registered Office: 804 Mast Quay, London, SE18 5NP
Shareholders: Michael Talabi; Devillers Muambamakasa
Officers: Devillers Muambamakasa [1990] Director/Insurance Underwriter; Michael Talabi [1991] Director/Project Manager

Marbella Cartel Ltd
Incorporated: 21 October 2014
Previous: Eden Corp Ltd
Registered Office: 132 Headfield Road, Dewsbury, W Yorks, WF12 9JH
Shareholders: Mohammed Ahmed Riaz; Sabbir Umar
Officers: Mohammed Ahmed Riaz [1990] Director

March Foods Limited
Incorporated: 26 January 2009 *Employees:* 145
Net Worth: £2,034,815 *Total Assets:* £4,238,437
Registered Office: 7 Martin Avenue, March, Cambs, PE15 0AY
Major Shareholder: Robert Alan Carruthers Belcher
Officers: Stephen Dor, Secretary; Robert Alan Carruthers Belcher [1955] Director; Ian Crosby [1978] Business Development Director; Stephen Dor [1973] Director/Accountant; James Paterson Robertson [1958] Director

Mariage Freres Royaume Uni Limited
Incorporated: 20 June 2012 *Employees:* 11
Net Worth Deficit: £559,403 *Total Assets:* £4,155,805
Registered Office: 38 King Street, London, WC2E 8JS
Shareholders: Kittichat Sangmanee; Peangjai Chanpanich
Officers: Franck Michel Desains [1960] Director [French]; Kittichat Sangmanee [1954] Director/Company President [Thai]

Marley and Barley Ltd
Incorporated: 23 February 2016
Registered Office: Clayton Farm, Church Lane, Peasmarsh, Rye, E Sussex, TN31 6XS
Shareholders: Stephen Charles Reeve; Jaqueline Reeve
Officers: Jaqueline Reeve [1947] Director/Farmer; Stephen Charles Reeve [1978] Director/Farmer

Marlish Waters Limited
Incorporated: 15 October 2013 *Employees:* 4
Net Worth: £77,938 *Total Assets:* £452,257
Registered Office: 17 Walkergate, Berwick upon Tweed, Northumberland, TD15 1DJ
Shareholders: Elizabeth Walton; Joseph Oliver Evans
Officers: Joseph Oliver Evans [1989] Director/Chemical Engineer; Elizabeth Walton [1954] Director/Farmer

Mawsons Traditional Drinks Limited
Incorporated: 1 February 2005
Net Worth Deficit: £134,395 *Total Assets:* £174
Registered Office: St Crispin House, St Crispin Way, Haslingden, Rossendale, Lancs, BB4 4PW
Officers: Joseph William Mawson [1934] Director/Shopkeeper; Stuart John Taylor [1986] Director/General Manager; Susan Heather Taylor [1960] Director/Company Secretary

Mayag Brands Ltd
Incorporated: 7 October 2016
Net Worth Deficit: £2,569 *Total Assets:* £10,326
Registered Office: 60 Hillcrest Road, London, E17 4AP
Major Shareholder: Abdullah Mustafa Mahmud
Officers: Abdullah Mustafa Mahmud [1972] Director/Entrepreneur

Maynard House Limited
Incorporated: 5 August 2003
Previous: Williamson Enterprises Limited
Net Worth: £79,295 *Total Assets:* £144,402
Registered Office: The Orchards, The Street, Bradfield Combust, Bury St Edmunds, Suffolk, IP30 0LP
Major Shareholder: Clive Edmund Williamson
Officers: Clive Edmund Williamson [1969] Director

MB Drinks Ltd
Incorporated: 15 January 2019
Registered Office: 5 Evington Lane, Leicester, LE5 5PQ
Major Shareholder: Noreen Mahboob
Officers: Noreen Mahboob [1985] Director

MCSS Investments Ltd
Incorporated: 25 January 2018
Net Worth: £100 *Total Assets:* £100
Registered Office: 7 Majendie Close, Speen, Newbury, Berks, RG14 1QX
Shareholders: Melanie Victoria Millin; Craig Ian Coleman
Officers: Melanie Victoria Millin [1980] Director

ME Letric Ltd
Incorporated: 29 August 2014
Net Worth: £8,572 *Total Assets:* £12,914
Registered Office: 25 Millfield, Livingston, W Lothian, EH54 7AR
Officers: Andy Murray [1972] Director/Electrical

Mello Drinks Ltd
Incorporated: 23 September 2011
Net Worth Deficit: £85,015 *Total Assets:* £92,310
Registered Office: 53 Fountain Street, Manchester, M2 2AN
Shareholders: Shahab Natanzi; Rose Aldean
Officers: Rose Aldean [1987] Director; Sophie Lund [1987] Director; Dr Shahab Natanzi [1982] Director

The Mendip Bottle Limited
Incorporated: 25 May 2006
Registered Office: Bishopbrook House, Cathedral Avenue, Wells, Somerset, BA5 1FD
Major Shareholder: Edward Charles Hay
Officers: Anna Hay, Secretary; Edward Charles Hay [1976] Director; Sarah Jane Hay [1973] Director

Mendip Hills Mineral Water Limited
Incorporated: 22 December 2004
Registered Office: Carscliffe, Upper Draycott Road, Cheddar, Somerset, BS27 3YL
Shareholder: Tabitha Sarah-Jane Urch
Officers: Virginia Urch, Secretary; David Lawrence Urch [1951] Director; Duncan Winston Urch [1980] Director; Tabitha Sarah-Jane Urch [1978] Director

Mendip Hills Spring Water Limited
Incorporated: 22 December 2004
Registered Office: Carscliffe, Upper Draycott Road, Cheddar, Somerset, BS27 3YL
Shareholder: Tabitha Sarah-Jane Urch
Officers: Virginia Urch, Secretary; David Lawrence Urch [1951] Director; Duncan Winston Urch [1980] Director; Tabitha Sarah-Jane Urch [1978] Director

The Meon Spirit Company Ltd
Incorporated: 8 April 2013
Net Worth Deficit: £65,241 *Total Assets:* £158,721
Registered Office: Hill Farm, Droxford Road, Swanmore, Southampton, SO32 2PY
Major Shareholder: Dominic William Swinburne Dobson
Officers: Dominic William Swinburne Dobson [1977] Director/Chartered Surveyor

Merrily Mulled Ltd
Incorporated: 27 May 2016
Net Worth Deficit: £19,069 *Total Assets:* £5,772
Registered Office: 77 St Gabriels Road, London, NW2 4DU
Officers: Charlotte Laroque Bendel [1977] Director; Margaret Linn Rothstein [1950] Director [Canadian]; Nicholas Roy Sandler [1964] Director

Merrydown PLC
Incorporated: 22 November 1946 *Employees:* 1
Net Worth: £26,722,968 *Total Assets:* £51,247,252
Registered Office: 5230 Valiant Court, Delta Way, Brockworth, Gloucester, GL3 4FE
Parent: SHS Group Ltd
Officers: Arthur William Richmond, Secretary; Elaine Birchall [1966] Director [Irish]; Arthur William Richmond [1966] Director/Accountant; Joseph Sloan [1946] Director/Group Chairman

Methuselah 969 Limited
Incorporated: 10 August 1995
Registered Office: 95 Grassendale Avenue, Plymouth, PL2 2JP
Officers: Roger James Mitchell, Secretary/Counsellor; Rachael Jane Mitchell [1968] Director/Manager; Caroline Jane Turner [1951] Director/Health & Nutrition

Metro Drinks Limited
Incorporated: 25 October 1999 *Employees:* 8
Net Worth: £413,432 *Total Assets:* £1,325,904
Registered Office: The Workshop, Endlewick House, Arlington, E Sussex, BN26 6RU
Shareholders: Paul Jonathan Bendit; Frances Katherine Bendit
Officers: Frances Bendit, Secretary; Frances Katherine Bendit [1960] Director/Company Secretary; Paul Jonathan Bendit [1959] Director

Microbiome Technologies Limited
Incorporated: 31 July 2017
Registered Office: 50 Galley Hill View, Bexhill on Sea, E Sussex, TN40 1SX
Major Shareholder: Hon Adam Smith
Officers: Hon Adam Smith [1964] Director

Middle Way Ltd.
Incorporated: 29 March 2017
Net Worth Deficit: £7,183 *Total Assets:* £32,153
Registered Office: Unit 12 Levenside Business Court, 21 Levenside Road, Vale of Leven Industrial Estate, Dumbarton, G82 3PE
Major Shareholder: Gavin David Monson
Officers: Catriona Monson [1989] Director; Gavin David Monson [1989] Director

Mighty Drinks Ltd.
Incorporated: 5 December 2018
Registered Office: Kemp House, 160 City Road, London, EC1V 2NX
Major Shareholder: Tina Tzu-Ming Chen
Officers: Tina Tzu-Ming Chen [1992] Director/Drinkpreneur [American]

Mighty Flames Ltd
Incorporated: 14 June 2017
Registered Office: 122 Hawthorn Road, Kingstanding, Birmingham, B44 8PX
Major Shareholder: Evol McKenzie
Officers: Evol McKenzie [1971] Director [Jamaican]; Claudine Sterling [1978] Assistant Director

Mildenhall Bottling Company Limited
Incorporated: 29 October 2018
Registered Office: Hedge House, Hangersley Hill, Hangersley, Ringwood, Hants, BH24 3JW
Major Shareholder: Christopher Berriman Martin
Officers: Christopher Berriman Martin [1952] Director/Farmer; Victor Bernard Wheeler [1944] Director/Builder

Milkshake and Co London Limited
Incorporated: 4 November 2016
Registered Office: 29 Halesowen Drive, Elstow, Bedford, MK42 9GG
Major Shareholder: Arshpreet Singh Sibia
Officers: Arshpreet Singh Sibia [1979] Director [Indian]

Miss Cola UK Limited
Incorporated: 3 October 2015
Net Worth: £100 *Total Assets:* £100
Registered Office: Flat 801, Jute Court, 58 Abbey Road, Barking, Essex, IG11 7FT
Officers: Olumolawa Oludotun Olusi [1977] Director [Nigerian]

Mission Juice Ltd
Incorporated: 29 January 2016
Net Worth Deficit: £5,406
Registered Office: 7 Chandler Close, Bath, BA1 4EG
Major Shareholder: Tom David Tigwell
Officers: Tom David Tigwell [1994] Director/Owner

Miximex Limited
Incorporated: 30 October 2014
Net Worth Deficit: £9,008 *Total Assets:* £4,048
Registered Office: 14 Guildown Avenue, Guildford, Surrey, GU2 4HB
Major Shareholder: David Theodoor de Jong
Officers: David Theodoor de Jong [1987] Managing Director [Dutch]

Mobay Drinks Ltd
Incorporated: 2 October 2018
Registered Office: 57 Coldharbour Road, Croydon, Surrey, CR0 4DY
Major Shareholder: Joshua Ferguson
Officers: Joshua Ferguson [1999] Director/Entrepreneur

Molly Rose Drinks Ltd
Incorporated: 2 July 2018
Registered Office: 82 Victory Avenue, Gretna, Dumfries & Galloway, DG16 5DR
Major Shareholder: Claire McLean
Officers: Claire McLean [1977] Managing Director

Momo Kombucha Ltd
Incorporated: 10 April 2017
Registered Office: 20-22 Wenlock Road, London, N1 7GU
Major Shareholder: Joshua Puddle
Officers: Joshua Puddle [1985] Director

Monarch Beverages Limited
Incorporated: 9 October 2013
Registered Office: 43 Boulton Road, Reading, Berks, RG2 0NU
Major Shareholder: Benjamin Paul Baker
Officers: Benjamin Paul Baker [1974] Director [Australian]

Monster Energy Europe Limited
Incorporated: 9 October 2007 *Employees:* 389
Net Worth: £31,493,468 *Total Assets:* £53,013,208
Registered Office: Unit 51 Metropolitan Park, Bristol Road, Greenford, Middlesex, UB6 8UP
Officers: Neil Shirley, Secretary; Guy Philip Carling [1977] Director; Rodney Cyril Sacks [1949] Director [American]; Hilton Schlosberg [1952] Director; Neil Shirley [1962] Director/VP Finance

Montecrysto Limited
Incorporated: 4 September 2015
Registered Office: 59 Grange Avenue, Bradford, BD3 7BE
Major Shareholder: Hassan Jahangir Ahmed
Officers: Hassan Jahangir Ahmed [1992] Director

Montgomery Waters Limited
Incorporated: 19 August 1996 *Employees:* 66
Previous: The Montgomery Natural Spring Water Company Limited
Net Worth: £3,156,188 *Total Assets:* £13,048,339
Registered Office: The Exchange Fiveways, Temple Street, Llandrindod Wells, Powys, LD1 5HG
Parent: Delfin Investments Limited
Officers: Sallie Amanda Attwell [1964] Director; David Paul Delves [1960] Director/Supermarket Manager; Gilroy Donald Delves Mbe [1937] Director/Supermarket Proprietor; Andrew Michael McAdam [1965] Director/Bottled Water & Drinks Manufacturer

Moor Organics Limited
Incorporated: 8 March 2007 *Employees:* 2
Net Worth: £118,577 *Total Assets:* £562,626
Registered Office: Mall House, The Mall, Faversham, Kent, ME13 8JL
Shareholders: John Moor; Nick Moor
Officers: John Moor, Secretary/Farmer; John Moor [1932] Director/Farmer; Nicholas Moor [1960] Director/Farmer

Moores of Warwick Limited
Incorporated: 6 October 2017
Registered Office: Arkham, 9 Emscote Road, Warwick, CV34 4PH
Major Shareholder: Martin Keith Moore
Officers: Lorraine Moore [1967] Director/Manager; Martin Keith Moore [1960] Director/Accountant

Moorland Mist Limited
Incorporated: 25 August 1995
Registered Office: 95 Grassendale Avenue, Plymouth, PL2 2JP
Officers: Roger James Mitchell, Secretary; Julia Christine Cider [1970] Director/Teacher; Rachael Jane Mitchell [1968] Director/Manager

Morgan's Exclusive Ltd
Incorporated: 12 January 2012
Registered Office: 70 Carmichael Road, London, SE25 5LX
Officers: Joan Sharon Lloye Geen [1960] Managing Director

Moringa Superfoods UK Limited
Incorporated: 4 April 2018
Registered Office: Moringa House, 11 Alderlands Close, Crowland, Peterborough, PE6 0BS
Shareholders: Eirlys Sian Arulanantham; Amit Arulanantham
Officers: Amit Arulanantham [1980] Director [Indian]; Eirlys Sian Arulanantham [1972] Director

Morninglory Ltd
Incorporated: 16 February 2018
Registered Office: Tudor Close, Newby Bridge, Ulverston, Cumbria, LA12 8LZ
Major Shareholder: Robert Clarke
Officers: Robert Clarke [1991] Director/Accountant

Moss Cider Limited
Incorporated: 20 February 2012
Net Worth: £3,623 *Total Assets:* £38,295
Registered Office: 12 Jordan Street, Liverpool, L1 0BP
Major Shareholder: Joseph Paul Weeks
Officers: Joseph Paul Weeks [1973] Director

Mossdoli Ltd
Incorporated: 4 October 2017
Net Worth Deficit: £930 *Total Assets:* £336
Registered Office: 27 Old Gloucester Street, London, WC1N 3AX
Officers: Mariama Tounkara [1982] Director [French]

Mother Juice Ltd
Incorporated: 30 September 2015 *Employees:* 8
Net Worth: £35,212 *Total Assets:* £145,539
Registered Office: Unit 1 Canalside, Here East, London, E20 3BS
Shareholders: Charles Christopher Hill; Charles Patrick Hill
Officers: Charles Christopher Hill [1987] Director/Consultant; Charles Patrick Hill [1984] Director/Business Consultant

Mother Kombucha Ltd
Incorporated: 9 November 2017
Registered Office: Flat 10, Fletcher House, Milton Garden Estate, London, N16 8TP
Major Shareholder: Wendle Nightingale
Officers: Anita Nightingale, Secretary; Wendle Nightingale [1968] Director

Mother Nature's Drinks Limited
Incorporated: 27 July 2017
Registered Office: 20-22 Wenlock Road, London, N1 7GU
Major Shareholder: Christiana Iliya
Officers: Christiana Iliya [1991] Director

Mother Root Ltd
Incorporated: 16 May 2017
Net Worth Deficit: £15,783 *Total Assets:* £1,768
Registered Office: 7 Muschamp Road, London, SE15 4EG
Major Shareholder: Bethan Higson
Officers: Bethan Higson [1986] Director/Business Development Manager

Mount Valley Beverages Ltd
Incorporated: 20 July 2018
Registered Office: 36 Alie Street, London, E1 8DA
Major Shareholder: Mohammed Ali
Officers: Mohammed Ali [1975] Director; Omar Majid [1985] Director

Mourne Mist Bottled Water Company Ltd
Incorporated: 13 December 2004 *Employees:* 5
Net Worth: £169,013 *Total Assets:* £269,385
Registered Office: Newcel Group Offices, Milltown Industrial Estate, Greenan Road, Warrenpoint, Co Down, BT34 3FN
Parent: Newcel Paper Converters Limited
Officers: Eunan McGurk, Secretary; Feithlinn McCullagh [1961] Director; Kevin Christopher McCullagh [1991] Operations Director [Irish]; Eunan McGurk [1964] Director

Mr Fitzpatrick's Limited
Incorporated: 23 August 2010 *Employees:* 6
Net Worth: £363,153 *Total Assets:* £475,900
Registered Office: Unit 7 The Courtyard, 270 Grane Road, Haslingden, Lancs, BB4 4PB
Officers: Benjamin John Alderson [1977] Director; Shirley Alderson [1956] Director; Christopher James Law [1959] Director; Shaun Morley [1966] Director

Mr Freeze (Europe) Limited
Incorporated: 12 June 2008
Registered Office: Citrus Grove, Sideley, Kegworth, Derby, DE74 2FJ
Parent: Cooke Bros Holdings Limited
Officers: David John Saint [1964] Managing Director

Mr Holmes Flavored Syrups Ltd
Incorporated: 12 October 2017
Registered Office: Suite 9, Rockfield House, Darwen Road, Bromley Cross, Bolton, Lancs, BL7 9DX
Officers: Dean Carl Holmes [1983] Managing Director

Mr. Whitehead's Drinks Company Ltd.
Incorporated: 30 January 2012
Registered Office: Windmill Farm, Colemore Lane, Colemore, Alton, Hants, GU34 3PY
Major Shareholder: Alexander Whitehead
Officers: Alexander Whitehead [1971] Director/Drinks Producer

Muirhall Water Limited
Incorporated: 28 February 2014
Previous: Muirhall Spring Water Limited
Net Worth: £100 *Total Assets:* £190,235
Registered Office: Muirhall Farm, Auchengray, Carnwath, Lanark, ML11 8LL
Shareholders: Keith Douglas Love; Christopher John Walker
Officers: Dr Keith Douglas Love [1966] Director; Christopher John Walker [1964] Director

P Mulrine and Sons Sales (U.K.) Limited
Incorporated: 18 August 2016 *Employees:* 6
Net Worth Deficit: £828,630 *Total Assets:* £1,284,538
Registered Office: 78 Peacock Road, Sion Mills, Strabane, Co Tyrone, BT82 9NP
Major Shareholder: Peter Mulrine
Officers: Peter Mulrine, Secretary; Malachy Magee [1971] Director [Irish]; Peter Mulrine [1960] Director [Irish]

My Little Potion Ltd
Incorporated: 9 May 2018
Registered Office: Flat 7, 5 Inverness Street, London, NW1 7HB
Major Shareholder: Charlotte Veronique M Mernier
Officers: Charlotte Veronique M Mernier [1988] Director/Osteopath [Belgian]

My Living Water UK Ltd
Incorporated: 27 July 2012
Net Worth Deficit: £28,660 *Total Assets:* £14,950
Registered Office: 2 Syon Close, Abbey Meads, Swindon, Wilts, SN25 4TZ
Shareholders: Nicholas James Cameron; Miki Cameron
Officers: Miki Cameron [1973] Director [Japanese]; Nicholas James Cameron [1971] Director

My Mum's Ltd
Incorporated: 27 March 2012
Registered Office: Flat A, 6 Shackleton Road, Southall, Middlesex, UB1 2JA
Officers: Christine Ingrid Francis [1970] Director/Drinks Distributor

Mylkman Ltd
Incorporated: 16 October 2017
Registered Office: The Nuthouse, 58 Containerville, Corbridge Crescent, London, E2 9EZ
Shareholders: Vbites Ventures Limited; Jamie Chapman
Officers: Jamie Chapman [1984] Director/Founder and Owner; Rachel Lucy Harrison [1991] Director/Owner; Heather Anne Mills [1968] Director

N'ife Limited
Incorporated: 16 February 2018
Registered Office: Flat 26, Mennie House, Royal Herbert Pavilions, Gilbert Close, London, SE18 4PR
Shareholders: Joy Temitayo Salaja; Olaitan Alabi
Officers: Olaitan Alabi [1985] Director/Co-owner; Joy Temitayo Salaja [1990] Co-Owner/Director [Irish]

Nachure Ltd
Incorporated: 15 July 2015
Registered Office: 35 Chaldon Way, Coulsdon, Surrey, CR5 1DJ
Major Shareholder: Naveed Aslam
Officers: Naveed Aslam [1970] Director

Nairamalt UK Limited
Incorporated: 4 April 2018
Registered Office: Flat 801, Jute Court, 58 Abbey Road, Barking, Essex, IG11 7FT
Major Shareholder: Olumolawa Oludotun Olusi
Officers: Olumolawa Oludotun Olusi [1977] Director [Nigerian]

The Naivasha Tonic Company Ltd
Incorporated: 30 June 2016
Net Worth: £100 *Total Assets:* £100
Registered Office: 11 Laura Place, Bath, BA2 4BL
Shareholders: Harald Eric Bret; Peter Meacock
Officers: Harald Eric Bret [1979] Director [French]; Peter Meacock [1958] Director

Naneau Limited
Incorporated: 8 March 2018
Registered Office: Tremain House, 8 Maple Drive, Kings Worthy, Winchester, Hants, SO23 7NG
Major Shareholder: Nicholas Joslin
Officers: Nicholas Joslin [1961] Director

Nari Palm Juice Beverages Ltd
Incorporated: 1 December 2015
Net Worth: £201 *Total Assets:* £249
Registered Office: 75 Bradstowe House, Headstone Road, Harrow, Middlesex, HA1 1EH
Officers: Adetola Adebukunla James-Odukoya [1991] Managing Director

Narino Limited
Incorporated: 10 March 2011
Previous: HM Land Solutions Limited
Registered Office: Horsley House, Tilford, Farnham, Surrey, GU10 2AJ
Shareholder: Edward Grellier Colby
Officers: Paula Marie Hopkins, Secretary; Grant Nicholas Walker [1973] Director; John Plenderleith Walker [1940] Director

The National Forest Spring Water Company Limited
Incorporated: 29 April 2002 *Employees:* 13
Net Worth Deficit: £41,606 *Total Assets:* £696,938
Registered Office: 370-374 Nottingham Road, Newthorpe, Nottingham, NG16 2ED
Major Shareholder: David William Smith
Officers: Alexandra Smith, Secretary/Curtain Designer; David William Smith [1952] Director/Farmer; Samuel Isaac Smith [1992] Director

The Natural Food and Drink Company Limited
Incorporated: 19 December 2017
Registered Office: 12 Dewe Lane, Burghfield, Reading, Berks, RG30 3SU
Major Shareholder: Ketan Harshad Joshi
Officers: Dr Ketan Joshi, Secretary; Dr Ketan Harshad Joshi [1961] Director

The Natural Fruit and Beverage Company Limited
Incorporated: 13 June 2001 *Employees:* 58
Net Worth: £825,842 *Total Assets:* £4,363,959
Registered Office: 1 Anthony Road, Largs, N Ayrshire, KA30 8EQ
Parent: LL Equity Limited
Officers: Henry John Jagielko, Secretary/Accountant; Alexander Bulloch [1927] Director; Carol Anne Bulloch [1956] Director; Henry John Jagielko [1952] Director/Accountant; Alexander Reynolds [1955] Director

Natural Juicing Company Ltd
Incorporated: 5 January 2016
Registered Office: ASM House, 103a Keymer Road, Hassocks, W Sussex, BN6 8QL
Shareholders: Gemma Louise Harding; James Robert Harding
Officers: Gemma Louise Harding [1982] Director; James Robert Harding [1982] Director/Engineer; Angus James Warner [1979] Director; Stephanie Warner [1982] Director

Naturally Buzzin Energy Products Ltd
Incorporated: 16 February 2017
Registered Office: 5 West Street, Okehampton, Devon, EX20 1HQ
Shareholders: Przemyslaw Kobuszewski; Simon David Weekes
Officers: Simon David Weekes, Secretary; Przemyslaw Kobuszewski [1979] Director [Polish]; Simon David Weekes [1986] Director

Nature's Fountain Limited
Incorporated: 17 April 2014
Registered Office: 6 Clarendon Place, London, W2 2NP
Major Shareholder: Ravinder Kullar
Officers: Ravinder Kullar [1988] Director

Nele Drinks Limited
Incorporated: 14 August 2017
Registered Office: 21 Racavan Road, Broughshane, Ballymena, Co Antrim, BT42 4PH
Major Shareholder: Niall Edward Lloyd Esler
Officers: Niall Edward Lloyd Esler [1985] Director/Solicitor

Neptune SA Ltd
Incorporated: 12 March 2018
Registered Office: Mays Grove Cottage, Mays Lane, Dedham, Colchester, Essex, CO7 6EW
Officers: Antanas Sadauskas [1965] Director [Lithuanian]

Nerissimo Luxury Espresso Ltd
Incorporated: 18 June 2018
Registered Office: 59 Bonnygate, Cupar, Fife, KY15 4BY
Major Shareholder: Giorgio Cozzolino Cozzolino
Officers: Giorgio Cozzolino Cozzolino [1964] Director [Italian]

Ness Scotland Ltd
Incorporated: 23 April 2015
Registered Office: Beinn Bhurie, 3 Hillpark Brae, Munlochy, Ross & Cromarty, IV8 8PL
Major Shareholder: John Philip Oag
Officers: John Arthur Bridges [1945] Director/Retired Civil Engineer; John Philip Oag [1970] Director/Sales

Nestle Waters (UK) Holdings Limited
Incorporated: 4 September 1998
Registered Office: 1 City Place, Gatwick, W Sussex, RH6 0PA
Parent: Nestle Holdings (U.K.) PLC
Officers: Michel Beneventi [1971] Managing Director of Nestle Waters UK [Swiss]; Charles David Hardy Roberts [1974] Director/Factory Manager; Richard James Shaw [1974] Director/Management Accountant

Nestle Waters GB Limited
Incorporated: 30 October 1986
Registered Office: 1 City Place, Gatwick, W Sussex, RH6 0PA
Parent: Buxton Mineral Water Limited
Officers: Michel Beneventi [1971] Managing Director Nestle Waters UK [Swiss]; David Steven McDaniel [1968] Finance Director; Charles David Hardy Roberts [1974] Director/Factory Manager; Richard James Shaw [1974] Director/Management Accountant

Nestle Waters UK Limited
Incorporated: 12 January 1989 *Employees:* 262
Net Worth: £6,706,000 *Total Assets:* £72,126,000
Registered Office: 1 City Place, Gatwick, W Sussex, RH6 0PA
Parent: Nestle UK Ltd.
Officers: Michel Beneventi [1971] Managing Director Nestle Waters UK [Swiss]; Charles David Hardy Roberts [1974] Director/Factory Manager; Richard James Shaw [1974] Director/Management Accountant

Neu Water Limited
Incorporated: 17 October 2017
Registered Office: c/o Harris & Co Consultants Limited, 5 Oak Tree Court, Cardiff Gate Business Park, Pontprennau, Cardiff, CF23 8RS
Major Shareholder: Ian Laing
Officers: Ian Laing [1960] Director

UK Manufacturers of Soft Drinks

Neue Water Limited
Incorporated: 15 January 2018
Registered Office: 42 Ballater Road, London, SW2 5QR
Major Shareholder: Michael Lowers
Officers: Michael Lowers [1982] Director [New Zealander]

New Earth Ventures Ltd
Incorporated: 31 March 2016
Registered Office: 234 Great Knightleys, Basildon, Essex, SS15 5EY
Shareholders: Eleanor Grant; Aslam Sulaiman
Officers: Eleanor Grant [1981] Director; Aslam Sulaiman [1972] Director [Sri Lankan]

New Forest Spring Water Distribution Limited
Incorporated: 11 May 2017 Employees: 2
Net Worth: £216,008 Total Assets: £220,429
Registered Office: Spring House, Blind Lane, South Gorley, Hants, SP6 2PW
Officers: Kevin David Cowell [1963] Director; Simon Reed [1970] Director

New Forest Spring Water Limited
Incorporated: 11 February 2011 Employees: 6
Net Worth Deficit: £11,879 Total Assets: £192,695
Registered Office: Spring House, Blind Lane, South Gorley, Hants, SP6 2PW
Shareholders: Kevin David Cowell; Arthur Eugene Dunne
Officers: Kevin David Cowell [1963] Director/Sales Executive; Simon Reed [1970] Production Director

New Life Water Limited
Incorporated: 3 July 2017
Registered Office: 2 Croft Avenue, Otley, W Yorks, LS21 2AX
Major Shareholder: Laraine Helen Barnes
Officers: Laraine Helen Barnes [1968] Director/Water Manufacturer

NFSG Ltd.
Incorporated: 24 October 2014 Employees: 3
Net Worth: £98,452 Total Assets: £128,246
Registered Office: c/o Harbour Key Limited, Midway House, Staverton Technology Park, Herrick Way, Staverton, Cheltenham, Glos, GL51 6TQ
Officers: Stephen Raymond Wilkinson [1965] Director/Self Employed Builder; William James Wilkinson [1991] Director/Self Employed Musician

NGN Distribution Limited
Incorporated: 1 October 2003 Employees: 4
Net Worth: £940,418 Total Assets: £1,597,197
Registered Office: Alexander Partnership, Barclays Bank Chambers, 18 High Street, Tenby, Pembrokeshire, SA70 7HE
Major Shareholder: David Gary Owen
Officers: David Gary Owen, Secretary/Director; Annette Owen [1960] Director; David Gary Owen [1959] Director

Nichols PLC
Incorporated: 28 March 1929 Employees: 242
Net Worth: £99,322,000 Total Assets: £127,396,000
Registered Office: Laurel House, Woodlands Park, Ashton Road, Newton-le-Willows, St Helens, Merseyside, WA12 0HH
Officers: Timothy John Croston, Secretary; Timothy John Croston [1963] Finance Director; John Anthony Gittins [1960] Director; Helen Margaret Keays [1964] Director; Marnie Jane Millard [1964] Director; Andrew Paul Milne [1973] Group Commercial Director; Peter John Nichols [1949] Non-Executive Director Chairman

Nix & Kix Ltd
Incorporated: 20 October 2014
Net Worth: £448,123 Total Assets: £535,077
Registered Office: 86-90 Paul Street, London, EC2A 4NE
Shareholders: Julia Kessler; Kerstin Robinson
Officers: Matthew John Cushen [1969] Director; Julia Kessler [1983] Director/Founder [German]; Kerstin Robinson [1983] Director [German]; John Bernard Stapleton [1964] Director [Irish]; Kin-Man Suen [1981] Director/Financial Controller [Australian]

No Longer Bax Botanics Limited
Incorporated: 12 September 2018
Registered Office: 1 Thornton Bridge Cottages, Thornton Bridge, Helperby, York, YO61 2RH
Shareholders: Rosemary Jane Badger Bax; Christopher Martin Bax
Officers: Christopher Martin Bax [1966] Director; Rosemary Jane Badger Bax [1964] Director

The Noisy Drinks Co Ltd
Incorporated: 14 August 2006
Net Worth: £968,769 Total Assets: £968,769
Registered Office: Laurel House, Woodlands Park, Ashton Road, Newton-le-Willows, Merseyside, WA12 0HH
Parent: Nichols PLC
Officers: Timothy John Croston, Secretary; Tim John Croston [1963] Director

Norbev Limited
Incorporated: 26 June 2000 Employees: 123
Net Worth: £5,328,056 Total Assets: £15,103,629
Registered Office: 100 Railway Street, Ballymena, Co Antrim, BT42 2AF
Officers: Rachel McCann, Secretary; Shona Jane Blythe [1977] Technical Director; Ciaran Joseph Doherty [1969] Operations Director [Irish]; James Crawford Harkness [1964] Director; Rachel Katherine McCann [1977] Finance Director [Irish]

Norfolk Cordial Ltd
Incorporated: 5 December 2012
Net Worth Deficit: £7,785 Total Assets: £71,443
Registered Office: 19 The Street, Matlaske, Norwich, NR11 7AQ
Shareholders: John Dumeresq McFarlane; Georgina Amy Rodwell
Officers: Georgina Amy Rodwell, Secretary; John Dumeresq McFarlane [1972] Managing Director; Georgina Amy Rodwell [1986] Finance and Manufacturing Director

Northern Citrus Products Limited
Incorporated: 8 June 1967 Employees: 8
Net Worth: £116,311 Total Assets: £502,968
Registered Office: Cocker Avenue, Poulton Industrial Estate, Poulton-le-Fylde, Blackpool, Lancs, FY6 8JU
Major Shareholder: Andrew Joseph Smith
Officers: Andrew Joseph Smith, Secretary; Stephen Michael Houghton [1968] Director/Sales Representative; Andrew Joseph Smith [1964] Director/Sales Representative

Northumbrian Ice Cream Company Limited
Incorporated: 31 January 1994 Employees: 38
Net Worth: £2,036,745 Total Assets: £5,799,730
Registered Office: Wansbeck Business Park, Rotary Parkway, Ashington, Northumberland, NE63 8QW
Shareholders: Allison Goldfinch; Paul John Goldfinch
Officers: Allison Goldfinch [1975] Director; Margaret Goldfinch [1936] Director; Paul John Goldfinch [1973] Director; Peter John Goldfinch [1934] Director; Kieran Anthony O'Connor [1961] Director; Michael Reid [1980] Director

Norwegian Glacier Water Limited
Incorporated: 15 January 2009 *Employees:* 2
Net Worth Deficit: £51,434 *Total Assets:* £542
Registered Office: Roland House, Princes Dock Street, Hull, HU1 2LD
Major Shareholder: Yaseen Altabtabaei
Officers: Yaseen Abdul Mohsen Altabtabaei [1971] Director [Kuwaiti]; Anond Jarand Ronjom [1969] Director [Norwegian]

Nourish Foods Limited
Incorporated: 18 August 2015
Net Worth Deficit: £32,401 *Total Assets:* £156,903
Registered Office: 4 Dawson Street, Armagh, BT61 7QT
Shareholders: Rhian Alys Horwill; Michael Gerald Lennon
Officers: Rhian Alys Horwill, Secretary; Rhian Alys Horwill [1979] Director; Michael Generald Lennon [1976] Director [Irish]

Nozbo Drinks Limited
Incorporated: 23 January 2017
Registered Office: 15 Hutcheon Low Drive, Aberdeen, AB21 9WH
Officers: Solomon Igboayaka [1976] Director/Process Engineer

NR Enterprise Limited
Incorporated: 6 September 2018
Registered Office: 60 Hartismere Road, London, SW6 7UD
Major Shareholder: Nick James Hird
Officers: Robert Mark Peter Bennett-Baggs [1986] Director and Company Secretary; Nick James Hird [1989] Director

Nude & Rude Ltd
Incorporated: 25 May 2017 *Employees:* 1
Net Worth Deficit: £2,514 *Total Assets:* £1,000
Registered Office: 28 Burleigh Road, Enfield, Middlesex, EN1 1NY
Major Shareholder: Samuel Rosenheim
Officers: Samuel Rosenheim [1981] Director

Nude Drinks Limited
Incorporated: 15 May 2017
Registered Office: Flat 2, 17 Snowdon Road, Bournemouth, BH4 9HL
Major Shareholder: Thomas Frank Bradshaw
Officers: Thomas Frank Bradshaw [1992] Director

Nutrapharm Ltd
Incorporated: 9 May 2017
Registered Office: 9 Denton Drive, West Bridgford, Nottingham, NG2 7FS
Officers: Gavin Gresswell [1972] Director; Paul Settle [1970] Director; Simon Wills [1969] Director

Nutricana Ltd
Incorporated: 18 October 2018
Registered Office: 20-22 Wenlock Road, London, N1 7GU
Major Shareholder: Habib Miah
Officers: Habib Miah [1990] Director/Founder & CEO

O.T.C Beverages Limited
Incorporated: 8 August 2018
Registered Office: 34 Westway, Caterham on the Hill, Caterham, Surrey, CR3 5TP
Major Shareholder: Shirley White
Officers: Shirley White [1963] Director/Consultant

Oakdale Spring Limited
Incorporated: 3 October 2012
Registered Office: Harrogate Water Brands, Harlow Moor Road, Harrogate, N Yorks, HG2 0QB
Parent: Harrogate Water Brands Limited
Officers: Anthony Joseph Cain [1948] Director; James Anthony Cain [1973] Director; Robert James Pickering [1964] Director

Obeliver Drinks Limited
Incorporated: 11 May 2012
Net Worth Deficit: £31,083 *Total Assets:* £16,394
Registered Office: 48 Albert Road, South Norwood, London, SE25 4JE
Major Shareholder: Obed Oliver Ofori Kingful
Officers: Obed Oliver Ofori Kingful [1980] Director/Accountant

Ocean Tears Ltd
Incorporated: 7 February 2019
Registered Office: R2 Rapide Studios, Penn Street, Amersham, Bucks, HP7 0PX
Shareholders: Louise Claire Lloyd; Ian Michael Minton
Officers: Louise Claire Lloyd [1981] Director; Ian Michael Minton [1982] Director

Ocentek Ltd
Incorporated: 23 October 2018
Registered Office: 3 Rose Avenue, Mitcham, Surrey, CR4 3JS
Major Shareholder: Raviraja Sebastiampillai
Officers: Raviraja Sebastiampillai [1992] Director/Entrepreneur [Sri Lankan]

Office Beverages Ltd
Incorporated: 2 July 2014
Registered Office: Waters Edge, 2 Burghley Court, Winterbourne, Bristol, BS36 1LR
Major Shareholder: Peter John Brooks
Officers: Peter John Brooks, Secretary; Peter John Brooks [1961] Director/Sales

Office Watercoolers (S.W.) Limited
Incorporated: 10 August 2001 *Employees:* 37
Net Worth: £1,953,775 *Total Assets:* £2,329,478
Registered Office: Unit 5 Rivermead, Dean Road, Yate, Glos, BS37 5NH
Major Shareholder: Peter John Brooks
Officers: Peter John Brooks [1961] Director/Sales

Old WCS (Bottlers) Limited
Incorporated: 14 October 2011 *Employees:* 1
Previous: WCS (Bottlers) Limited
Net Worth Deficit: £140,954
Registered Office: Unit B, 3, Livingstone Boulevard, Blantyre, S Lanarks, G72 0BP
Shareholders: Cott Corporation; Water Coolers (Scotland) Limited
Officers: Brian Richard Macpherson [1971] Director

Omega EFA Limited
Incorporated: 19 February 2001
Net Worth: £85,705 *Total Assets:* £156,107
Registered Office: Spring House, 1 Well Lane, Yealand Redmayne, Carnforth, Lancs, LA5 9SX
Major Shareholder: Robin Jeremy Higgens
Officers: Caroline Elizabeth Higgens, Secretary; Robin Jeremy Higgens [1958] Director

One Co. of Harrogate Ltd
Incorporated: 17 February 2016
Net Worth: £8,815 *Total Assets:* £8,815
Registered Office: 37 Otley Road, Killinghall, Harrogate, N Yorks, HG3 2DN
Shareholders: Johnathan Eaton Charles Slater; John Melvyn Slater; Norman Anthony Slater
Officers: Johnathan Eaton Charles Slater, Secretary; Dr John Melvyn Slater [1953] Commercial Director; Johnathan Eaton Charles Slater [1983] Managing Director; Dr Norman Anthony Slater [1953] Technical Director

Orchid Drinks Limited
Incorporated: 9 January 1992
Net Worth: £12,764,000 *Total Assets:* £14,113,000
Registered Office: Breakspear Park, Breakspear Way, Hemel Hempstead, Herts, HP2 4TZ
Parent: Britvic Soft Drinks Limited
Officers: Judith Moore, Secretary; Mathew James Dunn [1974] Director/Chief Financial Officer; Peter Simon Litherland [1964] Director/Chief Executive; Alexandra Clare Thomas [1974] Director/General Counsel and Company Secretary

The Original Drinks and Food Company Ltd
Incorporated: 27 November 1990
Net Worth: £2,067,569 *Total Assets:* £2,432,643
Registered Office: 123 Cross Lane East, Gravesend, Kent, DA12 5HA
Major Shareholder: James Edwards
Officers: James Edwards, Secretary; Claire Elizabeth Edwards [1962] Director; James Edwards [1954] Director/Marketing Person

The Original Drinks Company Ltd.
Incorporated: 20 December 1989
Registered Office: Barnfield Farm, Gravesend Road, Wrotham, Kent, TN15 7JR
Major Shareholder: James Edwards
Officers: James Edwards, Secretary; James Edwards [1954] Director

The Original Free Drinks Company Limited
Incorporated: 27 February 2019
Registered Office: 37 Warren Street, London, W1T 6AD
Major Shareholder: Redmond Antony Guy Johnson
Officers: Redmond Antony Guy Johnson [1970] Director

The Original Somerset Certified Water Supply Company Limited
Incorporated: 6 August 1990
Registered Office: Hollow End Farm, Lippiatt Lane, Shipham, Somerset, BS25 1QY
Major Shareholder: Christopher David George Cooper
Officers: Christopher David George Cooper, Secretary; Nicola Jane Armour [1973] Director; Christopher David George Cooper [1946] Director

Originalsip Ltd
Incorporated: 27 April 2017
Net Worth: £4,158 *Total Assets:* £17,260
Registered Office: 10 Rutland Gardens, London, N4 1JP
Shareholder: Antonio Pescatori
Officers: Antonio Pescatori [1990] Director/Rectifier [Italian]

Our Northern Stars Limited
Incorporated: 1 October 2018
Registered Office: 2 Prospect Terrace, Eighton Banks, Gateshead, Tyne & Wear, NE9 7YE
Major Shareholder: Grainne Marie Fegan
Officers: Grainne Marie Fegan [1970] Director/Project Manager

Outfox Drinks Ltd
Incorporated: 27 October 2016
Net Worth: £38,272 *Total Assets:* £54,554
Registered Office: Timsons Business Centre, Bath Road, Kettering, Northants, NN16 8NQ
Major Shareholder: Jessica Hook
Officers: Jessica Hook [1986] Director; Paul Henry Soanes [1970] Director

Outsider Drinks Ltd.
Incorporated: 20 April 2017
Net Worth Deficit: £7,380 *Total Assets:* £970
Registered Office: 45a Maryland Square, London, E15 1HF
Major Shareholder: Eoghan Joseph Conway
Officers: Eoghan Joseph Conway [1988] Director/Beverages

The Oxford Juice Company Ltd
Incorporated: 9 May 2018
Registered Office: 34 Victor Street, Oxford, OX2 6BT
Shareholders: Sphelo Sphephelo Skhumbuzo Madlala; Akeem Trinity Perry Williams
Officers: Akeem Trinity Perry Williams, Secretary; Sphelo Sphephelo Skhumbuzo Madlala [1989] Director/Manager [South African]

Oxidize Limited
Incorporated: 8 January 2018
Registered Office: Kemp House, 160 City Road, London, EC1V 2NX
Major Shareholder: Shine Prakash
Officers: Shine Prakash [1983] Director [Indian]

Package Water Solutions Limited
Incorporated: 24 January 2019
Registered Office: 26 The Mallards, Southport, Merseyside, PR9 8RJ
Major Shareholder: Mark Robert Newby
Officers: Mark Robert Newby [1965] Director

Paisley Drinks Co. Ltd
Incorporated: 4 June 2018
Registered Office: 1 MacDowall Street, Paisley, Renfrewshire, PA3 2NB
Major Shareholder: Brian O'Shea
Officers: Brian O'Shea [1981] Managing Director

Panacea Drinks Ltd
Incorporated: 21 March 2016 *Employees:* 1
Net Worth Deficit: £30,575
Registered Office: Titanic Suites, 55-59 Adelaide Street, Belfast, BT2 8FE
Major Shareholder: Kelly Victoria Neill
Officers: Kelly Victoria Neill [1979] Director

Papas Mineral Company Ltd
Incorporated: 6 February 2015 *Employees:* 3
Net Worth: £17,426 *Total Assets:* £35,643
Registered Office: 39 Bayview Road, Bangor, Co Down, BT19 6AR
Major Shareholder: Christopher Wayne Adair
Officers: Christopher Wayne Adair [1977] Director

Paradise Drinks Co. Limited
Incorporated: 25 February 2019
Registered Office: Suite 19, Maple Court, Grove Park, Maidenhead, Berks, SL6 3LW
Officers: Marcis Alfred Dzelzainis [1982] Director; Luke McFayden [1987] Director; Trowbridge George McKay [1983] Director [New Zealander]; Michael Sager [1983] Director [Swiss]

Paradise Rum Limited
Incorporated: 16 January 2019
Registered Office: 3 Logan Close, Enfield, Middlesex, EN3 5NL
Shareholder: Nathan Brown
Officers: Nathan Brown [1993] Director; Kianne Ward [1994] Director

Pass The Baton Limited
Incorporated: 19 January 2006
Registered Office: 12 Rutland Place, Worcester, WR5 3UR
Major Shareholder: Georgina Louise Hopkinson
Officers: Stuart Hopkinson, Secretary; Georgina Louise Hopkinson [1967] Director/General Manager

Pearl Soft Drinks Limited
Incorporated: 16 May 2006 *Employees:* 2
Net Worth Deficit: £27,018 *Total Assets:* £11,162
Registered Office: 59 Brasenose Road, Bootle, Merseyside, L20 8HE
Shareholders: Daniel Stephen Bates; Jamie Thomas Bates
Officers: John Burke [1953] Director

Peel and Spice Ltd
Incorporated: 29 June 2017
Registered Office: The Croft, Butts Road, Ashover, Chesterfield, Derbys, S45 0AZ
Shareholders: Richard Forbes Barltrop; Sabrina Rose Brooks
Officers: Richard Forbes Barltrop [1992] Director; Sabrina Rose Brooks [1991] Director

Pembrokeshire Cider Limited
Incorporated: 24 March 2016
Net Worth: £15,553 *Total Assets:* £31,168
Registered Office: 6 Commons Road, Pembroke, SA71 4EB
Shareholders: David Michael Halsted; Jonathan Ashley Ryan; Christopher Gordon Scourfield
Officers: David Michael Halsted [1959] Director; Jonathan Ashley Ryan [1967] Director

Penning Power & Water Limited
Incorporated: 19 February 2001
Net Worth: £1,331,013 *Total Assets:* £1,438,103
Registered Office: The Estate Office, Fonthill Bishop, Salisbury, Wilts, SP3 5SH
Major Shareholder: Alastair John Margadale of Islay
Officers: Simon Neil Fowler, Secretary; Lord Alastair John Margadale of Islay [1958] Director/Landowner

Pentire Drinks Limited
Incorporated: 24 May 2018
Registered Office: 64 Fairholme Road, London, W14 9JY
Major Shareholder: Alistair Edward Frost
Officers: Alistair Edward Frost [1989] Director

Permeske Ltd
Incorporated: 14 August 2018
Registered Office: 86 Honey Hall Road, Liverpool, L26 1TQ
Major Shareholder: Ian Jones
Officers: Ian Jones [1985] Director/Consultant

Persian Roze Ltd
Incorporated: 18 February 2019
Registered Office: 140 Ontario Point, 28 Surrey Quays Road, London, SE16 7EF
Major Shareholder: Nona Keyhani
Officers: Nona Keyhani [1987] Director/Lawyer [Swedish]

Pharmaco Group Limited
Incorporated: 6 April 2018
Registered Office: Kemp House, 160 City Road, London, EC1V 2NX
Shareholders: Roy Salmons; Nutresco Limited
Officers: Roy Salmons [1945] Director

Phoenix School Drinks Ltd
Incorporated: 11 January 2013 *Employees:* 4
Net Worth: £5,430 *Total Assets:* £74,098
Registered Office: 101 Langdale Close, Rainham, Kent, ME8 7AF
Shareholder: Sharron Sylvester
Officers: Sharron Silvester, Secretary; Sharron Silvester [1967] Director

Phoenix Water Coolers Limited
Incorporated: 9 February 2009 *Employees:* 4
Net Worth: £7,292 *Total Assets:* £56,757
Registered Office: c/o South Staffordshire PLC, Green Lane, Walsall, W Midlands, WS2 7PD
Parent: Office Watercoolers Limited
Officers: Jason Richard Goodwin, Secretary; Adrian Peter Page [1965] Director; Kenneth Skelton [1965] Managing Director

Phutures Limited
Incorporated: 16 July 2018
Registered Office: Kemp House, 160 City Road, London, EC1V 2NX
Major Shareholder: James Mitchell
Officers: James Mitchell [1957] Director/Manager

Pickle Shot Limited
Incorporated: 29 January 2018
Registered Office: Safestore Building, Colima Avenue, Sunderland Business Park, Sunderland, Tyne & Wear, SR5 3XF
Major Shareholder: Jeffrey Ewart Knowles
Officers: Jeffrey Ewart Knowles [1959] Director

Piff Juice Limited
Incorporated: 9 May 2018
Registered Office: 529 Woodborough Road, Mapperly, Nottingham, NG3 5FR
Major Shareholder: Craig Jonathon Chance
Officers: Craig Jonathon Chance [1976] Director

Pitstop Coffee Limited
Incorporated: 27 March 2015
Previous: Twaste Limited
Net Worth: £12,992 *Total Assets:* £17,655
Registered Office: 18 Florence Road, Ealing, London, W5 3TX
Major Shareholder: James Vernon Hatfield
Officers: James Vernon Hatfield [1969] Director

Pivotal Drinks Ltd
Incorporated: 9 October 2018
Registered Office: 71-75 Shelton Street, London, WC2H 9JQ
Shareholder: Robert Andrew Hughes
Officers: Robert Andrew Hughes [1974] Director; Edward Marsden [1983] Director

PJ Kombucha Limited
Incorporated: 4 October 2017
Net Worth Deficit: £104,202 *Total Assets:* £40,238
Registered Office: Unit 5 Park Road, Hockley, Birmingham, B18 5HB
Major Shareholder: Patrick Michael O'Connor
Officers: Patrick Michael O'Connor [1988] Director [Irish]

Plenish Cleanse Ltd
Incorporated: 20 June 2012 *Employees:* 14
Net Worth: £224,260 *Total Assets:* £1,647,191
Registered Office: Unit 24, W10 Studios, 2-4 Exmoor Street, London, W10 6BD
Shareholders: Pembroke VCT; Kara Rosen
Officers: Leon Edward Diamond [1977] Director [Australian]; Brian Maloney [1969] Director; Kara Rosen [1977] Director [American]; Andrew Daniel Wolfson [1969] Director

Point Blank Cold Brew Ltd
Incorporated: 23 July 2014
Net Worth Deficit: £112,360 *Total Assets:* £38,887
Registered Office: c/o Optimal Accountancy Limited, 301a Sunderland Road, South Shields, Tyne & Wear, NE34 6RB
Shareholder: Josh William Thompson
Officers: Bryan David Griffiths [1966] Finance Director; Tom Mitchell [1981] Finance Director; Joshua Thompson [1975] Director

Pointeer Ltd
Incorporated: 18 September 2018
Registered Office: 43 The Calls, St Peters House, Leeds, LS2 7EY
Shareholders: David John Rushton; Stefan Amato
Officers: Stefan Amato, Secretary; Stefan Amato [1987] Director; Henry Robert Brighton Crofts [1989] Director; David John Rushton [1987] Director

Polar Krush Limited
Incorporated: 27 November 1998
Net Worth: £2 *Total Assets:* £2
Registered Office: Wansbeck Business Park, Rotary Parkway, Ashington, Northumberland, NE63 8QW
Major Shareholder: Paul John Goldfinch
Officers: Paul John Goldfinch [1973] Director; Kieran Anthony O'Connor [1961] Director; Michael Reid [1980] Director

Polconut Ltd
Incorporated: 28 June 2017
Registered Office: Flat 10, Palmera House, Field End Road, Ruislip, Middlesex, HA4 9NB
Officers: Kaludura Saiuri Wijesiri [1986] Director/Management Accountant; Punith Wijesiri [1987] Director/Human Resources Professional

Pomepure Ltd
Incorporated: 7 September 2016
Registered Office: 9 Cheam Road, Epsom, Surrey, KT17 1SP
Major Shareholder: Rashik Nagar
Officers: Nickolas Evangelopoulos [1956] Sales Director [Greek]; Rashik Nagar [1948] Director

Poo Tang Crisps Limited
Incorporated: 10 April 2016
Registered Office: Flat 4, 59 Ashgrove, Bradford, BD7 1BL
Officers: Hader Ali Sabir [1980] Managing Director

Pop in Tea Limited
Incorporated: 1 October 2018
Registered Office: 26 Chinchilla Drive, Hounslow, Middlesex, TW4 7NP
Major Shareholder: Daniel Junior Dailey
Officers: Daniel Junior Dailey [1981] Director/Civil Engineer

Poptails Limited
Incorporated: 29 June 2012
Net Worth Deficit: £52,807 *Total Assets:* £100
Registered Office: 14 Gray's Inn Road, London, WC1X 8HN
Major Shareholder: Assad Khan
Officers: Assad Khan [1979] Director

Portable Marketing Solutions Ltd
Incorporated: 22 August 2017
Registered Office: Flat 47, Phoenix Court, Chertsey Road, Feltham, Middlesex, TW13 4RN
Major Shareholder: Akil Porter
Officers: Akil Porter [1989] Director/Marketing Manager [American]

Portavadie Distillery Limited
Incorporated: 25 July 2007 *Employees:* 1
Net Worth: £71,709 *Total Assets:* £1,110,483
Registered Office: Craig Lodge, Ostel Bay, Tighnabruaich, Argyll & Bute, PA21 2AH
Major Shareholder: Sarah Stow
Officers: George James Riddell, Secretary; Alexander Bulloch [1927] Director; Sarah Stow [1963] Director

Positive Potions Limited
Incorporated: 25 September 2017
Registered Office: The Estate Office, Bodorgan, Anglesey, LL62 5LP
Major Shareholder: Candida Meyrick
Officers: Candida Meyrick [1970] Director

Post Hoc Ergo Propter Hoc Limited
Incorporated: 4 August 2008
Net Worth Deficit: £7,348
Registered Office: 1 Hillside Court, Hillside Road, St Albans, Herts, AL1 3QP
Major Shareholder: Ian William Escritt
Officers: Ian Escritt [1974] Director

Pouchlink Ltd
Incorporated: 14 September 2012
Net Worth Deficit: £21,427 *Total Assets:* £388,109
Registered Office: 7a Station Approach, Northwood, Middlesex, HA6 2XN
Officers: Anuj Joshi [1990] Director/Analyst

Power Juice Limited
Incorporated: 23 January 2006
Registered Office: 1 Ardgowan Road, London, SE6 1AJ
Major Shareholder: Horace Muhammad
Officers: Horace Muhammad [1963] Director

The Powerful Water Co Ltd
Incorporated: 18 July 2013
Previous: CBL Brands Limited
Registered Office: Riverside Industrial Estate, Riverside Road, Sunderland, Tyne & Wear, SR5 3JG
Parent: Clearly Drinks Group Limited
Officers: Michael Alan Howard [1969] Director; Damian Jon Stevenson [1967] Director

Prana Drinks Limited
Incorporated: 29 September 2015
Registered Office: Ground Floor Retail Unit, 114 Albany Road, Cardiff, CF24 3RU
Officers: Adam El Tagoury [1980] Director/Entrepreneur

Precision Hydration Limited
Incorporated: 14 April 2011 *Employees:* 4
Net Worth: £250,294 *Total Assets:* £271,471
Registered Office: 43 Saffron Drive, Christchurch, Dorset, BH23 4LR
Major Shareholder: Andrew Victor Blow
Officers: Andrew Victor Blow [1978] Director/Sports Scientist; Jonathan Christopher Tye [1993] Director/Operations Manager

Press London Ltd
Incorporated: 22 January 2013 *Employees:* 18
Net Worth: £144,712 *Total Assets:* £1,009,984
Registered Office: 64 New Cavendish Street, London, W1G 8TB
Shareholder: Edward Joseph Foy
Officers: Steven James Clark [1965] Director; Edward Joseph Foy [1982] Director; Georgina Sarah Emily Reames [1984] Director

Pressure Coolers Limited
Incorporated: 10 June 1999
Previous: Water Coolers Limited
Net Worth: £384,332 *Total Assets:* £1,762,930
Registered Office: 67-69 Nathan Way, London, SE28 0BQ
Major Shareholder: Matthew Richard Mitchison
Officers: Matthew Mitchison, Secretary; Matthew Mitchison [1960] Director/Water Coolers

Prime Sun Limited
Incorporated: 8 June 2015
Registered Office: Endurance House, 71 Sumner Road, Croydon, Surrey, CR0 3LN
Officers: Deji Mann Toyinbo [1989] Managing Director

Princes Gate Spring Water Limited
Incorporated: 31 October 2013 *Employees:* 50
Net Worth: £2,203,635 *Total Assets:* £14,847,811
Registered Office: The Well Fields, Princes Gate, Narbeth, Pembrokeshire, SA67 8JD
Parent: Nestle S.A.
Officers: Michel Beneventi [1971] Director/General Manager [Swiss]; Charles David Hardy Roberts [1974] Director/Factory Manager; Richard James Shaw [1974] Director/Accountant

Princes Gate Water Limited
Incorporated: 3 August 2001 *Employees:* 50
Net Worth: £1,522,991 *Total Assets:* £13,554,308
Registered Office: The Well Fields, Princes Gate, Narbeth, Pembrokeshire, SA67 8JD
Parent: Princes Gate Spring Water Limited
Officers: Michel Beneventi [1971] Director/General Manager [Swiss]; Endaf Edwards [1974] Director/General Manager; Charles David Hardy Roberts [1974] Director/Factory Manager; Richard James Shaw [1974] Director/Accountant

Proper Good Brands Limited
Incorporated: 4 July 2018
Registered Office: 1 Beauchamp Court, 10 Victors Way, Barnet, Herts, EN5 5TZ
Major Shareholder: Harpreet Mair
Officers: Harpreet Mair [1980] Director

Pump House Water Ltd
Incorporated: 12 September 2017
Registered Office: The Pump House, Main Street, West Hagbourne, Didcot, Oxon, OX11 0NB
Shareholder: William Giles Jenssen
Officers: Tobias Mark Jenssen [1971] Director; William Giles Jenssen [1969] Director

Punchline Ltd
Incorporated: 2 May 2018
Registered Office: 20a Southbrook Road, London, SE12 8LQ
Shareholders: Amari Boothe; Curtis Dixon; Ryan Banton
Officers: Ryan Banton [1987] Director; Amari Boothe [1989] Director; Curtis Dixon [1989] Director/Accounts Manager

Pura Panela Ltd
Incorporated: 6 April 2017
Registered Office: USE, 210 Portobello, Sheffield, S1 4AE
Major Shareholder: Natalia Welch
Officers: Natalia Welch [1985] Director/Founder [Colombian]

Pura Vita Drinks Ltd.
Incorporated: 27 May 2016
Registered Office: 27G Streatham Hill, Streatham High Road, Lambeth, London, SW16 1DT
Major Shareholder: Venelina Ivanova Gerginska
Officers: Venelina Gerginska [1986] Director/Entrepreneur [Bulgarian]

Pure Choice Watercoolers Limited
Incorporated: 24 September 1990
Registered Office: Unit D, Fleming Centre, Fleming Way, Crawley, W Sussex, RH10 9NN
Parent: Eden Springs UK Limited
Officers: Brian Richard Macpherson [1971] Director

The Pure Dartmoor Water Company Limited
Incorporated: 31 October 2011
Net Worth: £2,853 *Total Assets:* £23,686
Registered Office: The Water Shed, Mitchelcombe, Holne, Newton Abbot, Devon, TQ13 7SP
Officers: Mark Eden [1968] Director

Pure Spring Aqua Ltd
Incorporated: 20 March 2018
Registered Office: Unit 6b, 255 Water Road, Wembley, Middlesex, HA0 1JW
Major Shareholder: Amir Abbas Ahmadi Moghaddam
Officers: Amir Abbas Ahmadi Moghaddam [1997] Director

Purity Soft Drinks Limited
Incorporated: 20 December 1939 *Employees:* 72
Net Worth: £5,255,610 *Total Assets:* £14,429,173
Registered Office: Mounts Road, Wednesbury, W Midlands, WS10 0BU
Parent: Juiceburst Limited
Officers: Sarah Jane Baldwin [1970] Director/Chief Executive Officer

Qibla Cola (Beverages) Ltd
Incorporated: 13 February 2008
Registered Office: 1 Pennington Way, Coventry, Warwicks, CV6 5TJ
Major Shareholder: Mohammed Iqbal Khan
Officers: Mohammed Iqbal Khan, Secretary; Mohammed Iqbal Khan [1967] Director

Qiblah Beverages Limited
Incorporated: 26 October 2018
Registered Office: Impulse House, Westgatehill Street, Tong, Bradford, W Yorks, BD4 0SJ
Major Shareholder: Azr Abdul Quaddus
Officers: Azr Abdul Quaddus [1964] Director

Qiblah Products Limited
Incorporated: 2 November 2018
Registered Office: Impulse House, Westgatehill Street, Tong, Bradford, W Yorks, BD4 0SJ
Major Shareholder: Azr Abdul Quaddus
Officers: Azr Abdul Quaddus [1964] Director

Qishui Limited
Incorporated: 20 April 2018
Registered Office: Keepers, Longfords, Minchinhampton, Stroud, Glos, GL6 9AN
Major Shareholder: Henry Edward Stephen Davidson Binns
Officers: Henry Edward Stephen Davidson Binns [1997] Director

Quad Juices Limited
Incorporated: 11 October 2016
Net Worth: £5,500 *Total Assets:* £5,500
Registered Office: 210-211 Carter Place, London, SE17 2TF
Major Shareholder: Nii Ellis Affum Mensah Larnyoh
Officers: Nii Affum Larnyoh [1969] Director/Software Developer; Nii Affum Larnyoh [1969] Director/Software Developer

Radnor Hills Mineral Water Company Ltd
Incorporated: 3 October 1996 *Employees:* 165
Net Worth: £21,168,308 *Total Assets:* £31,864,320
Registered Office: Heartsease, Knighton, Powys, LD7 1LU
Major Shareholder: William Walter Watkins
Officers: Penelope Sue Butler, Secretary; Penelope Susan Butler [1960] Director; Julian Guy Rogers-Coltman [1961] Director; William Walter Watkins [1965] Director/Farmer

Rainbow Beverages Ltd
Incorporated: 15 November 2018
Registered Office: Kemp House, 160 City Road, London, EC1V 2NX
Shareholders: Amar Akram; Adil Mohammed Rafique
Officers: Amar Akram [1975] Director/Self Employed

Rainbow Carousel Soft Drinks Limited
Incorporated: 23 May 2001 *Employees:* 6
Net Worth: £27,614 *Total Assets:* £176,082
Registered Office: 5 Beaubridge Business Park, Heath Road, Skegness, Lincs, PE25 3ST
Shareholders: Michael John Davison; Yvonne Mary Davison
Officers: Yvonne Mary Davison, Secretary/Accountant; Michael John Davison [1958] Director/Refrigeration Engineer; Yvonne Mary Davison [1959] Director/Accountant

Raviom Limited
Incorporated: 2 January 2018
Registered Office: Kemp House, 160 City Road, London, EC1V 2NX
Major Shareholder: Bhaskar Nath
Officers: Aditi Nath, Secretary; Vishwa Nath, Secretary; Aditi Nath [1998] Director [Indian]; Bhaskar Nath [1994] Director/Businessman [Indian]; Vishwa Nath [1957] Director/Businessman [Indian]

Raw Is More Ltd.
Incorporated: 18 September 2015 *Employees:* 3
Net Worth Deficit: £32,448 *Total Assets:* £8,499
Registered Office: 3 Millwood Street, London, W10 6EH
Major Shareholder: Gabriel Bean
Officers: Victoria Bean, Secretary; Gabriel Bean [1993] Director/Founder; Brynmor Joe Ferris [1993] Director

H.D.Rawlings Limited
Incorporated: 13 May 1891
Registered Office: Breakspear Park, Breakspear Way, Hemel Hempstead, Herts, HP2 4TZ
Parent: Britvic Soft Drinks Limited
Officers: Judith Moore, Secretary; Mathew James Dunn [1974] Director/Chief Financial Officer; Peter Simon Litherland [1964] Director/Chief Executive; Alexandra Clare Thomas [1974] Director/General Counsel and Company Secretary

Razoo Limited
Incorporated: 30 July 2015
Net Worth Deficit: £9,062 *Total Assets:* £292
Registered Office: Lower Ground Floor, 40 Bloomsbury Way, London, WC1A 2SE
Shareholders: Andrew James Darragh Field; Rosheeka Dilhani Amarasekara Field
Officers: Andrew James Darragh Field [1980] Director [Australian]; Rosheeka Dilhani Amarasekara Field [1981] Director [Australian]

Real Natural UK Ltd
Incorporated: 16 October 2018
Registered Office: 61 Bridge Street, Kington, Herefords, HR5 3DJ
Major Shareholder: Graham Markham
Officers: Graham Markham [1984] Director [British/Canadian]

The Really Wild Drinks Company Limited
Incorporated: 7 May 1992
Registered Office: Breakspear Park, Breakspear Way, Hemel Hempstead, Herts, HP2 4TZ
Parent: Orchid Drinks Limited
Officers: Judith Moore, Secretary; Mathew James Dunn [1974] Director/Chief Financial Officer; Peter Simon Litherland [1964] Director/Chief Executive; Alexandra Clare Thomas [1974] Director/General Counsel and Company Secretary

Rebel Drinks (London) Limited
Incorporated: 15 September 2014
Net Worth: £2,395 *Total Assets:* £15,199
Registered Office: 167-169 Great Portland Street, London, W1W 5PF
Major Shareholder: Daniel Mark Boulter
Officers: Daniel Mark Boulter [1985] Director

Rebel Drinks Accra Limited
Incorporated: 29 January 2018
Registered Office: 167-169 Great Portland Street, London, W1W 5PF
Officers: Daniel Mark Boulter [1985] Director; Sarah Eleanor Nicole Meurisse [1972] Director

Red Bandit Limited
Incorporated: 8 March 2018
Registered Office: Union International Drinks Corporation, Bridge House, 64-72 Mabgate, Leeds, LS9 7DZ
Major Shareholder: Diane Wilson
Officers: Diane Wilson [1944] Director/Company Formation Agent Semi-Retired

Red Devil Energy Drinks Limited
Incorporated: 19 January 1995
Net Worth Deficit: £2,983,000
Registered Office: Breakspear Park, Breakspear Way, Hemel Hempstead, Herts, HP2 4TZ
Parent: Orchid Drinks Limited
Officers: Judith Moore, Secretary; Mathew James Dunn [1974] Director/Chief Financial Officer; Peter Simon Litherland [1964] Director/Chief Executive; Alexandra Clare Thomas [1974] Director/General Counsel and Company Secretary

Red Dragon Water Limited
Incorporated: 19 April 2005
Net Worth: £155,770 *Total Assets:* £463,677
Registered Office: 9 Greenways, Haywards Heath, W Sussex, RH16 2DT
Officers: Mercedes Travis Brewer, Secretary/Lawyer [American]; Frederic Peter Brewer [1940] Director/Financial Consultant; Mercedes Travis Brewer [1942] Director/Lawyer [American]

Red Steel Ltd
Incorporated: 13 June 2016
Registered Office: 200a High Street, Montrose, Angus, DD10 8PH
Officers: Martyn Turner [1968] Director

Refresco (Nelson) Limited
Incorporated: 22 March 1988
Previous: Cott (Nelson) Limited
Registered Office: Citrus Grove, Sideley, Kegworth, Derby, DE74 2FJ
Shareholder: Refresco Nelson (Holdings) Limited
Officers: David John Saint [1964] Managing Director

Refresco Beverages UK Limited
Incorporated: 28 November 1919 *Employees:* 842
Previous: Refresco Gerber UK Limited
Net Worth: £29,383,000 *Total Assets:* £185,803,008
Registered Office: Mallard Court, Express Park, Bridgwater, Somerset, TA6 4RN
Officers: Pieter Willem Van Meeteren, Secretary; Aart Cornelis Duijzer [1963] Managing Director [Dutch]; Johannes Henricus Wilhelmus Roelofs [1963] Managing Director [Dutch]; David John Saint [1964] Director/Executive

Refresco Developments Limited
Incorporated: 14 March 2013
Previous: Cott Developments Limited
Registered Office: Citrus Grove, Sideley, Kegworth, Derby, DE74 2FJ
Shareholder: Cott Beverages Limited
Officers: David John Saint [1964] Managing Director

Refresco Drinks UK Limited
Incorporated: 14 July 1993 *Employees:* 1,121
Previous: Cott Beverages Limited
Net Worth: £583,336,000 *Total Assets:* £751,484,992
Registered Office: Citrus Grove, Sideley, Kegworth, Derby, DE74 2FJ
Parent: Pride Foods Limited
Officers: Aart Duijzer [1963] Director [Dutch]; Hans Roelofs [1963] Director [Dutch]; David John Saint [1964] Managing Director

Refresh Brands Limited
Incorporated: 12 November 2013 *Employees:* 1
Net Worth Deficit: £115,344 *Total Assets:* £189,457
Registered Office: Timsons Business Centre, Bath Road, Kettering, Northants, NN16 8NQ
Major Shareholder: Rahi Daneshmand
Officers: Rahi Daneshmand [1988] Director

The Refreshing Drinks Company Limited
Incorporated: 21 February 2019
Registered Office: Kemp House, 160 City Road, London, EC1V 2NX
Officers: Simon Galea, Secretary; Paul Archard [1964] Director; Aneil Bedi [1967] Director; Simon David Galea [1961] Director; Taner Ozsumer [1986] Director

Refreshing Intercepted Limited
Incorporated: 30 July 2018
Registered Office: Jubilee House, East Beach, Lytham St Annes, Lancs, FY8 5FT
Officers: Richard Brittain [1983] Director/Recruiter; Justin Lee Steenhuisen [1981] Director

Regency Tonic Ltd
Incorporated: 2 August 2016
Net Worth Deficit: £7,475 *Total Assets:* £7,300
Registered Office: 66 Montgomery Street, Hove, E Sussex, BN3 5BE
Officers: Richard David Keeling [1983] Director; Charles David Osborne [1984] Director

Rejuvenation Water Ltd
Incorporated: 25 March 2015
Net Worth: £20,285 *Total Assets:* £78,248
Registered Office: c/o Bennett Brooks & Co Limited, Suite 345, 50 Eastcastle Street, London, W1W 8EA
Major Shareholder: Kristopher Ingham
Officers: Kristopher Ingham, Secretary; Carlo Geoffrey Buckley [1980] Director/UK Sales Manager; Garreth Hodgson [1971] Director; Kristopher Ingham [1985] Director/Business Owner; Cedric Marc Littman [1958] Director/Consultant; Daniel Smaller [1957] Director

Reluminate Ltd
Incorporated: 13 August 2018
Registered Office: Apartment 603, 1 Palace Place, London, SW1E 5BJ
Major Shareholder: Yulia Gladshteyn
Officers: Yulia Gladshteyn [1992] Managing Director [Cypriot]

Rhythm Nutrition Ltd
Incorporated: 19 October 2017
Registered Office: 21 Grange Road, Peterborough, PE3 9DR
Officers: Maya Qureshi [1981] Director [Spanish]; Yasir Qureshi [1983] Director

Ribble Valley Soft Drinks Limited
Incorporated: 1 July 2002 *Employees:* 6
Net Worth: £20,635 *Total Assets:* £192,997
Registered Office: 288 Church Street, Blackpool, Lancs, FY1 3QA
Shareholders: James Gordon Warnock; Karen Anne Warnock
Officers: Karen Anne Warnock [1961] Director/Soft Drinks Manufacturer

Rigdeplot Ltd
Incorporated: 14 August 2018
Registered Office: 18 Ffordd Ellen, Craig-Cefn-Parc, Swansea, SA6 5RZ
Major Shareholder: Leeanne McCreadie-Blake
Officers: Leeanne McCreadie-Blake [1994] Director/Consultant

Rio Coffee Limited
Incorporated: 1 July 2015
Registered Office: Construction House, Runwell Road, Wickford, Essex, SS11 7HQ
Shareholders: Jacqueline Finch; James Andrew Finch
Officers: Jacqueline Finch [1961] Director; James Andrew Finch [1961] Director

Roar Loud Limited
Incorporated: 8 August 2018
Registered Office: 65 College Road, London, SW19 2BP
Major Shareholder: Dino Pereira
Officers: Dino M C Pereira [1977] Director [Portuguese]

UK Manufacturers of Soft Drinks

Robinsons (Finance) No.2 Limited
Incorporated: 23 September 2010
Net Worth: £295,417,984 *Total Assets:* £295,481,984
Registered Office: Breakspear Park, Breakspear Way, Hemel Hempstead, Herts, HP2 4TZ
Officers: Judith Moore, Secretary; Mathew James Dunn [1974] Director/Chief Financial Officer; Peter Simon Litherland [1964] Director/Chief Executive; Alexandra Clare Thomas [1974] Director/General Counsel and Company Secretary

Robinsons Soft Drinks Limited
Incorporated: 4 November 1994
Net Worth: £205,435,008 *Total Assets:* £371,625,984
Registered Office: Breakspear Park, Breakspear Way, Hemel Hempstead, Herts, HP2 4TZ
Parent: Britvic Soft Drinks Limited
Officers: Judith Moore, Secretary; Mathew James Dunn [1974] Director/Chief Financial Officer; Peter Simon Litherland [1964] Director/Chief Executive; Alexandra Clare Thomas [1974] Director/General Counsel and Company Secretary

Rock's Organic Limited
Incorporated: 22 April 2002 *Employees:* 15
Net Worth: £1,306,668 *Total Assets:* £2,479,535
Registered Office: The Estate Office, Sutton Scotney, Winchester, Hants, SO21 3JW
Parent: 3V Natural Foods Limited
Officers: James Richard Willmott Ashton [1962] Director/Food and Drink Consultant; Elaine Birchall [1966] Director [Irish]; Neil William Butler [1963] Director/Accountant; Chris Lillie [1977] Director; Arthur William Richmond [1966] Director; Russell Alexander Smart [1963] Director

Rockbarr Limited
Incorporated: 7 November 1995 *Employees:* 8
Net Worth: £123,270 *Total Assets:* £325,722
Registered Office: Greengate, Middleton, Manchester, M24 1RU
Major Shareholder: Mark Adrian Currie
Officers: Mark Adrian Currie, Secretary; Mark Adrian Currie [1961] Director

Rocktails Drinks Limited
Incorporated: 12 February 2013 *Employees:* 3
Previous: Frozen Rocktails Limited
Net Worth Deficit: £499,636 *Total Assets:* £76,040
Registered Office: Netley House, Harrowbarrow, Callington, Cornwall, PL17 8BG
Major Shareholder: Christopher George Yandell
Officers: Christopher George Yandell [1981] Director

Rocx Energy Ltd
Incorporated: 20 January 2017
Registered Office: The Carlson Suite, Vantage Point Business Village, Mitcheldean, Glos, GL17 0DD
Major Shareholder: Oliver Roy Bennett
Officers: Oliver Bennett, Secretary; Oliver Roy Bennett [1992] Director

Roiss Mineral Water Limited
Incorporated: 22 December 2017
Registered Office: 14 Balmoral Close, Heanor, Derbys, DE75 7SN
Major Shareholder: Hugo Rodrigo Valdes Vera
Officers: Hugo Rodrigo Valdes Vera [1973] Director

Rok Natural Energy Limited
Incorporated: 13 September 2010
Registered Office: Rok House, Kingswood Business Park, Holyhead Road, Albrighton, Staffs, WV7 3AU
Parent: Rok Stars PLC
Officers: James Lee Kendrick [1969] Director

Roo Drinks Limited
Incorporated: 9 March 2017
Net Worth Deficit: £4,904
Registered Office: c/o Taylor Whittakes Accountancy Ltd, 46 Dovecote Lane, Sprighead, Oldham, Lancs, OL4 4SW
Shareholders: Stephen Glynn Williams; John Hodgson
Officers: John Hodgson [1968] Director; Stephen Glynn Williams [1967] Director

Rootfire Ltd
Incorporated: 23 January 2019
Registered Office: 84 Rye Road, Hoddesdon, Herts, EN11 0HP
Shareholders: Alexandra Fiske Harrisson; Alexandre Pierre Bidaut
Officers: Alexandra Fiske Harrisson [1977] Director/Accountant

Roots Soda Limited
Incorporated: 30 October 2012
Net Worth Deficit: £193,919 *Total Assets:* £29,039
Registered Office: Unit 13 New Broompark, Edinburgh, EH5 1RS
Major Shareholder: Mark Pool
Officers: Mark Pool [1978] Director/Entrepreneur

Rosemary Water Limited
Incorporated: 15 November 2016 *Employees:* 10
Net Worth: £181,309 *Total Assets:* £528,207
Registered Office: Ground Floor, 6 Burnsall Street, London, SW3 3ST
Major Shareholder: David Spencer-Percival
Officers: Richard James Pindar [1990] Director; David Spencer-Percival [1971] Director

Rubicon Drinks Limited
Incorporated: 14 September 1981
Net Worth: £80,284,000 *Total Assets:* £82,823,000
Registered Office: Crossley Drive, Magna Park, Milton Keynes, Bucks, MK17 8FL
Parent: A.G. Barr P.L.C.
Officers: Julie Anne Barr, Secretary; Stuart Lorimer [1966] Finance Director; Roger Alexander White [1965] Director

Russia Cola Limited
Incorporated: 2 January 2014
Registered Office: Third Floor, 207 Regent Street, London, W1B 3HH
Major Shareholder: Vincent Boueshaghi
Officers: Vincent Boueshaghi [1976] Director/Engineer [French]

Ruudz Limited
Incorporated: 21 May 2007
Net Worth Deficit: £469 *Total Assets:* £30
Registered Office: 4-5 King Square, Bridgwater, Somerset, TA6 3YF
Shareholders: Clive Graham John Birnie; Martyn James Shiner; Mark Robin Steele-Mortimer
Officers: Martyn James Shiner, Secretary; Clive Graham John Birnie [1968] Director/Marketing Executive; Martyn James Shiner [1963] Director/Accountant; Mark Robin Steele-Mortimer [1966] Director

Ryan-Knight Enterprises Limited
Incorporated: 21 December 2018
Registered Office: 3 Coronation Cottages, Jubilee Road, Worth, Deal, Kent, CT14 0DW
Major Shareholder: Danielle Samantha May Ryan-Knight
Officers: Danielle Samantha May Ryan-Knight [1992] Director/Carer

Ryd Food & Drinks Limited
Incorporated: 29 August 2014
Net Worth Deficit: £13,291 *Total Assets:* £35,544
Registered Office: Small Meadow, Sturt Green, Holyport, Maidenhead, Berks, SL6 2JF
Shareholders: Yvonne May Levy; Ramon Ashley Levy-Vassie; Dianne Nadine Irish-Tavares
Officers: Dianne Nadine Irish-Tavares [1964] Director; Ramon Ashley Levy-Vassie [1988] Director; Yvonne Levy-Vassie [1954] Director

Saapos Ltd
Incorporated: 14 December 2011
Registered Office: 32 Spinnells Road, Harrow, Middlesex, HA2 9RA
Officers: Collin Carr [1972] Director [Jamaican]

Sacred Springs Water Company Limited
Incorporated: 19 February 2013
Net Worth Deficit: £80,225 *Total Assets:* £15,804
Registered Office: Knapp Farm, Birdlip Hill, Witcombe, Glos, GL3 4SL
Major Shareholder: Paul Anthony Matthews
Officers: Paul Anthony Matthews, Secretary; Paul Anthony Matthews [1957] Director/Property Manager; Phillip James Matthews [1958] Director/Heating Engineer

Saffron Water Limited
Incorporated: 21 June 2018
Registered Office: 13 Mornington Avenue, London, W14 8UJ
Major Shareholder: Keyvan Fathalizadeh
Officers: Keyvan Fathalizadeh [1986] Director

Saft Drinks Ltd
Incorporated: 17 May 2018
Registered Office: 6 Dukes Lane, Gerrards Cross, Bucks, SL9 7JZ
Major Shareholder: Katarina Eva Birgitta Tencor
Officers: Katarina Eva Birgitta Tencor [1990] Director

Saftiaray & Co Limited
Incorporated: 3 September 2013
Registered Office: 5 Luxfield Road, London, SE9 4EZ
Officers: Jean Bailey [1953] Director

Sai Water UK Limited
Incorporated: 19 February 2019
Registered Office: 1 Conifer Way, Wembley, Middlesex, HA0 3QP
Shareholder: Firoz Dulobo
Officers: Amitkumar Bhavsar [1982] Director/Self Employed [Indian]; Firoz Dulobo [1976] Director [Portuguese]; Mehul Rana [1980] Director/Self Employed [American]

Saicho Ltd.
Incorporated: 15 May 2017
Registered Office: BDO, Regent House, Clinton Avenue, Nottingham, NG5 1AZ
Shareholders: Xiao Nan Natalie Chiu; Charles George Winkworth-Smith
Officers: Dr Xiao Nan Natalie Chiu [1990] Director/Scientist [Hong Kong]; Dr Charles George Winkworth-Smith [1987] Director/Scientist

Saint Patricks Ltd
Incorporated: 15 February 2018
Registered Office: 20-22 Wenlock Road, London, N1 7GU
Major Shareholder: Patrick Hayden
Officers: Patrick Hayden [1987] Director/Founder

Salad Passion Foods Ltd
Incorporated: 27 May 2015
Registered Office: 8 Oulton Close, London, E5 9PQ
Shareholder: Tamara Maddix
Officers: Tamara Maddix, Secretary; Wayne Maddix, Secretary; Tamara Maddix [1981] Production Director [Jamaican]; Wayne Maddix [1976] Production Director

Salcombe Cider Company Ltd
Incorporated: 5 December 2016
Registered Office: Holwell Farm, South Huish, Kingsbridge, Devon, TQ7 3EQ
Major Shareholder: Duncan Walker Burnett
Officers: Duncan Walker Burnett [1986] Director/Cider Maker

Salicaria Ltd
Incorporated: 20 August 2018
Registered Office: 62 Westfield Court, Redcar, Cleveland, TS10 5QZ
Major Shareholder: Michael Hoyle
Officers: Michael Hoyle [1982] Director/Consultant

Saltcoats Mineral Water Company Limited
Incorporated: 28 August 2018
Registered Office: Greenhead Farm, Grassyards Road, Kilmarnock, E Ayrshire, KA3 6HG
Major Shareholder: Gordon McCulloch

Samco Retail Ltd
Incorporated: 6 July 2007
Net Worth Deficit: £57,057 *Total Assets:* £35,745
Registered Office: Unit I, Victoria Works, Barton Road, Dukinfield, Cheshire, SK16 4US
Major Shareholder: Bilal Aziz
Officers: Lubna Aziz, Secretary; Bilal Aziz [1968] Director

Sansu Drinks Ltd
Incorporated: 15 May 2013
Net Worth Deficit: £78,082 *Total Assets:* £56,768
Registered Office: Unit 76, 275 New North Road, London, N1 7AA
Officers: Jung-Yeun Hahn [1954] Director/Administrator [South Korean]

The Santa Monica Company Ltd
Incorporated: 2 June 2017
Net Worth Deficit: £28,782 *Total Assets:* £9,218
Registered Office: Millshaw, Ring Road, Leeds, LS11 8EG
Major Shareholder: Oliver William Roderick Evans
Officers: Oliver William Roderick Evans [1996] Director/Chairman

Scheckter's Organic Beverages Limited
Incorporated: 29 June 2010 *Employees:* 3
Net Worth Deficit: £1,748,593 *Total Assets:* £1,662,964
Registered Office: D1, The Courtyard, Alban Park, Hatfield Road, St Albans, Herts, AL4 0LA
Officers: Owen Charles Phillips [1959] Director

UK Manufacturers of Soft Drinks   dellam

Schnapps Limited
Incorporated: 25 May 2018
Registered Office: Bridge House, 64-72 Mabgate, Leeds, LS9 7DZ
Major Shareholder: Robert (Elias) Wilson
Officers: Robert Elias Wilson [1941] Director/Company Formation Agent

Schweppes International Limited
Incorporated: 17 August 1923 *Employees:* 94
Net Worth: £357,152,096 *Total Assets:* £453,451,424
Registered Office: 7 Albemarle Street, London, W1S 4HQ
Parent: Suntory Beverage & Food Limited
Officers: Patrick David Blake [1977] Finance Director [Irish]; Sylvie Bouvet Ep. Toole [1971] Director/Supply Operations Manager [French]; Diego de Blas Bravo [1963] Director/Chief Legal Officer [Spanish]; Louis-Francois Amand Gombert [1967] Director/Senior General Manager Global Finance [French]; Jaime Antonio Mussons Freixas [1961] Director/Chief Marketing Officer [Spanish]; Jonathan Mark Roberts [1966] Managing Director; Jennegien Willemina Schnieders [1967] Director/Legal Executive [Dutch]; Tetsu Tanaka [1967] Director/Chief of Staff to SBFE CEO [Japanese]

Scops Drinks Limited
Incorporated: 16 June 2010
Net Worth Deficit: £75,046 *Total Assets:* £2,704
Registered Office: Dean Court, Lower Dean, Buckfastleigh, Devon, TQ11 0LT
Major Shareholder: Gabriel Luscombe David
Officers: Gabriel Luscombe David [1965] Director

The Scotch Water Company Limited
Incorporated: 11 June 1992
Registered Office: 1a Guthrie Street, Carnoustie, Angus, DD7 6EL
Officers: Robin Phillips Grant, Secretary; Robin Phillips Grant [1939] Director/General Manager

Scotod Ltd
Incorporated: 17 January 2018
Net Worth Deficit: £4,597 *Total Assets:* £5,429
Registered Office: 15 Jellicoe Avenue, Belfast, BT15 3FZ
Major Shareholder: Scott Todd
Officers: Scott Todd [1987] Director

Sea Buck Limited
Incorporated: 7 May 2018
Registered Office: Red Willows, Dynas la Road, St Ives, Cornwall, TR26 2BU
Shareholders: Timothy John Symons; Charles Henry Symons; Mark Louis James Rule
Officers: Mark Louis James Rule [1982] Director/Restaurateur; Charles Henry Symons [1983] Director/Restaurateur; Timothy John Symons [1957] Director/Restaurateur

Seafire Brewing Co. Ltd
Incorporated: 22 February 2019
Registered Office: 10 Seafire Place, Dalgety Bay, Dunfermline, Fife, KY11 9GY
Major Shareholder: Kiera Browne
Officers: Kiera Browne [1982] Director/Chief Executive

Seasons Soft Drinks Limited
Incorporated: 29 May 1997
Net Worth: £49,341 *Total Assets:* £351,440
Registered Office: 9 Vantage Point, Howley Park Road, East Morley, Leeds, LS27 0SU
Shareholders: Christina McCool; Ian Parish; Belinda Ruth Parish
Officers: Christina McCool, Secretary; Richard Christopher McCool [1967] Director/Accountant; Ian Parish [1955] Managing Director

Seed Lab Ltd.
Incorporated: 8 April 2017
Net Worth Deficit: £827 *Total Assets:* £143
Registered Office: 49 Queens Road, Cheltenham, Glos, GL50 2LX
Shareholders: William Martin; Waseem Brare
Officers: Waseem Brare [1989] Managing Director; William Martin [1986] Managing Director

Sejuiced Limited
Incorporated: 13 April 2004
Net Worth: £80,766 *Total Assets:* £103,593
Registered Office: Arch 1, Block G, Chartwell Business Park, 61-65 Paulet Road, London, SE5 9HW
Major Shareholder: Sylvia Marie Garvin
Officers: Sylvia Marie Garvin, Secretary/General Manager; Sylvia Marie Garvin [1974] Director/General Manager

Sekforde Drinks Limited
Incorporated: 13 May 2016
Net Worth: £83,826 *Total Assets:* £124,766
Registered Office: First Floor, 10 Temple Back, Bristol, BS1 6FL
Major Shareholder: Sarah Emily Talula White
Officers: Sarah Emily Talula White [1985] Director/Advertising Executive

Seltza Ltd
Incorporated: 23 June 2016
Registered Office: Endrick Hub, 151 Buchanan Street, Balfron, Stirlingshire, G63 0TE
Officers: Martha MacKenzie, Secretary; Martha MacKenzie [1976] Director/Sales Person; Petra Margareta Wetzel [1974] Director [German]

Sendivogius Limited
Incorporated: 8 June 2018
Registered Office: 9 Christopher Street, London, EC2A 2BS
Major Shareholder: Piotr Jan Jedrzejewski
Officers: Piotr Jan Jedrzejewski [1983] Managing Director [Polish]

The Sensible Drinks Company Ltd
Incorporated: 20 August 2014 *Employees:* 1
Net Worth Deficit: £96,315 *Total Assets:* £22,975
Registered Office: 9 Moorlands Court, Spring Meadows, Darwen, Lancs, BB3 3LQ
Shareholder: Glenn Roberts
Officers: Glenn Roberts [1960] Director

Septimus Spyder Soft Drinks Limited
Incorporated: 9 October 1995
Net Worth Deficit: £75,641 *Total Assets:* £87,314
Registered Office: 54 Yew Tree Avenue, Lichfield, Staffs, WS14 9UA
Major Shareholder: Roger John Schmid
Officers: Roger John Schmid, Secretary; Ellen Frania Crosby [1978] Director

Session Brewing Co. Limited
Incorporated: 19 June 2017
Registered Office: Mount Noddy, Church Lane, Danehill, Haywards Heath, W Sussex, RH17 7EY
Major Shareholder: Rufus Wilkinson
Officers: Rufus Giles Wilkinson [1995] Director/Student

SGRIC Limited
Incorporated: 23 February 2016
Registered Office: Flat 3, 103 Ross Road, London, SE25 6TS
Major Shareholder: Prince Tikare
Officers: Prince Tikare [1969] Director/Architect/Entrepreneur

The Shakespeare Spring Water Company Limited
Incorporated: 1 July 1994
Registered Office: The Cedars, Stoneleigh Road, Bubbenhall, Warwicks, CV8 3BT
Officers: Maxine Jones, Secretary; Malcolm Jones [1949] Director/Chartered Surveyor; Maxine Jones [1960] Director/Secretary

Shandy Shack Ltd
Incorporated: 14 August 2018
Registered Office: 18 The Parkway, Southampton, SO16 3PQ
Shareholders: Frederick Joseph York Gleadowe; Edward Stapleton; Thomas Peter Stevens
Officers: Dr Frederick Joseph York Gleadowe [1991] Managing Director; Edward Stapleton [1992] Managing Director; Dr Thomas Peter Stevens [1991] Managing Director

Sharewater Ltd
Incorporated: 14 November 2014
Net Worth Deficit: £5,220
Registered Office: Flat 15, 272 Cambridge Heath Road, London, E2 9DA
Major Shareholder: Ahmed Amarouch
Officers: Ahmed Amarouch [1988] Director [German]

Ben Shaws Dispense Drinks Limited
Incorporated: 14 June 1928
Registered Office: Laurel House, 3 Woodlands Park, Newton-le-Willows, Merseyside, WA12 0HH
Parent: Nichols PLC
Officers: Timothy John Croston, Secretary; Timothy John Croston [1963] Director

Shepley Spring Limited
Incorporated: 9 July 1996 *Employees:* 59
Net Worth: £7,454,720 *Total Assets:* £11,338,697
Registered Office: Eastfield Mills, The Knowle, Shepley, Huddersfield, W Yorks, HD8 8EA
Parent: Penmoor UK Ltd
Officers: Jason Barlow [1972] Director; Andrew Peykoff II [1976] Director/Executive [American]; Kenneth Ratzlaff [1968] Director/Executive [American]; Rali Sanderon [1976] Director/Executive [American]; Charles Alistair Smith [1969] Director; James Maxwell Smith [1971] Director; John Selwyn Smith [1942] Director

Shindig Promotions Ltd
Incorporated: 22 May 2017
Registered Office: 2 Beechlodge Park, Warrenpoint, Co Down, BT34 3NA
Shareholders: James Stephen McAteer; Shan McAteer
Officers: James Stephen McAteer [1957] Director/Entrepreneur [Irish]; Shan McAteer [1980] Director/Therapist [Irish]

Shlurpies Ltd.
Incorporated: 22 February 2018
Registered Office: 16 Court Farm Road, Northolt, Middlesex, UB5 5HQ
Major Shareholder: Stefania Amodeo
Officers: Stefania Amodeo [1994] Director/Entrepreneur

Shop-Local-UK Ltd
Incorporated: 17 August 2016
Net Worth: £1 *Total Assets:* £1
Registered Office: Unit 1 Fairview Industrial Park, Marsh Way, Rainham, Essex, RM13 8UH
Major Shareholder: Shamir Bihal
Officers: Shamir Bihal [1974] Director

Showerings Cider Mill Ltd
Incorporated: 14 July 2016
Net Worth Deficit: £360,544 *Total Assets:* £2,506,517
Registered Office: St Catherine's Court, Berkeley Place, Clifton, Bristol, BS8 1BQ
Parent: Brothers Drinks Co. Limited
Officers: Iain David Glen [1969] Finance Director; Jonathan Showering [1962] Director; Matthew Herbert Showering [1964] Director

Shrubb Ltd
Incorporated: 26 June 2018
Registered Office: Allensbank, Providence Hill, Narberth, Pembrokeshire, SA67 8RF
Shareholders: Ashley James Calvert; Elinor Beverly Alexandra Tourlamain
Officers: Ashley James Calvert [1969] Director/Business Consultant; Elinor Beverly Alexandra Tourlamain [1975] Director/Self Employed

Signpost Brewery Ltd
Incorporated: 13 September 2018
Registered Office: 71-75 Shelton Street, London, WC2H 9JQ
Shareholders: David Berkeley Buchanan Kenning; Tobias Edward Burney Kenning
Officers: David Berkeley Buchanan Kenning [1951] Director; Tobias Edward Burney Kenning [1988] Director

Silver Spa Limited
Incorporated: 26 March 2007
Registered Office: Limberlost, Eastbourne Road, Halland, Lewes, E Sussex, BN8 6PU
Major Shareholder: Chris Magness
Officers: Christopher Stanley Magness, Secretary; Christopher Stanley Magness [1949] Director

Simple Nature Limited
Incorporated: 10 February 2016
Net Worth: £700 *Total Assets:* £700
Registered Office: 1 Billesley, Alcester, Warwicks, B49 6NE
Major Shareholder: Oak Aaron Kerby-Steele
Officers: Oak Kerby-Steele, Secretary; Oak Kerby-Steele [1995] Director

Simpson's Beverage Supply Company Limited
Incorporated: 30 September 1948 *Employees:* 32
Net Worth: £1,795,191 *Total Assets:* £2,822,880
Registered Office: Unit 1 Chiswick Grove, Blackpool, Lancs, FY3 9EU
Parent: Simpsons Holdings Limited
Officers: James Simpson, Secretary; Adrian Simpson [1986] Director; Caleb Simpson [1978] Director; Generald Whitworth Simpson [1947] Director/Mineral Water Manufacturer; James Simpson [1970] Director/Production Manager; Jason Simpson [1981] Director

SIP Kombucha Ltd
Incorporated: 2 January 2019
Registered Office: 21 Fresson Road, Stevenage, Herts, SG1 3QU
Major Shareholder: William Donald Hornby
Officers: Caroline Nicole Hornby [1983] Marketing Director [Swedish/Norwegian]; William Donald Hornby [1980] Director/Chief Executive

Sips MCR Ltd
Incorporated: 12 February 2019
Registered Office: Flat 7, Elite Close, Manchester, M8 9FL
Major Shareholder: Yissochor Dov Merlin
Officers: Yissochor Dov Merlin [1995] Director/General Manager

UK Manufacturers of Soft Drinks

Sipsup Limited
Incorporated: 17 August 2018
Registered Office: Wey Court West, Union Road, Farnham, Surrey, GU9 7PT
Major Shareholder: Edward Swete
Officers: Edward Swete [1981] Managing Director

SK Global Brands Ltd
Incorporated: 30 June 2017
Registered Office: Third Floor, 207 Regent Street, London, W1B 3HH
Major Shareholder: Michael Peter Olesker
Officers: Michael Peter Olesker [1949] Director

Skep Drinks Limited
Incorporated: 16 August 2018
Registered Office: 24 St Albans Road, Colchester, Essex, CO3 3JQ
Major Shareholder: Chris Adam Strong
Officers: Chris Adam Strong [1980] Creative Director

Skwishee Ltd
Incorporated: 7 August 2017
Registered Office: 7 Glass Street, Markinch, Glenrothes, Fife, KY7 6DP
Shareholders: Raza Rehman; Harris Shahzad Aslam
Officers: Harris Shahzad Aslam [1996] Director; Raza Rehman [1990] Director

Sleek Still Scottish Water Limited
Incorporated: 13 February 2017
Net Worth Deficit: £13,947 *Total Assets:* £33,953
Registered Office: My Edinburgh Life, 13-14 Rosebery Crescent, Edinburgh, EH12 5JY
Shareholder: Nathanael Sinue Slijkhuis
Officers: Nathanael Sinue Slijkhuis [1996] Director [Dutch]

Slimmers World Sports Drinks Limited
Incorporated: 10 March 2018
Registered Office: Union International Drinks Corporation, Bridge House, 64-72 Mabgate, off Regent Street, Leeds, LS9 7DZ
Major Shareholder: Diane Wilson
Officers: Diane Wilson [1944] Director/Company Formation Agent Semi-Retired

SLO Good Living Ltd
Incorporated: 3 February 2016
Net Worth Deficit: £8,351 *Total Assets:* £1,020
Registered Office: Unit 204, 28 Old Brompton Road, London, SW7 3SS
Shareholders: Paul Martin Krepski; Colleen Woo
Officers: Paul Martin Krepski [1982] Director/Finance

Slush Puppie Limited
Incorporated: 16 June 1945 *Employees:* 88
Net Worth: £6,632,496 *Total Assets:* £13,844,823
Registered Office: Slush Puppie Ltd, Coronation Road, Cressex Business Park, High Wycombe, Bucks, HP12 3TA
Parent: Ralph Peter's and Sons Ltd
Officers: Susanne Treacher, Secretary; Alan Raymond Beaney [1962] Director/Chairman; Laura Peters [1988] Director/Stock Manager; Mark Jeffrey Peters [1958] Director

Smilk Limited
Incorporated: 15 February 2012
Registered Office: 2 Churchill Drive, Emsworth, Hants, PO10 7SL
Major Shareholder: Simon Flint
Officers: Simon Flint [1980] Director

Smith & Harrison Ltd
Incorporated: 12 September 2017
Registered Office: 316 Millhouses Lane, Sheffield, S11 9JD
Shareholders: Lynwen Rachel Harrison; Rachel Suzanne Smith
Officers: Lynwen Rachel Harrison [1969] Director; Rachel Suzanne Smith [1972] Director

SmithKline Beecham Limited
Incorporated: 24 January 1989 *Employees:* 1,333
Net Worth: £1,310,000,000 *Total Assets:* £2,496,000,000
Registered Office: 980 Great West Road, Brentford, Middlesex, TW8 9GS
Parent: GlaxoSmithKline Finance PLC
Officers: Victoria Anne Whyte, Secretary; Simon Paul Dingemans [1963] Director

SMJ Beverages Limited
Incorporated: 27 October 1992
Net Worth Deficit: £24,332 *Total Assets:* £222
Registered Office: St Bride's House, 10 Salisbury Square, London, EC4Y 8EH
Major Shareholder: Aleem Mohammed
Officers: Moreland Mohammed, Secretary; Doctor Aleem Mohammed [1951] Director/Medical Doctor [Trinidadian]

Smoother Spirits Limited
Incorporated: 13 July 2006 *Employees:* 1
Net Worth: £141,749 *Total Assets:* £337,555
Registered Office: 76 Dumbarton Road, Clydebank, W Dunbartonshire, G81 1UG
Shareholder: Graeme John Lindsay
Officers: Graeme John Lindsay [1965] Director; Zihni Erhan Rustem Tatar [1964] Director

So-Real Foods Ltd
Incorporated: 13 September 2012
Registered Office: 24 McNeil Road, Camberwell, London, SE5 8PL
Major Shareholder: Umar Abdullah
Officers: Umar Abdullah, Secretary; Umar Abdullah [1958] Director/Trader

Soak Coffee Ltd
Incorporated: 13 January 2017
Net Worth: £9,977 *Total Assets:* £9,977
Registered Office: 1 Kernaghan Court, Hillsborough, Co Down, BT26 6RN
Major Shareholder: Geoffrey William Barr
Officers: Geoffrey William Barr [1993] Director/Entrepreneur

Sobare Limited
Incorporated: 9 August 2017
Net Worth: £100 *Total Assets:* £20,361
Registered Office: 12 Upper Berkeley Street, London, W1H 7QD
Officers: Selina Jane Norfolk [1962] Director/Consultant

Sober Drinks Limited
Incorporated: 29 August 2017
Registered Office: 13 Merlin Crescent, Newport, NP19 7LF
Major Shareholder: Richard Pollentine
Officers: Richard Pollentine [1985] Director/Owner

The Soda Factory Limited
Incorporated: 9 June 2017
Net Worth Deficit: £6,768 *Total Assets:* £637
Registered Office: 3 Wellesley Road, Liverpool, L8 3SU
Officers: Hami David Harbridge [1988] Director/Management and Trading of Soft Drink Beverages; Dr Bimal Karmakar [1969] Director/Management and Trading of Soft Drink Beverage

Soda Folk Ltd
Incorporated: 10 July 2013
Net Worth: £84,780 *Total Assets:* £328,685
Registered Office: Suite 210, Fountain Court, 2 Victoria Square, St Albans, Herts, AL1 3TF
Major Shareholder: Kenneth Farrell Graham
Officers: Kenneth Graham [1982] Sales Director [American]

Sodahouseco Limited
Incorporated: 22 August 2018
Registered Office: 13 Montpellier Arcade, Cheltenham, Glos, GL50 1SU
Major Shareholder: Michele Carole Bodart
Officers: Michele Carole Bodart [1960] Director/Chief Executive

Soft N Sweet Ltd
Incorporated: 12 October 2015
Net Worth: £527,873 *Total Assets:* £619,012
Registered Office: Henleaze House, 13 Harbury Road, Bristol, BS9 4PN
Major Shareholder: Essin Khan
Officers: Essin Khan [1991] Trading Director

Soho Juice Co Ltd
Incorporated: 3 February 2015 *Employees:* 4
Net Worth Deficit: £137,701 *Total Assets:* £33,466
Registered Office: 1st Floor, 25 Lexington Street, London, W1F 9AH
Major Shareholder: Paul Martin Barnes
Officers: Paul Martin Barnes [1953] Director/Chartered Certified Accountant

Solar Cola Limited
Incorporated: 24 January 2005
Net Worth: £60 *Total Assets:* £67,217
Registered Office: Solar House, Lime Park, Herstmonceux, E Sussex, BN27 1RF
Officers: Briggette Madge Odell Dusart [1957] Director/Administration; Christina Dusart [1988] Director/Artist; Katie Dusart [1985] Director/Office Manager

Solo Coffee Ltd
Incorporated: 1 April 2016
Previous: Antler and Bird Limited
Net Worth: £6,290 *Total Assets:* £36,710
Registered Office: Bramleys, Bournes Green, Stroud, Glos, GL6 7NL
Shareholders: Alexander Kimberley John Foss Sims; Theo Garcia-Minaur
Officers: Alexander Foss Sims [1989] Director; Theo Garcia-Minaur [1995] Director

Sopro Drinks Ltd
Incorporated: 3 January 2018
Registered Office: Gateshead International Business Centre, Mulgrave Terrace, Gateshead, Tyne & Wear, NE8 1AN
Parent: Brainwave Brands Ltd
Officers: Nikola Hrstic [1959] Director; Richard Frederick Veltrop-Baister [1981] Director

South West Juice Co. Ltd
Incorporated: 7 January 2015
Previous: PRSMCO Ltd
Net Worth: £100 *Total Assets:* £100
Registered Office: 120 High Road, East Finchley, London, N2 9ED
Major Shareholder: Marcus Prosch
Officers: Marcus Prosch [1976] Director/Management [German]

The Southdowns Natural Water Ltd
Incorporated: 10 May 2006
Registered Office: Windsor House, Park Road, Southbourne, Hants, PO10 8NY
Shareholders: Ian Gavin Charles Windsor; Kathryn Denise Windsor
Officers: Ian Gavin Charles Windsor, Secretary; Ian Gavin Charles Windsor [1954] Director; Kathryn Denise Windsor [1956] Director

Southdowns Water Co Ltd
Incorporated: 28 May 2013 *Employees:* 9
Net Worth: £69,715 *Total Assets:* £338,135
Registered Office: Windsor House, Clovelly Road, Southbourne, Emsworth, Hants, PO10 8PF
Major Shareholder: William Thomas Gregory Windsor
Officers: William Thomas Gregory Windsor [1985] Director

Southern Table Water Company Limited (The)
Incorporated: 12 January 1948
Registered Office: Breakspear Park, Breakspear Way, Hemel Hempstead, Herts, HP2 4TZ
Parent: Britvic Soft Drinks Limited
Officers: Judith Moore, Secretary; Mathew James Dunn [1974] Director/Chief Financial Officer; Peter Simon Litherland [1964] Director/Chief Executive; Alexandra Clare Thomas [1974] Director/General Counsel and Company Secretary

Space Chef Ltd
Incorporated: 4 January 2019
Registered Office: 35 East Crescent, Sneyd Green, Stoke on Trent, Staffs, ST1 6ES
Major Shareholder: Oakley Blue Anderson
Officers: Oakley Blue Anderson [1997] Director/Shop Assistant

Peter Spanton Drinks Ltd
Incorporated: 30 July 2014 *Employees:* 7
Net Worth: £201,095 *Total Assets:* £374,302
Registered Office: 18 Iliffe Yard, London, SE17 3QA
Officers: Ceri Passmore, Secretary; Darryl John Burton [1964] Managing Director; Barrie Haley Moore [1954] Investment Director; Ceri Elizabeth Passmore [1972] Director/Producer; Peter Charles Spanton [1955] Director/Drink Designer; William Job Stern [1970] Director/Managing Partner

Sperrin Springs Limited
Incorporated: 5 October 2000
Net Worth: £31,060 *Total Assets:* £181,665
Registered Office: 31 Carrigullen Road, Strabane, Co Tyrone, BT82 8PN
Officers: Raymond Moan, Secretary; Eunice Gloria Moan [1955] Director/Housewife; Raymond Moan [1951] Director/Farmer

Speyside Glenlivet (HSL) Company Limited
Incorporated: 12 December 2008 *Employees:* 9
Net Worth: £188,000 *Total Assets:* £543,000
Registered Office: Stirling Street, Blackford, Perthshire, PH4 1QA
Officers: Mark Alexander Steven, Secretary; Maher Altajir [1957] Director/Businessman [Emirati]; Leslie Montgomery [1963] Director

Spirit of Shanti Ltd
Incorporated: 11 September 2018
Registered Office: 12 Turnpike Way, Rothley, Leicester, LE7 7SU
Major Shareholder: Layla Marissa Lawford
Officers: Layla Marissa Lawford [1987] Director

UK Manufacturers of Soft Drinks dellam

Sportential Limited
Incorporated: 15 August 2016
Net Worth: £1 Total Assets: £1
Registered Office: Wilson Business Park, 1 Queen Elizabeth Avenue, Hillington Park, Glasgow, G52 4NQ
Shareholders: Iain Wilson; Iain Wilson
Officers: Iain Wilson [1953] Director; Iain Wilson [1978] Director

Spring Cool Soft Drinks Limited
Incorporated: 6 August 2008
Net Worth Deficit: £211,580
Registered Office: 100 Railway Street, Ballymena, Co Antrim, BT42 2AF
Major Shareholder: James Crawford Harkness
Officers: Rachel McCann, Secretary; James Crawford Harkness [1964] Director

Spring Water (Devon) Limited
Incorporated: 29 September 2010
Net Worth Deficit: £79,126 Total Assets: £139,667
Registered Office: 3rd Floor, Vyman House, 104 College Road, Harrow, Middlesex, HA1 1BQ
Shareholders: Jeremy Wright; Marilyn Poole; Steve Littley
Officers: Steven Belford Littley [1969] Director; Marilyn Poole [1959] Director; Jeremy Wright [1962] Director

Spruce Water Limited
Incorporated: 18 February 2019
Registered Office: 125 Gassiot Road, London, SW17 8LD
Major Shareholder: Jonathan Philip Cazaly
Officers: Jonathan Philip Cazaly [1989] Director

Square Root London Limited
Incorporated: 21 November 2013 Employees: 16
Net Worth Deficit: £23,376 Total Assets: £171,353
Registered Office: 449a Railway Arches, Amhurst Road, London, E8 2AJ
Shareholders: Edward Taylor; Robyn Louise Simms
Officers: Robyn Simms [1990] Director; Edward Taylor [1988] Director

Squish Squash Limited
Incorporated: 13 September 2013
Registered Office: 4 Harford Close, Chippenham, Wilts, SN15 3PY
Shareholder: Matthew Steven Harvey
Officers: Matthew Steven Harvey [1979] Director/Owner; Simon James Herbert [1978] Director; Adrian Christopher Stockil [1965] Director of Sales

Sqwish Squash Limited
Incorporated: 23 October 2012
Registered Office: 4 Harford Close, Chippenham, Wilts, SN15 3PY
Shareholder: Matthew Steven Harvey
Officers: Matthew Steven Harvey [1979] Director

SRP Equipe Limited
Incorporated: 8 September 2017
Registered Office: 100 Horseshoe Crescent, Birmingham, B43 7BL
Shareholder: Lateef Elford-Alliyu
Officers: Saido Berahino [1993] Director/Sports Person; Lateef Elford-Alliyu [1992] Director/Retail; Romaine Sawyers [1991] Director/Sports Person

St. Davids Spring Water Company Limited
Incorporated: 14 July 2005
Net Worth: £1 Total Assets: £1
Registered Office: Bryn Gwynfa Farm, Carmel, Caernarfon, Gwynedd, LL54 7AP
Major Shareholder: Michael Rees Thomas
Officers: Diana Wendy Rees Thomas, Secretary; Michael Rees Thomas [1950] Director/Consultant

The Start-Up Drinks Lab Limited
Incorporated: 13 June 2017
Net Worth: £121,474 Total Assets: £206,699
Registered Office: Unit 4 Building D, Kelburn Business Park, Port Glasgow, Inverclyde, PA14 6BL
Shareholders: Craig Robert Strachan; Hannah Magdaline Fisher
Officers: John Ross Brodie [1964] Director; Hannah Magdaline Fisher [1983] Marketing Director; Craig Robert Strachan [1988] Finance Director

Steep Soft Drinks Company Ltd
Incorporated: 29 January 2016
Net Worth: £2,663 Total Assets: £6,663
Registered Office: 73 Temperance Street, Manchester, M12 6HU
Shareholders: Liam Adrian Willday; Laura Jane Smith
Officers: Laura Jane Smith [1991] Director; Liam Adrian Willday [1991] Director

Stonehenge Spring Water Limited
Incorporated: 24 September 2014
Registered Office: The Old Mill, Netheravon, Salisbury, Wilts, SP4 9QB
Shareholders: Stig Anker Andersen; Anna Marie Andersen
Officers: Anna Marie Andersen [1954] Director/Administrator [Danish]; Stig Anker Andersen [1958] Director/Brewer [Danish]

Storefast Solutions Limited
Incorporated: 23 March 2007 Employees: 22
Net Worth: £803,431 Total Assets: £1,923,409
Registered Office: Ochard House, Courtyard V, Springhead Enterprise Park, Northfleet, Kent, DA11 8HN
Shareholders: Sharon Claretta Angela Kirby; John Kirby; Nicholas Kirby
Officers: Sharon Claretta Angela Kirby, Secretary; Nicholas Kirby [1981] Director; Sharon Claretta Angela Kirby [1957] Director

Story Drinks Limited
Incorporated: 17 April 2014
Registered Office: Lifford Hall, Lifford Lane, Kings Norton, Birmingham, B30 3JN
Major Shareholder: Julian Wilfrid Sollom
Officers: Julian Wilfrid Sollom [1964] Director

Strada Soft Drinks Ltd
Incorporated: 4 September 2018
Registered Office: 392 St Helens Road, Bolton, Lancs, BL3 3RR
Major Shareholder: Salim Majid Patel
Officers: Salim Majid Patel [1988] Director/Consultant

Strawhill Estate Spirits Company Ltd
Incorporated: 4 October 2017
Registered Office: McCleary & Company Ltd, Quaker Buildings, High Street, Lurgan, Craigavon, Co Armagh, BT66 8BB
Shareholders: Norman Mark Pearson; Gregory Berry
Officers: Adam Berry [1995] Director/Student; Norman Mark Pearson [1974] Director

Sugen Frooth Limited
Incorporated: 18 May 2016
Registered Office: 3 Westwood Old Road, Liskeard, Cornwall, PL14 6DG
Officers: Alan James Hunt, Secretary; Alan James Hunt [1971] Director/Vigneron

Sumo Drinks Ltd
Incorporated: 30 April 2008
Net Worth: £348 *Total Assets:* £700
Registered Office: Gateshead International Business Centre, Mulgrave Terrace, Gateshead, Tyne & Wear, NE8 1AN
Major Shareholder: Richard Frederick Veltrop-Baister
Officers: Richard Frederick Baister, Secretary; Richard Frederick Baister [1981] Director; Nikola Hrstic [1959] Director

Suncrest Associates Limited
Incorporated: 3 June 1983 *Employees:* 4
Net Worth: £195,755 *Total Assets:* £385,165
Registered Office: J S House, Moorcroft Drive, Wednesbury, W Midlands, WS10 7DE
Parent: Primegreen Properties Limited
Officers: Karndeep Singh Khera, Secretary; Karndeep Singh Khera [1980] Director; Lakhvinder Singh Khera [1974] Director

Sunfresh Soft Drinks Limited
Incorporated: 18 September 1925
Registered Office: Breakspear Park, Breakspear Way, Hemel Hempstead, Herts, HP2 4TZ
Parent: Britvic Soft Drinks Limited
Officers: Judith Moore, Secretary; Mathew James Dunn [1974] Director/Chief Financial Officer; Peter Simon Litherland [1964] Director/Chief Executive; Alexandra Clare Thomas [1974] Director/General Counsel and Company Secretary

Suntory Beverage & Food South Africa Limited
Incorporated: 14 October 2013 *Employees:* 42
Net Worth: £1,275,471 *Total Assets:* £4,755,399
Registered Office: 2 Longwalk Road, Stockley Park, Uxbridge, Middlesex, UB11 1BA
Parent: Orangina Schweppes Holding B.V
Officers: Rory Mathew Brennan [1974] Director/General Manager of Business Development [Irish]; Natasha Chetty [1983] Director [South African]; Chandrashekhar Arvind Mundlay [1962] Director [Indian]

Super Nuva Ltd
Incorporated: 1 October 2013 *Employees:* 4
Net Worth Deficit: £10,145 *Total Assets:* £212,330
Registered Office: Manderson House, 5230 Valiant Court, Gloucester, GL3 4FE
Parent: Beverage Brands (U.K.) Limited
Officers: Arthur William Richmond, Secretary; Elaine Birchall [1966] Director [Irish]; Gemma Iris Pond [1981] Director; Christine Renier [1968] Director/Entrepreneur [French]; Arthur William Richmond [1966] Director

Superfoods Nutrition Ltd
Incorporated: 6 September 2018
Registered Office: 27 Old Gloucester Street, London, WC1N 3AX
Major Shareholder: Nicholas Fratini
Officers: Nicholas Fratini, Secretary; Nicholas Fratini [1983] Director Self Employed

Surrey Food and Drink Innovation Limited
Incorporated: 14 June 2012
Registered Office: 38 Staneway, Ewell, Epsom, Surrey, KT17 1PN
Major Shareholder: Philip George Naom Moseley
Officers: Dr Philip George Naom Moseley [1933] Managing Director

The Sussex Mobile Coffee Company Limited
Incorporated: 4 February 2014
Net Worth: £15,136 *Total Assets:* £18,752
Registered Office: 4 Sussex Business Village, Lake Lane, Barnham, Bognor Regis, W Sussex, PO22 0AL
Shareholder: Steven Wilson
Officers: Steven Wilson, Secretary; Nikki Wilson [1967] Director; Stephen Wilson [1957] Director

Sutton Spring Limited
Incorporated: 14 June 2004 *Employees:* 8
Net Worth: £180,776 *Total Assets:* £473,368
Registered Office: 3 Railway Court, Ten Pound Walk, Doncaster, S Yorks, DN4 5FB
Major Shareholder: Robert James Booth
Officers: Cheryl Tracey Booth, Secretary; Cheryl Tracey Booth [1966] Director; Robert James Booth [1964] Director/Farmer

Swalevalley Springwater Limited
Incorporated: 28 November 2006
Net Worth: £16,912 *Total Assets:* £23,450
Registered Office: Buena Vista, Swale View Caravan Park, Richmond, N Yorks, DL10 4SF
Shareholders: Andrew Philip Carter; Eileen Lamont Carter
Officers: Eileen Lamont Carter, Secretary/Caravan Site Operator; Andrew Philip Carter [1954] Director/Caravan Site Operator; Eileen Lamont Carter [1959] Director/Caravan Site Operator

Swallow Drinks South West Ltd
Incorporated: 28 August 2008 *Employees:* 9
Net Worth: £178,651 *Total Assets:* £602,348
Registered Office: Unit 4, 9 Evercreech Way, Walrow Estate, Highbridge, Somerset, TA9 4AR
Shareholders: Elliott Johnson; Adrian Davis
Officers: Elliott Johnson, Secretary; Adrian Davis [1971] Director; Elliott Johnson [1977] Director

Sweet Leaves Ltd
Incorporated: 20 November 2018
Registered Office: Clyst End, Clyst St George, Exeter, EX3 0RB
Major Shareholder: George Robert Wheatley
Officers: George Robert Wheatley [1995] Director/Student

Sweet Memoirs Limited
Incorporated: 21 February 2012
Registered Office: Suite 27A, 23 Wharf Street, London, SE8 3GG
Officers: Fernand Kwasi Frimpong Jnr [1990] Director; Fernand Kwasi-Frimpong [1960] Director

Sweet Sally Limited
Incorporated: 12 September 2013
Net Worth Deficit: £45,396 *Total Assets:* £26
Registered Office: 4 Capricorn Centre, Cranes Farm Road, Basildon, Essex, SS14 3JJ
Major Shareholder: Gwendolyn Nicole Vaughan
Officers: Gwendolyn Nicole Vaughan [1980] Director [American]

Swing Top Limited
Incorporated: 9 April 2014
Registered Office: 15 Arlington Court, Stourbridge, W Midlands, DY8 1NN
Major Shareholder: Mitchell James Lowe
Officers: Mitchell James Lowe [1991] Director/Trainee Accountant

Swithland Spring Water Limited
Incorporated: 6 November 1998 *Employees:* 22
Net Worth: £455,864 *Total Assets:* £906,652
Registered Office: c/o Mr Brian Beeby, Hall Farm, Swithland, Loughborough, Leics, LE12 8TQ
Major Shareholder: Brian Joseph Beeby
Officers: Janet Margaret Beeby, Secretary/Administrator; Brian Joseph Beeby [1950] Director; Janet Margaret Beeby [1954] Director/Administrator; James Burke [1953] Director/Restaurateur

Syncrobia Ltd
Incorporated: 12 November 2018
Registered Office: 20-22 Wenlock Road, London, N1 7GU
Major Shareholder: Sean Michael Bates
Officers: Sean Michael Bates [1990] Director/Chemical Engineer

Syrup Junkie Limited
Incorporated: 18 February 2014 *Employees:* 2
Net Worth: £342 *Total Assets:* £8,329
Registered Office: 2 Purley View Terrace, Sanderstead Road, South Croydon, Surrey, CR2 0PJ
Shareholder: Corene Joan Gdanitz
Officers: Corene Joan Gdanitz [1980] Director/Waitress [New Zealander]; Laszlo Ormay [1986] Director/Waiter [Hungarian]

Bertrand Tailor Limited
Incorporated: 25 May 2017
Registered Office: 178 Seven Sisters Road, London, N7 7PX
Shareholders: Nikolaos Konstantinou; Georgios Drakakis-Kastrinakis
Officers: Nikolaos Konstantinou [1974] Director

Talent Drinks Ltd
Incorporated: 6 February 2017
Net Worth Deficit: £47,607 *Total Assets:* £12,100
Registered Office: Suite 1, 5 Hercules Way, Leavesden Park, Watford, Herts, WD25 7GS
Major Shareholder: Daniel James Welling
Officers: Daniel James Welling [1975] Director

Tanfield Springs Ltd
Incorporated: 16 January 2019
Registered Office: Tanfield Lodge, West Tanfield, Ripon, N Yorks, HG4 5LE
Major Shareholder: Richard William Bourne-Arton
Officers: Richard William Bourne-Arton [1966] Managing Director

Tani-Mola Enterprise Ltd
Incorporated: 19 May 2011
Net Worth Deficit: £42,299 *Total Assets:* £282
Registered Office: 1 Macmillan Court, 309 Ruislip Road East, Greenford, Middlesex, UB6 9FH
Major Shareholder: Christopher Tani-Mola Adrian John
Officers: Christopher Tani-Mola Adrian John [1980] Director/Founder

Tapwater Corporation Limited
Incorporated: 20 February 2017
Registered Office: 98 Cae Morfa, Neath, W Glamorgan, SA10 6EH
Major Shareholder: David Lloyd Richards
Officers: David Lloyd Richards [1979] Director

Tarka Springs Limited
Incorporated: 8 June 2000 *Employees:* 15
Net Worth: £362,096 *Total Assets:* £1,649,132
Registered Office: Little Comfort, Langtree, Torrington, Devon, EX38 8NY
Shareholders: Neil Scott Folland; Sarah Jane Folland
Officers: Neil Scott Folland [1966] Director; Sarah Jane Folland [1967] Director

Tassology Limited
Incorporated: 4 December 2018
Registered Office: 49 The Green House, Green Lanes, London, N16 9BU
Major Shareholder: Francis Oyewole
Officers: Francis Oyewole [1991] Director

Tasteuk Limited
Incorporated: 12 October 2018
Registered Office: 89 Russell Lane, London, N20 0BA
Major Shareholder: Mert Ali Tasci
Officers: Mert Ali Tasci [1978] Director [Turkish]

Tasty Kameleon Ltd
Incorporated: 19 September 2018
Registered Office: 20-22 Wenlock Road, London, N1 7GU
Shareholders: Felix-Johannes Peter Otto Kress von Wendland; Marcelle Michelle Georgina Maria von Wendland
Officers: Felix-Johannes Peter Otto Kress Von Wendland [1974] Director [German]; Marcelle Michelle Georgina Maria Von Wendland [1970] Director [German]

Taut (UK) Limited
Incorporated: 31 May 2002
Registered Office: Crossley Drive, Magna Park, Milton Keynes, Bucks, MK17 8FL
Parent: A.G. Barr P.L.C.
Officers: Julie Anne Barr, Company Secretary; Stuart Lorimer [1966] Finance Director; Roger Alexander White [1965] Director

TBD Brew Co Ltd
Incorporated: 31 October 2018
Registered Office: 3rd Floor, Arnott House, 12-16 Bridge Street, Belfast, BT1 1LU
Major Shareholder: Peter David Barrett
Officers: Dr Peter David Barrett [1976] Director

Tea GB International Limited
Incorporated: 4 October 2016
Registered Office: 49 Upper Selsdon Road, South Croydon, Surrey, CR2 8DG
Officers: Paul Abdul-Abbass Audu [1966] Director/Consultant; Sharon Johnson [1962] Director/Consultant

Tea Rocks Ltd
Incorporated: 14 June 2017
Registered Office: 18 Westerham Road, Keston, Kent, BR2 6HU
Major Shareholder: Victoria Hewlett
Officers: Victoria Hewlett [1973] Director

Teabase Ltd
Incorporated: 6 November 2018
Registered Office: P O Box 606663, 49 The Green House, Green Lanes, London, N16 9BU
Parent: Darj Ltd
Officers: Francis Oyewole [1991] Director

Temperance Drinks Limited
Incorporated: 26 January 2017
Registered Office: Sitwell Barn, The Square, Long Itchington, Southam, Warwicks, CV47 9PE
Officers: Richard Jonathan Phillips [1980] Director

The Temperance Spirit Company Ltd
Incorporated: 6 July 2015 *Employees:* 4
Net Worth: £7,771 *Total Assets:* £52,508
Registered Office: Bay Horse Farm, Thorlby, Skipton, N Yorks, BD23 3LL
Shareholder: Ian Mark Ackroyd
Officers: Ian Mark Ackroyd [1957] Director; Kai Arter [1970] Director; Brendan Gerard Duckworth [1954] Director

Thames Vintage Ltd
Incorporated: 10 September 2014
Registered Office: 32a Edenvale Street, London, SW6 2SF
Major Shareholder: George Still
Officers: George Still [1978] Director

Theodore Global Limited
Incorporated: 20 February 2018
Registered Office: The Incuba, 1 Brewers Hill Road, Dunstable, Beds, LU6 1AA
Shareholders: Janet Theodore; Nicola Roberts
Officers: Nicola Roberts [1987] Director; Bethany Theodore [1995] Director; Janet Ann Theodore [1962] Director/Family Practitioner

Think Drinks Limited
Incorporated: 15 November 2010 *Employees:* 11
Net Worth: £686,000 *Total Assets:* £1,154,000
Registered Office: Unit 6 Mill Batch Farm, East Brent, Highbridge, Somerset, TA9 4JN
Shareholders: Thomas James Gane Collins; John Roger Gane Collins; John Collins; Michael Stewart Vowles; Tom Collins
Officers: John Roger Gane Collins [1982] Director; Thomas James Gane Collins [1980] Director; Gonzalo Alonso Trujillo [1970] Director/Accountant; Michael Stewart Vowles [1968] Director/Operations Manager

Third Wave Coffee Ventures Ltd
Incorporated: 5 May 2015 *Employees:* 1
Net Worth: £76,134 *Total Assets:* £91,328
Registered Office: 6th Floor, 49 Peter Street, Manchester, M2 3NG
Major Shareholder: Joseph Patrick Devereux-Kelly
Officers: Joseph Patrick Devereux-Kelly [1992] Managing Director

Thirstea Drinks Limited
Incorporated: 30 March 2017
Registered Office: 157b Chatham Street, London, SE17 1PA
Major Shareholder: Rok Lasan
Officers: Rok Lasan [1985] Director [Slovenian]

Thirsty Beasts Drinks Ltd
Incorporated: 16 February 2017
Registered Office: 27a Priory Road, Newbury, Berks, RG14 7QS
Officers: Daniel James Smith [1978] Director

Thirsty Planet Limited
Incorporated: 10 November 2006
Net Worth: £1 *Total Assets:* £38,260
Registered Office: Thirsty Planet Limited, Harlow Moor Road, Harrogate, N Yorks, HG2 0QB
Officers: Anthony Joseph Cain [1948] Director; James Anthony Cain [1973] Director; Simon David Knaggs [1966] Operations Director; Robert James Pickering [1964] Director; Damien Michael Wilkinson [1969] Finance Director

Thirsty Soft Drinks Ltd
Incorporated: 2 March 2007 *Employees:* 4
Previous: 4 Square Wholesale Ltd
Net Worth Deficit: £13,937 *Total Assets:* £99,278
Registered Office: Unit I, Victoria Works, Barton Road, Dukinfield, Cheshire, SK16 4US
Officers: Lubna Aziz, Secretary; Bilal Aziz [1968] Director

This Is Holy Water Limited
Incorporated: 6 May 2016
Net Worth Deficit: £46,168 *Total Assets:* £53,380
Registered Office: c/o Bottling International Ltd T/A Bottling UK, Unit 8 Triumph Trading Estate, Tariff Road, London, N17 0EB
Officers: Gina Marghrtha Geoghegan [1983] Director [Swedish]; Lee Thomas John Jeffries [1981] Director/Business Owner; Marc Mendoza [1960] Director/Consultant; Luke James Montgomery-Smith [1989] Director/Event Producer

Three Cents Ltd
Incorporated: 11 September 2017 *Employees:* 2
Net Worth: £317,100 *Total Assets:* £639,151
Registered Office: 1 Kings Avenue, London, N21 3NA
Officers: Georgios Bagkos [1984] Director [Greek]; Athanasios Kyriakopoulos [1969] Director [Canadian]

Three Spirit Drinks Ltd
Incorporated: 8 November 2018
Registered Office: 150 Wharfedale Road, Winnersh Triangle, Berks, RG41 5RB
Parent: Beyond Alcohol Ltd
Officers: Meeta Gournay [1980] Director

Nelly Tickner Drinks Co. Ltd
Incorporated: 13 July 2016
Net Worth: £319 *Total Assets:* £408
Registered Office: Kemp House, 160 City Road, London, EC1V 2NX
Major Shareholder: Andrew Jones
Officers: Michaela MacIntyre, Secretary; Andrew Jones [1972] Director

Timeless Drinks Ventures Ltd
Incorporated: 21 January 2016
Net Worth Deficit: £50,616 *Total Assets:* £7,356
Registered Office: 26 Meadow Place, London, SW8 1XZ
Shareholders: Zoltan Szucs-Farkas; Simon Charles Hamilton Rucker
Officers: Simon Charles Hamilton Rucker [1970] Director; Zoltan Szucs-Farkas [1968] Director

Tiny Mighty People Ltd
Incorporated: 20 April 2018
Registered Office: 71-75 Shelton Street, Covent Garden, London, WC2H 9JQ
Major Shareholder: Melissa Price
Officers: Melissa Price, Secretary; Melissa Price [1975] Director

Titonic Ltd
Incorporated: 6 August 2018
Registered Office: Unit 11 Lowes Industrial Estate, 31 Ballynahinch Road, Carryduff, Co Down, BT8 8EH
Officers: Robert Stewart [1947] Director

Tizer Limited
Incorporated: 15 April 1936
Registered Office: Crossley Drive, Magna Park, Milton Keynes, Bucks, MK17 8FL
Parent: A.G. Barr P.L.C.
Officers: Julie Anne Barr, Company Secretary; Stuart Lorimer [1966] Finance Director; Roger Alexander White [1965] Director/Chief Executive

TMF Trading Limited
Incorporated: 3 August 2018
Registered Office: Colebrooke House, 10-12 Gaskin Street, London, N1 2RY
Major Shareholder: Theodore Freedman
Officers: Theodore Freedman [1990] Director/Solicitor

Total Water Solutions Limited
Incorporated: 13 May 2014
Previous: Cott Ventures Limited
Net Worth: £44,883,000 *Total Assets:* £87,678,000
Registered Office: c/o Aimia Foods Limited, Penny Lane, Haydock, St Helens, Merseyside, WA11 0QZ
Shareholder: Cott Ventures UK Limited
Officers: Jason Robert Ausher [1973] Director [American]; Claire Duffy [1976] Director/Solicitor; Steven Kitching [1964] Director; Matthew James Vernon [1975] Director

Tovali Limited
Incorporated: 23 December 1958 *Employees:* 9
Net Worth: £189,549 *Total Assets:* £1,056,041
Registered Office: Tovali Works, Glanyrafon Road, Carmarthen, SA31 3AR
Shareholder: Eurwyn George Harries
Officers: Cynthia George Davies, Secretary; Cynthia George Davies [1945] Director/Company Secretary; Karen Louise Davies [1969] Director/Bank Employee; Eurwyn George Harries [1947] Director

Trederwen Springs 2008 Limited
Incorporated: 13 December 2007 *Employees:* 28
Net Worth: £2,409,477 *Total Assets:* £5,310,754
Registered Office: The Factory, Llansantffraid-ym-Mechain, Powys, ST22 6SY
Officers: Janet Elizabeth Tinsley, Secretary; David Paul Tinsley [1956] Director; John Derek Tinsley [1954] Director

Trip Drink Ltd
Incorporated: 19 February 2019
Registered Office: Unit 5 Drakes Courtyard, 291 Kilburn High Road, London, NW6 7JR
Major Shareholder: Daniel Francis El Khoury
Officers: Daniel Francis El Khoury [1987] Director [Irish]

Trove International Limited
Incorporated: 7 December 2015
Registered Office: 3rd Floor, Cavendish House, 18 Cavendish Square, London, W1G 0PJ
Officers: Emeraba Afaoma Tony-Uzoebo [1974] Director/Accountant

Tulchan Spring Water Limited
Incorporated: 18 August 2004
Registered Office: Morton Fraser LLP, 5th Floor, Quartermile Two, 2 Lister Square, Edinburgh, EH3 9GL
Parent: Tulchan Sporting Estates Limited
Officers: Natalia Sidorenco [1976] Director

Turn Global Ltd
Incorporated: 27 February 2015
Registered Office: 20-22 Wenlock Road, London, N1 7GU
Shareholder: Greger Faye
Officers: Greger Faye [1965] Director [Norwegian]; Alexander Hosp [1973] Director [Austrian]

Two B Limited
Incorporated: 29 January 1999
Net Worth Deficit: £123,702 *Total Assets:* £192
Registered Office: Suite 1, 3rd Floor, 11-12 St James's Square, London, SW1Y 4LB
Shareholders: Jean-Claude Billa; Jean Brignone
Officers: Jean Claude Billa [1958] Director/Representant [French]

Two Brothers Beverage Company Limited
Incorporated: 7 September 2015
Registered Office: 2 Shelton Gardens, Cropwell Bishop, Nottingham, NG12 3GX
Shareholder: Christopher Benjamin Thorpe
Officers: Christopher Benjamin Thorpe [1986] Director; Daniel Thorpe [1984] Director

Two Keys Ltd
Incorporated: 6 November 2018
Registered Office: 1 Knightsbridge Green, London, SW1X 7NE
Shareholders: Jack Herlihy; James Thomas Simpson
Officers: Jack Michael Herlihy [1986] Director; James Thomas Simpson [1981] Director

Two2Three2Four Ltd
Incorporated: 29 February 2016 *Employees:* 3
Net Worth: £7,661 *Total Assets:* £8,459
Registered Office: 12 Cullen Close, Yateley, Hants, GU46 6HB
Shareholders: Leigh Morris Howard Tilley; Mark Andrew Hainy; Mark Andrew Hainy; Leigh Morris Howard Tilley
Officers: John Gosler [1955] Art Director; Mark Andrew Hainy [1978] Director; Leigh Morris Howard Tilley [1975] Director

Ty Nant Spring Water Limited
Incorporated: 14 November 1988
Net Worth Deficit: £55,032 *Total Assets:* £3,366,041
Registered Office: Bethania, Llanon, Ceredigion, SY23 5LS
Officers: Hywel John Davies, Secretary; Pietro Biscaldi [1958] Managing Director [Italian]

Ugly Brands Limited
Incorporated: 29 January 2015 *Employees:* 13
Net Worth Deficit: £72,380 *Total Assets:* £179,676
Registered Office: 30 Oval Road, London, NW1 7DE
Shareholders: Green Park Brands LP; Hugh William Thomas; Joseph William Benn
Officers: Joseph William Benn [1988] Director; Livio Bisterzo [1981] Director/Senior Executive [Italian]; Christopher Paul Britton [1957] Director; Alexander Frederick Nurnberg [1985] Director/Investment Manager; Hugh William Thomas [1989] Director

UK Blue Ribbon Group Beer Co., Ltd
Incorporated: 2 November 2018
Registered Office: Unit G25, Waterfront Studios, 1 Dock Road, London, E16 1AH
Major Shareholder: Xiuyun Wang
Officers: Xiuyun Wang [1960] Director [Chinese]

UK Brighton Food & Nutrition Research Centre Ltd
Incorporated: 13 August 2018
Registered Office: Unit G25, Waterfront Studios, 1 Dock Road, London, E16 1AH
Major Shareholder: Xingzhong Deng
Officers: Xingzhong Deng [1986] Director [Chinese]

UK Dorset Ltd
Incorporated: 5 May 2017
Registered Office: 71-75 Shelton Street, Covent Garden, London, WC2H 9JQ
Major Shareholder: Saidabror Gulyamov
Officers: Shamagdiev Abdurasul [1987] Director [Uzbek]

UK Premium Brands Limited
Incorporated: 14 September 2017
Net Worth: £2,237 *Total Assets:* £2,250
Registered Office: 2nd Floor, 154 Bishopsgate, London, EC2M 4LN
Major Shareholder: Georgios Konstantinos Chatzimanolis
Officers: Georgios Konstantinos Chatzimanolis [1974] Director/Businessman [Greek]

Ultra Beauty Limited
Incorporated: 9 April 2014
Net Worth: £21,366 *Total Assets:* £21,366
Registered Office: 175b Purves Road, London, NW10 5TH
Shareholder: Suzannah Denise Hartley Baker
Officers: Suzannah Denise Hartley Baker [1981] Director/Beauty Retailer; Kevin Alexander Kewley [1981] Director/Investment Banker

Unique Drinks Limited
Incorporated: 13 November 2017
Registered Office: 36 Carlton Road, Bolton, Lancs, BL1 5HY
Shareholders: Christopher James Farnworth; Ryan Moore
Officers: Chris James Farnworth [1985] Director/Manager; Ryan Moore [1986] Director/Manager

Upper Harglodd Farm Ltd
Incorporated: 13 June 2018
Registered Office: Upper Harglodd, St Davids, Haverfordwest, Pembrokeshire, SA62 6BX
Shareholders: Mark Wyn Raymond Evans; Emma Sarah Evans
Officers: Emma Sarah Evans [1981] Director/Local Government Officer; Mark Wyn Raymond Evans [1979] Director/Farmer

The Urban Cordial Company Limited
Incorporated: 6 March 2015 *Employees:* 1
Net Worth Deficit: £10,688 *Total Assets:* £13,279
Registered Office: 5 Technology Park, Colindeep Lane, London, NW9 6BX
Major Shareholder: Natasha Steele
Officers: Natasha Steele [1987] Managing Director

Us 4 Slush Limited
Incorporated: 15 June 2004
Net Worth: £160,063 *Total Assets:* £347,388
Registered Office: Ground Floor, Avalon, 26-32 Oxford Road, Bournemouth, BH8 8EZ
Major Shareholder: David Paul Fish
Officers: David Paul Fish [1963] Director

V-Storm Energy Ltd
Incorporated: 11 December 2018
Registered Office: Rose Cottage, The Green, Ellington, Huntingdon, Cambs, PE28 0AQ
Major Shareholder: George William Harriman-Hardy
Officers: George William Harriman-Hardy [1992] Director/Accounts Manager

Vero Drinks Ltd
Incorporated: 14 March 2017 *Employees:* 2
Net Worth Deficit: £28,411 *Total Assets:* £198
Registered Office: 45b Langham Road, London, N15 3QX
Major Shareholder: Nicholas Oakes
Officers: Nicholas Oakes [1986] Director/Sustainable Finance Specialist

Vida Water Ltd
Incorporated: 11 February 2019
Registered Office: 32 Church Road, Hove, E Sussex, BN3 2TE
Major Shareholder: Ben David Walton
Officers: Ben David Walton [1995] Director/Consultant

The Village Orchard Ltd
Incorporated: 23 January 2017
Registered Office: 3 Everdon Park, Heartlands Business Park, Daventry, Northants, NN11 8YJ
Parent: Chaplin and Chaplin Holdings Ltd
Officers: Jonathan George Llewellyn Chaplin [1961] Director/Businessman

Vine Springs Ltd
Incorporated: 23 October 2018
Registered Office: 20-22 Wenlock Road, London, N1 7GU
Major Shareholder: Denzel Mensah
Officers: Denzel Mensah [1978] Director/Taxi Driver

Vitamin Brands Ltd.
Incorporated: 25 May 2004
Net Worth: £3,553,956 *Total Assets:* £3,581,257
Registered Office: Building 4, Chiswick Park, 566 Chiswick High Road, London, W4 5YE
Parent: Pepsico Inc
Officers: Victoria Elizabeth Evans, Secretary; Joanne Kerry Averiss [1963] Director/VP Law; Victoria Elizabeth Evans [1970] Director/Solicitor; Andrew John MacLeod [1962] Director/Solicitor; Claire Ellen Stone [1969] Finance Director; Andrew Williams [1960] Director/General Manager

The Vitapure Drinks Company Limited
Incorporated: 18 May 2017
Registered Office: Chapel House, 1 Chapel Street, Guildford, Surrey, GU1 3UH
Major Shareholder: Ian Paul Webb
Officers: Ian Paul Webb [1961] Director

Vitosha Wine Ltd
Incorporated: 10 January 2019
Registered Office: 7 Victoria Road, Alton, Hants, GU34 2DH
Shareholders: Umesh Prasad; Neelesh Prasad
Officers: Umesh Prasad [1965] Director

Vitte Nutrition Ltd
Incorporated: 21 September 2018
Registered Office: Unit A, Gainsborough Studios East, 1 Poole Street, London, N1 5ED
Shareholders: Oliver James Thirlwell-Pearce; Phoebe Thirlwell-Pearce
Officers: Oliver James Thirlwell-Pearce [1989] Director; Phoebe Thirlwell-Pearce [1989] Director

Viva Riva Beverage Company Limited
Incorporated: 11 March 2018
Registered Office: Union International Drinks Corporation, Bridge House, 64-72 Mabgate, Leeds, LS9 7DZ
Major Shareholder: Diane Wilson
Officers: Diane Wilson [1944] Director/Company Formation Agent Semi-Retired

Vivo Viva Beverages Limited
Incorporated: 6 March 2018
Registered Office: Union International Drinks Corporation, Bridge House, 64-72 Mabgate, Leeds, LS9 7DZ
Major Shareholder: Robert (Elias) Wilson
Officers: Diane Wilson [1944] Director/Company Formation Agent Semi-Retired; Robert Wilson [1941] Director (CEO)

Vivo Water Ltd
Incorporated: 3 January 2018
Registered Office: 22 Sceptre House, Malcolm Road, London, E1 4HP
Major Shareholder: Linda Anna Mabrouk
Officers: Linda Anna Mabrouk [1977] Director [Swedish]

Vyking Energy Limited
Incorporated: 25 July 2016
Net Worth Deficit: £16,167 *Total Assets:* £35,004
Registered Office: 15 Niffany Gardens, Skipton, N Yorks, BD23 1SZ
Major Shareholder: Nicholas Jonathan Asquith Cawood
Officers: Jonathan Nicholas Asquith Cawood [1961] Director

Wake Drinks Ltd
Incorporated: 7 June 2016
Net Worth Deficit: £3,803 *Total Assets:* £8,176
Registered Office: 3 Grove Road, Wrexham, Clwyd, LL11 1DY
Shareholder: Alexander Charles Buckley
Officers: Alex Buckley [1973] Director

Wake Energy Drinks Limited
Incorporated: 3 July 2014
Net Worth Deficit: £48,738 *Total Assets:* £4,546
Registered Office: 3 Grove Road, Wrexham, Clwyd, LL11 1DY
Shareholder: Alexander Buckley
Officers: Alex Buckley [1973] Director; Claire Buckley [1970] Director

Wardle Spring Water Company Limited
Incorporated: 9 February 1994 *Employees:* 7
Net Worth: £9,590 *Total Assets:* £53,442
Registered Office: William Gregson House, off Crossfield Road, Wardle, Rochdale, Lancs, OL12 9JW
Shareholders: Dawn Elizabeth Smith; Lee Craig Peter Hardman; Elisabeth Doreen Hardman
Officers: Lee Craig Peter Hardman, Secretary/Business Manager; Lee Craig Peter Hardman [1961] Director/Business Manager; Dawn Elizabeth Smith [1965] Director/Bookkeeper

J Water Disabled Children Limited
Incorporated: 9 July 2018
Registered Office: 13 Patience Avenue, Seaton Burn, Newcastle upon Tyne, NE13 6HF
Major Shareholder: James Man
Officers: James Manager [1965] Director

Water Group Ltd
Incorporated: 4 September 2018
Registered Office: 6 Station Road, Brompton on Swale, Richmond, N Yorks, DL10 7SN
Major Shareholder: Sarah Marie Larby
Officers: Sarah Marie Larby [1991] Director/Supply Chain Manager

The Water Guru Limited
Incorporated: 22 February 2017
Net Worth: £175 *Total Assets:* £175
Registered Office: Restdale House, 32-33 Foregate Street, Worcester, WR1 1EE
Parent: Crack of Dawn Limited
Officers: Richard William Bailey [1974] Director/Advisor

The Water Shop Limited
Incorporated: 10 August 2004
Registered Office: Carscliffe, Upper Draycott Road, Cheddar, Somerset, BS27 3YL
Officers: Virginia Urch, Secretary; David Lawrence Urch [1951] Director; Duncan Winston Urch [1980] Director; Tabitha Sarah-Jane Urch [1978] Director; Virginia Urch [1952] Director

Waterful Ltd
Incorporated: 21 June 2018
Registered Office: 33 Ashpole Avenue, Wootton, Bedford, MK43 9EG
Shareholders: Richard Sofer; Ilona Rose Yvonne Sofer
Officers: Richard Sofer [1978] Managing Director

Watermarket Limited
Incorporated: 13 August 2014
Registered Office: Carscliff Farm, Upper Draycott Road, Cheddar, Somerset, BS27 3YL
Officers: Duncan Urgh [1980] Director; Tabitha Urgh [1978] Director

Waters & Robson Holdings Limited
Incorporated: 24 February 2003 *Employees:* 5
Net Worth: £2,110,184 *Total Assets:* £2,110,184
Registered Office: 1a Wimpole Street, London, W1G 0EA
Parent: The Coca-Cola Company
Officers: Ingrid Natalie Cope [1972] Director/Solicitor; Scott Edward Roche [1964] Finance Director [Canadian]; Ruben Christiaan Stephaan Rutten [1977] Finance Director [Belgian]; Margaret Ann Stewart [1972] HR Director [Irish]; Jonathan Mark Woods [1968] Director/Franchise Operations Manager

Watkins Drinks Limited
Incorporated: 27 March 2018
Registered Office: Timsons Business Centre, Bath Road, Kettering, Northants, NN16 8NQ
Shareholders: Thomas Watkins; Nicholas James Watkins
Officers: Claire Elizabeth Smith [1963] Director/Investor [Swiss]; Nicholas James Watkins [1986] Director; Thomas Watkins [1991] Director

We Are Haps Ltd
Incorporated: 3 February 2016
Net Worth Deficit: £691 *Total Assets:* £6,856
Registered Office: Lytchett House, 13 Freeland Park, Wareham Road, Lytchett Matravers, Dorset, BH16 6FA
Major Shareholder: Rik Turner
Officers: Rik William Turner [1987] Director/Strategist

Westmoor Botanicals Limited
Incorporated: 22 November 2018
Registered Office: 132 Ravenstone Drive, Greetland, Halifax, W Yorks, HX4 8DY
Shareholder: Philip George Scoley
Officers: Helen Rose-Marie Scoley [1966] Director/Teacher; Philip George Scoley [1962] Director/Management Consultant

Wet Beverages (Global) Ltd
Incorporated: 14 September 2015
Registered Office: Greville House, 11 Abbey Hill, Kenilworth, Warwicks, CV8 1LU
Major Shareholder: Michael Daniel Adams
Officers: Michael Daniel Adams [1957] Director

Whimble Mineral Water & Brewing Co. Ltd.
Incorporated: 24 August 1995
Registered Office: West Lodge, Rainbow Street, Leominster, Herefords, HR6 8DQ
Major Shareholder: Eric Michael Kinsey-Jones
Officers: Olwen Kinsey Jones, Secretary; Eric Michael Kinsey Jones [1941] Director/Farmer

R.White & Sons Limited
Incorporated: 20 July 1894
Registered Office: Breakspear Park, Breakspear Way, Hemel Hempstead, Herts, HP2 4TZ
Parent: Britvic Soft Drinks Limited
Officers: Judith Moore, Secretary; Mathew James Dunn [1974] Director/Chief Financial Officer; Peter Simon Litherland [1964] Director/Chief Executive; Alexandra Clare Thomas [1974] Director/General Counsel and Company Secretary

James White Drinks Ltd
Incorporated: 7 June 1989 *Employees:* 32
Net Worth: £5,445,056 *Total Assets:* £6,707,049
Registered Office: Whites Fruit Farm, Helmingham Road, Ashbocking, Ipswich, Suffolk, IP6 9JS
Major Shareholder: Lawrence Stuart Mallinson
Officers: Anne Mallinson, Secretary; Angela Marie Christine Mallinson [1960] Director/Classical Music Agent; Lawrence Stuart Mallinson [1957] Managing Director

White Smoke Distillery Ltd
Incorporated: 8 November 2017
Registered Office: Ilex, Ufford Place, Ufford, Woodbridge, Suffolk, IP13 6DR
Major Shareholder: Ben Bewley-Pope
Officers: Ben Bewley-Pope [1983] Director/Businessman

Whollywater Ltd
Incorporated: 11 July 2018
Registered Office: 20-22 Wenlock Road, London, N1 7GU
Major Shareholder: Dawna Diane Henson
Officers: Dawna Diane Henson [1968] Director/Solicitor

Wild Cat Energy Drink Ltd
Incorporated: 24 October 2011
Net Worth Deficit: £130,582 *Total Assets:* £31,069
Registered Office: 24 High View Close, Vantage Park, Leicester, LE4 9LJ
Shareholders: Kassam Barkatali Rajani; Hasnein Dhirani
Officers: Gurminder Singh Basra [1970] International Sales Director; Shantilal Chauhan [1946] Director/Microbiologist; Hasnein Dhirani [1975] Director; Kassam Barkatali Rajani [1974] Director; Shubnit Singh Rehal [1993] Operations Director

Wild Husk Limited
Incorporated: 14 March 2018
Registered Office: 8 Bridle Close, Maidenhead, Berks, SL6 7RR
Major Shareholder: Jack Gerard Bennet
Officers: Jack Gerard Bennet [1994] Director

Wild Life Botanicals Ltd
Incorporated: 28 February 2019
Registered Office: 20-22 Wenlock Road, London, N1 7GU
Major Shareholder: Jonathan Paul Steadman Archer
Officers: Jonathan Paul Steadman Archer [1966] Director

Wildeve Ltd
Incorporated: 19 April 2018
Registered Office: 163a High Street, Lewes, E Sussex, BN7 1XU
Major Shareholder: Amanda Jane Saurin
Officers: Amanda Jane Saurin [1964] Director

Willimott House Limited
Incorporated: 17 October 2011
Net Worth Deficit: £76,547 *Total Assets:* £29,010
Registered Office: First Floor, Unit 7 Waterside, Hamm Moor Lane, Addlestone, Surrey, KT15 2SN
Major Shareholder: Benjamin Koffi Vigno Agboli
Officers: Benjamin Koffi Vigno Agboli [1969] Director; Pamela Maud Phyllis Agboli [1979] Director

Willow Water Limited
Incorporated: 17 August 2005
Net Worth: £1,280,000 *Total Assets:* £2,159,000
Registered Office: The Sovereign Distillery, Wilson Road, Huyton Business Park, Knowsley, Merseyside, L36 6AD
Shareholders: Judith Margaret Halewood; Ian Alan Douglas; Halewood Wines and Spirits PLC
Officers: Peter Gary Eaton [1960] Director; Stewart Andrew Hainsworth [1969] Director/Group CEO; Judith Margaret Halewood [1951] Director; Alan William Robinson [1965] Director/Accountant; Lee Andrew Tayburn [1974] Director of Production

Wisdom Superfoods CIC
Incorporated: 6 July 2017
Registered Office: 56 Kimmeridge Road, Oxford, OX2 9RQ
Officers: Mbakeh Camara [1986] Director/Social Entrepreneur [Gambian]; Natasha Jane Robinson [1980] Director/Social Entrepreneur

The Wise Herb Company Limited
Incorporated: 19 December 2017
Registered Office: 12 Dewe Lane, Burghfield, Reading, Berks, RG30 3SU
Major Shareholder: Ketan Harshad Joshi
Officers: Carolynne Yew Kiew Joshi [1959] Director; Dev Ketan Kong Joshi [1994] Director; Jay Ketan Kong Joshi [1992] Director; Dr Ketan Harshad Joshi [1961] Director

Wolfe's Drinks Limited
Incorporated: 19 December 2017
Registered Office: 22a Caldwell Street, London, SW9 0EL
Officers: Giles Andrew David Robinette, Secretary; Giles Andrew David Robinette [1962] Director/Accountant; Bronwyn Elizabeth Wolfe [1960] Director/Chef

Woodchester Enterprises Limited
Incorporated: 4 March 1999 *Employees:* 38
Net Worth: £5,672,775 *Total Assets:* £16,070,285
Registered Office: Manderson House, 5230 Valiant Court, Delta Way, Gloucester Business Park, Brockworth, Gloucester, GL3 4FE
Parent: Bottlegreen Holdings Limited
Officers: Arthur Richmond, Secretary; Elaine Birchall [1966] Director [Irish]; Arthur William Richmond [1966] Director/Accountant; Karen Salters [1970] Director

Woodford & Warner Limited
Incorporated: 21 July 2009
Net Worth Deficit: £132,862 *Total Assets:* £2,131
Registered Office: 4 Eastholm, Letchworth Garden City, Herts, SG6 4TN
Major Shareholder: Sarah Elizabeth Moore
Officers: Sarah Elizabeth Moore [1973] Director

Wotar Ltd
Incorporated: 16 August 2018
Registered Office: 327a Oakleigh Road North, London, N20 0RJ
Major Shareholder: Steven Keith Green
Officers: Steven Keith Green [1965] Director/Property Developer

UK Manufacturers of Soft Drinks   dellam

Wow Food and Drinks Ltd
Incorporated: 9 May 2014 *Employees:* 8
Net Worth: £240,576 *Total Assets:* £719,670
Registered Office: 20 Vestry Street, London, N1 7RE
Shareholder: Portchester Equity Limited
Officers: Oliver John Dickinson [1991] Director; David Christopher Harbord [1961] Managing Director; John Mark Swales [1956] Finance Director

WTRplus Ltd
Incorporated: 28 February 2018
Registered Office: 58 Boundstone Lane, Lancing, W Sussex, BN15 9QP
Major Shareholder: Joe Zoutewelle
Officers: Joe Zoutewelle [1986] Director

Wunder Workshop Ltd
Incorporated: 4 June 2014
Net Worth: £7,531 *Total Assets:* £50,538
Registered Office: 20-22 Wenlock Road, London, N1 7GU
Shareholders: Thomas Sothers Smale; Zoe Petrovna Lind Van't Hof
Officers: Zoe Lind Van't Hof [1988] Director [Dutch]; Thomas Smale [1990] Director

Xite Beverages Limited
Incorporated: 22 December 2017
Registered Office: The Carlson Suite, Vantage Point Business Village, Mitcheldean, Glos, GL17 0DD
Major Shareholder: Oliver Roy Bennett
Officers: Oliver Roy Bennett [1992] Director

Xite Energy Limited
Incorporated: 21 February 2017
Net Worth Deficit: £575,891 *Total Assets:* £68,687
Registered Office: Vantage Point Business Village, Mitcheldean, Glos, GL17 0DD
Officers: Oliver Roy Bennett [1992] Director

Xorb Energy Limited
Incorporated: 21 February 2017
Registered Office: The Carlson Suite, Vantage Point Business Village, Mitcheldean, Glos, GL17 0DD
Major Shareholder: Oliver Roy Bennett
Officers: Oliver Roy Bennett [1992] Director

Xtreme Energy Group Limited
Incorporated: 24 October 2016 *Employees:* 1
Net Worth Deficit: £11 *Total Assets:* £31,451
Registered Office: 1 St Margarets Terrace, 1 St Margarets Road, Cheltenham, Glos, GL50 4DT
Shareholder: Connor Victor Crotchett
Officers: Conner Victor Crotchett [1974] Director [Irish]; Angela Jewkes [1969] Director

Yarty Cordials Limited
Incorporated: 28 May 2014
Net Worth: £10,900 *Total Assets:* £15,100
Registered Office: 5 St Georges, Rodney Road, Southsea, Hants, PO4 8SS
Shareholders: David Edward Mugridge; Jayne Mugridge
Officers: Jayne Mugridge, Secretary; David Edward Mugridge [1961] Director; Jayne Mugridge [1965] Director and Company Secretary

Yeast Meets West Limited
Incorporated: 31 August 2017
Registered Office: 12 Dale Street, London, W4 2BL
Shareholders: Michael Stuart Eldridge; Freya Louise Twigden
Officers: Michael Stuart Eldridge [1966] Director; Freya Louise Twigden [1994] Director

Yee Energy Ltd
Incorporated: 19 September 2018
Registered Office: 56 Furtherwood Road, Oldham, Lancs, OL1 2QN
Shareholders: Bradley Ray; Jack Petty
Officers: Jack Petty [1995] Director; Bradley Ray [1996] Director/Banker

Yemsmoothies Ltd
Incorporated: 2 February 2016
Net Worth Deficit: £1,954
Registered Office: 14 Morten Close, London, SW4 8LG
Officers: Oluwatoyin Kehinde, Secretary; Oluyemisi Kehinde [1977] Director/Consultant

Yo! Cola Ltd
Incorporated: 14 April 2010
Registered Office: 3 Chiltern Green, Flackwell Heath, High Wycombe, Bucks, HP10 9AJ
Major Shareholder: Andrew James Powney
Officers: Andrew Powney [1965] Director/Proprietor

Yorkshire Soft Drinks Ltd
Incorporated: 31 May 2018
Registered Office: Impulse House, Impulse Direct, Westgatehill Street, Bradford, W Yorks, BD4 0SJ
Officers: Azr Abdul Quaddus [1964] Director

Your Mind Body Soul Limited
Incorporated: 3 October 2018
Registered Office: 41 Stanhope Gardens, London, N4 1HY
Major Shareholder: Steve Palanyandi
Officers: Steve Palanyandi [1984] Director

Your Water Ltd
Incorporated: 16 May 2018
Registered Office: 7 Church Avenue, Easton, Bristol, BS5 6DY
Major Shareholder: Nathan Christopher Stokes
Officers: Nathan Christopher Stokes [1989] Director

Youthenergy Drinks Ltd
Incorporated: 11 May 2016
Registered Office: 61 Bridge Street, Kington, Herefords, HR5 3DL
Major Shareholder: Amandas Kate Freeman
Officers: Amanda Kate Freeman [1970] Director; Hollyann Freeman [1991] Director/Recruitment Consultant

Youthenergy East Africa Limited
Incorporated: 24 September 2018
Registered Office: 61 Bridge Street, Kington, Herts, HR5 3DL
Officers: Maxwell Benjamin [1957] Director; Amanda Kate Freeman [1970] Director; Jason Carl Freeman [1971] Director; Ocan Bob Mabelle [1959] Director/Architect; Joab James Ngesa [1956] Director

The Yummy Juice Company Limited
Incorporated: 26 July 2017
Registered Office: Tish Press and Company, 27 Cambridge Park, London, E11 2PU
Major Shareholder: Frances Colman
Officers: Clive Ivan Colman [1957] Director; Frances Colman [1933] Director

Yuyo Drinks Ltd
Incorporated: 15 July 2013 *Employees:* 2
Previous: Teatonics Beverages Ltd
Net Worth Deficit: £18,766 *Total Assets:* £24,651
Registered Office: 4 Well Lane, Enmore Green, Shaftesbury, Dorset, SP7 8LP
Shareholders: Charles Gordon Grummitt; Rosie Marteau
Officers: Rosie Marteau, Secretary; Rosie Marteau [1986] Director/Translator

Zaas Limited
Incorporated: 21 August 2013
Net Worth: £5,601 *Total Assets:* £5,601
Registered Office: Rourke House, Watermans Business Park, The Causeway, Staines upon Thames, Middlesex, TW18 3BA
Major Shareholder: Sonya Haque Zaman
Officers: Sonya Haque Zaman [1983] Director [Bangladeshi]

Zero Proof International Limited
Incorporated: 27 September 2018
Registered Office: Enterprise House, Beeson's Yard, Bury Lane, Rickmansworth, Herts, WD3 1DS
Major Shareholder: Carl Fane Hartmann
Officers: Darko Atijas, Secretary; Carl Fane Hartmann [1983] Director [Australian]; Mark Seymour Livings [1980] Director [Australian]

Zero Proof UK Limited
Incorporated: 12 December 2018
Registered Office: Enterprise House, Beesons Yard, Bury Lane, Rickmansworth, Herts, WD3 1DS
Parent: Zero Proof International Limited
Officers: Christopher Simon Best, Secretary; Peter Graham Gates [1966] Director [Australian]; Mark Seymour Livings [1980] Director [Australian]

Zilch Ltd
Incorporated: 8 June 2016
Registered Office: 14 Fox Hedge Way, Sharnbrook, Bedford, MK44 1JR
Officers: Ben David Evans [1997] Director

Zion Manufacturing Ltd
Incorporated: 7 August 2018
Registered Office: 52 Lobelia Lane, Cringleford, Norwich, NR4 7JU
Major Shareholder: Gavin Paul Caird
Officers: Gavin Paul Caird [1977] Director/Consultant

Zireson Enterprises Limited
Incorporated: 1 May 2018
Registered Office: 24 Fairmead Rise, Northampton, NN2 8PP
Major Shareholder: Bahati Gaspard Bahizire
Officers: Bahati Gaspard Bahizire [1973] Director [Congolese]

Zombie Energy Limited
Incorporated: 8 May 2017
Registered Office: 27 Medomsley Road, Consett, Co Durham, DH8 5HE
Shareholders: Neil Johnson; Ian Harry Ashby
Officers: Ian Harry Ashby [1979] Director; John Paul Dyer [1974] Director; Neil Johnson [1970] Director; Keith Opie [1962] Director

Zowell Ltd
Incorporated: 19 July 2018
Registered Office: 55 Ingledew Road, London, SE18 1AP
Shareholders: Chukuka Ebinum; Maria Shoniregun
Officers: Chukuka Ebinum [1992] Director; Maria Shoniregun [1989] Director

Zuddha Water Limited
Incorporated: 8 November 2017
Registered Office: 9 Ullswater Road, Melton Mowbray, Leics, LE13 0LS
Shareholders: Peter John Mayes; Bobby Mark Sheldrake
Officers: Peter John Mayes [1966] Director/Marketing; Bobby Mark Sheldrake [1973] Director/Project Manager

Index of Directorships

Abdon, Anna Caroline
Linsenlinsen Limited

Abdullah, Umar
So-Real Foods Ltd

Abdullah-Hucker, Randa
Hullabaloos Lemonade Limited

Abdurasul, Shamagdiev
UK Dorset Ltd

Aboud, Sara Jennifer
Aqua Hebrides Limited

Abraham, Malcolm Joseph
Citrosoft Drinks Limited

Abraham, Patricia Anne
Citrosoft Drinks Limited

Abramovitz, Bailey
Fonthill Waters Limited

Ackroyd, Ian Mark
The Temperance Spirit Co Ltd

Adair, Christopher Wayne
Papas Mineral Co Ltd

Adamo, Olusoji
BODI Products Limited

Adams, Michael Daniel
Wet Beverages (Global) Ltd

Adamson, Mark Kevin
Cawingredients Limited

Adcock, John Keith
Adcocks Drinks Co Ltd

Ademola, Adekunle Akanji
Fruito Beverages (Africa) Ltd
Fruito Soft Drinks Limited

Adeosun, Adebayo
Anglo African Food & Beverages Holding

Adu, Aklane
Elan League UK Ltd

Adu, Babatunde
Elan League UK Ltd

Aga Khan, Kendra
The Cure Project Limited

Agbeyo, Tolulope Ayomide
Burble Foods and Beverages Ltd
Cornfield Foods and Beverages Ltd

Agboli, Benjamin Koffi Vigno
Willimott House Limited

Agboli, Pamela Maud Phyllis
Willimott House Limited

Ahluwalia, Harminder Singh
Innovative Drinks Ltd

Ahmad, Faraz
Cold Bru Tea Limited

Ahmad, Zaheer
Fruitfilm Limited

Ahmadi Moghaddam, Amir Abbas
Pure Spring Aqua Ltd

Ahmed, Bilal
Double Apple Ltd

Ahmed, Hassan Jahangir
Montecrysto Limited

Ahmed, Osman
Cold Bru Tea Limited

Akcicek, Polat Cosar
Adaquo H20 Ltd

Akoto, Adwoa Kuffour
AA Group Holdings Ltd

Akram, Amar
Rainbow Beverages Ltd

Al Khyami, Ali
CBDMEhealthy Limited

Al Tajir, Maher
Lothian Shelf (674) Limited

Al Tajir, Mohammed Mahdi
Highland Spring Limited
Hope Sixteen (No.87) Limited

Al-Tajir, Maher
Gleneagles Spring Water Co Ltd.

Alabi, Olaitan
N'ife Limited

Alalia, Savannah
Kingdon Callea Ltd

Aldean, Rose
Mello Drinks Ltd

Alderson, Benjamin John
Mr Fitzpatrick's Limited

Alderson, Shirley
Mr Fitzpatrick's Limited

Aleksandrova, Anna
Enterprises Beyond Reason Ltd

Ali, Mohammed
Mount Valley Beverages Ltd

Ali, Sharmarke Haydar
Ammo Your Ammunition to Greatness

Alkhalifa, Khalifah Mohamed Ateyatalla
HD Water Limited

Allana, Huma
Coca-Cola European Partners GB Ltd

Allen, Mark Jason Keith
Bladud Spring Limited

Allen, Rachel Ingeborg Mary
Bladud Spring Limited

Altabtabaei, Yaseen Abdul Mohsen
Norwegian Glacier Water Ltd

Altajir, Khalid Mohamed Mahdi
Highland Spring Limited

Altajir, Maher
Highland Spring Limited
Hope Sixteen (No.87) Limited
Speyside Glenlivet (HSL) Co Ltd

Amarouch, Ahmed
Sharewater Ltd

Amato, Stefan
Pointeer Ltd

Amodeo, Stefania
Shlurpies Ltd.

Amponsah, Vivian
Cornny Drinks Limited

Amponsah, Yaw
Cornny Drinks Limited

Anand, Rooney
JB Drinks Holdings Limited

Andersen, Anna Marie
Stonehenge Spring Water Ltd

Andersen, Stig Anker
Stonehenge Spring Water Ltd

Anderson, Oakley Blue
Space Chef Ltd

Anderson, Thomas Alexander
Limonada Mathe Limited

Anderson, William John Edward
Hike Coffee Ltd

Andrews, Michael John
Artisan Drinks Co Ltd

Arbib, Benjamin Guy
Better Fresh Limited

Archard, Paul
The Refreshing Drinks Co Ltd

Archer, Jonathan Paul Steadman
Wild Life Botanicals Ltd

Armour, Nicola Jane
The Original Somerset Certified Water Supply Co

Armstrong, Peter
Goodlives Panacea Blend Ltd

Armstrong, Peter Michael
Thomas Hardy Kendal Limited

Arter, Kai
The Temperance Spirit Co Ltd

Arulanantham, Amit
Moringa Superfoods UK Limited

Arulanantham, Eirlys Sian
Moringa Superfoods UK Limited

Arweny, David
Avid Stacc Ltd

Ashby, Ian Harry
Zombie Energy Limited

Ashraf, Tasadduq Ali
411 Beverages Limited
Freez Global Ltd.

Ashton, James Richard Willmott
Rock's Organic Limited

Aslam, Harris Shahzad
Skwishee Ltd

Aslam, Naveed
Aillo Ltd
Nachure Ltd

Athwal, Kamaljit
Big Time Soft Drinks Limited

Athwal, Mohinder Singh
Big Time Soft Drinks Limited

Atkinson, Samantha
Mambo Drinks Limited

Attwell, Sallie Amanda
Montgomery Waters Limited

Audu, Paul Abdul-Abbass
Chocquers Limited
Choquers Limited
Tea GB International Limited

Augustin, Bethael
B + K Augustin Limited

Augustin, Kim
B + K Augustin Limited

Ausher, Jason Robert
Cott Ventures UK Limited
Decantae Mineral Water Limited
Total Water Solutions Limited

Averiss, Joanne Kerry
Vitamin Brands Ltd.

Averre, Jayne Tracy
The Gourmet Water Co Ltd

Averre, Raymond James
The Gourmet Water Co Ltd

Aweys, Mohamed
Dangercode Ltd

Ayson, Rannie
Aberrucia Ltd

Ayub, Asif
Chilled Water Ltd

Aziz, Bilal
Samco Retail Ltd
Thirsty Soft Drinks Ltd

Azouri, Ilan
Flow 33 UK Limited

Bagkos, Georgios
Three Cents Ltd

Bahadur, Omar
Faraday Drinks Ltd

Bahizire, Bahati Gaspard
Zireson Enterprises Limited

Bailey, Ashley
Henny and Joes Ltd

Bailey, Emma
Cardinal Drinks Ltd

Bailey, Jean
Saftiaray & Co Limited

Bailey, Margaret
Hartpury Heritage Trust

Bailey, Richard William
The Water Guru Limited

Bain, Katie May
Devon Soda Co Limited

Bainn, Candy Mary
Inmind Care Services Ltd

Baister, Richard Frederick
Sumo Drinks Ltd

Baker, Benjamin Paul
Monarch Beverages Limited

Baker, Charisse
East London Juice Co Ltd

Baker, Suzannah Denise Hartley
Ultra Beauty Limited

Bakhaty, Omar Sharif Mohamed
Etoh Studio Limited

Baldwin, Sarah Jane
JB Drinks Holdings Limited
JB Drinks Limited
Purity Soft Drinks Limited

Ball, Jasbinder Singh
Good Beverage Co Ltd

Ballantyne, Sharon Anna
Ballantyne McLean Limited

Banks, Christopher Nigel
Cracker Drinks Co. Limited

Banks, Samuel N K
AB Vaults Group Limited

Banton, Ryan
Punchline Ltd

Barker, Ben Lewis
Artemis Brew Ltd

Barlow, Jason
Shepley Spring Limited

Barltrop, Richard Forbes
Peel and Spice Ltd

Barnes, Laraine Helen
New Life Water Limited

Barnes, Paul Martin
Soho Juice Co Ltd

Barnshaw, Gary Mark
Goodness Brands Ltd

Barr, Geoffrey William
Soak Coffee Ltd

Barr, Julie Anne
Robert Barr Limited

Barr, William Robin Graham
A.G. Barr P.L.C.

Barratt, Susan Verity
A.G. Barr P.L.C.

Barrett, Peter David, Dr
TBD Brew Co Ltd

Barwell, Matthew Robert
Britvic Soft Drinks Limited

Basra, Gurminder Singh
Wild Cat Energy Drink Ltd

Basra, Suresh Kumar
Can of Wagon Ltd

Bass, Michael Peter Andrew
Calyx Drinks Ltd

Bates, Sean Michael
Syncrobia Ltd

Bax, Christopher Martin
Bax Botanics Limited
No Longer Bax Botanics Limited

Bax, Rosemary Jane Badger
Bax Botanics Limited
No Longer Bax Botanics Limited

Bean, Gabriel
Raw Is More Ltd.

Beaney, Alan Raymond
Slush Puppie Limited

Beard, Charles Rowden
Grown-Up Foods Ltd

Beaumont, Ian Christopher
ICB Advisory Limited

Bedi, Aneil
The Refreshing Drinks Co Ltd

Beeby, Brian Joseph
Swithland Spring Water Limited

Beeby, Janet Margaret
Swithland Spring Water Limited

Beech, Christopher
LUHV Drinks Limited
LUHV Limited

Beer, Nicholas
Kuka Coffee Ltd

Belcher, Robert Alan Carruthers
March Foods Limited

Bell, Andrew Mark
BFT Drinks Limited

Bell, Robert
The Live Kindly Drinks Co Ltd

Bello, Nurudeen
Bello's World Limited

Bendel, Charlotte Laroque
Merrily Mulled Ltd

Bendit, Frances Katherine
Metro Drinks Limited

Bendit, Paul Jonathan
E D Resources Limited
Folkington's (Middle East) Ltd
Metro Drinks Limited

Beneventi, Michel
Buxton Mineral Water Limited
Nestle Waters (UK) Holdings Ltd
Nestle Waters GB Limited
Nestle Waters UK Limited
Princes Gate Spring Water Ltd
Princes Gate Water Limited

Benjamin, Maxwell
Youthenergy East Africa Ltd

Benn, Joseph William
Ugly Brands Limited

Bennet, Jack Gerard
Wild Husk Limited

Bennett, Oliver Roy
Rocx Energy Ltd
Xite Beverages Limited
Xite Energy Limited
Xorb Energy Limited

Bennett, Richard Donald John
Mad Dog Drinks Limited

Bennett-Baggs, Robert Mark Peter
NR Enterprise Limited

Bennink, Jan
Coca-Cola European Partners PLC

Berahino, Saido
SRP Equipe Limited

Berger, Dominic Peter Clive
Halo Drinks Co Ltd
Liverpool Canning Co Ltd

Berman, Bradley
Dash Brands Ltd

Bernard, Deirdre
Heather Spring Water Limited

Bernard, Stanley Ian
Heather Spring Water Limited

Berry, Adam
Strawhill Estate Spirits Co Ltd

Bese, Lajos Janos
Juicy Brands (UK) Ltd.

Best, Reece
H2go Drinks Ltd

Best, William Trevorian Stuart
Bloody Drinks Limited

Bewley-Pope, Ben
White Smoke Distillery Ltd

Bhangle, Sarbjeet Singh
Innovative Drinks Ltd

Bhavsar, Amitkumar
Sai Water UK Limited

Bihal, Shamir
Shop-Local-UK Ltd

Billa, Jean Claude
Two B Limited

Binder, Doran Barry
The Crag Spring Water Limited

Binder, Melissa
Aquacan Limited

Binder, Melissa Jane
The Crag Spring Water Limited

Binns, Henry Edward Stephen Davidson
Brewberry Limited
Qishui Limited

Birch, Patrick, Dr
Birch Boost Ltd

Birchall, Elaine
Beverage Brands (U.K.) Limited
Bottle Green Drinks Co Ltd
Bottlegreen Holdings Limited
Caledonian Bottlers PLC
Merrydown PLC
Rock's Organic Limited
Super Nuva Ltd
Woodchester Enterprises Ltd

Birnie, Clive Graham John
Ruudz Limited

Biscaldi, Pietro
Ty Nant Spring Water Limited

Bisterzo, Livio
Ugly Brands Limited

Blackler, Paul
Hippo & Hedgehog Ltd

Blake, Patrick David
Schweppes International Ltd

Blow, Andrew Victor
Precision Hydration Limited

Blythe, Shona Jane
Norbev Limited

Bodart, Michele Carole
Inginius Limited
Sodahouseco Limited

Bomer, Sarah
CMB Water Limited

Bomer, William
CMB Water Limited

Bond, Tara Michelle
Jolly's Drinks Limited

Booker, Gary
Koala Karma UK Limited

Booth, Cheryl Tracey
Sutton Spring Limited

Booth, Robert James
Sutton Spring Limited

Boothe, Amari
Punchline Ltd

Boueshaghi, Vincent
Russia Cola Limited

Boulter, Daniel Mark
Rebel Drinks (London) Limited
Rebel Drinks Accra Limited

Bourne-Arton, Richard William
Tanfield Springs Ltd

Bouvet Ep. Toole, Sylvie
Schweppes International Ltd

Bowden, John Arthur
Kuka Coffee Ltd

Bowen, Christopher Peter
Karkade Drinks Limited

Bowen, Lisa Margaret
The Do Drink Co Ltd

Boyadjian, Igor Pierre
Liver Health UK Ltd.

Boydall, Hannah Mary
Boydall Limited

Boydall, Patrick Vincent
Boydall Limited

Bradley, Jeffrey Charles Richard
Hidden Orchard Ltd

Bradshaw, Christopher John
Kingsley Beverage Limited

Bradshaw, Thomas Frank
Nude Drinks Limited

Brady, Siobhan Cathrina Maria
GB Heritage Ltd

Brare, Waseem
Seed Lab Ltd.

Bray, Ian David
Fentimans Ltd.

Brennan, Rory Mathew
Suntory Beverage & Food South Africa Ltd

Bret, Harald Eric
The Naivasha Tonic Co Ltd

Brewer, Frederic Peter
Red Dragon Water Limited

Bridgens, Stephen Christopher
Belvoir Fruit Farms Drinks Holdings
Belvoir Fruit Farms Limited

Bridges, John Arthur
Ness Scotland Ltd

Brittain, Richard
Refreshing Intercepted Limited

UK Manufacturers of Soft Drinks dellam

Britton, Christopher Paul
Ugly Brands Limited

Brodie, John Ross
The Start-Up Drinks Lab Ltd

Brooks, Peter John
Office Beverages Ltd
Office Watercoolers (S.W.) Ltd

Brooks, Sabrina Rose
Peel and Spice Ltd

Broughton, Daniel James
Dalston's Soda Co Ltd

Brown, Charles Duncan
Highlands Pride Ltd.

Brown, David Charles Alexander
The Goodnatured Co Ltd.

Brown, Edward Finnbar
Finn Capital Ltd

Brown, Hadley-James Henry
Frey Drinks Limited

Brown, Heloise
The Goodnatured Co Ltd.

Brown, John Walter James
Core Fruit Products Limited

Brown, Jonathan Michael
Fonthill Waters Limited

Brown, Nathan
Paradise Rum Limited

Browne, Kiera
Seafire Brewing Co. Ltd

Bryan, Duane
The Bily Co Limited

Buba, Amina
Kapyani Limited

Buckley, Alex
Wake Drinks Ltd
Wake Energy Drinks Limited

Buckley, Carlo Geoffrey
Rejuvenation Water Ltd

Buckley, Claire
Wake Energy Drinks Limited

Buddhasingh, Carl
Anglo African Food & Beverages Holding

Bulloch, Alexander
The Natural Fruit and Beverage Co Ltd
Portavadie Distillery Limited

Bulloch, Carol Anne
The Natural Fruit and Beverage Co Ltd

Burchardt, Harald Peter
Liver Health UK Ltd.

Burke, James
Swithland Spring Water Limited

Burke, John
Pearl Soft Drinks Limited

Burke, Michael
Fuctivino Ltd

Burkhardt, Elizabeth
Cawingredients Limited

Burleton, Karen Marie
Everything But The Cow Limited

Burnett, Duncan Walker
Salcombe Cider Co Ltd

Burris, Joseph
Bennu Rising Ltd.

Burrough, Nathan Paul
Bon Accord Soft Drinks Limited

Burrows, Richard Alan
Jolly's Drinks Limited

Burton, Darryl John
Peter Spanton Drinks Ltd

Bush, Nicholas Benjamin, Dr
Enrj Drinks Ltd

Bushell, William Thomas
Copper Stag Ltd

Butler, Neil William
Rock's Organic Limited

Butler, Penelope Susan
Radnor Hills Mineral Water Co Ltd

Bye, Ian Jonathan
Just Bee Drinks Limited

Byerley, Callum James
Botanical Soda Works Limited

Cain, Anthony Joseph
HSW Limited
Harrogate Spring Water Limited
Oakdale Spring Limited
Thirsty Planet Limited

Cain, James Anthony
Harrogate Spring Water Limited
Oakdale Spring Limited
Thirsty Planet Limited

Caird, Gavin Paul
Zion Manufacturing Ltd

Callan, Raymond
The Diesel Brewing Co Ltd.

Calvert, Ashley James
Shrubb Ltd

Camara, Mbakeh
Wisdom Superfoods CIC

Cameron, Miki
My Living Water UK Ltd

Cameron, Nicholas James
My Living Water UK Ltd

Campbell, Eion
CMB Water Limited

Carbutt, Jack Francis de Montmorency
Duo Drinks Ltd

Carling, Guy Philip
Monster Energy Europe Limited

Carr, Collin
Saapos Ltd

Carrington, Alexander Nicholas
Carrington's Coffee Co Ltd

Carter, Andrew Philip
Swalevalley Springwater Ltd

Carter, Eileen Lamont
Swalevalley Springwater Ltd

Carty, Simon
Amino Drinks Limited

Cashin, James Frederick
El Natural Ltd

Catton, Mark Jonathan
Little Miracles Drinks Limited

Catton, Mark Jonathan
Little Miracles (International) Ltd

Cawood, Jonathan Nicholas Asquith
Vyking Energy Limited

Cawthray, Andrew James
DRII Limited
Dry Beverages Limited
Cawingredients Limited

Cawthray, Susan
Cawingredients Limited

Cazaly, Jonathan Philip
Spruce Water Limited

Challinor, Lewis Dan
Bright Smoothies Ltd

Chance, Craig Jonathon
Piff Juice Limited

Chaplin, Jonathan George Llewellyn
Core Beverage Equipment Ltd
The Village Orchard Ltd

Chapman, Holly Bridget
Hartpury Heritage Trust

Chapman, James Roger
Hartpury Heritage Trust

Chapman, Jamie
Mylkman Ltd

Chapman, Robin
The East India Company Indian Tonic Water

Charlton, David
Fentimans Ltd.

Chatzimanolis, Georgios Konstantinos
UK Premium Brands Limited

Chauhan, Shantilal
Wild Cat Energy Drink Ltd

Chauhan, Suniti Kiransinh
Britvic PLC

Cheetham, David Paul
Lowe Bros. (Cardiff) Limited

Chen, Tina Tzu-Ming
Mighty Drinks Ltd.

Cheta, Ghomdim Jose Fabrice
Guffaw Ltd

Chetty, Natasha
Suntory Beverage & Food South Africa Ltd

Chiu, Xiao Nan Natalie, Dr
Saicho Ltd.

Chondrorizos, Georgios
Creative Properties and Investments Ltd
Evogue Limited

Chopra, Kuldip
Green Leaf Liquids Limited

Choraria, Sanjeev Kumar
A & S Specialist Supplies Ltd.

Christodoulou, Eleftherios
Icely Done Drinks Limited

Cider, Julia Christine
Clearly Devon Limited
Moorland Mist Limited

Clamp, Robert William
Birken Tree (Scotland) Limited

Clark, Michael
Coca-Cola European Partners GB Ltd

Clark, Peter Charles
Dexos Drinks Limited
Kolibri Drinks Limited

Clark, Steven James
Press London Ltd

Clark, Susan Michelle
Britvic PLC

Clarke, John Henry
Kimpton Apple Press Limited

Clarke, Lisa Christine
Chia Food (York) Limited

Clarke, Robert
Morninglory Ltd

Clement, Lisa Jane
Everything But The Cow Limited

Clemes, Nathan McKenzie
Happy Curations Limited

Cliffe, Odili Anthony
Buatoc Limited

Cobbett, Benjamin Peter
Impact Sports Science Limited

Cocogne, Jonathann
The Bread Drink Lab Limited

Coker, William Joseph
Green Room Brands Limited

Cole, John
Jurassic Water Limited

Coley, Simon Cosmo
Karma Cola UK Ltd

Colley, Andrew George
Eastcott Drinks Ltd

Colling, Valerie
Karma Water Co Ltd
Love Tide Water Limited

Collins, John Roger Gane
Think Drinks Limited

Collins, Thomas James Gane
Think Drinks Limited

Collins, Timothy
Fielding Dairies Limited

Collis, Christopher James
Elfie Drinks Co Ltd

Collis, Elvis Anthony
Highdrate Ltd

Colman, Clive Ivan
The Yummy Juice Co Ltd

Colman, Frances
The Yummy Juice Co Ltd

Condron, Janice Grace
Chastity Limited

Conway, Eoghan Joseph
Outsider Drinks Ltd.

Cooke, Martin James
Gingercool Limited

Cooper, Andrew [1979]
Horizon (Contract Drinks) Ltd

Cooper, Andrew [1944]
Burnswell Spring (Mauchline) Ltd

Cooper, Andrew James
Juice Man Limited

Cooper, Carol
Cotton & Cane Ltd

Cooper, Christopher David George
The Original Somerset Certified Water Supply Co

Cooper, Craig Bryan
Fiji Water (UK) Limited

Cooper, Daniel
Dayla Limited

Cooper, Steven William
Artisan Drinks Co Ltd

Cooper, Timothy John
Dayla Holdings Limited
Dayla Limited

Cope, Ingrid Natalie
Coca-Cola International Sales Ltd
Waters & Robson Holdings Ltd

Coppel, Andrew Maxwell
Cambrian Soft Drinks Limited

Corrigan, Howard James
Captains Original Ltd

Cowell, Kevin David
New Forest Spring Water Distribution Ltd
New Forest Spring Water Ltd

Cox, Gavin Lloyd
Benefit Water Ltd

Cozzolino, Giorgio Cozzolino
A & C Green Food and Beverage Ltd
Nerissimo Luxury Espresso Ltd

Craig, Giles Augustus
BODI Products Limited

Cram, Stephen
Goodness Brands Ltd

Crame, Janet Pamela Winifred
Ankerwycke Water Limited

Crame, Jeremy Hugh
Ankerwycke Water Limited

Crawford, Kelly
Armagh Juice Co Ltd

Crespo Benitez, Francisco Javier
Coca-Cola European Partners PLC

Crickmore, Gavin Paul
Diageo Great Britain Limited

Crispini, Nick Alessandro
BTW Drinks Ltd

Crocker, Matt
Berrington Spring Water Ltd

Crofts, Henry Robert Brighton
Pointeer Ltd

Crosby, Ellen Frania
Septimus Spyder Soft Drinks Ltd

Crosby, Ian
March Foods Limited

Cross, Christine
Coca-Cola European Partners PLC

Croston, Tim John
The Noisy Drinks Co Ltd

Croston, Timothy John
Beacon Drinks Limited
Dayla Liquid Packing Limited
Just Bee Drinks Limited
Nichols PLC
Ben Shaws Dispense Drinks Ltd

Crotchett, Conner Victor
Innovate Energy Drinks Ltd
Xtreme Energy Group Limited

Cruickshank, William
W.& J.Cruickshank and Co Ltd

Cubuk, Arin
Boosted Tea (UK) Ltd.

Curran, Jamie
Boosted Tea (UK) Ltd.

Currie, Mark Adrian
Rockbarr Limited

Cushen, Matthew John
Nix & Kix Ltd

Cuvalcioglu, Pervin
Artemis Import & Export Ltd

Da Camara, Jose Manuel
Kingsley Beverage Limited

Dailey, Daniel Junior
Pop in Tea Limited

Dali, Christen
Lifeline Holdings Limited

Daly, John Patrick
Britvic PLC

Daneshmand, Rahi
Refresh Brands Limited

Daniels-Dada, Will Afolabi
Elementhree Ltd

Daurella, Sol
Coca-Cola European Partners PLC

David, Gabriel Luscombe
Luscombe Drinks Limited
Scops Drinks Limited

David, Venetia
Luscombe Drinks Limited

Davidson, Mark
Artisan Drinks Co Ltd

Davies, Cynthia George
Tovali Limited

Davies, Karen Louise
Tovali Limited

Davies, Serge
Green Monkey Drinks Ltd

Davis, Adrian
Swallow Drinks South West Ltd

Davis, Benjamin James
GB Refreshments Limited

Davison, Michael John
Rainbow Carousel Soft Drinks Ltd

Davison, Yvonne Mary
Rainbow Carousel Soft Drinks Ltd

De Blas Bravo, Diego
Schweppes International Ltd

De Haas, Joyce Michelle
Double Dutch Ltd.

De Haas, Raissa Catherina
Double Dutch Ltd.

De Jong, David Theodoor
Miximex Limited

De Ruijt, Tanita
Jamu Kitchen Ltd

De Silva, Asanka
Liver Health UK Ltd.

Decaux, Hortense
Limonada Mathe Limited

Deeley, Andrew Stephen
Fitch Brew Co Ltd.

Delves Mbe, Gilroy Donald
Montgomery Waters Limited

Delves, David Paul
Montgomery Waters Limited

Den Hollander, Leendert Pieter
Coca-Cola European Partners GB Ltd

Deng, Xingzhong
UK Brighton Food & Nutrition Research Centre

Desains, Franck Michel
Mariage Freres Royaume Uni Ltd

Devereux-Kelly, Joseph Patrick
Third Wave Coffee Ventures Ltd

Dexter, Roy Ian Lawson
Fillongley Spring Water Ltd
Fillongley Ventures Limited

Dhirani, Hasnein
Wild Cat Energy Drink Ltd

Diamond, Leon Edward
Plenish Cleanse Ltd

Dickinson, Oliver John
Wow Food and Drinks Ltd

Dingemans, Simon Paul
SmithKline Beecham Limited

Diniz, Rogerio Correia
Kingsley Beverage Limited

Dixon, Curtis
Punchline Ltd

Dobson, Dominic William Swinburne
The Meon Spirit Co Ltd

Doherty, Ciaran Joseph
Norbev Limited

Dollive, Matthew
Barncrofts of London Limited

Donnelly, Kevin Ronald
Counterpoint Wholesale (NI) Ltd

Dor, Stephen
March Foods Limited

Doubleday, Edward
Bax Farm Juice Ltd

Doubleday, Oliver Christopher
Bax Farm Juice Ltd

Doubleday, Oliver Peter, Dr
Bax Farm Juice Ltd

Doubleday, Philip
Bax Farm Juice Ltd

Dougan, Kieran
40 Kola Ltd

Dougan, Sarah
Grown-Up Foods Ltd

Douws, Kevin Jean-Frederic
ABI SAB Group Holding Limited

Dover, Alexander Thomas
Bitter Salvation Ltd

Dover, Alexandra Lynette
Bitter Salvation Ltd

Down, Rachel Susan
Boil and Broth Ltd

Down, Simon Edward
Boil and Broth Ltd

Drogba, Danielle
Deedee's Kitchen Limited

Drohan, Mel
Coca-Cola HBC Northern Ireland Ltd

Drury, Pauline
Hartpury Heritage Trust

Drysdale, Colin Jonathon
Allson Sparkle Limited

Drysdale, Nicola
Allson Sparkle Limited

Duckworth, Brendan Gerard
The Temperance Spirit Co Ltd

Duffy, Claire
Cott Ventures UK Limited
Decantae Mineral Water Limited
Total Water Solutions Limited

Duffy, Liam
Classic Holdings Limited
Classic Mineral Water Co Ltd

Duijzer, Aart
Refresco Drinks UK Limited

Duijzer, Aart Cornelis
04021465 Limited
Refresco Beverages UK Limited

Dulobo, Firoz
Sai Water UK Limited

Dumelie, Johann
Akme Coffee Limited

Dunkerley, John
Glucofit Limited

Dunn, Mathew James
Britannia Soft Drinks Limited
British Vitamin Products Ltd
Britvic Asset Company No.1 Ltd
Britvic Asset Company No.2 Ltd
Britvic Asset Company No.3 Ltd
Britvic Asset Company No.4 Ltd
Britvic Beverages Limited
Britvic Corona Limited
Britvic International Investments
Britvic International Support Services
Britvic Overseas Limited
Britvic PLC
Britvic Soft Drinks Limited
Counterpoint Wholesale (NI) Ltd
Greenbank Drinks Co Ltd
Hooper,Struve & Co Ltd
Idris Limited
London Essence Co Ltd
Orchid Drinks Limited
H.D.Rawlings Limited
The Really Wild Drinks Co Ltd
Red Devil Energy Drinks Ltd
Robinsons (Finance) No.2 Ltd
Robinsons Soft Drinks Limited
Southern Table Water Co Ltd
Sunfresh Soft Drinks Limited
R.White & Sons Limited

Dupont Dudley, Aude Marie Claude Jacques
Blossoms Syrup Limited

Dusart, Briggette Madge Odell
Solar Cola Limited

Dusart, Christina
Solar Cola Limited

Dusart, Katie
Solar Cola Limited

Dye, Tom Alexander Scott
Herbal Fusions Ltd

Dyer, Colin John
Just Water Limited

Dyer, John Paul
Zombie Energy Limited

Dyer, Pauline Dianne
Just Water Limited

Dzelzainis, Marcis Alfred
Paradise Drinks Co. Limited

Eaton, Peter Gary
Willow Water Limited

Ebinum, Chukuka
Zowell Ltd

Eccleshare, Christopher William
Britvic PLC

Eden, Mark
The Pure Dartmoor Water Co Ltd

Edmunds, James Matthew Crayden
Diageo Great Britain Limited

Edwards, Claire Elizabeth
The Original Drinks and Food Co Ltd

Edwards, Donya
Drinks-on-Draught Limited

Edwards, Endaf
Princes Gate Water Limited

Edwards, Huw Pritchard
Ice Cube Tea Ltd

Edwards, James
Desert Island Drinks Limited
The Original Drinks Co Ltd.
The Original Drinks and Food Co Ltd

Edwards, Philip Aubrey
Alcarelle Holdings Limited
Alcarelle Limited

Egbune, Freedom Ikechukwu, Rev
ECF Global Ltd

Egen, Caitlin Mary
Honu Sodas UK Limited

Egen, Gregg Michael
Honu Sodas UK Limited

Ejaz, Muhammad
Chaiwala Limited

El Khoury, Daniel Francis
Trip Drink Ltd

El Tagoury, Adam
Prana Drinks Limited

Eldridge, Michael Stuart
Yeast Meets West Limited

Elford-Alliyu, Lateef
SRP Equipe Limited

Elliot, Colin David
Cambrian Soft Drinks Limited

Elliott, John
Kul-Kis Limited

Elliott, Rosemary Francis
Kul-Kis Limited

English, Julie
Birdhouse Tea Co Ltd

English, Rebecca Lauren
Birdhouse Tea Co Ltd

Entwisle, Nicholas Mark Warwick
HYP Water Ltd

Escritt, Ian
Post Hoc Ergo Propter Hoc Ltd

Esler, Niall Edward Lloyd
Nele Drinks Limited

Evangelopoulos, Nickolas
Pomepure Ltd

Evans, Adrian Eliot
Hydration Station Ltd

Evans, Ben David
Zilch Ltd

Evans, Emma Sarah
Upper Harglodd Farm Ltd

Evans, John
Hedgerow Soft Drinks Ltd

Evans, John Griffiths
Hartpury Heritage Trust

Evans, Joseph Oliver
Marlish Waters Limited

Evans, Mark Wyn Raymond
Upper Harglodd Farm Ltd

Evans, Oliver William Roderick
The Santa Monica Co Ltd

Evans, Victoria Elizabeth
Vitamin Brands Ltd.

Fachler, Jason
Bespokery Ltd

Farmer, Robert
Jurassic Spring Water Ltd

Farnham, Henry Robert Spencer
Bloody Drinks Limited

Farnworth, Chris James
Unique Drinks Limited

Farquhar, Alexander Ross
Fionnar Springs Ltd.

Farrell, David John
Faractive Limited

Fathalizadeh, Keyvan
Saffron Water Limited

Faust, Nina
Faustian Ltd

Faye, Greger
Turn Global Ltd

Fegan, Grainne Marie
Our Northern Stars Limited

Felton, Andrew James
Ipro Sport Exports Limited

Fennessy, Sharon Lynnette
Diageo Great Britain Limited

Ferguson, Joshua
Mobay Drinks Ltd

Ferran, Javier
Coca-Cola European Partners PLC

Ferris, Brynmor Joe
Raw Is More Ltd.

Ficsor, Laszlo
Budaquelle Beverages International Ltd

Field, Andrew James Darragh
Razoo Limited

Field, Rosheeka Dilhani Amarasekara
Razoo Limited

Fildes, Gregory
Baroncroft Ltd

Finan, Irial
Coca-Cola European Partners PLC

Finch, Jacqueline
Rio Coffee Limited

Finch, James Andrew
Rio Coffee Limited

Findlay, Norma Jane
Edinburgh Kombucha Ltd

Fiordilino, Brigidino
H Two Eau International Ltd

Fish, David Paul
Us 4 Slush Limited

Fisher, Hannah Magdaline
The Craft Soft Drinks Community Ltd
The Start-Up Drinks Lab Ltd

Fitchett, Emily
Fitch Brew Co Ltd.

FitzGenerald, Megan
JW Production Limited

Fitzgibbons, Francis William
Belvoir Fruit Farms Limited

Flint, Simon
Smilk Limited

Folland, Neil Scott
Tarka Springs Limited

Folland, Sarah Jane
Tarka Springs Limited

Fomychov, Andrew
Acqua Eterna Ltd
Acqua Nordica Ltd

Forward, Eaoifa
Boo-Chi Limited

Foss Sims, Alexander
Solo Coffee Ltd

Foster, Max
Frey Drinks Limited

Fox, Vernon
Lough Neagh Distillers - 1837 Ltd

Foy, Edward Joseph
Press London Ltd

Frampton, Emma
The Juice Collective Limited

France, Denis
Handmade Cider Co Ltd

Francis, Christine Ingrid
My Mum's Ltd

Franke, Teresa Elizabeth
Ferment Revolution Limited

Fratini, Nicholas
Superfoods Nutrition Ltd

Freedman, Theodore
TMF Trading Limited

Freeman, Amanda Kate
Youthenergy Drinks Ltd
Youthenergy East Africa Ltd

Freeman, Hollyann
Youthenergy Drinks Ltd

Freeman, Jason Carl
Youthenergy East Africa Ltd

Freeman, Richard Antony
Lovely Drinks Limited

Frehley, Steven
Jeffrey's Tonic Ltd

Frieman, Ron Zev
Eden Springs UK Limited

Frimpong Jnr, Fernand Kwasi
Sweet Memoirs Limited

Frost, Alistair Edward
Pentire Drinks Limited

Fuller, Jonathan Mark
BFT Drinks Limited

Gaal, Elena
Ellive Ltd

Gaal, Gyorgy Eduard
Ellive Ltd

Gabriel, Joel
Essence PH10 Limited

Gagneja, Radha Nagrecha
Exotic Beverages Limited

Gale, Tracey Jayne
Galactogen Products Limited

Galea, Simon David
The Refreshing Drinks Co Ltd

Gallagher, John Stephen
Ella Drinks Limited

Galvin, Mark
Drinks for Beauty Ltd

Gammell, Damian Paul
Coca-Cola European Partners PLC

Garba, Ibrahim Abubakar
Ayge Limited

Garcia, Christophe
Britvic EMEA Limited

Garcia-Minaur, Theo
Solo Coffee Ltd

Gardner, Clare Louise
Impact Sports Science Limited

Garvey, Emma
Alive Beverages Limited

Garvin, Sylvia Marie
Sejuiced Limited

Gates, Peter Graham
Zero Proof UK Limited

Gaveau, Nathalie Laurence
Coca-Cola European Partners PLC

Gdanitz, Corene Joan
Syrup Junkie Limited

Geary, Brian Samuel
Antrim Hills Spring Water Co Ltd

Geary, Peter Jonathon
Antrim Hills Spring Water Co Ltd

Geary, Rosemary Wilson
Antrim Hills Spring Water Co Ltd

Gee, Patrick Robert Cooper
Llanllyr Water Co Ltd

Geen, Joan Sharon Lloye
Morgan's Exclusive Ltd

Geoghegan, Gina Marghrtha
This Is Holy Water Limited

Gerginska, Venelina
Pura Vita Drinks Ltd.

Gerrard, Clare Susannah
Ferment Revolution Limited

Gibbs-Sawyers, Gillian
Koolvibes Limited

Gibson, Craig
Ginsecco Ltd

Gibson, David Channing
Canncrest Drinks Limited

Gilani, Rohail
Alive Water Ltd

Gill, Navinder Kaur
LVS Bottling Limited

Gill, Salinder Kaur
KGN London Ltd

Gilland Robinson, Christine
Holos London Ltd

Giorgio, Nick
CBDMEhealthy Limited

Girdler, James Oliver
Ember Drinks Ltd.

Gittins, John Anthony
Nichols PLC

Gladshteyn, Yulia
Reluminate Ltd

Glaisher, George Woulfe
Glaisher & Ames Ltd

Gleadowe, Frederick Joseph York, Dr
Shandy Shack Ltd

Gleave, Amanda Louise Duran
Ammacus Trading Limited

Gleave, Simon
Lytewater Limited

Gleave, Simon Andrew
Ammacus Trading Limited

Glen, Iain David
Showerings Cider Mill Ltd

Gold, Jonathan Paul
Karma Water Co Ltd

Goldfinch, Allison
Blue Raspberry Investments Ltd
Northumbrian Ice Cream Co Ltd

Goldfinch, Margaret
Northumbrian Ice Cream Co Ltd

Goldfinch, Paul John
Blue Raspberry Investments Ltd
Northumbrian Ice Cream Co Ltd
Polar Krush Limited

Goldfinch, Peter John
Northumbrian Ice Cream Co Ltd

Gombert, Louis-Francois Amand
Lucozade Ribena Suntory Exports Ltd
Schweppes International Ltd

Gomez-Trenor Aguilar, Alvaro
Coca-Cola European Partners PLC

Gonzales, Ralph Christian
Agilebody Ltd

Good, Nicholas Paul
Dorset Ginger Co Ltd

Good, Timea
Dorset Ginger Co Ltd

Gordon, Hamish Christian
The Driver's Drinks Co Ltd

Gorna, Barbara Elizabeth
Bad Girls Brew Limited

Gosler, John
Two2Three2Four Ltd

Gould, Jessica Katharine
Brain Fud Ltd

Gournay, Meeta
Three Spirit Drinks Ltd

Gournay, Meeta Sethna
Beyond Alcohol Ltd

Govaerts, Frank
Coca-Cola European Partners GB Ltd

Grace, Jordan
Loft 68 Vintage Ltd

Grafham, Robert John
Highlands Pride Ltd.

Graham, Kenneth
Soda Folk Ltd

Graham, Neil Osbern Nigel
Devonia Water Ltd

Graham, Nicholas
Hoods Cordial Ltd

Graham, Richard Paul
Britvic Soft Drinks Limited

Grainger, Michael
Artio Foods Ltd

Grant, Charlotte Mary Maconarchy
Hedgerow Cordials Limited

Grant, Eleanor
New Earth Ventures Ltd

Grant, Hewitt
The Juice Doctor Limited

Grant, Robin Phillips
The Scotch Water Co Ltd

Grant, Stuart James
The Ice People Limited

Green, Bruce Philip
5 Hour Energy Limited

Green, Steven Keith
Wotar Ltd

Gregory, Damian
Adapt Kombucha Limited

Gresswell, Gavin
Nutrapharm Ltd

Griffiths, Bryan David
Point Blank Cold Brew Ltd

Griffiths, Martin Andrew
A.G. Barr P.L.C.

Griffiths, Terry Baugh
Liquid Ice Water Co Ltd

Grimwood, Andrew Rupert
Channel Island Water Limited

Grove-Stephensen, Berenge Nathalie
Bliiss Ltd

Grover, Clayton Ritchard
Dr.Shot Ltd.

Groves, Thomas James
Faultless Drinks Limited

Gubbanna, Shashidhar Kalenahalli
Havok Energy Drink. Ltd

Guest, Mary Elizabeth
Lucozade Ribena Suntory Exports Ltd
Lucozade Ribena Suntory Ltd

Guglia, Eugen
Lionade Ltd

Gwillim, Rupert William Conroy
Corduroy Ideas Limited

Hahn, Jung-Yeun
Sansu Drinks Ltd

Hainsworth, Stewart Andrew
Willow Water Limited

Hainy, Mark Andrew
Two2Three2Four Ltd

Hajjar, Martina Angelova
Dry Drinks and Teas Co Ltd

Halewood, Judith Margaret
Willow Water Limited

Hall, Felicity Eleanor
Distillers Tonic Limited

Hallsworth, Kay
Explorer Coffees Ltd

Hallsworth, Neil
Explorer Coffees Ltd

Halsted, David Michael
Pembrokeshire Cider Limited

Hamilton, Emma
The Country Garden Drinks Co Ltd

Hamilton, Matthew James
The Country Garden Drinks Co Ltd

Hamilton, Victoria
Alive Beverages Limited

Hannaway, Christopher John
Infinite Session Ltd

Hannaway, Thomas Eamon
Infinite Session Ltd

Harbord, David Christopher
Wow Food and Drinks Ltd

Harbridge, Hami David
The Soda Factory Limited

Harding, Gemma Louise
Natural Juicing Co Ltd

Harding, James Robert
Natural Juicing Co Ltd

Harding, Peter John
Lucozade Ribena Suntory Ltd

Hardman, Lee Craig Peter
Wardle Spring Water Co Ltd

Hardy, Simon Richard Francis
Fonthill Waters Limited

Harkness, Bruce
Maine Soft Drinks Limited

Harkness, Derrick
Maine Soft Drinks Limited

Harkness, James Crawford
Norbev Limited
Spring Cool Soft Drinks Ltd

Harkness, Jonathan
Maine Soft Drinks Limited

Harkness, Priscilla Ann
Maine Soft Drinks Limited

Harkness, Samuel
Maine Soft Drinks Limited

Harnden, Charles Michael
Charlie T's Ltd

Harnden, Karin
Charlie T's Ltd

Harper, Joseph
Just Bee Drinks Limited

Harries, Eurwyn George
Tovali Limited

Harriman-Hardy, George William
V-Storm Energy Ltd

Harrington, Charlotte Sera
Belu Water Limited

Harrison, Bernadette
Bouncing Biotics Ltd

Harrison, Hannah
Cawingredients Limited

Harrison, Lynwen Rachel
Smith & Harrison Ltd

Harrison, Peter Richard
Cawingredients Limited
DRII Limited
Dry Beverages Limited

Harrison, Rachel Lucy
Mylkman Ltd

Harrisson, Alexandra Fiske
Rootfire Ltd

Hartmann, Carl Fane
Zero Proof International Ltd

Hartridge, Charlotte Amelia
Hartridges Limited

Hartridge, Christopher Simon
Hartridges Limited

Hartridge, Edward Thomas
Hartridges Limited

Harvey, Matthew Steven
Squish Squash Limited
Sqwish Squash Limited

Hassan, Ali
Berkeley Springs Limited

Hatch, Allison
Steven Hatch Operations Consultancy Ltd

Hatch, Steven
Steven Hatch Operations Consultancy Ltd

Hatfield, James Vernon
Pitstop Coffee Limited

Hatton, Daniel Paul
London Botanical Drinks Ltd

Havers, Matthew Graham
Kings Farm Foods Limited

Hawkins, Martin John
Hawkins Drinks Limited

Hay, Edward Charles
The Mendip Bottle Limited

Hay, Giles Aaron
IDC Irish Drinks Co. Ltd

Hay, Sarah Jane
The Mendip Bottle Limited

Hayden, Patrick
Saint Patricks Ltd

Haynes, Kerryn Louise
Diageo Great Britain Limited

He, Hua, Dr
Ideas 2 Launch Limited

Heath, Josh Dion Bradley
Enso Goods Limited

Heginbottom, David
Diageo Great Britain Limited

Heilbron, Vincent Soe On
Better Fresh Limited

Heller, Keith Louis
Everything But The Cow Limited

Hemmings, Lee Bruce
Belvoir Fruit Farms Limited

Henry, Keith
Henrysuper Roots Drinks Ltd

Henson, Dawna Diane
Whollywater Ltd

Henton, Rachel Ann
Galactogen Products Limited

Herbert, Simon James
Squish Squash Limited

Herd, Charles Alexander
Edinburgh Tonic Ltd

Heritage, Lynn
Heritage Health Organics Ltd

Heritage, Yvonne
Heritage Health Organics Ltd

Herlihy, Jack Michael
Two Keys Ltd

Hewlett, Victoria
Tea Rocks Ltd

Higgens, Robin Jeremy
Omega EFA Limited

Higson, Bethan
Mother Root Ltd

Hill, Augustus David
Duo Drinks Ltd

Hill, Charles Christopher
Mother Juice Ltd

Hill, Charles Patrick
Mother Juice Ltd

Hill, Ronald Andrew
Cocomojo Group Limited

Hill, Simon
Fossick Limited

Hindle, Helen Victoria
Kendal Cordials Limited

Hinge, Carla
Kingsley Beverage Limited

Hird, Nick James
NR Enterprise Limited

Hirst, Timothy Norman
Fake Brews Ltd

Ho, Elaine Emily
Lupe Kombucha Ltd.

Hobson, Simon Paul
CBD Tonic & Mixers Limited

Hodge, Craig
Amor Food and Beverages Holdings Ltd

Hodges, Graham
The Fizzbang Beverage Co Ltd

Hodgkins, Gareth Liam
Juice Junkies Limited

Hodgson, Garreth
Rejuvenation Water Ltd

Hodgson, Geoffrey Mark
Clearly Drinks Limited

Hodgson, John
Roo Drinks Limited

Hoefer, Helge
Evo Drinks Europe Ltd

Hoey, David Paul
Elite Global Nutrition Limited

Hoey, Luke Dominic
Elite Global Nutrition Limited

Holloway, Rupert
Bowser Limited
Bowser Properties Limited
Bowser Tonic Limited

Holmes, Dean Carl
Mr Holmes Flavored Syrups Ltd

Holt, Andrew David
Cawingredients Limited

Hook, Jessica
Outfox Drinks Ltd

Hooper, Clive Alastair
Britvic Soft Drinks Limited

Hopkinson, Georgina Louise
Pass The Baton Limited

Hoque, Radhwan
Ad Hoque Ltd

Hornby, Caroline Nicole
SIP Kombucha Ltd

Hornby, William Donald
SIP Kombucha Ltd

Horwill, Rhian Alys
Nourish Foods Limited

Hosp, Alexander
Turn Global Ltd

Houghton, Stephen Michael
Northern Citrus Products Ltd

Hounsell, Ronald Mark
Kingshill Mineral Water Ltd.

Howard, Michael Alan
Clearly Drinks Limited
The Powerful Water Co Ltd

Howard, Richard Geoffrey
Kingdon Callea Ltd

Howell, Adrian
Carbon Drinks Limited

Hoyle, Michael
Salicaria Ltd

Hrstic, Nikola
Brainwave Brands Ltd
Sopro Drinks Ltd
Sumo Drinks Ltd

Hucker, Leigh
Hullabaloos Lemonade Limited

Hudson, Paul Thomas
Fuse Drinks Ltd

Hughes, Robert Andrew
Pivotal Drinks Ltd

Hughes, Stephen
Clear Green Water Limited

Hughes-Davies, George
Daily Dose Ltd
Juice Supply Limited

Hulme, Andrew Grahame
Flavour Master Limited

Humann, Philip
Coca-Cola European Partners PLC

Hunt, Alan James
Sugen Frooth Limited

Hunter, Joseph Michael Mead
Alive & Kicking Fermented Foods Ltd

Hussain, Danyal Adam
Distinate Ltd

Hussain, Mazeer
Boostvitaminwater Ltd

Hussain, Shaban
Green Monkey Drinks Ltd

Hutchison, Craig
Celtic Soul Drinks Limited

Idun, Nanaesi
Belle Beverages Ltd

Igboayaka, Solomon
Nozbo Drinks Limited

Iles, Christoper
Cure T.H.A.S.D. Limited

Iliya, Christiana
Mother Nature's Drinks Limited

Imo, Kelechi Kenneth
Big Daddy Beverages Limited

Ingham, Kristopher
Rejuvenation Water Ltd

Ingram II, Orrin Henry
Coca-Cola European Partners PLC

Irish-Tavares, Dianne Nadine
Ryd Food & Drinks Limited

Irving, Charles Graham
Ibis Organics Limited

Irving, William Graham
Ibis Organics Limited

Ismail, Djahit
Goldbucks Limited

Iverson, Barry Bernard
CMB Water Limited

Jabrane, Thomas Aymen, Dr
Livitus Limited

Jacob, Jerome Tagore
Mangogo Ltd

Jacoby, James Daniel
Conscious Drinks Limited

Jacoby, Vanessa Tanis
Conscious Drinks Limited

Jagielko, Henry John
The Natural Fruit and Beverage Co Ltd

Jago, Jolyon Paul
Alcohol Free Drinks Limited

James-Odukoya, Adetola Adebukunla
Nari Palm Juice Beverages Ltd

Jaminska, Marissa
Interactive World Ltd

Jaminski, Bogdan
Interactive World Ltd

Jamison, Antonia Alexandra
Happy Curations Limited

Jarasunas, Simas
ARSJ Holding Ltd

Jarrett, Pearl Ann
Jarrett Health Limited

Jay, Melvin George William
Gunna Drinks Limited

Jedrzejewski, Piotr Jan
Sendivogius Limited

Jeffries, Lee
Jeffries Group Ltd

Jeffries, Lee Thomas John
Bottling International Ltd
This Is Holy Water Limited

Jennings, Andrew Willfred Mark
Benu Distribution Limited

Jenssen, Tobias Mark
Pump House Water Ltd

Jenssen, William Giles
Pump House Water Ltd

Jervis, Stephen
The Elaychi Tea Co Ltd

Jess, Allan
Braveau Limited

Jess, David Campbell
Braveau Limited

Jewkes, Angela
Xtreme Energy Group Limited

Jhooty, Manjit
Green Monkey Drinks Ltd

Jiang, Jiali
Bright Barley Co Ltd

Jiang, Sibil
ABI SAB Group Holding Limited

Johansson, Bjorn Filip Botvid
Eliya Europe Ltd

John, Christopher Tani-Mola Adrian
Tani-Mola Enterprise Ltd

Johnson, Adebowale
413 Limited

Johnson, Elliott
Brown Box Trading Co Ltd
Swallow Drinks South West Ltd

Johnson, Neil
Zombie Energy Limited

Johnson, Neville
Johnson Supplies UK Ltd

Johnson, Redmond Antony Guy
The Original Free Drinks Co Ltd

Johnson, Rhys
Crosby Beverages Ltd

Johnson, Saul
Lucid Beverage Research Ltd

Johnson, Sharon
Chocquers Limited
Choquers Limited
Tea GB International Limited

Johnson, Thomas
Coca-Cola European Partners PLC

Johnstone, Michael Robert
Elsenham Water Limited

Jollivet, Alexander Edward
The Craft Mixers Co Ltd

UK Manufacturers of Soft Drinks dellam

Jones, Andrew
Nelly Tickner Drinks Co. Ltd

Jones, Christopher Blair
The Bloomberry Juice Co Ltd

Jones, David Hugh
Mambo Drinks Limited

Jones, Eliza Miranda Maurice
Chosan Drinks Ltd

Jones, Ian
Permeske Ltd

Jones, Khaleelah Estella-Jean, Dr
Lifeline Holdings Limited

Jones, Lewis
Kombuchaye Ltd

Jones, Malcolm
The Shakespeare Spring Water Co Ltd

Jones, Maxine
The Shakespeare Spring Water Co Ltd

Jones, Rachel Louise
Connect Beverages Ltd

Jones, Sarah Jane
The Bloomberry Juice Co Ltd

Jong, Hessel Douwe De
Britvic EMEA Limited

Joshi, Anuj
Pouchlink Ltd
Green Drink (GB) Ltd

Joshi, Carolynne
Innorbit Ltd

Joshi, Carolynne Yew Kiew
The Wise Herb Co Ltd

Joshi, Dev Ketan Kong
The Food and Drink Development Co Ltd
Innorbit Ltd
The Wise Herb Co Ltd

Joshi, Jay Ketan Kong
The Food and Drink Development Co Ltd
Innorbit Ltd
The Wise Herb Co Ltd

Joshi, Ketan Harshad, Dr
The Food and Drink Development Co Ltd
Happy Curations Limited
The Natural Food and Drink Co Ltd
The Wise Herb Co Ltd

Joshi, Ketan, Dr
Innorbit Ltd

Joshi, Keval
The Earth Plant Co Ltd

Joslin, Nicholas
Naneau Limited

Juozapaityte, Juste
Alitasa Ltd

Kaffo, Olalekan Kamorudeen
Cen Bottling Co Ltd

Kain, Michael Colin
Distillers Tonic Limited

Kang, Ravinder Kaur
Big Time Soft Drinks Limited

Kannan, Munjurpet Narayanan
Hildon Limited

Karakas, Ramazan
Beyaz Kartal Ltd

Karmakar, Bimal, Dr
The Soda Factory Limited

Kato, Archard Lwihula
Alko Vintages UK Ltd

Katona, Jonathan Alexander
Kompassion Ltd

Kaur, Kashmir
Big Time Soft Drinks Limited

Kay, Michael Dennis
Kali Engineering Ltd

Keays, Helen Margaret
Nichols PLC

Keeling, Richard David
Regency Tonic Ltd

Kehinde, Oluyemisi
Yemsmoothies Ltd

Kelly, Eamon Charles
Beechvale Natural Water Ltd

Kelly, Maureen Elizabeth
Beechvale Natural Water Ltd

Kemp, Fiona
Gallybird Tonic Co Ltd

Kemp, Jonathan David
A.G. Barr P.L.C.

Kendrick, James Lee
Rok Natural Energy Limited

Kennedy, Damien
D & G Drinks Ltd

Kenning, David Berkeley Buchanan
Signpost Brewery Ltd

Kenning, Tobias Edward Burney
Signpost Brewery Ltd

Kerby-Steele, Oak
Simple Nature Limited

Kerr, Paul Jonathan
Double Dutch Ltd.

Kessler, Julia
Nix & Kix Ltd

Kewley, Kevin Alexander
Ultra Beauty Limited

Keyhani, Nona
Persian Roze Ltd

Khan, Assad
Poptails Limited

Khan, Essin
Soft N Sweet Ltd

Khan, Mohammed Iqbal
Qibla Cola (Beverages) Ltd

Khan, Muhammad Saad
Biofresh Cosmos Ltd

Khan, Uzma
Ma3 Drinks Ltd

Khan, Zubaida
Immunoguardian Ltd

Khanduja, Pradeep
Fab World Limited

Khera, Karndeep Singh
Suncrest Associates Limited

Khera, Lakhvinder Singh
Suncrest Associates Limited

Khimani, Davendra Parbat
Exotic Beverages Limited

King, Aniko
Kore Kombucha Ltd

King, Geoffrey Nigel John
Kore Kombucha Ltd

King, Helen Olukemi
Dakena-One International Ltd

King, Matthew John
Belu Water Limited

Kingful, Obed Oliver Ofori
Obeliver Drinks Limited

Kingsley-Bates, Paul
Kingsley Partners Limited

Kingsley-Bates, Rebecca Louise
Kingsley Partners Limited

Kinnaird, Michael
Aqua Hebrides Limited

Kinsey Jones, Eric Michael
Whimble Mineral Water & Brewing Co Ltd

Kirby, Nicholas
Storefast Solutions Limited

Kirby, Sharon Claretta Angela
Storefast Solutions Limited

Kitching, Jon-Paul
Alyke Health Limited
Gooddrop Supply Co. Limited

Kitching, Steven
Cott Ventures UK Limited
Decantae Mineral Water Limited
Total Water Solutions Limited

Knaggs, Simon David
Harrogate Spring Water Limited
Thirsty Planet Limited

Knight, Brian
Fonthill Waters Limited

Knowles, Jeffrey Ewart
Pickle Shot Limited

Knowles, Karen Margaret
Bon Accord Soft Drinks Limited

Knox, Christopher Royston
Gran Steads Ginger Limited

Knox, Rosemary Ann
Gran Steads Ginger Limited

Kobuszewski, Przemyslaw
Naturally Buzzin Energy Products Ltd

Konstantinou, Nikolaos
Bertrand Tailor Limited

Kontos, Andros
Drinks-on-Draught Limited

Kostadinchev, Yavor
Bigla Brewing Co Ltd

Krepski, Paul Martin
SLO Good Living Ltd

Kress Von Wendland, Felix-Johannes Peter Otto
Tasty Kameleon Ltd

Kullar, Ravinder
Nature's Fountain Limited

Kwasi-Frimpong, Fernand
Sweet Memoirs Limited

Kyriakopoulos, Athanasios
Three Cents Ltd

Laginaf, Mohsin
B4Sport Ltd.

Laing, Ian
Neu Water Limited

Laithwaite, Jake Christopher
Bless Up Beverages Ltd

Lal, Aneil
The Lemon Factory Ltd

Lander, Oonagh Chloe
The Babywater Co Ltd

Lane, Clare Louise
Hill Holme Juice Ltd

Lane, Nigel Peter
Hill Holme Juice Ltd

Langford, Marian Tracey
Alder Spring Limited

Lansley, Jonathon Mark
The Live Kindly Drinks Co Ltd

Lapham, James
Dayla Limited

Lapham, Peter Brine
Dayla Limited

Larby, Sarah Marie
Water Group Ltd

Larnyoh, Nii Affum
Quad Juices Limited

Lartey, Hermina Korko
Korko Limited

Lasan, Rok
Thirstea Drinks Limited

Laskey, Ben John
Cornish Kombucha Limited

Lasme, Nathanael
GO4 Beverages Limited

Laurie, Guy Steven
Common Goods Group Limited

Law, Christopher James
Mr Fitzpatrick's Limited

Lawal, Ade Teslim
Keizen SDK Ltd

Lawford, Layla Marissa
Spirit of Shanti Ltd

Lawson, Donald Sinclair
Love Tonic Ltd

Lawson, Rory Gordon MacGregor
D & G Drinks Ltd

Leary, James
ECIG Retail Europe Limited

Leek, Abigail
House of Symbols Ltd

Leigh, Gary Simon
Gaia Brands Ltd

Lendak, Boris
Admete Ltd

Lennon, Michael Generald
Nourish Foods Limited

Leonard, Simon Maxwell Saul
Just Bee Drinks Limited

Leoni Sceti, Patrick William Elio
Flower of Life Ltd

LesbIreland, Robert Carl
Ice2u Ltd

Lettice, Claire
Botanical Alchemy Ltd
J B Bowler Ltd

Lettice, Susan Claire
The Botanical Drinks Co Ltd

Levy, Joseph Julian
Jeffries Group Ltd

Levy-Vassie, Ramon Ashley
Ryd Food & Drinks Limited

Levy-Vassie, Yvonne
Ryd Food & Drinks Limited

Lewis, Mark Peter
Blending and Bottling Solutions Ltd

Lewis, Oliver Daniel
Blending and Bottling Solutions Ltd

Lewis, Rhodri Alun
Berrington Pure Spring Water Ltd
Berrington Spring Water Ltd

Lewis, Tracy Jane
Blending and Bottling Solutions Ltd

Leyshon, Sioned Haf
Hendre Distillery Ltd

Liban, Julian
Common Goods Group Limited

Libano Daurella, Alfonso
Coca-Cola European Partners PLC

Ligertwood, Andrew
Drink Better Limited

Ligertwood, Gillian
Drink Better Limited

Lilley, Dashiel Reuben
Beyond Alcohol Ltd

Lillie, Chris
Rock's Organic Limited

Lincoln, Darren
Kendal Brewery Ltd

Lind Van't Hof, Zoe
Wunder Workshop Ltd

Lindsay, Graeme John
Smoother Spirits Limited

Linnebank, Justin Lyndan
Common Goods Group Limited

Lintaru, Alexandru
Lintaru DGL Ltd

Litherland, Peter Simon
Britannia Soft Drinks Limited
British Vitamin Products Ltd
Britvic Asset Company No.1 Ltd
Britvic Asset Company No.2 Ltd
Britvic Asset Company No.3 Ltd
Britvic Asset Company No.4 Ltd
Britvic Beverages Limited
Britvic Corona Limited
Britvic International Investments
Britvic Overseas Limited
Britvic PLC
Britvic Soft Drinks Limited
Greenbank Drinks Co Ltd
Hooper,Struve & Co Ltd
Idris Limited
London Essence Co Ltd
Orchid Drinks Limited
H.D.Rawlings Limited
The Really Wild Drinks Co Ltd
Red Devil Energy Drinks Ltd
Robinsons (Finance) No.2 Ltd
Robinsons Soft Drinks Limited
Southern Table Water Co Ltd
Sunfresh Soft Drinks Limited
R.White & Sons Limited

Littley, Steven Belford
Spring Water (Devon) Limited

Littman, Cedric Marc
Rejuvenation Water Ltd

Liveras, Luke John
Liveras Limited

Livings, Mark Seymour
Zero Proof International Ltd
Zero Proof UK Limited

Lloyd, Louise Claire
Ocean Tears Ltd

Loftsson, Birgir
Acqua Nordica Ltd

Lorimer, Stuart
Robert Barr Limited
A.G. Barr P.L.C.
Mandora St. Clements Limited
Rubicon Drinks Limited
Taut (UK) Limited
Tizer Limited

Losada, Daniel Jessid
B20 Water Ltd

Louw, Mellenefi Van Wyk
Coca-Cola Holdings Africa Ltd

Love, Keith Douglas, Dr
Muirhall Water Limited

Lovell, John James Clifford
Cracker Drinks Co. Limited

Lowe, Anthony James
Equilibrium Food & Drink Ltd

Lowe, Mitchell James
Swing Top Limited

Lowers, Michael
Neue Water Limited

Loxton, Jennifer Louise, Dr
Edible Hedgerow Ltd

Lund, Sophie
Mello Drinks Ltd

Luscombe, Timothy Lawrence
Club Consultants Ltd

Lynch, Karen Jane
Belu Water Limited

Lyons, Ivor Samuel
Jumpin' Juice Limited

Mabelle, Ocan Bob
Youthenergy East Africa Ltd

Mabrouk, Linda Anna
Vivo Water Ltd

MacCaskill, William
Isle of Skye Spring Water Co Ltd

MacDougall, Scott
House of Balmoral Ltd

MacKay, Hugh Kenneth St Clair
MacKay & Partners (UK) Limited

MacKenzie, Martha
Seltza Ltd

MacLeod, Andrew John
Vitamin Brands Ltd.

Macpherson, Brian Richard
Eden Springs UK Limited
Old WCS (Bottlers) Limited
Pure Choice Watercoolers Ltd

Madden, Richard James
Kingshill Mineral Water Ltd.

Maddix, Tamara
Salad Passion Foods Ltd

Maddix, Wayne
Salad Passion Foods Ltd

Maddocks, Bernadette Frances
Hon Limited

Madlala, Sphelo Sphephelo Skhumbuzo
The Oxford Juice Co Ltd

Maduemezia, Toju
Keizen SDK Ltd

Maerker, Max
Evo Drinks Europe Ltd

Magee, Malachy
P Mulrine and Sons Sales (U.K.) Ltd

Magness, Christopher Stanley
Silver Spa Limited

Magraw, Annette Denise
Fruit Diversity Limited

Magraw, James Edmund Grenville
Fruit Diversity Limited

Mahatme, Matthew Devendra
Lixir Ltd

Mahboob, Noreen
MB Drinks Ltd

Mahmud, Abdullah Mustafa
Mayag Brands Ltd

Mair, Harpreet
Proper Good Brands Limited

Majid, Omar
Mount Valley Beverages Ltd

Malcolmson, James
Enhance Drinks Ltd

Mallinson, Angela Marie Christine
James White Drinks Ltd

Mallinson, Lawrence Stuart
James White Drinks Ltd

Maloloy On, Kate
Cybora Ltd

Maloney, Brian
Plenish Cleanse Ltd

Man, James
J Water Disabled Children Ltd

Mani, Leona Bodina
Good Water Trading Ltd

Mann Toyinbo, Deji
Prime Sun Limited

Manners, Richard John Peverel
Belvoir Fruit Farms Drinks Holdings
Belvoir Fruit Farms Limited
Belvoir Natural Drinks Co Ltd

Mansour, Ali
Bolbol Imports Ltd

Marchant, Samuel
Hangin Drinks Limited

Margadale of Islay, Alastair John, Lord
Penning Power & Water Limited

Maris, Dirk Stany Urbain Jozef Ghislain
Konings Juices & Drinks UK Ltd

Markham, Graham
Real Natural UK Ltd

Marks, Scott James
The Intelligent Brews Co Ltd

Marr, Bridget Stickney
Blue Keld Springs Limited

Marr, Charles Roger
Blue Keld Springs Limited

Marr, Philip Edward
Blue Keld Springs Limited

Marsden, Edward
Pivotal Drinks Ltd

Marsh, Hilary Jane
Genius Drinks Limited

Marteau, Rosie
Yuyo Drinks Ltd

Martin, Adam Alexander
Destructive Lines Ltd

Martin, Christopher Berriman
Mildenhall Bottling Co Ltd

Martin, Paul
Kingshill Mineral Water Ltd.

Martin, Rebecca
Mag Marketing Limited

Martin, William
Seed Lab Ltd.

Martingell, Sam Edmund
Kombucha Kat Ltd

Mason, Niall Aadya
Alkali Water Limited

Mathew, Paul
London Botanical Drinks Ltd

Matthews, Kevin John
Fillongley Spring Water Ltd
Fillongley Ventures Limited

Matthews, Paul Anthony
Sacred Springs Water Co Ltd

Matthews, Phillip James
Sacred Springs Water Co Ltd

Mattu, Sukhveer Singh
Drinkology Limited

Mawson, Joseph William
Mawsons Traditional Drinks Ltd

Mayes, Peter John
Zuddha Water Limited

Mazibuko, Mpumelelo
Coca-Cola Holdings Africa Ltd

McAdam, Andrew Michael
Montgomery Waters Limited

McAteer, James Stephen
Shindig Promotions Ltd

McAteer, Shan
Shindig Promotions Ltd

McCall, Hamish Spencer Murray
Better Fresh Limited

McCall, Jonathan
Ginsecco Ltd

McCann, Rachel Katherine
Norbev Limited

McCanta, Joseph Michael
Coast Drinks Ltd

McCarthy, Robert Barry
Be Gemwater Limited

McClounie, Ruth
Ayrshire Springs Limited

McClounie, William
Ayrshire Springs Limited

McClounie, William Lindsay
Ayrshire Springs Limited

McCool, Richard Christopher
Seasons Soft Drinks Limited

McCreadie-Blake, Leeanne
Rigdeplot Ltd

McCullagh, Feithlinn
Mourne Mist Bottled Water Co Ltd

McCullagh, Kevin Christopher
Mourne Mist Bottled Water Co Ltd

McDaniel, David Steven
Nestle Waters GB Limited

McDonald, Neil Alexander Shand
Hydrade Drinks Limited

McDougall, James
K K Draught Drinks Limited

McElherron, Ronan
Ardmore Spring Water Limited

McFarlane, John Dumeresq
Norfolk Cordial Ltd

McFayden, Luke
Paradise Drinks Co. Limited

McGannan, Benjamin Raymond Stanley
Hawk Spring Water (S.E.) Ltd

McGeown, Amanda
Healthy Juice Co (NI) Ltd

McGhee, Mary Rose
Hartpury Heritage Trust

McGovern, Daniel Alexander Albert
Man Up Energy Limited

McGurk, Eunan
Mourne Mist Bottled Water Co Ltd

McHoul, Ian Philip
Britvic PLC

McKay, Trowbridge George
Paradise Drinks Co. Limited

McKeever, Toby Peter
Lucozade Ribena Suntory Ltd

McKenna, Margherita
Belfast Bottle Co Ltd

McKenna, Nicholas
Belfast Bottle Co Ltd

McKenzie, Evol
Mighty Flames Ltd

McKinlay, Charles Thomson
Edinburgh Artesian Water Co Ltd

McLean, Cary
Ballantyne McLean Limited

McLean, Claire
Molly Rose Drinks Ltd

McSharry, Fiona
Eauvolution Limited

McTaggart, Donald Emmanuel
Ardross Castle Water Co Ltd

Meacock, Peter
The Naivasha Tonic Co Ltd

Mead, James Darrin
JDM Enterprises Ltd

Mee, Lydia
Ballmax Beverage Co Limited

Meester, Jay Douglas
Creamright Products, Ltd

Meghzifene, Mehdi
Aqua Arbore Ltd.

Memmott, Andrew Lewis
A.G. Barr P.L.C.

Mendoza, Marc
This Is Holy Water Limited

Mensah, Denzel
Vine Springs Ltd

Mensah, Edwin Kwaku Broni, Dr
Give Me Tap Limited

Mercer, Charlotte Tatiana Mary
Beyond Alcohol Ltd

Merlin, Yissochor Dov
Sips MCR Ltd

Mernier, Charlotte Veronique
My Little Potion Ltd

Metcalfe, Polly Anna
Blue Keld Springs Limited

Meurisse, Sarah Eleanor Nicole
Rebel Drinks Accra Limited

Meyer, Adrien
Limonada Mathe Limited

Meyrick, Candida
Positive Potions Limited

Miah, Habib
Nutricana Ltd

Michaels, Simon Phillip
Lady Eden Ltd
Lord Eden Beverages Ltd
Lord Eden Ltd

Millard, Marnie Jane
Nichols PLC

Millichip, Graham Stanley
Birmingham Soft Drinks Association Ltd

Millin, Melanie Victoria
MCSS Investments Ltd

Mills, Heather Anne
Mylkman Ltd

Milne, Andrew Paul
Nichols PLC

UK Manufacturers of Soft Drinks dellam

Minton, Ian Michael
Halo Drinks Co Ltd
Liverpool Canning Co Ltd
Ocean Tears Ltd

Mire, Antimo Farid
Areea Limited

Mitchell, James
Phutures Limited

Mitchell, Jason
Ashridge Cider Limited

Mitchell, Rachael Jane
Clearly Devon Limited
Methuselah 969 Limited
Moorland Mist Limited

Mitchell, Simon James
Floreana Ltd

Mitchell, Tom
Point Blank Cold Brew Ltd

Mitchison, Matthew
Pressure Coolers Limited

Moan, Eunice Gloria
Sperrin Springs Limited

Moan, Raymond
Sperrin Springs Limited

Moed, Roy Uziel
H20miles Ltd

Mohajerani, Hoda
Chakra Chai Limited

Mohammed, Aleem, Doctor
SMJ Beverages Limited

Monson, Catriona
Middle Way Ltd.

Monson, Gavin David
Middle Way Ltd.

Montgomery, Leslie
Gleneagles Spring Water Co Ltd.
Highland Spring Limited
Hope Sixteen (No.87) Limited
Lothian Shelf (674) Limited
Speyside Glenlivet (HSL) Co Ltd

Montgomery-Smith, Luke James
This Is Holy Water Limited

Moor, John
Moor Organics Limited

Moor, Nicholas
Moor Organics Limited

Moore, Barrie Haley
Peter Spanton Drinks Ltd

Moore, Lorraine
Moores of Warwick Limited

Moore, Martin Keith
Moores of Warwick Limited

Moore, Ryan
Unique Drinks Limited

Moore, Sarah Elizabeth
Woodford & Warner Limited

Moors, Anne Marina
Konings Juices & Drinks UK Ltd

Morgan, Declan Daniel
Counterpoint Wholesale (NI) Ltd

Morgan, Frederick Lindsay
International Soft Drinks Ltd

Morley, Shaun
Mr Fitzpatrick's Limited

Morphet, Charles David
Alder Spring Limited

Morphet, Stanley
Alder Spring Limited

Morren, Gary Ronald
Love Tonic Ltd

Morris, Jordan Lewis Ayrton
Bless Up Beverages Ltd

Morrison, Christopher John
Karma Cola UK Ltd

Morrison, Matthew John
Karma Cola UK Ltd

Mortimer, Edmund
Enterprises Beyond Reason Ltd

Morton, Janet
Danjan Ventures Ltd

Moseley, Philip George Naom, Dr
Surrey Food and Drink Innovation Ltd

Moulding, Jamie
Grace Under Pressure Ltd

Moulding, Jessica Mary
Grace Under Pressure Ltd

Muambamakasa, Devillers
Marah Drinks Limited

Mugridge, David Edward
Yarty Cordials Limited

Mugridge, Jayne
Yarty Cordials Limited

Muhammad, Horace
Power Juice Limited

Mulrine, Peter
P Mulrine and Sons Sales (U.K.) Ltd

Mundlay, Chandrashekhar Arvind
Suntory Beverage & Food South Africa Ltd

Murphy, John Martin
Fillongley Spring Water Ltd

Murray, Andrew
K K Draught Drinks Limited

Murray, Andy
ME Letric Ltd

Mussons Freixas, Jaime Antonio
Lucozade Ribena Suntory Ltd
Schweppes International Ltd

Mustacioara, Ionut Alexandru
Alexionut Ltd

Nadur, Sophia
Ideas 2 Launch Limited

Nagar, Rashik
Pomepure Ltd

Nanthakumar, Thurairajasingam
Emery Brand Ltd

Natanzi, Shahab, Dr
Mello Drinks Ltd

Nath, Aditi
Raviom Limited

Nath, Bhaskar
Raviom Limited

Nath, Vishwa
Raviom Limited

Ndunda, Joel
Adapt Kombucha Limited

Neill, Kelly Victoria
Panacea Drinks Ltd

Neufelt, Panayiotis
Artathlon Beverages Limited
Artathlon Water Limited

Newby, Mark Robert
Package Water Solutions Ltd

Newman, Anthony
APE2O Limited

Newton, Maurice
Bottling International Ltd

Ngesa, Joab James
Youthenergy East Africa Ltd

Nguyen, Vian Nga
Drinks for Beauty Ltd

Nichols, Peter John
Nichols PLC

Nicholson, Alan William
Falcon Soft Drinks Limited

Nicholson, Victoria Rosina Kathleen
Falcon Soft Drinks Limited

Nicoll, Rodryke
Chastity Limited

Nicolson, John Ross
A.G. Barr P.L.C.

Nightingale, Wendle
Mother Kombucha Ltd

Nijran, Perjeet
The Lemon Factory Ltd

Njai, Isatou
Hippo & Hedgehog Ltd

Norfolk, Selina Jane
Sobare Limited

Norris, Alyn
The Happy Gut Hut Limited

Nottay, Jaskarn
Healthy Hemp Products Ltd

Nulens, Luc Leon Alfons
Konings Juices & Drinks UK Ltd

Nunes, Angela
Innovate Energy Drinks Ltd

Nurnberg, Alexander Frederick
Ugly Brands Limited

Nutt, David
Alcarelle Holdings Limited
Alcarelle Limited

O'Brien, Duncan Anthony Daniel Benedict
Dalston's Soda Co Ltd

O'Connor, Kieran Anthony
Northumbrian Ice Cream Co Ltd
Polar Krush Limited

O'Connor, Patrick Michael
PJ Kombucha Limited

O'Flaherty, Patrick John
Booost Trading Limited

O'Neill, Karen Margaret
Booost Trading Limited

O'Reilly, Kelly
Juice Fabulous Ltd

O'Shea, Brian
Paisley Drinks Co. Ltd

Oag, John Philip
Loch Ness Drinks Ltd
Loch Ness Limited
Loch Ness Tonic Ltd
Loch Ness Tonic Water Ltd
Loch Ness Water Ltd
Ness Scotland Ltd

Oakes, Nicholas
Vero Drinks Ltd

Obateru, Kayode Akinsola
Jellani Ltd

Oenga, Elkanah Ondieki
Alko Vintages UK Ltd

Ogunrinde, Raphael Adesina
Calyx Drinks Ltd

Okpapi, John Ikhaobomhe
Endurance Juice Co Ltd

Okpapi, Michael Osizimhete
Endurance Juice Co Ltd

Olali, Odi
Crosby Beverages Ltd

Olaoye, Oyedele Abidemi
Livitus Limited

Olesker, Michael Peter
SK Global Brands Ltd

Olufemi-Dada, Olufunmilayo
Elementhree Ltd

Olusi, Olumolawa Oludotun
Afrimalt International Limited
Miss Cola UK Limited
Nairamalt UK Limited

Omar, Shekha Ahmed
Clearwater Drink Limited

Omotosho, Bamidele, Dr
Jellani Ltd

Opie, Keith
Zombie Energy Limited

Ormay, Laszlo
Syrup Junkie Limited

Orr, Gem
Istok Foods Limited

Orren, David
Alcarelle Holdings Limited
Alcarelle Limited

Osammor, Marie Terez Laraba
Cen Bottling Co Ltd

Osborne, Charles David
Regency Tonic Ltd

Oughton, Neil Graham
Dr Go Ltd

Owen, Annette
NGN Distribution Limited

Owen, David Gary
NGN Distribution Limited

Oyewole, Francis
Darj Limited
Tassology Limited
Teabase Ltd

Ozsumer, Taner
The Refreshing Drinks Co Ltd

Pabial, Ravinder Paul
Green Leaf Liquids Limited

Page, Adrian Peter
Phoenix Water Coolers Limited

Palanyandi, Steve
Your Mind Body Soul Limited

Palmer, Daren Robert
The CBD Revolution Ltd

Palmer, Jordan John
Lixir Ltd

Palmer, Louise Jayne
Jeffrey's Tonic Ltd

Palmer, Philip Edward
Kixse Limited

Pampanga, Charise
Cantaker Ltd

Papadimitrakopoulos, Christos
Biofresh Cosmos Ltd

Parente, Fabrizio
Innovative Drinks Ltd

Parillon, Connie Petronella
Exoteeque Limited

Parish, Ian
Seasons Soft Drinks Limited

Parker, Richard Anthony
Jeffries Group Ltd

Parkins, Paul Andrew
Belvoir Fruit Farms Limited

Parrot, Gabrielle
Birken Tree (Scotland) Limited

Parsons, Thomas David
Icetails Ltd

Partridge, Naomi Joy
Holos London Ltd

Partridge, Thomas Michael
Holos London Ltd

Passmore, Ceri Elizabeth
Peter Spanton Drinks Ltd

Patel, Hershil
Dips Dips Ltd

Patel, Hina
Diageo Great Britain Limited

Patel, Rahul
Distinate Ltd

Patel, Salim Majid
Strada Soft Drinks Ltd

Paterson, Rory
70s Booch Ltd

Pathak, Heman
Hello Coco Limited

Pattni, Davin
Aqua Burst Ltd

Pearce, David Charles
The Fizzbang Beverage Co Ltd
Fizzbang Ltd

Pearce, Sarah Jane
Fizzbang Ltd

Pearson, Norman Mark
Strawhill Estate Spirits Co Ltd

Peerless, Andrew Graham
Inginius Limited

Pepper, Amber
115 Design Limited

Pepper, Matthew
115 Design Limited

Pereira, Dino M C
Roar Loud Limited

Perkey, Shane
Eden Springs UK Limited

Pescatori, Antonio
Originalsip Ltd

Peters, Laura
Slush Puppie Limited

Peters, Laura Rebecca
Eskimo Joe's Limited

Peters, Mark Jeffrey
Frozen Brothers Limited
Slush Puppie Limited

Petty, Jack
Yee Energy Ltd

Peykoff II, Andrew
Shepley Spring Limited

Phillips, Owen Charles
Scheckter's Organic Beverages Ltd

Phillips, Paul John
Falcon Soft Drinks Limited

Phillips, Richard Jonathan
Temperance Drinks Limited

Phillips, Ronan
D & G Drinks Ltd

Pickering, Robert James
Harrogate Spring Water Limited
Oakdale Spring Limited
Thirsty Planet Limited

Pike, Angela Cecilia
J.H.P Foods Limited

Pike, John Henry
J.H.P Foods Limited

Pillai, Vandana
Bounce Back Drinks Limited

Pindar, Richard James
Rosemary Water Limited

Pintaldi, Jacopo
Limonada Mathe Limited

Plimmer, Aine Mary
A & S Specialist Supplies Ltd.

Polack, Richard Kirk
Be Gemwater Limited
Malvern Bottling Works Limited

Pollentine, Richard
Sober Drinks Limited

Pond, Gemma Iris
Super Nuva Ltd

Pool, Mark
Roots Soda Limited

Poole, Marilyn
Spring Water (Devon) Limited

Popov, Igor
Global Functional Drinks UK Ltd

Portelli, Neville John
Happy Curations Limited

Porter, Akil
Portable Marketing Solutions Ltd

Powell, Pamela
A.G. Barr P.L.C.

Powney, Andrew
Yo! Cola Ltd

Prakash, Shine
Oxidize Limited

Prasad, Umesh
Vitosha Wine Ltd

Preston, Noah
Agua Fresca Ltd.

Price, Melissa
Tiny Mighty People Ltd

Prince, Kate Rebecca
Made By Brave Limited
Made By Noble Limited

Prince, Simon Charles
Made By Noble Limited

Pritchard, Dawn
Beau Drinks Ltd

Pritchard, Joanne Claire
Imprint Marketing Ltd

Pritchett, Gregory
Fillongley Spring Water Ltd
Fillongley Ventures Limited

Prosch, Marcus
South West Juice Co. Ltd

Puckrin, Nicholas Edward
Aqua Arbore Ltd.

Puddle, Joshua
Momo Kombucha Ltd

Puno, Laila
Awlgold Ltd

Qasim, Intisar
Evoca Enterprises Limited

Quaddus, Azr Abdul
Qiblah Beverages Limited
Qiblah Products Limited
Yorkshire Soft Drinks Ltd

Quintanilla Del Mar, Jonathan
Amaize Drinks Limited

Qureshi, Maya
Rhythm Nutrition Ltd

Qureshi, Yasir
Rhythm Nutrition Ltd

Rabani, Idrees
Macro Munch Ltd

Radcliffe, Roxanne
Kings Farm Foods Limited

Rafferty, Caoimhin Michael
Functional Beverages Ltd

Rajani, Kassam Barkatali
Wild Cat Energy Drink Ltd

Ralston Jordan, Gillian
Azerbaijan Juices Limited

Ramirez, Hernando
Luxbev Limited

Rana, Mehul
Sai Water UK Limited

Rana, Omer Ahmed
HD Water Limited

Raskino, Luke Dominic
Delicious Retail Ltd

Rasul, Sohail Anwar
Cracker Drinks Co. Limited

Ratkevicius, Andrius
ARSJ Holding Ltd

Ratzlaff, Kenneth
Shepley Spring Limited

Rauter, Horst Werner
The Divine Water Co Ltd

Rauter, James Werner
The Divine Water Co Ltd

Rauter, Sylvia Christine
The Divine Water Co Ltd

Ray, Bradley
Yee Energy Ltd

Read, William Edward
Genie Drinks Ltd

Reames, Georgina Sarah Emily
Press London Ltd

Reed, Simon
New Forest Spring Water Distribution Ltd
New Forest Spring Water Ltd

Reeve, Jaqueline
Marley and Barley Ltd

Reeve, Stephen Charles
Marley and Barley Ltd

Rehal, Shubnit Singh
Wild Cat Energy Drink Ltd

Rehman, Raza
Skwishee Ltd

Reid, Michael
Northumbrian Ice Cream Co Ltd
Polar Krush Limited

Reidy, Gerard Anthony
Green Room Brands Limited

Rendell, Benjamin Phillip
Berrington Pure Spring Water Ltd
Berrington Spring Water Ltd

Renier, Christine
Super Nuva Ltd

Reynolds, Alexander
The Natural Fruit and Beverage Co Ltd

Riaz, Mohammed Ahmed
Marbella Cartel Ltd

Richards, David Lloyd
Tapwater Corporation Limited

Richardson, Benjamin
Berrington Spring Water Ltd

Richmond, Arthur
Bottle Green Drinks Co Ltd

Richmond, Arthur William
Beverage Brands (U.K.) Limited
Bottlegreen Holdings Limited
Caledonian Bottlers PLC
Merrydown PLC
Rock's Organic Limited
Super Nuva Ltd
Woodchester Enterprises Ltd

Rigg, Edward
Ed's Trading Limited

Ritchie, David James
A.G. Barr P.L.C.

Robert, Carol
Lucozade Ribena Suntory Exports Ltd
Lucozade Ribena Suntory Ltd

Roberts, Charles David Hardy
Buxton Mineral Water Limited
Nestle Waters (UK) Holdings Ltd
Nestle Waters GB Limited
Nestle Waters UK Limited
Princes Gate Spring Water Ltd
Princes Gate Water Limited

Roberts, Glenn
The Sensible Drinks Co Ltd

Roberts, Jonathan Mark
Schweppes International Ltd

Roberts, Nicola
Theodore Global Limited

Roberts, Sarah Elisabeth
Ffynnon Wen Springs Limited

Robertson, James Paterson
March Foods Limited

Robinette, Giles Andrew David
Wolfe's Drinks Limited

Robinson, Alan William
Willow Water Limited

Robinson, Benjamin Edward
Jeffrey's Tonic Ltd

Robinson, Garry
Ikoyi Chapmans Limited

Robinson, Garry Mark
Chapmans Drinks Limited

Robinson, Kerstin
Nix & Kix Ltd

Robinson, Maureen Stella
Jeffrey's Tonic Ltd

Robinson, Michael Edward
Jeffrey's Tonic Ltd

Robinson, Michael John
Ikoyi Chapmans Limited

Robinson, Natasha Jane
Wisdom Superfoods CIC

Robinson, Nicholas
H2can Ltd

Robson, Eldon Arthur
Fentimans Ltd.

Robson, Peter
The Drinks Group Holdings Ltd

Roche, Scott Edward
Coca-Cola International Sales Ltd
Waters & Robson Holdings Ltd

Rodwell, Georgina Amy
Norfolk Cordial Ltd

Roelofs, Hans
Refresco Drinks UK Limited

Roelofs, Johannes Henricus Wilhelmus
Refresco Beverages UK Limited

Rogers, Jacob Alexander
Flower of Life Ltd

Rogers-Coltman, Julian Guy
Radnor Hills Mineral Water Co Ltd

Rolls, Charles Timothy
Fevertree Limited

Romaine, Samuel Paul
Lixir Ltd

Romans, Seth
Llanllyr Water Co Ltd

Ronjom, Anond Jarand
Norwegian Glacier Water Ltd

Rosen, Kara
Plenish Cleanse Ltd

Rosenheim, Samuel
Nude & Rude Ltd

Rothstein, Margaret Linn
Merrily Mulled Ltd

Rotllant Sola, Mario
Coca-Cola European Partners PLC

Routley, Damian Guy
Good Remedy Limited

Rowntree, Rachel Mary
Koala Karma UK Limited

Royal, Anne-Marie
Hafod Water Limited

Royal, Christopher Howard
Hafod Water Limited

Royal, David Howard
Hafod Water Limited

Rozenson, Rafael
The Healthy Protein Co Ltd.

Rubin, Mindel Deborah
Burst Drink Limited

Rucker, Simon Charles Hamilton
Timeless Drinks Ventures Ltd

Ruffman, Callum
Brewski Coffee Ltd

Rule, Mark Louis James
Sea Buck Limited

Rushton, David John
Pointeer Ltd

Russell, Elizabeth Ann
Dr.Shot Ltd.

Rutten, Ruben Christiaan Stephaan
Coca-Cola International Sales Ltd
Waters & Robson Holdings Ltd

Ryan, Jonathan Ashley
Pembrokeshire Cider Limited

Ryan-Knight, Danielle Samantha May
Ryan-Knight Enterprises Ltd

Sabir, Hader Ali
Poo Tang Crisps Limited

Sacks, Rodney Cyril
Monster Energy Europe Limited

Sadauskas, Antanas
Neptune SA Ltd

Saddiq, Anjam
Exotica Beverages Ltd

Safhill, Colette
Goat Drinks Ltd

Sager, Michael
Paradise Drinks Co. Limited

Sagoo, Ranjeet Singh
Gurkhatise Limited

Saint, David John
Calypso Soft Drinks Limited
Mr Freeze (Europe) Limited
Refresco (Nelson) Limited
Refresco Beverages UK Limited
Refresco Developments Limited
Refresco Drinks UK Limited

Salaja, Joy Temitayo
N'ife Limited

Salem, Sophia
Fizzy Bugz Limited

Salloway, Helen Claire
Derbyshire Mineral Waters Ltd

Salloway, Stephen Michael
Derbyshire Mineral Waters Ltd

Salmons, Roy
Pharmaco Group Limited

Salters, Karen
Bottle Green Drinks Co Ltd
Bottlegreen Holdings Limited
Woodchester Enterprises Ltd

Sanchez Real, Jose Ignacio Comenge
Coca-Cola European Partners PLC

Sanderon, Rali
Shepley Spring Limited

Sandhu, Ravinder Singh
Drinks Cubed Ltd

Sandler, Nicholas Roy
Merrily Mulled Ltd

Sanford, Troy Peter
Bless Up Beverages Ltd

Sanghera, Boota
Healthy Well Being Products Ltd

Sangmanee, Kittichat
Mariage Freres Royaume Uni Ltd

Sanno, Takayuki
Lucozade Ribena Suntory Ltd

Sansom, David John
Lowe Bros. (Cardiff) Limited

Satayaprakorb, Arnon
Alpha Energy Drink Limited

Saurin, Amanda Jane
Wildeve Ltd

Sawyers, Michael
Koolvibes Limited

Sawyers, Romaine
SRP Equipe Limited

Scarborough, Ian
Humble Bumble Ltd

Schlosberg, Hilton
Monster Energy Europe Limited

Schnieders, Jennegien Willemina
Schweppes International Ltd

Schubert-Nicolas, Nicole
Ferment Revolution Limited

Scobey, Freddie
Genii Energy Ltd.

Scoley, Helen Rose-Marie
Westmoor Botanicals Limited

Scoley, Philip George
Westmoor Botanicals Limited

Scott, Jack Harry
Dash Brands Ltd

Screw You, Jeb
Boss of Bosses Global Limited

Screw You, Jebaraj
Cocaine Limited
London Fashion Industry Ltd

Sebastiampillai, Raviraja
Ocentek Ltd

Seddon, Karl Bradley
Fyba Ltd.

Sedman, Victoria Louise, Dr
Edible Hedgerow Ltd

Seguin, Matthieu Antoine Jean
Coca-Cola HBC Northern Ireland Ltd

Sehmi, Jatinder Singh
Magic Potion Energy Drinks International

Sell, Jan-Oliver
Bibax Limited

Senger, Frederik
Little Miracles (International) Ltd

Senior, Bob
The Diesel Brewing Co Ltd.

Settle, Paul
Nutrapharm Ltd

Sexton, Thomas
Hangin Drinks Limited

Shaw, Richard James
Buxton Mineral Water Limited
Nestle Waters (UK) Holdings Ltd
Nestle Waters GB Limited
Nestle Waters UK Limited
Princes Gate Spring Water Ltd
Princes Gate Water Limited

Shelden, Craig William
Lucozade Ribena Suntory Ltd

Sheldrake, Bobby Mark
Zuddha Water Limited

Sherick, Andrew Jonathan
Luxuryshakes Ltd

Shiels, Philomena Catherine
HH Frankly Irresistible Ltd

Shiner, Martyn James
Ruudz Limited

Shirley, Neil
Monster Energy Europe Limited

Shoniregun, Maria
Zowell Ltd

Showering, Jonathan
Showerings Cider Mill Ltd

Showering, Matthew Herbert
Showerings Cider Mill Ltd

Shparkovich, Pavel
Amazing Forest Limited

Sibia, Arshpreet Singh
Milkshake and Co London Ltd

Sidorenco, Natalia
Tulchan Spring Water Limited

Silvester, Sharron
Phoenix School Drinks Ltd

Simms, Robyn
Square Root London Limited

Simpson Brown, Wendy Dorothea
Core Fruit Products Limited

Simpson, Adrian
Simpson's Beverage Supply Co Ltd

Simpson, Caleb
Simpson's Beverage Supply Co Ltd

Simpson, Generald Whitworth
Simpson's Beverage Supply Co Ltd

Simpson, George Alexander
The Deeside Water Company (Holdings)
The Deeside Water Co Ltd

Simpson, James
Simpson's Beverage Supply Co Ltd

Simpson, James Thomas
Two Keys Ltd

Simpson, Jason
Simpson's Beverage Supply Co Ltd

Simpson, Javan
JSJuices Ltd

Simpson, Martin John
The Deeside Water Company (Holdings)
The Deeside Water Co Ltd

Simpson, Pete Freerunner
Ginsense Ltd

Simpson, Terence William
Juice Fabulous Ltd

Sitwell, Kamila Laura
Dexos Drinks Limited
Kolibri Drinks Limited

Sitwell, Vincent Lucien
Dexos Drinks Limited
Kolibri Drinks Limited

Skaanild, Nicolai Henrik
Green Room Brands Limited

Skelton, Kenneth
Phoenix Water Coolers Limited

Sklut, Avi David
Hildon Limited

Skurray, Dianne
Aqua Esse Limited

Slater, John Melvyn, Dr
One Co. of Harrogate Ltd

Slater, Johnathan Eaton Charles
One Co. of Harrogate Ltd

Slater, Norman Anthony, Dr
One Co. of Harrogate Ltd

Slijkhuis, Nathanael Sinue
Sleek Still Scottish Water Ltd

Sloan, Joseph
Beverage Brands (U.K.) Limited
Merrydown PLC

Smadja, Serge Noel
C02 Drinks Ltd

Smale, Thomas
Wunder Workshop Ltd

Smaller, Daniel
Rejuvenation Water Ltd

Smart, Russell Alexander
Rock's Organic Limited

Smith, Adam, Hon
Microbiome Technologies Ltd

Smith, Andrew Joseph
Northern Citrus Products Ltd

Smith, Charles Alistair
Shepley Spring Limited

Smith, Claire Elizabeth
Watkins Drinks Limited

Smith, Daniel James
Thirsty Beasts Drinks Ltd

Smith, David Jervis
Goodness Brands Ltd

Smith, David William
The National Forest Spring Water Co Ltd

Smith, Dawn Elizabeth
Wardle Spring Water Co Ltd

Smith, James Maxwell
Shepley Spring Limited

Smith, John Selwyn
Shepley Spring Limited

Smith, Laura Jane
Steep Soft Drinks Co Ltd

Smith, Lucy Madeleine
Funk Beverages Ltd

Smith, Nicholas Mark
Green Monkey Drinks Ltd

Smith, Rachel Suzanne
Smith & Harrison Ltd

Smith, Samuel Isaac
The National Forest Spring Water Co Ltd

Smith, Stephen Andrew
Britvic EMEA Limited

Smyth, Michael Patrick
Ipro Sport Exports Limited

Soanes, Paul Henry
Outfox Drinks Ltd

Soden, Thomas Edward
Destructive Lines Ltd

Sodha, Vishal
DRGN Global Ltd.

Sofer, Richard
Waterful Ltd

Sokol, Peter Alexander
Aquadog Mineral Water Ltd

Sollom, Julian Wilfrid
Story Drinks Limited

Sooch, Pardeep Singh
Endo Sport Ltd

Sosin, Igor
Freedrinks Limited

Sowemimo, Georgina
Kapyani Limited

Spanton, Peter Charles
Peter Spanton Drinks Ltd

Spayne, Daniel Shevek
Flower of Life Ltd

Spence, Michelle Jayne
Citrosoft Drinks Limited

Spencer-Percival, David
Rosemary Water Limited

Spooner, George Hugh Rynn Arthur
Kuka Coffee Ltd

Spooner, Ian
Decantae Mineral Water Limited

Spreadbury, James
Luscombe Drinks Limited

St. John Webster, Alexander
Genie Drinks Ltd

Stapleton, Edward
Shandy Shack Ltd

Stapleton, John Bernard
Nix & Kix Ltd

Steele, Natasha
The Urban Cordial Co Ltd

Steele-Mortimer, Mark Robin
Ruudz Limited

Steenhuisen, Justin Lee
Refreshing Intercepted Limited

Sterling, Claudine
Mighty Flames Ltd

Stern, William Job
Peter Spanton Drinks Ltd

Stevens, Barry John
Birmingham Soft Drinks Association Ltd
Horizon (Contract Drinks) Ltd

Stevens, David Barry
Horizon (Contract Drinks) Ltd

Stevens, Thomas Peter, Dr
Shandy Shack Ltd

Stevenson, Damian Jon
Clearly Drinks Limited
The Powerful Water Co Ltd

Steward, David John
Lurvills Delight Limited

Stewart, Margaret Ann
Coca-Cola International Sales Ltd
Waters & Robson Holdings Ltd

Stewart, Robert
Titonic Ltd

Still, George
Thames Vintage Ltd

Stockil, Adrian Christopher
Squish Squash Limited

Stokes, Nathan Christopher
Your Water Ltd

Stone, Claire Ellen
Vitamin Brands Ltd.

Stow, Sarah
Portavadie Distillery Limited

Strachan, Craig Robert
The Craft Soft Drinks Community Ltd
Foal Limited
The Start-Up Drinks Lab Ltd

Strong, Chris Adam
Skep Drinks Limited

Stukan, Natalia
Fuse Drinks Ltd

Stylianou, Kyriacos
CBDMEhealthy Limited

Suen, Kin-Man
Nix & Kix Ltd

Sugden, Andrew
Just Bee Drinks Limited

Sulaiman, Aslam
New Earth Ventures Ltd

Sullivan, James Paul
Eastcott Drinks Ltd

Summers, Christian John Cameron
Clayton's Cold Brewed Coffee Ltd

Sun, Hao
Hell Energy Ltd

Sura, Gurkirpal Singh
Ffynnon Carreg Limited

Sura, Kulveerpal Singh
Ffynnon Carreg Limited

Sutherland, Euan Angus
Britvic PLC

Swailes, Fiona Jayne
Bussl Limited

Swales, John Mark
Wow Food and Drinks Ltd

Sweeney, Michael Thomas
Captains Original Ltd

Swete, Edward
Liquid Fusion Limited
Sipsup Limited

Symons, Charles Henry
Sea Buck Limited

Symons, Timothy John
Sea Buck Limited

Szucs-Farkas, Zoltan
Timeless Drinks Ventures Ltd

Talabi, Michael
Marah Drinks Limited

Tanaka, Tetsu
Lucozade Ribena Suntory Ltd
Schweppes International Ltd

Tanzer, Felix
JF Rabbit Ltd

Taplin, James Richard Dominic
The Do Drink Co Ltd

Tasci, Mert Ali
Tasteuk Limited

Tatar, Zihni Erhan Rustem
Smoother Spirits Limited

Tayburn, Lee Andrew
Willow Water Limited

Taylor, Edward
Square Root London Limited

Taylor, James Andrew
Gut Drinks Ltd

Taylor, John William
21st Century Coke Co Ltd

Taylor, Joshua Delano
Kubera Group International Ltd

Taylor, Steven James
21st Century Coke Co Ltd

Taylor, Stuart John
Mawsons Traditional Drinks Ltd

Taylor, Susan Heather
Mawsons Traditional Drinks Ltd

Tencor, Katarina Eva Birgitta
Saft Drinks Ltd

Tenorio, Darwin
Crystalstore Ltd

Theakston, Nicholas Robert
Cracker Drinks Co. Limited

Theodore, Bethany
Theodore Global Limited

Theodore, Janet Ann
Theodore Global Limited

Thethy, Govind
Ice Factory Limited

Thirlwell-Pearce, Oliver James
Vitte Nutrition Ltd

Thirlwell-Pearce, Phoebe
Vitte Nutrition Ltd

Thomas, Alexandra Clare
Britannia Soft Drinks Limited
British Vitamin Products Ltd
Britvic Asset Company No.1 Ltd
Britvic Asset Company No.2 Ltd
Britvic Asset Company No.3 Ltd
Britvic Asset Company No.4 Ltd
Britvic Beverages Limited
Britvic Corona Limited
Britvic International Investments
Britvic International Support Services
Britvic Overseas Limited
Greenbank Drinks Co Ltd
Hooper,Struve & Co Ltd
Idris Limited
London Essence Co Ltd
Orchid Drinks Limited
H.D.Rawlings Limited
The Really Wild Drinks Co Ltd
Red Devil Energy Drinks Ltd
Robinsons (Finance) No.2 Ltd
Robinsons Soft Drinks Limited
Southern Table Water Co Ltd
Sunfresh Soft Drinks Limited
R.White & Sons Limited

Thomas, David Wyn
Anglesey Spring / Dwr Ffynnon Mon / Dwr Mon

Thomas, Hugh William
Ugly Brands Limited

Thomas, Michael Rees
Ffynnon Wen Springs Limited
St. Davids Spring Water Co Ltd

Thomlinson, Peter James
Lucozade Ribena Suntory Exports Ltd
Lucozade Ribena Suntory Ltd

Thompson, Dwayne
Kemetic Cooks Ltd

Thompson, Joshua
Point Blank Cold Brew Ltd

Thompson, Matthew William
Juice Dub Ltd.

Thomson, Anne
Ella Drinks Limited

Thorpe, Christopher Benjamin
Two Brothers Beverage Co Ltd

Thorpe, Daniel
Two Brothers Beverage Co Ltd

Tigwell, Tom David
Mission Juice Ltd

Tikare, Prince
SGRIC Limited

Tilley, Leigh Morris Howard
Two2Three2Four Ltd

Tinsley, David Paul
Trederwen Springs 2008 Limited

Tinsley, John Derek
Trederwen Springs 2008 Limited

Todd, Gary Alexander
Thomas Hardy Burtonwood Ltd

Todd, Iain
The Kingston upon Hull Liqour Co Ltd

Todd, Scott
Scotod Ltd

Tomei, Jenny
Bouncing Biotics Ltd

Tomlin, Henry Alexander
Berrington Pure Spring Water Ltd
Berrington Spring Water Ltd

Tomlinson, Alison
Just Drinking Water Ltd

Tomlinson, Neil David
Just Drinking Water Ltd

Tony-Uzoebo, Emeraba Afaoma
Trove International Limited

Tounkara, Mariama
Mossdoli Ltd

Tourlamain, Elinor Beverly Alexandra
Shrubb Ltd

Towse, David Andrew Charles
Get Nourished Limited

Travis Brewer, Mercedes
Red Dragon Water Limited

Trevitt, Graham
Herbal Fusions Ltd

Trezona, Guy Deacon
The Malvern Water Co Ltd

Trigg, Mark
The Fizzbang Beverage Co Ltd

Troughton, Helen
Armagh Juice Co Ltd

Troughton, Mark
Armagh Juice Co Ltd

Troughton, Philip
Armagh Juice Co Ltd

Trujillo, Gonzalo Alonso
Think Drinks Limited

Tucker, Caroline Mary
Glastonbury Spring Water Co Ltd

Tucker, David Peter
Glastonbury Spring Water Co Ltd

Tucker, Ian Christopher
Glastonbury Spring Water Co Ltd

Tucker, Prince Albert
Karma Cola UK Ltd

Turner, Caroline Jane
Methuselah 969 Limited

Turner, Martyn
Red Steel Ltd

Turner, Rik William
We Are Haps Ltd

Turner, Stephen John
ABI SAB Group Holding Limited

Twigden, Freya Louise
Yeast Meets West Limited

Twiss, David John
Life Science Limited

Tye, Jonathan Christopher
Precision Hydration Limited

Tyler, Liam Matthew
BFT Drinks Limited

Tyson, Annabelle Amy
Blue Keld Springs Limited

Tyson, Peter
Belu Water Limited

Uddin, Sheikh Mohammed Goyas
Green Foods International Ltd

Udeh, Mark
Brain Fud Ltd

Udeh, Philip Enyinnaya
Brain Fud Ltd

Ugradar, Zubair
Dove Foods Ltd

Unger, Anahita
Efcon UK Ltd

Unger, Elena
Efcon UK Ltd

Unger, Philip
Efcon UK Ltd

Unger, Samira
Efcon UK Ltd

Urch, David Lawrence
Bath Natural Mineral Water Ltd
Bath Natural Spring Water Ltd
Cheddar Mineral Water Limited
Cheddar Natural Mineral Water Ltd
Cheddar Natural Spring Water Ltd
Cheddar Spring Water Limited
Cheddar Water Limited
Cornish Organic Aloe Vera Ltd
Mendip Hills Mineral Water Ltd
Mendip Hills Spring Water Ltd
The Water Shop Limited

Urch, Duncan Winston
Bath Natural Mineral Water Ltd
Bath Natural Spring Water Ltd
Cheddar Mineral Water Limited
Cheddar Natural Mineral Water Ltd
Cheddar Natural Spring Water Ltd
Cheddar Spring Water Limited
Cheddar Water Limited
Mendip Hills Mineral Water Ltd
Mendip Hills Spring Water Ltd
The Water Shop Limited

Urch, Tabitha Sarah-Jane
Bath Natural Mineral Water Ltd
Bath Natural Spring Water Ltd
Cheddar Mineral Water Limited
Cheddar Natural Mineral Water Ltd
Cheddar Natural Spring Water Ltd
Cheddar Spring Water Limited
Cheddar Water Limited
Mendip Hills Mineral Water Ltd
Mendip Hills Spring Water Ltd
The Water Shop Limited

Urch, Virginia
Bath Natural Mineral Water Ltd
Bath Natural Spring Water Ltd
Cheddar Mineral Water Limited
Cheddar Natural Spring Water Ltd
Cheddar Spring Water Limited
Cheddar Water Limited
Cornish Organic Aloe Vera Ltd
The Water Shop Limited

Urgh, Duncan
Watermarket Limited

Urgh, Tabitha
Watermarket Limited

Vagg, Oliver
Hangin Drinks Limited

Valdes Vera, Hugo Rodrigo
Roiss Mineral Water Limited

Valdes-Vera, Hugo
Alcro Commercials Limited

Valdetaro Lins de Albuquerque, Carlos Gustavo
Better Fresh Limited

Van Geest, Ross Leonard
Mad Dog Drinks Limited

Van Harn, Jules
Healthy Thirst Drinks Limited

Van Ooijen, Frank Christoffel
Healthy Thirst Drinks Limited

Varela Hernandez, Maria Paz
Andina Coffee Co. Ltd

Vaughan, Gwendolyn Nicole
Sweet Sally Limited

Veltrop-Baister, Richard Frederick
Brainwave Brands Ltd
Sopro Drinks Ltd

Vernon, Matthew James
Cott Ventures UK Limited
Decantae Mineral Water Limited
Total Water Solutions Limited

Vickers, Ewan Brian
Gingercool Limited

Vig, Amandeep Kaur
Drinkology Limited

Vila Vives, Cristina
&Tailor Ltd

Vogel, Malte
Beverage Management Limited

Volf, Michael Joseph
The Gibraltar Gin Co Ltd

Von Wendland, Marcelle Michelle Georgina Maria
Tasty Kameleon Ltd

Voss, Neil Mark
Thomas Hardy Burtonwood Ltd
Thomas Hardy Holdings Limited
Thomas Hardy Kendal Limited

Vowles, Michael Stewart
Think Drinks Limited

Walker, Christopher John
Muirhall Water Limited

Walker, Ed Owen
Coca-Cola European Partners GB Ltd

Walker, Grant Nicholas
Narino Limited

Walker, John Plenderleith
Narino Limited

Wallington, John Frank
Llanllyr Water Co Ltd

Walsh, Alan
Artisan Drinks Co Ltd

Walsh, Catherine Anne
Botanical Soda Works Limited

Walton, Ben David
Vida Water Ltd

Walton, Elizabeth
Marlish Waters Limited

Wang, Xiuyun
UK Blue Ribbon Group Beer Co., Ltd

Warburton, Mark
Hawkshead Gin and Spirit Co Ltd

Warburton, Sally Louise
Fonthill Waters Limited

Ward, Jonathan Christopher
Thomas Hardy Burtonwood Ltd
Thomas Hardy Holdings Limited
Thomas Hardy Kendal Limited

Ward, Kianne
Paradise Rum Limited

Ward, Margaret Rae
Thomas Hardy Burtonwood Ltd
Thomas Hardy Holdings Limited
Thomas Hardy Kendal Limited

Warner, Angus James
Natural Juicing Co Ltd

Warner, Stephanie
Natural Juicing Co Ltd

Warnock, Karen Anne
Ribble Valley Soft Drinks Ltd

Warrillow, Timothy Daniel Gray
Fevertree Limited

Watkins, Nicholas James
Watkins Drinks Limited

Watkins, Thomas
Watkins Drinks Limited

Watkins, William Walter
Hedgerow Soft Drinks Ltd
Radnor Hills Mineral Water Co Ltd

Watkinson, Matthew John
Ladybird (Drinks) Limited

Watson, Daniel
Bumblezest Limited

Watson, Richard Samuel
Coast Drinks Ltd

Watters, Gerard
Classic Holdings Limited
Classic Mineral Water Co Ltd

Watts, Garry
Coca-Cola European Partners PLC

Webb, Andrew John
The Juice Shed Co Ltd

Webb, Ian Paul
The Vitapure Drinks Co Ltd

Weekes, Simon David
Naturally Buzzin Energy Products Ltd

Weeks, Joseph Paul
Moss Cider Limited

Welbank, Sam James
Genii Energy Ltd.

Welch, Natalia
Pura Panela Ltd

Welling, Curtis
Coca-Cola European Partners PLC

Welling, Daniel James
Talent Drinks Ltd

Wells, Amanda Jane
Derbyshire Mineral Waters Ltd

Wells, Gary John
Derbyshire Mineral Waters Ltd

West, Russell Paul
Club Consultants Ltd

Western, Lea
Kixse Limited

Westropp, Anthony Henry
Belvoir Fruit Farms Drinks Holdings
Belvoir Fruit Farms Limited

Wetzel, Petra Margareta
Seltza Ltd

Wharton, Nicholas Barry Edward
A.G. Barr P.L.C.

Wharton, Nicholas Giles
Blue Keld Springs Limited

Wheatley, George Robert
Sweet Leaves Ltd

Wheeler, Victor Bernard
Mildenhall Bottling Co Ltd

White, Roger Alexander
A.G. Barr P.L.C.
Mandora St. Clements Limited
Rubicon Drinks Limited
Taut (UK) Limited
Tizer Limited

White, Sarah Emily Talula
Sekforde Drinks Limited

White, Shirley
O.T.C Beverages Limited

Whitehead, Alexander
Mr. Whitehead's Drinks Co Ltd.

Whitfield, Annelie
Made By Brave Limited

Wickens, Andrew, Rev
Calyx Drinks Ltd

Wiegman, Albert Edward Bernard
JB Drinks Holdings Limited
JB Drinks Limited

Wiggett, Thomas James
The Craft Mixers Co Ltd

Wijesiri, Kaludura Saiuri
Polconut Ltd

Wijesiri, Punith
Polconut Ltd

Wilkinson, Damien Michael
Harrogate Spring Water Limited
Thirsty Planet Limited

Wilkinson, Rufus Giles
Session Brewing Co. Limited

Wilkinson, Stephen Raymond
NFSG Ltd.

Wilkinson, Steven Christopher
Halo Drinks Co Ltd

Wilkinson, William James
NFSG Ltd.

Willday, Liam Adrian
Steep Soft Drinks Co Ltd

Williams, Alan John
Hendre Distillery Ltd

Williams, Andrew
Vitamin Brands Ltd.

Williams, Andrew Charles
Green Room Brands Limited

Williams, Bruce Andrew
Heather Ale Limited

Williams, Neville George
Barzy's Ltd

Williams, Novelette Ann-Marie
FYA Peppa Kitchen Ltd

Williams, Scott John
Heather Ale Limited

Williams, Stephen Glynn
Roo Drinks Limited

Williams, Victoria Nancy
Hendre Distillery Ltd

Williamson, Clive Edmund
Maynard House Limited

Williamson, Leon
Jeffries Group Ltd

Willis, Jonathan
Bladud Spring Limited

Wills, Simon
Nutrapharm Ltd

Wilson, Diane
Red Bandit Limited
Slimmers World Sports Drinks Ltd
Viva Riva Beverage Co Ltd
Vivo Viva Beverages Limited

Wilson, Iain [1978]
Sportential Limited

Wilson, Iain [1953]
Sportential Limited

Wilson, Nikki
The Sussex Mobile Coffee Co Ltd

Wilson, Robert
Cheese Burger Limited
Vivo Viva Beverages Limited

Wilson, Robert Elias
Schnapps Limited

Wilson, Stephen
The Sussex Mobile Coffee Co Ltd

Wimbourne, Suzanne Ellen Ruth
Carrington's Coffee Co Ltd

Windsor, Ian Gavin Charles
The Southdowns Natural Water Ltd

Windsor, Kathryn Denise
The Southdowns Natural Water Ltd

Windsor, William Thomas Gregory
Southdowns Water Co Ltd

Wingham, Damian Paul
Giantcandyco Limited

Winkworth-Smith, Charles George, Dr
Saicho Ltd.

Winsor, Lauren
Caraway and Peel Limited

Wolfe, Bronwyn Elizabeth
Wolfe's Drinks Limited

Wolfson, Andrew Daniel
Plenish Cleanse Ltd

Woodall, Guy, Dr
Healthy Thirst Drinks Limited

Woodall, Sheila Catherine
Healthy Thirst Drinks Limited

Woodman, Koby Gordon Roger
Bibax Limited

Woods, Jonathan Mark
Coca-Cola International Sales Ltd
Waters & Robson Holdings Ltd

Woodward, Paul James
Green Room Brands Limited

Worthington, Lance Barry
Freak Cocktails Ltd

Wright, Alexander William Lowndes
Dash Brands Ltd

Wright, Jeremy
Spring Water (Devon) Limited

Wright, Kelsey
Enchanted Forest Milks Limited

Yamazaki, Yuji
Lucozade Ribena Suntory Ltd

Yanakopoulos, Andreas
Creative Properties and Investments Ltd
Konon Limited

Yandell, Christopher George
Devon Soda Co Limited
Rocktails Drinks Limited

Yildirim, Fatih
Arosuk Ltd

Young, Daniel John
40 Kola Ltd

Yusuf, Hashi Ali
Dee's Greens Limited

Zaman, Sonya Haque
Zaas Limited

Zarkovic, Dragan
Freedrinks Limited

Zaveri, Hamza
Avobravo Limited
Leanteen Limited

Zeisler, Gabor
Diageo Great Britain Limited

Standard Industrial Classification
excluding
Manufacture of soft drinks; production of mineral waters and other bottled waters

01250 Growing of other tree and bush fruits and nuts
Moor Organics Limited

01270 Growing of beverage crops
Elan League UK Ltd

01280 Growing of spices, aromatic, drug and pharmaceutical crops
CBD Tonic & Mixers Limited

01610 Support activities for crop production
Bello's World Limited

01630 Post-harvest crop activities
Elan League UK Ltd

09100 Support activities for petroleum and natural gas mining
Elan League UK Ltd

10110 Processing and preserving of meat
Macro Munch Ltd

10200 Processing and preserving of fish, crustaceans and molluscs
ECF Global Ltd

10310 Processing and preserving of potatoes
Poo Tang Crisps Limited

10320 Manufacture of fruit and vegetable juice [27]
Ammo Your Ammunition to Greatness
Anglo African Food & Beverages Holding
Armagh Juice Co Ltd
Avobravo Limited
Bennu Rising Ltd.
Bright Smoothies Ltd
Chakra Chai Limited
Chocquers Limited
Crosby Beverages Ltd
Drinks Group Holdings Ltd
Ella Drinks Limited
Endurance Juice Co Ltd
Food and Drink Development Co Ltd
Grace Under Pressure Ltd
Handmade Cider Co Ltd
Healthy Thirst Drinks Limited
Hidden Orchard Ltd
Kemetic Cooks Ltd
Livitus Limited
Neptune SA Ltd
Oxford Juice Co Ltd
Plenish Cleanse Ltd
Razoo Limited
Refreshing Drinks Co Ltd
Trove International Limited
UK Dorset Ltd
Wise Herb Co Ltd

10390 Other processing and preserving of fruit and vegetables [11]
Alive & Kicking Fermented Foods Ltd
Ammo Your Ammunition to Greatness
Artio Foods Ltd
B + K Augustin Limited
Dakena-One International Ltd
Fab World Limited
Fruit Diversity Limited
Korko Limited
Pickle Shot Limited
Razoo Limited
Refreshing Drinks Co Ltd

10410 Manufacture of oils and fats
Salad Passion Foods Ltd

10511 Liquid milk and cream production
Chakra Chai Limited

10519 Manufacture of other milk products
Chakra Chai Limited
Faractive Limited
Food and Drink Development Co Ltd
Innorbit Ltd
Kings Farm Foods Limited
Mighty Drinks Ltd.
Wise Herb Co Ltd

10520 Manufacture of ice cream
Fossick Limited
Icetails Ltd
Woodford & Warner Limited

10611 Grain milling
Goodlives Panacea Blend Ltd

10612 Manufacture of breakfast cereals and cereals-based food
March Foods Limited
Natural Food and Drink Co Ltd
Space Chef Ltd

10710 Manufacture of bread; manufacture of fresh pastry goods and cakes
B + K Augustin Limited
Bespokery Ltd
Dove Foods Ltd
Morgan's Exclusive Ltd
Nature's Fountain Limited
Syrup Junkie Limited

10720 Manufacture of rusks and biscuits; manufacture of preserved pastry goods and cakes
Amor Food and Beverages Holdings Ltd
Korko Limited
Pass The Baton Limited
UK Brighton Food & Nutrition Research Centre

10821 Manufacture of cocoa and chocolate confectionery
Bily Co Limited
Chocquers Limited
Choquers Limited
Dove Foods Ltd
Made By Brave Limited
Poo Tang Crisps Limited
Soft N Sweet Ltd
Space Chef Ltd
Sweet Leaves Ltd

10822 Manufacture of sugar confectionery
Mr Freeze (Europe) Limited
Nude & Rude Ltd
Space Chef Ltd
Sweet Leaves Ltd

10831 Tea processing
Ibis Organics Limited
Innorbit Ltd
Kapyani Limited
Kompassion Ltd
Mighty Drinks Ltd.
Natural Food and Drink Co Ltd
Refreshing Intercepted Limited
Wise Herb Co Ltd
Yuyo Drinks Ltd

10832 Production of coffee and coffee substitutes
Burble Foods and Beverages Ltd
Carrington's Coffee Co Ltd
Cornfield Foods and Beverages Ltd
Lifeline Holdings Limited
Made By Brave Limited
Pitstop Coffee Limited
Surrey Food and Drink Innovation Ltd
UK Brighton Food & Nutrition Research Centre

10840 Manufacture of condiments and seasonings [12]
B + K Augustin Limited
Danjan Ventures Ltd
Dips Dips Ltd
Handmade Cider Co Ltd
Kapyani Limited
Kemetic Cooks Ltd
Korko Limited
Our Northern Stars Limited
Salad Passion Foods Ltd
Surrey Food and Drink Innovation Ltd
Woodford & Warner Limited
Yarty Cordials Limited

10850 Manufacture of prepared meals and dishes [10]
Birch Boost Ltd
Boil and Broth Ltd
Fab World Limited
Food and Drink Development Co Ltd
Istok Foods Limited
Kingsley Partners Limited
Macro Munch Ltd
Nude & Rude Ltd
Pass The Baton Limited
Surrey Food and Drink Innovation Ltd

10860 Manufacture of homogenized food preparations and dietetic food
Birch Boost Ltd
Chia Food (York) Limited
Taut (UK) Limited

10890 Manufacture of other food products n.e.c. [28]
Alcarelle Holdings Limited
Alcarelle Limited
Artio Foods Ltd
Avobravo Limited
Better Fresh Limited
Burble Foods and Beverages Ltd
Cheese Burger Limited
Cornfield Foods and Beverages Ltd
Cotton & Cane Ltd
Equilibrium Food & Drink Ltd
Fab World Limited
A & C Green Food and Beverage Ltd
Green Foods International Ltd
Guffaw Ltd
Johnson Supplies UK Ltd
Kemetic Cooks Ltd
Macro Munch Ltd
Marbella Cartel Ltd
Mello Drinks Ltd
Microbiome Technologies Ltd
Mylkman Ltd
Natural Food and Drink Co Ltd
Nutrapharm Ltd
Poo Tang Crisps Limited
Refreshing Drinks Co Ltd
Sweet Leaves Ltd
Tasty Kameleon Ltd
Woodford & Warner Limited

11010 Distilling, rectifying and blending of spirits [36]
Alko Vintages UK Ltd
Bitter Salvation Ltd
Botanical Alchemy Ltd
Caledonian Bottlers PLC
Country Garden Drinks Co Ltd
Diageo Great Britain Limited
Drinkology Limited
Equilibrium Food & Drink Ltd
Etoh Studio Limited
Gibraltar Gin Co Ltd
Ginsecco Ltd
Hawkshead Gin and Spirit Co Ltd
Hendre Distillery Ltd
Kendal Brewery Ltd
Kingston upon Hull Liqour Co Ltd
Koolvibes Limited
Liveras Limited
Loch Ness Drinks Ltd
London Botanical Drinks Ltd
Lough Neagh Distillers - 1837 Ltd
Luxbev Limited
Moores of Warwick Limited
Nele Drinks Limited
Neptune SA Ltd
Originalsip Ltd
Paradise Rum Limited
Portavadie Distillery Limited
Saint Patricks Ltd
Salcombe Cider Co Ltd
Sendivogius Limited
Start-Up Drinks Lab Limited
Strawhill Estate Spirits Co Ltd
Tea Rocks Ltd
UK Dorset Ltd
White Smoke Distillery Ltd
Willimott House Limited

11020 Manufacture of wine from grape
AB Vaults Group Limited
Alko Vintages UK Ltd
Amor Food and Beverages Holdings Ltd
Fruito Beverages (Africa) Ltd
Luxbev Limited
Vitosha Wine Ltd
Wild Life Botanicals Ltd

11030 Manufacture of cider and other fruit wines [25]
AB Vaults Group Limited
Ashridge Cider Limited
Crosby Beverages Ltd
Fruito Soft Drinks Limited
Ginsecco Ltd
Handmade Cider Co Ltd
Thomas Hardy Burtonwood Ltd
Thomas Hardy Holdings Limited
Thomas Hardy Kendal Limited
Hartpury Heritage Trust
Hawkins Drinks Limited
Hidden Orchard Ltd
Kendal Brewery Ltd
Kingston upon Hull Liqour Co Ltd
Marley and Barley Ltd
Merrydown PLC
Moss Cider Limited
Mr. Whitehead's Drinks Co Ltd.
Neptune SA Ltd
Pembrokeshire Cider Limited
Saint Patricks Ltd
Salcombe Cider Co Ltd
Showerings Cider Mill Ltd
Westmoor Botanicals Limited
Wild Life Botanicals Ltd

11040 Manufacture of other non-distilled fermented beverages [26]
Anglo African Food & Beverages Holding
Boil and Broth Ltd
Connect Beverages Ltd
Eastcott Drinks Ltd
Fruito Beverages (Africa) Ltd
Fruito Soft Drinks Limited
Genie Drinks Ltd
Ginsecco Ltd
Goat Drinks Ltd
Thomas Hardy Burtonwood Ltd
Thomas Hardy Holdings Limited
Thomas Hardy Kendal Limited
Hawkins Drinks Limited
Hawkshead Gin and Spirit Co Ltd
Icely Done Drinks Limited
Kingston upon Hull Liqour Co Ltd
Kombucha Kat Ltd
London Botanical Drinks Ltd
Magic Potion Energy Drinks International
Mobay Drinks Ltd
Momo Kombucha Ltd
Originalsip Ltd
SIP Kombucha Ltd
Saint Patricks Ltd
Vivo Water Ltd
Westmoor Botanicals Limited

11050 Manufacture of beer [24]
ABI SAB Group Holding Limited
Bad Girls Brew Limited
Bigla Brewing Co Ltd
Craft Soft Drinks Community Ltd
Crosby Beverages Ltd
A & C Green Food and Beverage Ltd
Thomas Hardy Burtonwood Ltd
Thomas Hardy Holdings Limited
Thomas Hardy Kendal Limited
Hawkins Drinks Limited
Heather Ale Limited
Infinite Session Ltd
Kendal Brewery Ltd
LVS Bottling Limited
Lough Neagh Distillers - 1837 Ltd
Luxbev Limited
Pointeer Ltd
Seafire Brewing Co. Ltd
Session Brewing Co. Limited
Shandy Shack Ltd
Signpost Brewery Ltd
Upper Harglodd Farm Ltd
Vitosha Wine Ltd
Westmoor Botanicals Limited

11060 Manufacture of malt
AB Vaults Group Limited
Buatoc Limited
Fruito Beverages (Africa) Ltd
Fruito Soft Drinks Limited

13921 Manufacture of soft furnishings
Tiny Mighty People Ltd

14131 Manufacture of other men's outerwear
London Fashion Industry Ltd
Session Brewing Co. Limited

14132 Manufacture of other women's outerwear
London Fashion Industry Ltd

14142 Manufacture of women's underwear
Goodnatured Co Ltd.

14190 Manufacture of other wearing apparel and accessories n.e.c.
Cocaine Limited
Portable Marketing Solutions Ltd

18203 Reproduction of computer media
Two2Three2Four Ltd

19201 Mineral oil refining
Ayge Limited

20140 Manufacture of other organic basic chemicals
HIH Frankly Irresistible Ltd
Phutures Limited

20420 Manufacture of perfumes and toilet preparations
AA Group Holdings Ltd
Pharmaco Group Limited

20530 Manufacture of essential oils
Faustian Ltd

21100 Manufacture of basic pharmaceutical products
Ad Hoque Ltd
Microbiome Technologies Ltd
Nutrapharm Ltd
Pharmaco Group Limited
SmithKline Beecham Limited

21200 Manufacture of pharmaceutical preparations
Pharmaco Group Limited

27900 Manufacture of other electrical equipment
Pressure Coolers Limited

28930 Manufacture of machinery for food, beverage and tobacco processing
Kubera Group International Ltd

32120 Manufacture of jewellery and related articles
Cocaine Limited

32990 Other manufacturing n.e.c.
AA Group Holdings Ltd
Goodnatured Co Ltd.
Morgan's Exclusive Ltd
My Living Water UK Ltd

33140 Repair of electrical equipment
Kali Engineering Ltd

35110 Production of electricity
Penning Power & Water Limited

36000 Water collection, treatment and supply
Artathlon Water Limited
Pump House Water Ltd

37000 Sewerage
Penning Power & Water Limited

41100 Development of building projects
Creative Properties and Investments Ltd
Konon Limited

42910 Construction of water projects
Kali Engineering Ltd
Zion Manufacturing Ltd

42990 Construction of other civil engineering projects n.e.c.
Admete Ltd

43999 Other specialised construction activities n.e.c.
Rockbarr Limited

45112 Sale of used cars and light motor vehicles
Ad Hoque Ltd

46140 Agents involved in the sale of machinery, industrial equipment, ships and aircraft
Kali Engineering Ltd

46170 Agents involved in the sale of food, beverages and tobacco
Aqua Esse Limited
Heather Ale Limited
Lady Eden Ltd
Lord Eden Ltd
Red Bandit Limited
Tea GB International Limited
Viva Riva Beverage Co Ltd

46190 Agents involved in the sale of a variety of goods
Aqua Esse Limited

46320 Wholesale of meat and meat products
Creative Properties and Investments Ltd
Evogue Limited
Konon Limited

46330 Wholesale of dairy products, eggs and edible oils and fats
Green Leaf Liquids Limited

46341 Wholesale of fruit and vegetable juices, mineral water and soft drinks [58]
413 Limited
Acqua Nordica Ltd
Alitasa Ltd
Alpha Energy Drink Limited
Artathlon Beverages Limited
Artathlon Water Limited
Artisan Drinks Co Ltd
B4Sport Ltd.
Bennu Rising Ltd.
Biofresh Cosmos Ltd
Birch Boost Ltd
Bright Smoothies Ltd
Budaquelle Beverages International Ltd
Club Consultants Ltd
Creative Properties and Investments Ltd
DRGN Global Ltd.
Driver's Drinks Co Ltd
Eliya Europe Ltd
Evogue Limited
Exoteeque Limited
Ferment Revolution Limited
Flow 33 UK Limited
Foal Limited
GB Heritage Limited
GO4 Beverages Limited
Gibraltar Gin Co Ltd
Green Foods International Ltd
H Two Eau International Ltd
Hello Coco Limited
Humble Bumble Ltd
Infinite Session Ltd
JSJuices Ltd
Konon Limited
Lord Eden Beverages Ltd
MB Drinks Ltd
Moringa Superfoods UK Limited
Mother Nature's Drinks Limited
N'ife Limited

Paisley Drinks Co. Ltd
Raw Is More Ltd.
Real Natural UK Ltd
Rocktails Drinks Limited
Saapos Ltd
Santa Monica Co Ltd
Seafire Brewing Co. Ltd
Sharewater Ltd
Simple Nature Limited
Sips MCR Ltd
Start-Up Drinks Lab Limited
Sweet Sally Limited
Temperance Drinks Limited
Theodore Global Limited
UK Brighton Food & Nutrition Research Centre
Vitte Nutrition Ltd
Vivo Viva Beverages Limited
J Water Disabled Children Ltd
Wild Cat Energy Drink Ltd
Your Water Ltd

46342 Wholesale of wine, beer, spirits and other alcoholic beverages [26]
Alko Vintages UK Ltd
Allson Sparkle Limited
Bad Girls Brew Limited
Bloody Drinks Limited
Burble Foods and Beverages Ltd
Citrosoft Drinks Limited
Cornfield Foods and Beverages Ltd
W.& J.Cruickshank and Co Ltd
Diageo Great Britain Limited
Gibraltar Gin Co Ltd
Green Leaf Liquids Limited
Infinite Session Ltd
Life Science Limited
Lough Neagh Distillers - 1837 Ltd
Mobay Drinks Ltd
Nele Drinks Limited
Portavadie Distillery Limited
Punchline Ltd
Seafire Brewing Co. Ltd
Shandy Shack Ltd
Bertrand Tailor Limited
Tasty Kameleon Ltd
Ty Nant Spring Water Limited
UK Blue Ribbon Group Beer Co., Ltd
Vitosha Wine Ltd
Wild Life Botanicals Ltd

46360 Wholesale of sugar and chocolate and sugar confectionery
Pura Panela Ltd
Tea GB International Limited

46370 Wholesale of coffee, tea, cocoa and spices
Carrington's Coffee Co Ltd
Goodnatured Co Ltd.
Kapyani Limited
Tea GB International Limited
Wild Husk Limited
Yuyo Drinks Ltd

46380 Wholesale of other food, including fish, crustaceans and molluscs
Green Foods International Ltd

46390 Non-specialised wholesale of food, beverages and tobacco [24]
Allson Sparkle Limited
Britannia Soft Drinks Limited
British Vitamin Products Ltd
Britvic Beverages Limited
Britvic Corona Limited
Britvic EMEA Limited
Britvic International Investments
Britvic Soft Drinks Limited
W.& J.Cruickshank and Co Ltd
Dayla Holdings Limited
Dayla Limited
Hooper,Struve & Co Ltd
Idris Limited
London Essence Co Ltd
Marbella Cartel Ltd
H.D.Rawlings Limited
Robinsons Soft Drinks Limited
Samco Retail Ltd
Shindig Promotions Ltd
Soft N Sweet Ltd
Southern Table Water Co Ltd
Sunfresh Soft Drinks Limited
Temperance Drinks Limited
R.White & Sons Limited

46420 Wholesale of clothing and footwear
SRP Equipe Limited

46520 Wholesale of electronic and telecommunications equipment and parts
Marbella Cartel Ltd

46900 Non-specialised wholesale trade
Acqua Eterna Ltd
Bello's World Limited
Beverage Brands (U.K.) Limited
Mourne Mist Bottled Water Co Ltd
Samco Retail Ltd
Tarka Springs Limited

47110 Retail sale in non-specialised stores with food, beverages or tobacco predominating
Alcro Commercials Limited
Delicious Retail Ltd
Positive Potions Limited

47190 Other retail sale in non-specialised stores
Faustian Ltd
GO4 Beverages Limited

47250 Retail sale of beverages in specialised stores [17]
Artathlon Beverages Limited
CBD Tonic & Mixers Limited
Havok Energy Drink. Ltd
Holos London Ltd
JDM Enterprises Ltd
Juice Collective Limited
Kubera Group International Ltd
Lady Eden Ltd
Lord Eden Beverages Ltd
Lord Eden Ltd
Neue Water Limited
Red Bandit Limited
Shindig Promotions Ltd

Slimmers World Sports Drinks Ltd
Viva Riva Beverage Co Ltd
Vivo Viva Beverages Limited
Wunder Workshop Ltd

47290 Other retail sale of food in specialised stores
Glaisher & Ames Ltd
JDM Enterprises Ltd
Pura Panela Ltd

47749 Retail sale of medical and orthopaedic goods in specialised stores (not incl. hearing aids) n.e.c.
Ayge Limited

47750 Retail sale of cosmetic and toilet articles in specialised stores
AA Group Holdings Ltd
Portable Marketing Solutions Ltd

47810 Retail sale via stalls and markets of food, beverages and tobacco products
Artathlon Beverages Limited
Bright Smoothies Ltd
Equilibrium Food & Drink Ltd
Holos London Ltd
Lady Eden Ltd
Lord Eden Beverages Ltd
Lord Eden Ltd
Momo Kombucha Ltd
Positive Potions Limited

47910 Retail sale via mail order houses or via Internet [12]
Aqua Esse Limited
Canncrest Drinks Limited
Cotton & Cane Ltd
Faractive Limited
Holos London Ltd
Istok Foods Limited
Portavadie Distillery Limited
Positive Potions Limited
Pura Panela Ltd
Rocktails Drinks Limited
Simple Nature Limited
Yuyo Drinks Ltd

47990 Other retail sale not in stores, stalls or markets
Canncrest Drinks Limited
Enterprises Beyond Reason Ltd

49410 Freight transport by road
Rockbarr Limited

52101 Operation of warehousing and storage facilities for water transport activities
Artathlon Water Limited

52103 Operation of warehousing and storage facilities for land transport activities
Rockbarr Limited
Storefast Solutions Limited

52290 Other transportation support activities
Pass The Baton Limited

56101 Licenced restaurants
Mighty Flames Ltd

56102 Unlicenced restaurants and cafes
Avid Stacc Ltd
Cotton & Cane Ltd
Goat Drinks Ltd
Syrup Junkie Limited

56103 Take-away food shops and mobile food stands
Bigla Brewing Co Ltd
Chocquers Limited
Choquers Limited
Ferment Revolution Limited
Mighty Flames Ltd
Seed Lab Ltd.

56210 Event catering activities
Ferment Revolution Limited
Marley and Barley Ltd
Mighty Flames Ltd
Moss Cider Limited
Sejuiced Limited

56290 Other food services [13]
Avid Stacc Ltd
Distinate Ltd
Divine Water Co Ltd
FYA Peppa Kitchen Ltd
Fizzbang Beverage Co Ltd
Goat Drinks Ltd
Jumpin' Juice Limited
Livitus Limited
Mylkman Ltd
Reluminate Ltd
Saapos Ltd
Saicho Ltd.
Tasteuk Limited

56302 Public houses and bars
Bigla Brewing Co Ltd
Shandy Shack Ltd

59112 Video production activities
Cocaine Limited

62011 Ready-made interactive leisure and entertainment software development
Two2Three2Four Ltd

62012 Business and domestic software development
Aillo Ltd
Nachure Ltd

62020 Information technology consultancy activities
Oxidize Limited
South West Juice Co. Ltd
Nelly Tickner Drinks Co. Ltd
Tiny Mighty People Ltd
Zaas Limited

62030 Computer facilities management activities
Interactive World Ltd

64204 Activities of distribution holding companies
Evo Drinks Europe Ltd

64301 Activities of investment trusts
Admete Ltd

64999 Financial intermediation not elsewhere classified
Admete Ltd

68209 Other letting and operating of own or leased real estate
115 Design Limited
ECF Global Ltd

69109 Activities of patent and copyright agents; other legal activities n.e.c.
Two B Limited

70100 Activities of head offices
Britvic International Investments
Britvic International Support Services
Britvic PLC
Dayla Holdings Limited
Diageo Great Britain Limited
Waters & Robson Holdings Ltd

70210 Public relations and communications activities
115 Design Limited

70229 Management consultancy activities other than financial management
Blending and Bottling Solutions Ltd
H Two Eau International Ltd
Hendre Distillery Ltd
ICB Advisory Limited
Ideas 2 Launch Limited
JDM Enterprises Ltd
Miximex Limited
Nelly Tickner Drinks Co. Ltd

71129 Other engineering activities
Fizzbang Beverage Co Ltd

72190 Other research and experimental development on natural sciences and engineering
Lucid Beverage Research Ltd
Nutrapharm Ltd
SmithKline Beecham Limited

74100 Specialised design activities
115 Design Limited
Tiny Mighty People Ltd

74909 Other professional, scientific and technical activities n.e.c.
Start-Up Drinks Lab Limited

74990 Non-trading company [11]
British Vitamin Products Ltd
Britvic Beverages Limited
Britvic Corona Limited
Hooper,Struve & Co Ltd
Idris Limited
London Essence Co Ltd
H.D.Rawlings Limited
Silver Spa Limited
Southern Table Water Co Ltd
Sunfresh Soft Drinks Limited
R.White & Sons Limited

77400 Leasing of intellectual property and similar products, except copyright works
H Two Eau International Ltd

82301 Activities of exhibition and fair organisers
Imprint Marketing Ltd

82920 Packaging activities
Artemis Import & Export Ltd

82990 Other business support service activities n.e.c.
Artisan Drinks Co Ltd
Elementhree Ltd
Fionnar Springs Ltd.
Galactogen Products Limited
Momo Kombucha Ltd
Nude & Rude Ltd
Storefast Solutions Limited
Bertrand Tailor Limited

84130 Regulation of and contribution to more efficient operation of businesses
Kubera Group International Ltd

85100 Pre-primary education
Morgan's Exclusive Ltd

85590 Other education n.e.c.
Ayge Limited
Inmind Care Services Ltd

86102 Medical nursing home activities
Ellive Ltd

86220 Specialists medical practice activities
Aillo Ltd
Nachure Ltd

86900 Other human health activities
Dakena-One International Ltd
Glaisher & Ames Ltd
Healthy Juice Co (NI) Ltd
Jarrett Health Limited

87200 Residential care activities for learning difficulties, mental health and substance abuse
Dakena-One International Ltd

88100 Social work activities without accommodation for the elderly and disabled
Inmind Care Services Ltd

90020 Support activities to performing arts
Dr Go Ltd

90030 Artistic creation
Healthy Hemp Products Ltd

94110 Activities of business and employers membership organisations
Alexionut Ltd
Craft Soft Drinks Community Ltd

94990 Activities of other membership organisations n.e.c.
Hartpury Heritage Trust

95110 Repair of computers and peripheral equipment
Raviom Limited

95210 Repair of consumer electronics
Raviom Limited

96090 Other service activities n.e.c.
Alexionut Ltd
Bello's World Limited
Raviom Limited

Printed in 8pt Nimbus Sans L

Designed by URW++ Design and Development GmbH

Dellam Publishing Limited

2 Heath Drive, Sutton, Surrey, SM2 5RP

Fax: 020 8770 7478   email: enquiries@dellam.com

SAN: 0177881   EAN/GLN: 5030670177882

www.ingramcontent.com/pod-product-compliance
Lightning Source LLC
Chambersburg PA
CBHW081115080526
44587CB00021B/3598